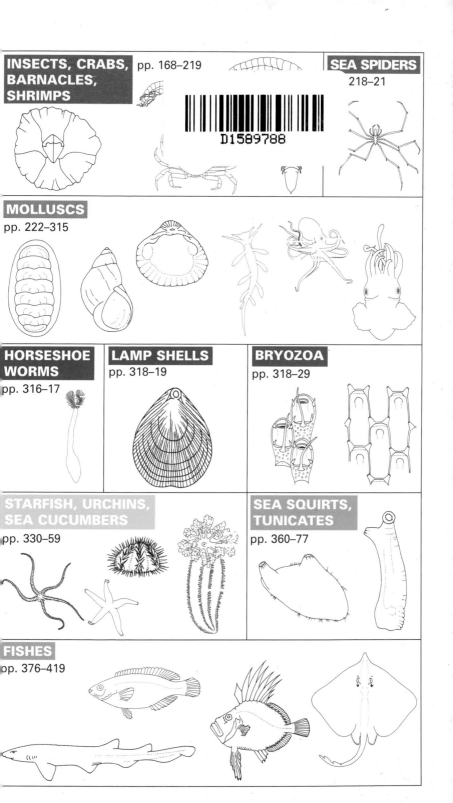

INSECTS, CRABS, BARNACLES, SHRIMPS pp. 168–219

SEA SPIDERS 218–21

D1589788

MOLLUSCS pp. 222–315

HORSESHOE WORMS pp. 316–17

LAMP SHELLS pp. 318–19

BRYOZOA pp. 318–29

STARFISH, URCHINS, SEA CUCUMBERS pp. 330–59

SEA SQUIRTS, TUNICATES pp. 360–77

FISHES pp. 376–419

Photographic Guide to the Sea and Shore Life
of Britain and North-west Europe

Photographic Guide to the Sea and Shore Life of Britain and North-west Europe

Ray Gibson
Benedict Hextall

OXFORD

UNIVERSITY PRESS

Great Clarendon Street, Oxford OX2 6DP

Oxford University Press is a department of the University of Oxford.
It furthers the University's objective of excellence in research, scholarship,
and education by publishing worldwide in

Oxford New York

Athens Auckland Bangkok Bogotá Buenos Aires
Cape Town Chennai Dar es Salaam Delhi Florence Hong Kong Istanbul
Karachi Kolkata Kuala Lumpur Madrid Melbourne Mexico City Mumbai
Nairobi Paris São Paulo Shangai Singapore Taipei Tokyo Toronto Warsaw

with associated companies in Berlin Ibadan

Published in the United States
by Oxford University Press Inc., New York

Text © Ray Gibson, Benedict Hextall, and Alex Rogers, 2001
Photographs © Benedict Hextall or other photographer where named
Line drawings © Ray Gibson

First published 2001

A catalogue record for this book is available from the British Library

Library of Congress Cataloging in Publication Data
(Data available)

ISBN 0 19 850709 7 (Pbk)
ISBN 0 19 850041 6 (Hbk)

Typeset by
Florence Production Ltd, Stoodleigh, Devon
Printed in Hong Kong

Contents

We would like to dedicate this book to our respective long-suffering wives, Jill, Sara, and Candida. Their tolerance was often severely tested, especially when the book seemed almost literally to be taking over our lives, but somehow they survived both it and us. You all fully deserve this dedication.

About this book

The shores and seas around the British Isles and north-western Europe are inhabited by an enormous variety of different plants and animals. Our aim, when writing this book, was simply to provide a guidebook to the marine life around the coasts of northern Europe and to present the common species that make up this striking diversity as they appear in the natural environment. We have relied on two main themes to guide us, first that most people simply wish to identify what they have found without having to delve too deeply into taxonomy, anatomy, or scientific terminology, and second that we should adopt a conservational approach and largely exclude species which can only be obtained by destroying their habitat. There are many different animals, and some whole groups of them, which are either microscopic in size or occupy habitats, such as sands and muds, in which they live permanently buried. Microscopic species mostly require both complex collection methods and specialist knowledge for their identification, and digging in sediments to find what animals live there destroys the very habitat in which they are living.

Many of the species are also far from either common or abundant; for example, more than 270 different species of marine amphipod crustaceans have been recorded around the British Isles, yet only a handful of types can be easily found. We have therefore largely restricted the content of this book to the species that are most frequently encountered; these are mostly illustrated with colour photographs of them in their natural habitat; their taxonomic position is indicated, brief descriptions are provided and, where necessary, simple line drawings are used as a supplementary aid to their identification. Key identificatory features are given, together with details of their known geographic distribution (supported with simple maps) and ecological habitat. Where an illustrated species may be mistaken for some other form, differences between them are also emphasised. At the same time, we have included examples of animal groups which, though they can be found by more diligent but non-destructive searching of seaweeds or rocky shores, tend to be less obvious, and in so doing, we have drawn attention to the far greater species diversity that exists around our shores.

Each taxonomic group of organisms is introduced with a short account of their major features. The use of some scientific terminology has been inevitable but this has been kept to a minimum and explanatory line drawings are included. The various groups and species have been dealt with in a taxonomic sequence, and for readers wishing to find out more details than can be included in a book such as this, key additional references are provided. For each species the scientific name and naming authority are listed, and if common names already exist these are given too; we have intentionally not invented common names for species which do not already have them. The use of scientific names is subject to certain rules and, for the benefit of the non-scientist, a brief explanation of the more important of these may be of benefit. A scientific name consists of two words; the first is the *genus* in which the organism belongs (generic name), the second is the *specific epithet* (specific name), the two words together comprising the *species name*. Thus, with the common limpet, whose species name is *Patella vulgata*, *Patella* is the generic name, *vulgata* the specific name. The naming authority is the name of the original person describing the organism as a new species. If the original species name given is still valid, as with *Patella vulgata*, then the naming authority (Linnaeus in this case) simply appears without parentheses; thus: *Patella vulgata* Linnaeus. If, however, the generic name for the species has been changed as a consequence of later taxonomic work, the naming authority should be placed within parentheses. An example of the latter case is seen with the common or edible cockle, originally described by Linnaeus under the name *Cardium edule* Linnaeus but now known as *Cerastoderma edule* (Linnaeus). In normal printing a scientific name should also always appear in *italics*.

Finally, the reader should note that not all species are equally common at all times of the day, or in all seasons of the year. Numerous animal species, for example, are more active during the night and thus rarely seen in daylight hours, whilst many seaweeds can only be found during the summer months and there is no point looking for them during winter.

The identification of a species should not be based entirely on its coloration, though there are notable exceptions to this generalisation, particularly with certain species of sea slugs (nudibranch molluscs) and a few species of ribbon worms (nemerteans) which have beautiful and highly characteristic colour patterns. For most organisms, colour may vary with the age and sex of the individual, with what it has fed upon, or according to whether it has been uncovered by low tides for several successive days or for some other reason. Shape and size, habitat type, and specifically mentioned features should thus be used in conjunction with the coloured illustrations to identify individuals you have found. If you cannot identify what you have found with the aid of this book, do not be concerned. The diversity of marine animals and plants is so great that precise identification requires years of experience and access to modern scientific literature, and equipment such as microscopes. Finally, we hope that this book transmits to others the thrill and excitement all three of us feel when walking on a shore, or diving and seeing a new and beautiful marine creature for the first time.

Photography

Obtaining good, clear photographs of animals and plants within their natural environment was the underlying prerequisite to this book. Below is a brief summary of the equipment used to take the photographs for this book.

Underwater photographs were achieved using a Nikon F4s in an Aquatica cast-aluminium housing with a 60mm Macro lens. This equipment is reliable, very tough and optically superb. By replacing the normal viewfinder with an oversized viewfinder, the housing allowed full-frame reflex viewing whilst wearing a mask. The 'standard' lens for 'close-up' photography was the Nikon 60mm Macro lens. This proved highly versatile offering rapid autofocus and allowing a reproduction ration of 1:1, ie life size. Sea & Sea underwater flash guns provided the artificial light necessary for close-up photography.

Although the Nikon/Aquatica equipment was used for the majority of the photographs, we also used Nikonos V cameras with a variety of lenses (15mm, 20mm, 28mm, 35mm and 80mm), extension tubes, close-up lenses and flashguns. While the Nikonos system is light-weight and optically superb, it does not offer the huge advantage of 'through-the-lens' framing, focusing and composition that the housed camera provides.

On land, we used Nikon F4s and F70 cameras, Nikon 60mm Macro lens, Benbo tripod, Nikon flashgun and remote shutter release. The tripod has waterproof legs and can be immersed in rock pools etc, enabling the camera to remain stable and dry.

Finally, the vast majority of the photographs were taken using Fujichrome Velvia slide film, a superb high definition film.

Introduction

Area of coverage

Although all of the species described in this book have been recorded from marine locations around the British Isles, their geographic distribution extends beyond our waters, often for very considerable distances. For the most part, however, we have dealt with an area roughly covering from the northern end of the Bay of Biscay to the Arctic Ocean coasts of Norway, and from the Danish, Dutch, Belgian, and French coasts of mainland Europe westwards to the margins of the continental shelf off the Irish Atlantic coast. Within this area fall the North Sea, Irish Sea, and English Channel. Within the area a wide range of physical conditions is found, ranging from the exposed western Irish coasts, subject to the influence of the open Atlantic Ocean, to the much more sheltered circumstances occurring in the southern part of the North Sea.

Excluding Northern Ireland, the British coastline has a length of about 10 708 km, encompassing virtually every type of temperate marine habitat from exposed intertidal rocky shores to estuarine mudflats, from brackish-water lagoons to sheltered subtidal sandy bays. Within each major habitat type a multitude of microhabitats exist. Rocky shores, for example, may consist of severely exposed rock platforms or cliff faces, or they may comprise outcrops of rock with muddy or sandy stretches between them in which boulders and stones are partially embedded. Sandy and muddy shores may have their sediments compacted and well sorted, or be semi-fluid and heterogeneous. Geology and climatic conditions in an area largely govern local conditions and are in turn reflected by the variety of flora and fauna found. Larger kelp seaweeds will not be found on muddy sediments, for they cannot attach themselves securely in such situations. Rock-boring bivalve molluscs will not be found unless the appropriate types of rock are available for them to live in. Interstitial invertebrates, who typically live between the sediment particles of sandy or muddy shores, will not be found on hard, bare rocky surfaces. Each species of animal and plant possesses its own particular range of ecological conditions within which it can survive and thrive, an ecological range which is directly affected by the local physical circumstances. Several categories of physical conditions that affect marine organisms can be identified; how they affect them depends partly upon what the effects are and partly on where the organisms live. Animals and plants living permanently submerged below low tide level will not be affected by the drying action of winds, any more than splash zone lichens will be subject to the influence of water currents. Although we can recognise individual environmental factors, such as intensity of sunlight, salinity, or substrate type, all are, to a greater or lesser extent, inter-dependent such that a change in one may enhance or reduce the effect of another. Of all the physical factors which can affect marine organisms, however, tidal cycles are probably the most significant in northern Europe.

Tides, environmental conditions, and shore regions

Tidal cycles are the result of the combined gravitational effects of the sun and moon upon waters of the seas and oceans, which cover more than 70% of the earth's surface. Three major tidal patterns can be recognised: diurnal, lunar monthly, and annual, but they can all be modified by meteorological or other conditions at any particular time or location.

The earth rotates about its north-south axis once every 24 hours, our moon orbits the earth once every 28 days, and the earth and moon together orbit the sun in an elliptical pathway once every year. Although the moon is very much smaller than the sun, its gravitational influence on the seas and oceans is greater because it is so much closer. The combination of the earth's rotation and the moon's gravitational pull on oceans and seas results in the typical diurnal tidal rhythm of two high and two low tides per day. However, during each 24-hour rotation by the earth, the moon is moving through 1/28 of its orbit so that its position relative to a fixed point on the earth's surface is changing. This results in tides becoming successively later, on average by about 50 minutes per day, so that a 2.00 p.m. high tide one day will be at 2.50 p.m. the next, and so on. The maximum distortion of the earth's oceanic waters occurs when the gravitational effects of the sun and moon are aligned (reinforce each other), which occurs with a new moon and full moon; that is, twice in every 28 days of the lunar cycle. At these times the highest high tides and the lowest low tides are produced (the maximum vertical movement of the sea between successive tidal states), called spring tides. When the gravitational effects of the sun and moon are at right angles to each other, the smallest vertical water movement between high and low water levels is found; that is, neap tides. The lunar monthly tidal cycle thus comprises, at 7-day intervals, successive spring, neap, spring, and neap tides. The annual tidal cycle results from the earth and moon orbiting the sun in an elliptical pathway, such that twice in a year (at spring and autumn equinoxes) the two are closer to the sun than at any other time, and twice (summer and winter solstices) they are farthest away. How much of an influence the sun's gravitational pull has on tidal cycles depends directly upon the distance between the earth and sun; the closer they are, the greater the effect on tides. So equinoctial spring tidal periods have a greater vertical water movement between high and low tide levels than other spring tides, whereas solstice spring tides have a smaller vertical range. The different tidal cycles enable shores to be divided up into three distinct regions, the upper, middle, and lower shore. The upper shore is uncovered by every low tide but is not submerged by high neap tides, the lower shore is covered by every high tide but not uncovered by low neap tides, and the mid-shore is covered and uncovered by every high and low tidal cycle. Figure 1 shows these tidal cycles in terms of the different low and high water levels which are used to define the three shore regions. Figure 2 is a representation of a predicted spring to neap tidal cycle.

Animals and plants living on the upper shore have to be able to survive long periods when they are not submerged, whereas lower shore organisms only have to tolerate short periods of emersion. Physical conditions are very different between the two extremes. When they are uncovered, these upper-shore fauna and flora are exposed to such factors as freshwater (rainfall), heating, and desiccation; animals that use dissolved oxygen for

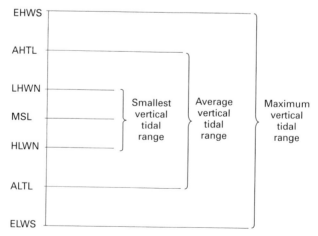

Fig. 1 A representation of the range of tides and levels on the shore. AHTL = average high tide level; ALTL = average low tide level; EHWS = extreme high water spring tide level; ELWS = extreme low water spring tide level; HLWN = highest low water neap tide level; LHWN = lowest high water neap tide level; MSL = mid-shore level.

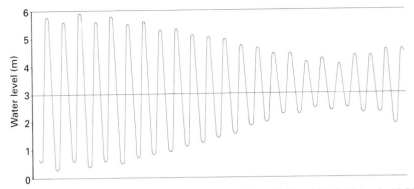

Fig. 2 The spring to neap tidal cycle and diurnal inequalities at Holyhead, North Wales, for 20-31 March 2000 (drawn from tidal predictions).

respiration may also have less oxygen available. Conversely, animals and plants living on the lower shore spend much more of their time submerged and are largely protected from these problems. Ecological factors are also important in the distribution of species. Predation and competition for space from other species can modify the levels on the shore at which an animal can survive. In other words, a species may be capable of surviving at a lower or higher level on the shore than

where it is normally found but cannot do so because other species living at this level overgrow or eat it. In addition, the supply and survival of young stages of animals and plants in an area, over time, can have a critical effect on the interaction between a species, the physical environment, and its competitors and predators. At any particular level on the shore the environmental conditions will be different from those found at another level, and one species of plant or animal will be better

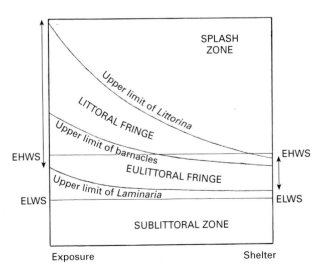

Fig. 3 The effect of exposure and shelter on the vertical extent of the littoral zone (shown by the arrow-headed vertical lines). Note that, as exposure increases, the vertical width of the littoral zone increases and moves higher above extreme low water spring tide level. Redrawn from Lewis (1964).

adapted to coping than another. Between tidal limits each species found living on the shore occupies the level to which it is best adapted, its zone. The vertical width of this zone depends upon many other environmental and ecological factors. Though best seen with surface-dwelling organisms on rocky shores, zonation happens on all types of beaches.

In the 1960s the theory of zonation was modified by using the presence of particular species of fauna and flora to subdivide shores into three biological zones: the littoral fringe, the eulittoral zone, and the sublittoral zone. The vertical extent of each of these zones varies from one shore to another according to the degree of exposure or shelter, and this basically depends on the amount of wave impact on the shore. An exposed shore is subject to powerful and destructive wave crash and water surge, whereas sheltered beaches are typified by gentle, lapping waves with virtually no surge effect. The gradient from exposure to shelter parallels the change from rocky to muddy shores, respectively. As exposure increases so the effects of seawater surge extend higher and higher up the shore. The biological significance of exposure in terms of how high on the shore organisms may be able to live is shown in Figure 3.

Types of shores and the shallow seas

A severely exposed rocky shore may have little life on it other than barnacles or other organisms capable of tenaciously holding on at their site of attachment. However, rocky shores, as a consequence of their great variability, generally tend to be biologically rich and diverse because they provide many ecological niches for organisms to colonise. Depending upon the geology (the type of rock and stratification), a rocky shore may be developed into a series of platforms and ledges, crevices and rockpools, or outcrops and overhangs; sediments may accumulate in crevices, boulders moved by wave action may form jumbled piles, or caves may be eroded by the action of sea water. The possible number of habitats, and therefore the variety of species to be found, are almost limitless.

At the other end of the exposure scale, muddy and sandy shores may at first seem to be marine deserts, with little immediate evidence of life. However, beneath the sediment surface there is often a rich infauna (animals living either burrowed into the sediment or inhabiting the water-filled spaces between the sediment particles). Often the size range of particles making up the beach, and how stable the shore is, determine the species composition in sandy and muddy situations; and though species diversity may be much smaller than on a rocky shore, individual species density may be very high. This is especially true when organic materials (detritus) are mixed up with the sediments, for detritus forms an important food resource for many different types of invertebrates (animals without backbones). Shingle or pebble beaches, however, tend to be biologically very poor for two main reasons: first, pebbles are easily rolled about by wave activity and, second, the volume of space between pebbles is far too big for water to be retained by capillarity when the shore is uncovered by the falling tide.

Sediment types can be categorised in various ways, from very well sorted (almost homogeneous) to poorly sorted (very heterogeneous) and compacted (consolidated), or loose (unconsolidated). Often they are identified by the size of particles they are composed of and particles are named according to their size range. The Phi Scale terminology (see table) was devised in the 1930s and is widely used in comparisons between sediments of different localities.

The shallow sublittoral regions covered by this book extend from extreme low water spring tide level to the edge of the continental shelf, at depths of 200–300 m. Within the area of coverage, the whole of the British Isles and Eire are fringed by a continental shelf, although there is a narrow channel about 600 m deep in parts of the Irish Sea. The entire English Channel and most of the North Sea are also over continental shelves, as are the north-western European coasts from north of the Bay of Biscay to just north of Denmark. Between Denmark and southern Norway deeper waters (more than 600 m) are encountered, whilst extending northwards

Scale of particle sizes

Name	Range (mm)	Phi Scale
Clay	0.0039	9
Silt	0.0039–0.0625	5–8
Very fine sand	0.0625–0.125	4
Fine sand	0.125–0.25	3
Medium sand	0.25–0.5	2
Coarse sand	0.5–1	1
Very coarse sand	1–2	0
Granule	2–4	−1
Small pebbles	4–8	−2
Medium pebbles	8–16	−3
Large pebbles	16–32	−4
Very large pebbles	32–64	−5
Cobbles	64–256	−6, −7
Boulders	256	−8

along the Norwegian coast the continental shelf is quite narrow.

Although many types of sublittoral habitat can be identified, the shallow seas over continental shelves provide a much more uniform environment, and organisms living subtidally are protected from many of the problems encountered by intertidal plants and animals. Most marine forms are quite incapable of surviving even short periods of emersion, with the result that species diversity in shallow seas is far higher than that found even on the richest rocky shores. However, one group of organisms, the algae, are limited by the diffusion of sunlight in seawater and are thus mostly found only close to the shoreline, for without sufficient light intensities they cannot photosynthesise. Shallower coastal waters, though much less variable in their physical conditions than intertidal regions, are nevertheless subject to some fluctuations in environmental conditions. Areas underwater can be subject to varying degrees of exposure to tidal currents. Water temperature within the area covered by this book varies according to season; off the Norwegian coast winter temperatures are typically 5°C or less but during August often rise to 13°C, whilst in the western parts of the English Channel winter and summer temperatures are, respectively, about 9°C and 17°C. Arctic species may thus be prevented by summer temperatures from penetrating into the more southerly parts of

the area covered, whilst boreal (warmer water) forms are likewise unable to move farther northwards because of the colder conditions during the winter months. The west coasts of Ireland and Scotland are influenced by the warm North Atlantic drift, which to some extent ameliorates low temperatures usually associated with temperate or cold temperate latitudes. Unlike deep oceanic waters, where salinity changes little, if at all, shallow coastal waters are subject to dilution by freshwater input from rivers and streams, especially during wet seasons or when winter snow and ice melt. For this reason coastal salinity tends to be less than that of oceanic waters and may fluctuate seasonally. The North Sea, for example, typically has a salinity of 34‰, though other regions, such as the south-eastern Irish Sea, into which the rivers Mersey and Ribble open, may be even lower. As well as bringing freshwater into the marine environment, rivers also carry sediment derived from terrestrial locations, which leads shallower inshore waters subject to estuarine discharge to be cloudier or muddier than deeper offshore regions. This cloudiness can be further enhanced by sewage and other industrial discharges and, in semi-landlocked areas such as the Irish Sea, pollution by waste chemicals or radioactive discharge can pose problems for a variety of animal life.

Coastal organisms broadly fall into one of two ecological types; they are either benthic, living most or all of their lives on or in the seabed, or they possess floating and swimming habits. As a broad generalisation, organisms which either float passively in the sea water or can swim but feebly are called planktonic forms and include a diverse variety of species, such as phytoplankton and the larval stages of many invertebrate forms, whereas animals capable of swimming powerfully enough to control their own direction of movement irrespective of current direction form the nektonic species, such as fishes, marine mammals, and many crustaceans. Several pelagic fishes spend much of their time on or close to the seabed, such forms being termed demersal. It is not uncommon for planktonic species, blown inshore by autumnal westerly gales, to be found stranded in intertidal rockpools or on the open beach, but the occurrence of such forms is both haphazard and random.

Looking for species

Whether searching beaches on foot when the tide is out, or snorkelling or scuba-diving, most people will easily find something they cannot immediately name. The more carefully and diligently one searches, the more one is likely to find unusual or less common species. One of our guiding principles in the production of this book has been that of being non-destructive to the environment. If it meant destroying a burrow to dig out some animal, tearing free a specimen of some alga, or breaking open a boulder to find what was living in deeper holes in its surface, we have not done it. People who find a plant or animal that they have not seen before often collect it for later identification; less rarely, though, do

they return the creature to its natural habitat. Indeed, often the very act of removing a marine animal or plant from its habitat, even for a short time, is enough to kill it. In using this book, then, try and think 'green'; take a conservational approach to your searching, and try to sketch or photograph what you have found, or make notes on its shape, size, colour, habitat, etc., rather than collect the plant or animal and then risk letting it die. It does no harm to remind oneself that life in the marine environment, as on land or in freshwater, is struggling to survive, often against high odds, and we should not add to the problems through careless or thoughtless actions.

We should also mention aspects of safety when beachcombing or diving. We strongly recommend that you never venture onto the shore by yourself. Even a relatively trivial accident can become a serious and life-threatening problem when faced with exposure or with the incoming tide. Always seek local advice before visiting an unfamiliar area so that you are aware of potential hazards. Think about letting somebody know where you are going and when to expect you back, ring the coastguard if necessary. Rocky shores are particularly dangerous as they can be very slippery and a fall can result in injury. However, sandy beaches can harbour quick sands or may be subject to very rapid incoming tides, leading to a possibility of becoming stranded. Divers should always be fully trained and only dive in areas suited to their experience and current levels of fitness. As with exploring the shore, they should never go alone.

The Guide

Plants (Kingdom Plantae)

Lichens

Lichens are compound plants, comprising **fungi** and **algae** living together symbiotically as a **thallus** (plants not separated into leaf, stem, and root). They are found in three main forms: **crustose** lichens form closely adhering encrustations on rocks and other suitable hard surfaces; **foliose** forms are generally flattened but composed of loosely attached lobes of thallus; **fruticose** lichens grow erect or hang down from a basal attachment and are simple or branched and often narrowly elongate. Lichen fruiting or **reproductive bodies**, found at appropriate times of the year, are typically fungal in nature. Although generally slow growing, lichens can cover large areas of shore, particularly in the supralittoral fringe or splash zone where they are most commonly found. Most are intolerant of full submergence, though a few species do occur as far down as the mid- to lower-shore.

FAMILY Pyrenulaceae

Caloplaca marina (Weddell) Zahlbruckner

Description · The upper surface of this lichen, which may form an irregular encrustation up to 10 cm or more across, is often covered with irregularly scattered coarse granules. The colour is typically distinctly orange, although individual growths may have a somewhat yellowish tinge. The reproductive bodies may be visible as smooth discs, the same colour as the rest of the lichen. **Habitat & ecology** · Often locally abundant in sunny positions, on sheltered shores *Caloplaca* may form a distinct band immediately above *Verrucaria* but increased wave activity results in the two lichens having an intermingled distribution. *Caloplaca* lives in the supralittoral fringe or splash zone associated with rocky shores, often forming numerous scattered patches of growth. **Similar species** · Easily confused with *Xanthoria parietina*.

Abundance & distribution
Usually abundant but less so or even absent from shaded or north-facing surfaces. Found on Atlantic coasts of northern Europe, the English Channel, and North Sea, it is an abundant species on most British rocky shores.

FAMILY Lecanoraceae

Lecanora atra (Hudson) Acharius **Black Shields**

Description · The thallus forms irregularly shaped encrusting patches, up to about 8 cm across, on rocky surfaces. The colour is typically a dirty greyish-white, although when reproducing the fruiting bodies appear as black nodular shapes, with grey rims, towards the middle of the colony. Each colony may be outlined by an indistinct blue-black line. **Habitat & ecology** · Common in the supralittoral fringe or splash zone of rocky shores, frequently associated with *Caloplaca*, *Ramalina*, and/or *Xanthoria*. On headlands exposed to a wide and poorly defined splash zone this lichen may overlap with the uppermost limits of *Verrucaria* and *Lichina*. **Similar species** · Resembles *Ochrolechia parella*, but this species tends to form rounded colonies, sometimes with whitish edges. The fruiting bodies are saucer-shaped and contain dusty grey or pinkish spores.

Abundance & distribution
Common round the British Isles, *L. atra* may occur on inland walls, roofs, and rocks some distance from the shore where conditions are severely exposed. Found throughout northern Europe.

Further reading

Ferry, B. W. & Sheard, J. W. (1969). Zonation of supralittoral lichens on rocky shores around the Dale Peninsula, Pembrokeshire. *Field Studies*, 3, 41–67.

Gilbert, O. (2000) Lichens. The New Naturalist Library No. 86. Harper Collins Publishers, 288pp.

Distinctive features
1. Thallus encrusting, flattish, not leafy.
2. Orange colour.

Distinctive features
1. Thallus encrusting, not leafy.
2. Greyish-white colour.

FAMILY **Lichinaceae**

Lichina pygmaea (Lightfoot) Agardh

Description · Easily mistaken for a very small seaweed, this lichen has a tufted and branched thallus up to about 1 cm tall and 2–3 cm in diameter. Branches may appear somewhat compressed or flattened. Reproductive bodies appear as swollen tips of branches. Typically a dark brownish-black or very deep reddish-brown. **Habitat & ecology** · One of the few true intertidal lichens around Britain, *Lichina* lives in the middle and upper levels of rocky shores, particularly on steep, southerly facing and well-drained surfaces, and is usually associated with the higher levels of barnacle colonies. On shores dominated by the barnacle *Semibalanus balanoides* the lichen extends above the upper barnacle limits, but when the dominant barnacle species is *Chthamalus stellatus* it is found entirely within the barnacle zone. **Similar species** · *L. confinis* closely resembles this species but is smaller, with more cylindrical branches, and more typically associated with the middle and upper regions of the *Verrucaria* belt.

Abundance & distribution
Fairly common, although unobtrusive, on exposed rocky shores around the British Isles. Found throughout northern Europe on Atlantic, Channel, and North Sea coasts. May be rare in southern North Sea because of lack of habitat.

FAMILY **Usneaceae**

Ramalina siliquosa (Hudson) Smith **Sea ivory**

Description · Thallus strap-like, tufted and branched, up to 5 cm or more tall, typically a pale greyish-green colour with minute white spots but when fruiting it has brownish-white or yellowish-grey disc-like bodies near the ends of the branches. The thallus, which is smooth and with a glossy surface, feels brittle and coarse to the touch. **Habitat & ecology** · Lives in the supralittoral fringe or splash zone on more or less any rocky surface, but does not extend below extreme high water spring tide level. On exposed headlands *Ramalina* may overlap the higher levels of *Lichina* and *Verrucaria* growth. **Similar species** · Growth form similar to the lichen *Roccella fuciformis*.

Abundance & distribution
Widespread on rocky shores all around the British Isles, often found some distance inland on buildings, stone walls, and boulders near severely exposed beaches. Found on the English Channel, North Sea, and Atlantic coasts of northern Europe.

FAMILY **Verrucariaceae**

Verrucaria maura Wahlenberg

Description · Easily mistaken for an oil spillage on rocks, it forms a thin, variably shaped and sized thallus closely adhering to substrate surfaces. Thallus surface often covered in fine cracks. Typically matt black, it may cover large areas of rocks and boulders. **Habitat & ecology** · Almost all types of rocky shores, missing/scarce only where rocks are soft, crumbly, or very cracked, where beach is loose shingle or mobile rocks, or in permanently damp situations. On very exposed shores *Verrucaria* belt is entirely above tide levels and 30 m or more above barnacle zone; on very sheltered beaches it may form a vertical band 30–100 cm wide, within reach of high spring tides. Can extend high into supralittoral fringe, especially on exposed shores, but lower limit in sheltered conditions fairly sharply defined. May extend down to about mean high water spring tide level, but lower limit of distribution affected by presence of barnacles, or algae such as *Porphyra*. Often associated with yellow lichen, *Caloplaca marina*. **Similar species** · *V. mucosa*.

Abundance & distribution
Very common on most rocky shores around the British Isles. It is distributed all around north-west Europe.

Distinctive features
1. Thallus tufted and branching.
2. Looks like a small seaweed.

Distinctive features
1. Tufted and branched, strap-like thallus.
2. Pale greyish-green colour.

Distinctive features
1. Black colour.
2. Flat, thinly encrusting thallus.

Xanthoria parietina (Linnaeus) Fries

Description · The thallus of this lichen forms irregularly shaped encrustations on rocks, often 10 cm or more in diameter, but it has a generally more obvious rough and leafy growth form than the orange-coloured *Caloplaca marina*, with which it may be found. **Habitat & ecology** · Although most commonly found in the splash zone or supralittoral fringe, often extending inland near exposed shores, it may form a distinct band just below *Ramalina siliquosa* in the extreme upper-shore zone. Its lower limits may overlap with both *Lichina pygmaea* and *Verrucaria maura* on shores where the splash zone is ill-defined, such as on rocky headlands. **Similar species** · May be confused with *Caloplaca marina*.

Abundance & distribution
Common in the supralittoral fringe of most rocky shores around the British Isles, this species is widespread throughout northern Europe.

Distinctive features

1. Thallus rough, forming somewhat leafy encrustations.
2. Vivid yellow colour.

Seaweeds and flowering plants

Marine algae vary enormously in size and complexity, ranging from single-celled microscopic forms to the typical intertidal and shallow sublittoral macroscopic seaweeds. Seaweeds typically grow from a **holdfast** (or **hapteron**), an attachment organ that may be a simple disc or a complex meshwork of **rhizoids** (root-like growths) for holding the plant securely to a firm surface. The remainder of the plant forms the **frond**, which may have an elongate single or branched form, possess a distinct stem (**stipe**) with a blade (**lamina**), or be profusely branched. The type of branching shown by the frond is often an aid to identification and may be **alternate**, **dichotomous**, **opposite**, or **whorled**. Branches may all occur in the same plane, spiral around a main stem, or extend off in different directions.

The macroscopic seaweeds often possess complex life-cycles; a **sporophyte** stage asexually produces **spores** that develop into a **gametophyte**, the sexually reproducing generation in the life-cycle. These alternating generations may look very different from each other (**heteromorphic**) or be very similar (**isomorphic**). Often the sporophyte is small and motile, and it is the gametophyte that comprises the typical seaweed found on the shore. The gameto- phytes may possess both male and female reproductive bodies on the same plant, or male and female plants may be separate, but the nature and position of the reproductive bodies is often helpful in the identification of macroscopic algae.

Algae are mainly classified according to the **photosynthetic pigments** they contain, and broadly fall into three groups: the **Chlorophyta** (**Chlorophyceae**) or green algae, the **Heterokontophyta** (**Phaeophyceae**) or brown algae, and the **Rhodophyta** (**Rhodophyceae**) or red algae. These groups have usually been regarded as classes but recent trends afford them phylum or division status.

Further reading

Burrows, E. M. (1991). *Seaweeds of the British Isles Volume 2 Chlorophyta*. Natural History Museum, London.

Dixon, P.S. and Irvine, L. M. (1977). *Seaweeds of the British Isles. Volume 1 Rhodophyta. Part 1 Introduction, Nemaliales, Gigartinales*. British Museum (Natural History), London.

Fletcher, R. L. (1987). *Seaweeds of the British Isles Volume 3 Fucophyceae (Phaeophyceae) Part 1*. British Museum (Natural History), London.

Irvine, L. M. (1983). *Seaweeds of the British Isles Volume 1 Rhodophyta Part 2A Cryptonemiales (sensu stricto) Palmariales, Rhodymeniales*. British Museum (Natural History), London.

Irvine, L. M. & Chamberlain, Y. M. (1994). *Seaweeds of the British Isles Volume 1 Rhodophyta Part 2B Corallinales, Hildenbrandiales*. The Natural History Museum, HMSO, London.

Parke, M. & Dixon, P. S. (1976). Checklist of British marine algae, third revision. *Journal of the Marine Biological Association of the United Kingdom*, **56**(3), 527–94.

Algae

Division Chlorophyta

Class Chlorophyceae (green algae)

The **Chlorophyta** are all shades of green, their colours ranging from a pale yellowish-green to a dark greenish-black or brownish-green, their

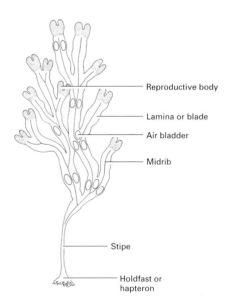

Fucus vesiculosus, a brown alga, showing the structures referred to in the text.

- Reproductive body
- Lamina or blade
- Air bladder
- Midrib
- Stipe
- Holdfast or hapteron

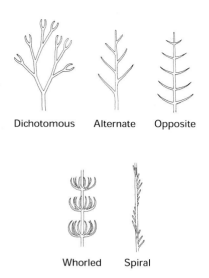

Dichotomous   Alternate   Opposite

Whorled   Spiral

Branching patterns found amongst the algae.

chlorophyll pigment not being hidden by the additional photosynthetic pigments found in the other groups. Green algae are often tolerant of difficult conditions, such as pollution or reduced salinity, and are commonly found in the upper half of intertidal regions, in brackish water, on beaches subject to freshwater run-off, growing on pier piles, or in splash-zone rock pools. Within intertidal regions green algae may be the most abundant seaweeds, though their often small size makes them less obvious than the brown algae. Upper-shore species subjected to strong sunlight for long periods of time are often **bleached** white. Green algae vary from minute, simple, unicellular plants to larger thread-like, tubular, or frond-like plants composed of many cells. Most species are less than about 20 cm in length, although a few may exceed this.

Division Heterokontophyta
Class Phaeophyceae (brown algae)

In this group the green chlorophyll pigment is typically masked by a brown pigment, **fucoxanthin**, which is better at absorbing the blue-green end of the light spectrum. Blue-green light penetrates deeper into sea water than other colours. A diverse group, the brown algae are typically among the largest seaweeds and intertidally the most obvious, several species living in distinct horizontal bands (**zones**) on rocky shores, though they also flourish in shallow sublittoral situations. All are multicellular and more usually associated with temperate marine habitats; few species can tolerate reduced salinities or higher temperatures. The Phaeophyceae contains some 1500 species arranged into 14 orders, of which the **Fucales** and **Laminariales** are perhaps the most familiar. However, the organisation and definition of higher systematic levels remains controversial and for this reason we have organised the brown algae according to families, based on information presented in Parke & Dixon (1976) and modified in Fletcher (1987).

Division Rhodophyta
Class Rhodophyceae (red algae)

Chlorophyll in the **Rhodophyta** is typically masked by the red pigment, **phycoerythrin**, and the blue pigment, **phycocyanin**, although the colour of the different species is very variable and may be almost anything from crimson, rose-red, pink, or violet to brown, green, or even black. In water, a few species are distinctly iridescent or fluorescent. Red algae are all multicellular and mostly of small to moderate size. They are the most tolerant of reduced light conditions and are therefore common under the canopies of kelps, and can survive in deeper waters than other types of plant. Many red seaweeds are intolerant of drying out or reduced salinities, and are thus mainly limited to permanent rock pools in the intertidal region, very damp areas under larger plants, or to sublittoral situations. There are more than 5000 known species, world-wide. Several groups within the phylum are **calcareous** or **coralline**, and often form hard, encrusting growths on rocks or other suitable surfaces. Some of the red algae are amongst the most difficult of seaweeds to identify reliably, and careful examination of specimens is usually needed.

DIVISION **Chlorophyta** | CLASS **Chlorophyceae**
ORDER **Ulotrichales**

FAMILY **Ulvaceae**

Blidingia minima (Nägeli Ex Kützing) Kylin

Description · Slender (up to 4 mm broad), dark green fronds up to 24 cm long. Fronds arise from a basal disc and are usually unbranched but may sometimes appear branched and inflated. Previously known as *Enteromorpha minima*. **Habitat & ecology** · Typically upper-shore, found on exposed and sheltered shores. Grows on rocks, boulders, pier pilings, harbour walls, or any suitable vertical hard surface. Tolerant of reduced salinities and occurs in estuaries or lagoons. Found throughout the year and in the Arctic may survive being frozen in ice. **Similar species** · Closely resembles *Enteromorpha linza* but is smaller, more delicate, and occasionally branched. *Blidingia* is also typically a darker green than the bright green *Enteromorpha*. *B. marginata* also similar but tends to form soft prostrate masses on the rock surface on upper shore and supralittoral. It may be mixed with *B. minima*. *B. chadefaudii* is usually unbranched and smaller (to 8 cm long). The disc of this species is formed by loosely associated branches. Positive identifications may require microscopic examination.

Abundance & distribution
Common. Found around all coasts of Britain and Ireland. Distributed from Spitzbergen to the Mediterranean.

Enteromorpha intestinalis (Linnaeus) Link

Description · Minute, disc-like holdfast giving rise to simple, unbranched (subsp. *intestinalis*) or branched (subsp. *compressa*) fronds, 10–30 cm to 1 m or more long. Fronds initially slender but gradually expand, forming hollow tubes up to 20 mm diameter but up to 6–7 cm or more in sheltered rock pools. Ends of fronds rounded, older plants often having crinkled appearance. Light to dark green, but during summer may be bleached white, especially around rock pools. **Habitat & ecology** · All exposures, upper shore to sublittoral, all year. On rock, in rock pools, on boulders, stones, shells, and harbour walls. Tolerates reduced salinities, common in estuaries and lagoons. *E. intestinalis intestinalis* more common on upper shore. The two subspecies reproduce together and are treated as conspecific ecotypes. **Similar species** · Identification of several similar *Enteromorpha* species requires microscopic examination. *E. prolifera* is very similar but in smaller specimens fronds tend to be same width for entire length. This species can appear like a mass of tangled threads.

Abundance & distribution
Common, often abundant. All coasts of Britain and Ireland. Distribution is more or less worldwide. In some parts of the world, such as China and Japan, *E. intestinalis* is sold as a food item.

Enteromorpha linza (Linnaeus) Agardh

Description · Growing to a length of 30–50 cm, the bright light or dark green unbranched fronds of this seaweed are hollow and cylindrical at their base but for most of their length appear somewhat flattened, sometimes crinkled along their borders. The base is very stipe-like and the seaweed abruptly or gently widens from this base to a width of up to 5 cm. The margins of the fronds possess the hollowed construction characteristic of *Enteromorpha* species, but this is only distinguishable in transverse sections examined under a microscope. **Habitat & ecology** · Found on all levels of rocky shores, growing on rock, on boulders, and in rock pools. Also occurs in brackish waters but tends to be more common in fully marine conditions. **Similar species** · Somewhat similar to *E. intestinalis* in being unbranched, the flattened appearance of the fronds of *E. linza* enable the two seaweeds to be distinguished from each other. Precise identification of *E. linza* may require microscopic examination.

Abundance & distribution
Common. Found around all coasts of Britain and Ireland. Distributed from the Arctic to the Mediterranean Sea, including Iceland and the Faeroe Islands. Also occurs in the western Atlantic and in the Pacific.

Distinctive features

1. Fronds dark green in colour.
2. Typically unbranched, sometimes slightly branched.
3. Found on upper-shore hard, vertical surfaces.

Distinctive features

1. Fronds branched or unbranched.
2. Fronds of mature plants are often irregularly inflated.
3. Width increases from base to middle of the frond.

Distinctive features

1. Frond appears flattened, at least for most of its length.
2. Unbranched.
3. Stipe-like base, from which the frond increases in width.

Ulva lactuca Linnaeus **Sea lettuce, green laver**

Description · Delicate, irregularly rounded, flat frond, growing from small, disc-like holdfast, up to 1 m or more long and often very wide. Margins of frond wavy, tending to split. Texture soft, may be firmer at base. Typically bright translucent green, but ranges from very pale to dark green. May appear dirty white when discharging spores. **Habitat & ecology** · All levels of rocky shores, on rock, boulders, or in rock pools, sublittoral to 15–20 m depth, present all year. Tolerates reduced salinities, found in estuaries and salt marshes. Thrives in shelter with abundant decaying plant material or sewage pollution, benefiting from increased nitrates, but grows well in unpolluted sea water. Does not favour more exposed shores, particularly in higher latitudes. Under very sheltered conditions may form extensive, unattached, floating masses. **Similar species** · Resembles *U. rigida*, but this has stiff texture. *U. olivascens* has flat, firm, olive green frond, often with small holes and longitudinal ribs near base, typical of shaded localities. *Monostroma* species also resemble *Ulva* but are generally small and arise from tubular base, mostly in rock pools.

Abundance & distribution
Very common. Occurs on all coasts of Britain and Ireland. Distributed almost worldwide. In some parts of world, such as China, is sold both as a food and medicine.

ORDER **Cladophorales**

FAMILY **Cladophoraceae**

Cladophora rupestris (Linnaeus) Kützing

Description · Densely tufted plants, up to 20 cm long, dark or bluish-green but dull. Profusely branched from holdfast, formed by plate of tiny rootlets. Typically, branching irregular but may be whorled or opposite. Stoutness, density, and arrangement of branches give the alga coarse feel. May spread in turf-like patches by means of short lateral runners from rhizoidal base. **Habitat & ecology** · All shore levels at all exposures. Often in rock pools, on rock, or in crevices. May form turfs under canopy of larger algae. Stunted plants may live in high-shore rock pools or splash zone. Abundant all year. **Similar species** · Up to 17 species of *Cladophora* in north-west Europe. Identification requires specialist knowledge and microscope. *C. albida* is common. It is very branched, delicate, up to 15 (rarely 50) cm long with spongy texture. Branches straight or curved, tapering towards ends that can have branchlets arranged like comb teeth. Attached by tiny rootlets. Whitish-yellow to bright olive green.

Abundance & distribution
Very common. All coasts of Britain and Ireland. Distributed from Arctic Norway to the Mediterranean, including Greenland, Iceland, the Faeroes, and Baltic Sea. Also on the east coast of Canada and USA as far south as Massachusetts.

ORDER **Codiales**

FAMILY **Codiaceae**

Codium bursa (Olivi) Agardh

Description · This alga appears as a velvety sphere of up to 30 cm in diameter. It is attached to the seabed by filaments. Colour is deep green. The inside of the sphere is packed with loose filaments. **Habitat & ecology** · Occurs subtidally on rock to 30 m depth, or more, but detached specimens may be found. **Similar species** · *C. adhaerens* resembles an encrusting, dark green, velvety mat, though it is not likely to be mistaken for this species.

Abundance & distribution
Occurs in southern and south-west Britain and Ireland where it is rare. Distributed southwards to the Mediterranean, Azores, and Canary Islands.

Distinctive features

1. Frond thin, leafy, and irregular in shape, generally resembling lettuce leaves in appearance.

Distinctive features

1. Profusely branched and tufted growth form.
2. Coarse to the touch.
3. Dark green colour.

Distinctive features

1. Spherical shape.
2. Velvety texture.

Codium fragile (Suringar) Hariot

Description · Seaweed composed of erect, dichotomously or irregularly branched fronds, 25 cm (subsp. *atlanticum*) to 1 m (subsp. *tomentosoides*) in length. Branches round in cross-section, but may be flattened beneath dichotomies of branches (subsp. *tomentosoides*). May be robust (subsp. *atlanticum*) or soft (subsp. *tomentosoides*). Surface with velvety texture. Fronds usually arise from spongy disc, several of which may fuse to form a mat. Colour varies from light (subsp. *atlanticum*) to dark green (subsp. *tomentosoides*). **Habitat & ecology** · Rocky shores from mid- to low-tide levels, in rock pools, or subtidally to depths of a few metres. The subspecies may be separate species. *C. fragile tomentosoides* was probably introduced from Japan in the 19th century. *C. fragile atlanticum* is found during spring and summer, *tomentosoides* all year round. **Similar species** · Closely resembles southern species, *C. tomentosum*. It is generally smaller, darker green, with more slender branches. The species can only be reliably separated by studies of internal morphology. *C. tomentosum* is present throughout the year, more common in winter.

Abundance & distribution
Common. All coasts of Britain and Ireland. Subsp. *atlanticum* more northern-living, as far south as Anglesey on west coast of Britain and Northumberland on east. Subsp. *tomentosoides* largely absent from Irish Sea but occurs in Northern Ireland and south-west Scotland. *C. fragile* distributed from Norway to

DIVISION Heterokontophyta | CLASS Phaeophyceae

FAMILY Ectocarpaceae

Ectocarpus siliculosus (Dillwyn) Lyngbye

Description · Fronds 12–30 cm long, consisting of many profusely branched and very slender filaments, forming a densely tangled tufted growth, developed from a creeping, filamentous holdfast. Tips of fronds not entangled. A hand lens will show the reproductive bodies, which may be borne on short branches or grow directly from the filaments; these are club-like and rounded, or elongate and pointed. Varies from yellowish to pale olive green. **Habitat & ecology·** On rocks and boulders from mid-to low-shore, extending sublittorally in shallow water. *E. siliculosus* may grow on other, larger seaweeds during the summer. At one time several separate species of *Ectocarpus* were recognised, but their differences were so small that the group is now regarded as a single aggregate form. **Similar species** · *Spongonema tomentosum*, but the fronds are made of more tightly entwined filaments, giving it a ropy or woolly appearance. It also tends to be duller in colour than *E. siliculosus*.

Abundance & distribution
Common. Occurs all around the coasts of Britain and Ireland. Distributed from Norway and the Baltic Sea to the Mediterranean.

FAMILY Corynophlaeaceae

Leathesia difformis (Linnaeus) Areschoug **Sea potato**

Description · Irregularly shaped, globular plant, usually up to 5 cm in diameter exceptionally 8 cm. At first the ball-like plant, attached by a short stipe, is solid, globose, and smooth, but soon hollows out to form a pale, almost translucent but shiny, convoluted bag often filled with sea water. Distinctly gelatinous texture. Colour is olive brown to yellowish-brown or amber. Thick plant walls. **Habitat & ecology** · Mid- to lower-shore regions, often in rock pools, usually attached to other algae, especially *Corallina officinalis*. More rarely found on rocks and boulders. Detached plants are often found floating partially submerged in intertidal rock pools. Annual plant found in spring and summer. **Similar species** · May be confused with *Colpomenia peregrina*, the oyster thief, particularly when dried out, but in life *Colpomenia* is thin-walled, more or less perfectly spherical and, though smooth-surfaced, is not shiny or gelatinous.

Abundance & distribution
Common. Occurs all around Britain and Ireland. Distributed from Norway and the Faeroes to the Mediterranean. Also occurs in South Africa, and the western Atlantic and Pacific Oceans.

South Africa. Other
subspecies occur in Indian
and Pacific Oceans.

Distinctive features

1. Dichotomously or
   irregularly branched
   fronds.
2. Fronds are generally
   round in cross-section
   with a velvety texture.

Distinctive features

1. Tangled, fine filaments,
   free towards their tips.
2. Forms 'cloudy', gelatinous
   tufts.
3. Yellowish or olive green
   colour.

Distinctive features

1. Irregular, globular, or
   ball-like shape, solid when
   young, later hollow; thick
   convoluted walls.
2. Pale olive brown to
   yellowish-brown.
3. Gelatinous.

FAMILY **Scytosiphonaceae**

Colpomenia peregrina (Sauvageau) Hamel
Oyster thief

Description · This alga appears as an erect, irregularly spherical, or sac-like hollow ball. It can grow to a diameter of up to 7–9 cm but is frequently smaller. When young, the plants are fleshy but often become furrowed, deflated, and torn when older. It is attached by a bundle of tiny rootlets. The texture is smooth on the outside and rough inside, and the colour is olive brown or greenish-brown. **Habitat & ecology** · The oyster thief is an introduced species, probably originating from the Pacific. It is found living on other plants and rock in rock pools from the upper middle shore to lower shore and subtidally to 3 m. When the algal thallus becomes filled with air it may lift the objects it is attached to and move them – hence its common name.

Abundance & distribution
Frequent, locally common. Occurs all around Britain and Ireland. Distributed at least from France to Norway.

Petalonia fascia (Müller) Kuntze

Description · Holdfast small and disc-like, or in form of a crust. From this grow one or more erect, flattened, lance-shaped, elongated but broad blades up to 15 cm (rarely 40 cm) high, 4 cm broad. Texture flaccid but blades solid; these widen from base and are rounded or tapered at top. Plant may be eroded at top and have ruffled edges. Light to dark greenish-brown or brown. **Habitat & ecology** · Middle to lower shore on rocks, or in rock pools and channels. Grows in sheltered to moderately exposed localities; tolerant of some sand cover and fluctuating salinities. Found throughout year but particularly common in late winter to spring. **Similar species** · Two other species of *Petalonia* occur in northern Europe, *P. filiformis* and *P. zosterifolia*. Both have much smaller and thinner blades than *P. fascia*. *Punctaria latifolia*, resembling *P. filiformis* but more membranous and slightly slimy, tends to grow on other plants. *Punctaria plantaginea* also similar but generally not as rounded as *P. fascia*, and tends to be deeply split longitudinally.

Abundance & distribution
Very common. Occurs all around Britain and Ireland. Distributed from Iceland and Norway to South Africa, including the Mediterranean. Also found in the western Atlantic and Pacific Oceans.

Ralfsia verrucosa (Areschoug) Agardh

Description · This alga forms a thick, encrusting thallus with an irregular outline, up to 10 cm across. The texture is generally leathery and lumpy. It is firmly attached to rock but the margins may often be easily raised with care. Is usually olive brown, dark brown to blackish-brown above and rust red coloured beneath. Several plants may grow into, or on top of, each other. Sometimes the plants have gelatinous wart-like structures that are reproductive. **Habitat & ecology** · Intertidal on all levels of the shore. It is found encrusted on rocks, and on shells of animals such as limpets, top-shells, mussels, and barnacles. *R. verrucosa* is particularly common in rock pools or in damp areas such as under *Fucus* canopies. It is the commonest of several encrusting brown algae species on European shores. **Similar species** · These tend to be thinner than *Ralfsia* and impossible to lift from the substrate intact; they include *Microspongium* species, *Petroderma* species, *Pseudolithoderma* species, and *Stragularia* species.

Abundance & distribution
Abundant. Occurs all around Britain and Ireland. Distributed from Iceland, Norway, and the Baltic to South Africa, including the Mediterranean and Black Seas. Also found in the western Atlantic, Pacific, and Indian Oceans, and Red Sea.

Distinctive features

1. Spherical or sac-like shape, generally hollow.
2. Texture on outside smooth, inside rough.

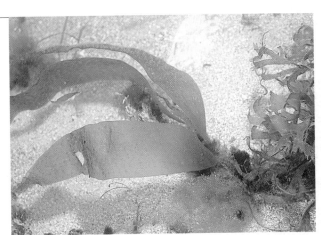

Distinctive features

1. One or more lance-shaped, flattened, blades.
2. Smooth surface but sometimes ruffled margins.
3. Rounded or tapered at top.

Distinctive features

1. Forms a thick brown encrusting thallus.
2. Leathery texture.
3. Sides of plant easy to raise intact.

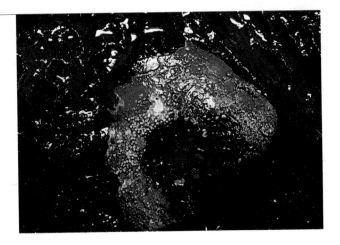

Scytosiphon lomentaria (Lyngbye) Link

Description · Consists of one or more erect tubular fronds arising from disc-like holdfast. Fronds soft, hollow, cylindrical, up to 40 cm long, generally gently tapering at the base and sharply ending at the top. Fronds may be flaccid or inflated; larger plants may be constricted at intervals along their length to resemble a chain of sausages. Yellow to dark brown or yellowish-green; may have a shiny appearance. **Habitat & ecology** · Lives on rock, often in pools or channels, from littoral fringe to lower shore and shallow sublittoral. Also found on shells, stones, and on *Zostera* species. Occurs throughout year but commonest in spring and summer. **Similar species** · *S. dotyi* resembles it but only grows to 14 cm, may feel slightly rigid to the touch, and does not have constrictions when mature. *Petalonia filiformis* and *Petalonia zosterifolia* also similar but solid rather than hollow. *Asperococcus fistulosus* similar and hollow but lacks obvious constrictions and is covered in dark brown spots. May also be mistaken for some *Enteromorpha* species.

Abundance & distribution
Common. Occurs all around Britain and Ireland. Distributed from Iceland, Norway, and the Baltic Sea to South Africa, including the Mediterranean and Black Seas.

FAMILY **Desmarestiaceae**

Desmarestia aculeata (Linneaus) Lamouroux

Description · Erect seaweed rising from small bulbous holdfast and regularly branching, alternately or oppositely. Main plant stem oval in cross-section, 3 mm wide at base, narrowing further up. Branches have alternate thorn-like branchlets. In summer only these are covered in 1–3 oppositely branched filaments, 2–4 mm long. Seaweed reaches 2 m in length. Green when young and cartilaginous to touch, light brown when older, and coarse and stiff. Summer filaments on branchlets are light brown. When these are shed plant has toothed appearance. **Habitat & ecology** · Intertidally on rock growing in lower middle-shore rock pools to the low shore, subtidally to 15 m or more. **Similar species** · *D. viridis* resembles *D. aculeata* but branching is opposite rather than alternate. Both have a similar distribution but *D. viridis* uncommon. *Arthrocladia villosa* is another erect, coarse seaweed but has distinctive regular whorls of hair-like filaments along stem and all branches. *Sporochnus pedunculatus* also similar but branchlets are small, bulbous, with tuft of filaments at end.

Abundance & distribution
Frequent. Occurs all around the British Isles and Ireland. Distributed from Norway to the Mediterranean, also Greenland, Iceland, the Faeroes, and the Baltic Sea. Also found in the western Atlantic and Indo-Pacific Oceans.

FAMILY **Chordaceae**

Chorda filum (Linnaeus) Stackhouse
Bootlace weed, mermaid's tresses, dead men's ropes, sea lace, cat gut

Description · A very distinctive seaweed, the slender, olive brown unbranched fronds, growing from a tiny holdfast, may reach a length of 3–6 m yet are only about 5–6 mm in diameter. The fronds are densely covered with short, colourless hairs, and are tough and slimy to the touch. Fronds of mature specimens are hollow and air-filled, a uniform width for most of their length but tapering at the extremities. **Habitat & ecology** · Very intolerant of desiccation, *Chorda filum* is most commonly found in sheltered situations, especially on gravelly sediments at depths of 3–30 m. It may sometimes be found growing in slightly brackish waters. Often dense communities of the seaweed form tangled masses which have been known to trap a swimmer. An annual summer alga, *Chorda filum* decays during the autumn and disappears in winter.

Abundance & distribution
Common, often abundant. Occurs all around the coasts of Britain and Ireland. Distributed north to Scandinavia.

Distinctive features

1. Erect tubular fronds.
2. Hollow and flaccid, or inflated.
3. Gently tapering base, sharply ending at top.
4. Larger plants with slight constrictions.

Distinctive features

1. Erect, coarse, stiff.
2. Stem oval in cross-section, alternately or oppositely branched.
3. Branches bear alternate, thorn-like, branchlets.
4. In summer branchlets have 1–3 oppositely branched filaments.

Distinctive features

1. Long, unbranched, whip-like frond.

FAMILY **Laminariaceae**

These are the kelps and two species, *Laminaria digitata* and *L. hyperborea*, form canopies that reduce light penetration to underlying plants. *L. digitata* tends to occur at or near to the low water mark, whereas *L. hyperborea* is generally a subtidal species that forms the dense kelp forests so familiar to divers. In more exposed areas these kelps may be replaced by *Alaria esculenta*, whereas in sheltered areas with unstable bottoms or in rock pools the opportunistic species *L. saccharina* may be found.

Laminaria digitata (Hudson) Lamouroux
Sea tangle, tangleweed, oarweed, sea girdle, horsetail kelp, devil's apron

Description · Attains lengths of 150 cm or more. Strong holdfast formed by cluster of branching, intertwined roots. Smooth-surfaced stipe, oval in cross-section, tough, flexible, up to 35–40 mm in diameter. When tide is out, seaweed lies flat. Distally, stipe becomes flattened and expands into a wide, flat, shiny, deep brown, or golden brown blade, up to 60 cm wide, divided into strap-like branches. Number of branches depends on exposure, plants on more exposed shores having more divisions. Blade of younger plants may be undivided and spear-shaped. Blade and stipe about equal length. **Habitat & ecology** · Important canopy forming alga, usually on exposed rocky coasts. Forms zone at ELWS tide levels, to 6 m or more in depth, growing on secure rocky surfaces. Smaller plants may live in deep permanent rock pools, up to mid-shore level. The complex holdfast shelters variety of animals and plants. **Similar species** · *L. hyperborea*. It stands up when tide recedes because of stiff stipe. This is round in cross-section, and in older individuals is covered by small, pimple-like growths.

Abundance & distribution
Common, locally abundant. Occurs on all British and Irish coasts. Distributed from Norway and the Baltic Sea to the Atlantic coast of Portugal and Spain.

Laminaria hyperborea (Gunnerus) Foslie **Cuvie**

Description · Holdfast a large cluster of branched roots up to 15–18 cm in diameter. Stipe 30–120 cm long, round in cross-section, up to 25 mm in diameter at base but tapering to half this before expanding into blade. Stipe stiff, so alga stands up when tide recedes and has roughened surface which, in older plants, is covered with small, pimple-like growths and frequently overgrown with other algae. Blade about same length as stipe, with smooth, shiny, leathery surface, dark or golden brown. Young blades may be undivided and oval but split deeply into strap-like branches as they grow. **Habitat & ecology** · Very important, canopy-forming alga, growing on rock at extreme lower shore to sublittoral depths of 25–30 m. Rarely uncovered by even lowest tides, but drooping fronds supported by inflexible stipes may be seen. Associated with exposed rather than sheltered shores. Stipes (= sea rods in Ireland) widely used in alginate industry. **Similar species** · *L. digitata*, but this has flexible, smooth stipe. *L. ochroleuca* also has smooth stipe and often yellow patch at blade base and is found in southwest of Britain and south to Atlantic coasts of Spain and Portugal.

Abundance & distribution
Common, locally abundant. Found all around British Isles and Ireland. Distributed from Norway and Baltic to Atlantic coasts of Spain and Portugal.

Distinctive features

1. Much-branched tough holdfast.
2. Stipe strong, smooth-surfaced, oval in cross-section, flexible.
3. Blade of frond broad, deeply divided into strap-like branches.

Distinctive features

1. Tough holdfast with numerous branches.
2. Stipe strong, nearly cylindrical, roughened and stiff.

Laminaria saccharina (Linnaeus) Lamouroux
Sea belt, poor man's weather glass, sugar kelp, oarweed

Description · Branched holdfast with tiered appearance, branches about 5 mm diameter at base, tapering towards tips. Stipe thin and smooth up to 30 cm or more length in older plants. At distal end it widens into a broad, unbranched, ribbon-like, wrinkled, yellowish-olive blade. This can become darker brown with age and has slightly undulate median strip, 20–25 mm wide, extending full length. Widths up to 15 cm and lengths up to 150 cm common; exceptionally may reach lengths of 9 m and widths of 45 cm.
Habitat & ecology · On rock and boulders on sheltered shores, low spring tide levels to sublittoral depths of several metres. Also grows in deeper, permanent mid- to lower-shore rock pools or on small rocks and stones on sand in sheltered areas. Dried fronds covered with sweet, whitish substance (thus sugar kelp) said to be enjoyed by horses. Collected fronds become soft and limp with approaching rain, or rigid and brittle in dry and sunny periods (hence poor man's weather glass).

Abundance & distribution
Common. Found all around the British Isles and Ireland. Distributed from Norway to Atlantic coasts of Spain and Portugal.

Saccorhiza polyschides (Lightfoot) Batters
Furbelows

Description · Largest European seaweed, may be 1.5–4.5 m long with blade of frond almost as broad. Young individuals attached by small disc but, as they grow, base of stipe develops into thick, fleshy, often bilobed, hemi-spherical structure, up to 25–30 cm in diameter, covered with tubercles. Stipe, short in juveniles, may attain length of 1 m or more and has charac-teristic single twist above holdfast. Stipe flattened, wavy margins giving corrugated appearance. Frond sharply widens from top of stipe with semi-circular to almost circular outline, deeply split almost to base into numerous broad straps. Frond covered with small tufts of hair. Typically rich reddish-brown to dark brown. **Habitat & ecology** · Attached to rock and secure boulders at low water spring tide level to shallow sublittoral depths, larger in size in deeper water. Most common on exposed shores but can be found at all exposures. **Similar species** · *Laminaria digitata* and *L. hyperborea*, but these easily distinguished by form of holdfast and stipe, and by lack of hairs on frond surface.

Abundance & distribution
Common. Occurs around all British and Irish coasts. Distributed from Norway to Atlantic coasts of Spain and Portugal and parts of the Mediterranean.

Undaria pinnatifida (Harvey) Suringar

Description · A large kelp with branched holdfast giving rise to a stipe. Just above the holdfast the stipe has very wavy edges giving it a corrugated appearance. Stipe gives rise to a blade that is flattened and lanceolate but broad and with a midrib. The margins of the blade are wavy. The overall size of this alga is 1.5–2 m long. The blade is dark brown. **Habitat & ecology** · An introduced species recently discovered in the Solent. It is generally subtidal, often growing on man-made structures such as pontoons in marinas. **Similar species** · This seaweed broadly resembles *Alaria esculenta* but the corrugated stipe is distinctive.

Abundance & distribution
Rare. Found in a small number of localities around the Solent in Southern Britain.

Distinctive features

1. Blade broad, thin, and very wrinkled.
2. Stipe slender and not very strong.
3. Holdfast branched, with tiered appearance.

Distinctive features

1. Holdfast of larger plants a fleshy hemisphere, often bilobed.
2. Stipe flattened, twisted once at base, with wavy margin.
3. Frond fan-like, semi-circular to almost circular, split into strap-like branches.

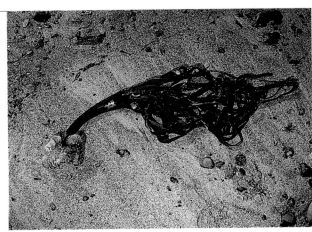

Distinctive features

1. Branched holdfast.
2. Stipe wavy or corrugated above holdfast.
3. Blade lanceolate and broad with a midrib.

FAMILY Alariaceae

Alaria esculenta (Linnaeus) Greville
Brown rib-weed, bladderlocks, badderlocks, dabberlocks, henware, murlin

Description · Stout, branched holdfast up to 8–9 cm across. Stipe, 5–15 cm long, rounded adjacent to holdfast becoming flattened towards frond. Stipe continues length of frond as a flat midrib. Towards base of stipe may be several small, lateral, club-shaped reproductive structures (pinnae). These are flattened with short stalks and a rounded end. Main fronds undivided, 60–180 cm long, 5–15 cm wide, with slightly frilled margins, often obliquely split from wave battering. Typically yellowish olive green, often with tiny brown spots which are tufts of microscopic hairs. **Habitat & ecology** · Typical of exposed rocky shores near extreme low water level or in shallow sublittoral situations. Can withstand wave battering and is an indicator of exposed conditions. Tends to grow slightly higher on shore than *Laminaria hyperborea*. Midrib eaten in parts of Scotland and Ireland. **Similar species** · May be mistaken for a kelp but can be easily distinguished from these by distinct midrib extending full length of frond.

Abundance & distribution
Common, sometimes abundant. Occurs around most coasts of Britain and Ireland but rare or absent in south-west Britain. Distributed from Scandinavia to the Channel, including Iceland and the Faeroes. Also occurs on the coast of North America.

FAMILY Stypocaulaceae

Halopteris scoparia (Linnaeus) Sauvageau

Description · This seaweed is formed of stiff, divided and subdivided threads forming 'cones' that resemble shaving brushes. These cones grow one on top of the other and the seaweed may be up to 15 cm long. In winter these may be worn and much reduced. **Habitat & ecology** · Grows on the lower shore and subtidally on rocks.

Abundance & distribution
Locally common. Occurs on southern and western coasts of Britain and Ireland, rare in the north. Distributed south to the Mediterranean.

FAMILY Dictyotaceae

Dictyopteris membranacea (Stackhouse) Batters

Description · This seaweed resembles a wrack. The frond arises from a disc-like holdfast. It is flat, branches dichotomously, and has a distinct midrib. The base of the frond may be torn or serrated to the midrib. Maximum length about 30 cm. Colour is a greenish- or yellowish-brown. **Habitat & ecology** · Found on rocks and stones from mid-low shore and subtidally to depths of 80 m. **Similar species** · *Dictyota dichotoma*, but it lacks a midrib. This species is more delicate than the cartilaginous wracks.

Abundance & distribution
Rare. Occurs in south-west Britain and Ireland. Distributed south to the Mediterranean.

Distinctive features

1. Broad, leaf-like frond with distinct midrib.
2. Yellowish-green frond.
3. Lateral, club-shaped reproductive bodies near base of stipe.

Distinctive features

1. Main stem of stiff, divided and subdivided threads.
2. Branches form 'cones' that resemble shaving brushes, one of top of the other.

Distinctive features

1. Wrack-like seaweed.
2. Disc-like holdfast.
3. Frond flat, dichotomously branched.
4. Distinct midrib.
5. Frond base may be serrated.

Dictyota dichotoma (Hudson) Lamouroux

Description · This seaweed arises from a disc-like holdfast. It has a delicate, flaccid, dichotomously branched frond lacking a midrib. Up to 30 cm in height, with branches 2–12 mm wide. A pale, translucent, olive green to brown colour, sometimes yellowish. May be iridescent. The terminal branches tend to be round-ended. **Habitat & ecology** · Occurs from the middle shore, on rocks, stones, and other plants. **Similar species** · Resembles *Dictyopteris membranacea* but this has a distinct midrib. Also similar to *Cutleria multifida* but this is a long and narrow plant and tends to be heavily spotted with brown.

Abundance & distribution
Common. Occurs in south-west Britain and Ireland, rare on other coasts. Distributed south to the Mediterranean.

FAMILY **Fucaceae**

The fucoid algae are amongst the dominant space-occupying plants on rocky shores in the temperate north-east Atlantic. On sheltered shores different species occupy different zones (called zonation). Just above the kelp zone, on the lower shore, *Fucus serratus* is found. Above this *F. vesiculosus* and *Ascophyllum nodosum* occur and finally, on the upper shore, the small species *F. spiralis* and then *Pelvetia canaliculata*. Generally, the higher on the shore a species occurs the greater its tolerance to harsh conditions, such as the drying effects of the sun and wind when the tide is out. Competition between different fucoids and predation by grazers such as limpets are also important in setting the zones at which the plants live. On more exposed shores, zonation becomes patchier, finally giving away to barnacle- and mussel-dominated rocks on the most exposed shores. *F. ceranoides* is a specialist coloniser of estuaries.

Ascophyllum nodosum (Linnaeus) Le Jolis
Egg wrack, knotted wrack, sea whistle, knobbed wrack, yellow tang

Description · May exceed 3 m in length but commonly less than half this. Fronds rounded for short distance from disc-like holdfast, but mostly distinctly flattened and dichotomously branched, without midrib. Usually dull, olive green, darkening to almost black when dried. At variable intervals, often 6–10 cm, frond enlarged to form spherical to elliptical air bladders, 4–5 cm long, frequently appearing damaged or with holes. Edges of fronds slightly notched at intervals, representing growing points for ordinary branches or short, slender branches which end in receptacles; golden yellow in male plants, olive yellow in females, swollen and covered in small knobs (papillae). **Habitat & ecology** · progressively replaced by *Fucus vesiculosus* as conditions become more exposed. Because of its large size and buoyancy, *Ascophyllum* requires a secure site, such as large boulders or base rock, for attachment. A short reddish-brown epiphytic alga, *Polysiphonia lanosa*, is very commonly found growing in tufts on the fronds. Plant's age may be estimated by counting number of air bladders along length of longest frond: after 1–2 years' growth each branch grows a single new bladder each year.

Abundance & distribution
Common, sometimes abundant. Occurs around all British and Irish coasts. Distributed from the English Channel, northwards to Norway.

Distinctive features

1. Flaccid seaweed with dichotomously branched frond.
2. No midrib.
3. Disc-like holdfast.

Distinctive features

1. No midrib on frond.
2. Variably sized air bladders arranged singly along frond.
3. Receptacles borne on slender branches.
4. Dichotomously branched.

Fucus ceranoides Linnaeus
Horned wrack

Description · Typically smaller (30–60 cm long, rarely 90 cm) than other *Fucus* species, not found with usual rocky shore intertidal *Fucus* zones. Stipe develops from small conical holdfast into flattened frond with narrow, prominent midrib. Fronds branch dichotomously, lateral branches usually narrower than main frond. Edges of fronds not toothed; plant lacks air bladders. Narrow reproductive bodies at forked tips of fronds, often forming fan-like groups. Olive brown or green. **Habitat & ecology** · Growing on rocks, boulders, or other secure structures at all shore levels, most commonly with reduced salinity, such as estuaries or coastline adjacent to river mouths. Generally does not form zones typical of fucoid and kelp seaweeds on open rocky coasts. **Similar species** · Resembles *F. spiralis*, but lacks typical twisted or spiral growth form of this species and does not form a distinct intertidal zone growing between *Pelvetia canaliculata* and *Ascophyllum nodosum*. Some forms of *F. vesiculosus* may lack bladders, but these are typical of exposed rocky coasts where *F. ceranoides* is not found. Small specimens of *F. vesiculosus* may be confused with *F. ceranoides*.

Abundance & distribution
Common, locally abundant. Found all around Britain and Ireland. Distributed from Norway to the Channel coasts of northern Europe.

Fucus serratus Linnaeus
Toothed wrack, saw wrack, serrated wrack, notched wrack, black wrack, prickly tang

Description · Distinctive, easily identified. Robust flattened frond, 15–20 mm wide and up to about 60 cm long; under ideal conditions may exceed 1 m. Holdfast tough, branched, giving rise to strong, short stipe from which fronds branch dichotomously or irregularly. Midrib prominent. Frond margins toothed or serrated, reminiscent of saw blade; tips of teeth pointing towards end of fronds, but often irregularly split by wave damage. No air bladders. Orange male and olive green or brown female reproductive bodies on different plants form swollen areas at ends of fronds. Fronds are covered in small tufts of white hairs issuing from minute pores (cryptostomata) scattered over surface. **Habitat & ecology** · On rocks and boulders two forms of *F. serratus* are recognised. Forma *angustifrons*, found under more exposed conditions, has narrow fronds up to 6 mm wide. Forma *latifolius* grows in very calm situations; it is short, with fronds 45–50 mm across.

Abundance & distribution
Abundant. Occurs around all coasts of Britain and Ireland. Distributed from the Baltic Sea to Atlantic coasts of Spain and Portugal.

Fucus spiralis Linnaeus
Spiral wrack, flat wrack, twisted wrack

Description · Discoid holdfast gives rise to short, rather flattened stipe. Frond flattened, dichotomously branched, 15–40 cm long, with distinct midrib, no air bladders, and untoothed margins. Wave damage commonly leads to torn frond edges. Plant characteristically exhibits twisted or spiral growth form, particularly towards ends of fronds, although not always apparent. Reproductive bodies distinct, varying from globular to egg-shaped granular structures carried on tips of branches. Reproductive bodies have narrow margin of frond around middle, i.e. margin of frond sterile. Their light orangey-brown contrasts with darker olive green of remainder of plant. **Habitat & ecology** · Important intertidally on rocky coasts, although often absent from more exposed habitats. On rocks in upper shore, spiral wrack frequently forms distinct zone immediately below *Pelvetia canaliculata*. Under adverse ecological conditions fronds may develop surface blisters, but these should not be mistaken for air bladders. In parts of Ireland a hot, salty-water infusion of sticky, swollen, mature reproductive bodies, known as 'jelly bags', used as cure for feet corns. **Similar species** · Confusable with bladderless variety of *F. vesiculosus* or *F. ceranoides*. However, margins of reproductive bodies in *F. spiralis* are sterile.

Abundance & distribution
Common, locally abundant. Occurs around all coasts of Britain and Ireland. Distributed from Norway to Atlantic coasts of Spain and Portugal. Also occurs in the Azores.

Distinctive features

1. Distinct midrib.
2. Margins of frond lamina not serrated.

Distinctive features

1. Fronds with distinct midrib.
2. Margins of fronds serrated or toothed.
3. No air bladders.

Distinctive features

1. Frond with conspicuous midrib, margins unserrated.
2. No air bladders.
3. Twisted or spiral growth form.

Fucus vesiculosus Linnaeus
Bladder wrack, bladder fucus, popweed, cutweed, kelpware, seawrack, pigweed, paddy tang

Description · Repeatedly forked frond, 20–120 cm or more long with distinct midrib and untoothed margins. Air bladders, arranged in pairs on either side of midrib, are about size of a pea, slightly oval or rounded, Sometimes single bladders occur on one side only or in groups of three or four. Reproductive bodies, at the end of branches, appear as bulbous, granular structures when fertile. These are yellowish-olive in females, orange in males. Plants olive green to olive brown. Appearance varies considerably, depending upon local ecological conditions. On exposed rocks, frond may be narrow (about 5 mm), without air bladders; this form known as *F vesiculosus linearis* or *evesiculosus*. Under extremely sheltered conditions bladder density may be so great as to be almost continuous along frond lamina. **Habitat & ecology** · Important intertidal canopy forming alga. Characteristically forms distinct mid-shore zone between *F. spiralis* and *F. serratus*. Grows on rocky surfaces, or securely embedded larger rocks and boulders. Although less frequently found on steeply sloping shores or on severely exposed beaches, the typical form may occur in regions too exposed for *Ascophyllum nodosum*. In areas of Scotland where fodder is scarce, the plant, locally called paddy tang, is sometimes fed to pigs, either as boiled mix with meal, or raw. **Similar species** · Bladderless variety resembles *F. spiralis*, although it lives on mid- rather than upper shore, generally in exposed areas. Unlike *F. spiralis*, reproductive bodies of *F. vesiculosus* lack sterile margins. Also resembles *F. ceranoides*, though this generally occurs in sheltered conditions with reduced salinities.

Abundance & distribution
Very common, often abundant. Distributed from Norway and the Baltic Sea to the Atlantic coasts of Spain and Portugal.

Pelvetia canaliculata (Linnaeus) Decaisne & Thuret
Channelled wrack, cow tang

Description · Small rounded holdfast grows into a short stipe which rapidly bifurcates to form fronds, 5–15 cm long and 5–6 mm wide, with a very characteristic channelled appearance caused by inrolling of the frond margins. There is no midrib and the plants possess neither air bladders nor cryptostomata (white hairs arising from pores). The swollen, ellipsoidal, granular, reproductive bodies are carried on the ends of the fronds which are deeply forked at their bases. Colour is dark greenish-brown, olive brown, or orangey-brown. May be blackish if very dried. **Habitat & ecology** · On rocks on the upper shore, sometimes above high water level, this alga forms a distinct zone above *Fucus spiralis*. Where never submerged by high water but regularly wetted by spray, it tends to be smaller, blackish, and brittle and may resemble the lichen *Lichina pygmaea*. Both sheep and cattle feed on this seaweed, cattle in particular, giving rise to the Scottish name of cow tang.

Abundance & distribution
Very common, locally abundant. Occurs all around the British Isles and Ireland. Distributed from Iceland and Norway south to the Atlantic coasts of Spain and Portugal.

Distinctive features

1. Fronds with distinct midrib.
2. Frond margins not serrated or toothed.
3. Air bladders on either side of midrib.

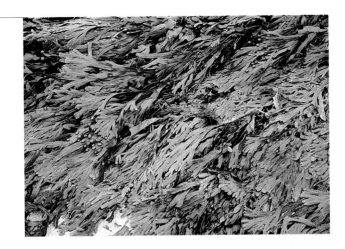

Distinctive features

1. Frond margins inrolled to form distinct longitudinal channels.
2. No midrib.
3. No cryptostomata.
4. No air bladders.

FAMILY **Himanthaliaceae**

Himanthalia elongata (Linnaeus) Gray
Thong weed, sea thong

Description · Young plants consist of small, glossy, olive brown club-shaped bodies about 5–6 mm wide; these grow into the typical short-stalked buttons, 25–40 mm in diameter, which have a distinctly concave upper surface. From the centre of these buttons the fertile frond, up to about 10 mm wide, forms an elongate, flattened, and strap-like structure which forks a few times and may reach a length of 2 m. During the spring and early summer the fronds, which are at other times a greenish-brown or yellowish-ochre colour, become mottled with brown spots. **Habitat & ecology** · Typically forms dense colonies on the lower shore below the *Fucus serratus* zone, or in shallow sublittoral situations, or in deep, permanent rock pools. The seaweed once known as *H. lorea* is now regarded as being the same species as *H. elongata*. **Similar species** · May be mistaken for *Chorda filum* but this species lacks the button-like holdfasts of *H. elongata*.

Abundance & distribution
Common, locally abundant. Found all around Britain and Ireland. Distributed from Norway to the Atlantic coasts of Spain and Portugal.

FAMILY **Cystoseiraceae**

Bifurcaria bifurcata Ross

Description · Also known as *Bifurcaria rotunda* and *B. tuberculata*, the main stem for its lower quarter is rounded and unbranched, but then branches alternately. Individual branches further divide unevenly, either irregularly or dichotomously, branchlets often being of different lengths. The brownish or dull olive brown fronds may be 30–60 cm long, the tips of the branches often bearing swollen and elongate fruiting bodies oval in cross-section. Single but irregularly spaced small, rounded air bladders may form along the main branches. **Habitat & ecology** · Generally found attached to rocks or boulders in shallow sublittoral waters, occurring inter-tidally only in permanent rock pools where it is never left exposed to the air. **Similar species** · In some ways resembling *Halidrys siliquosa* but can be easily distinguished from this form by the air bladders; in *Halidrys* these are borne on branches off the main stem and are rather like seed pods with about ten internal compartments.

Abundance & distribution
May be locally common. Occurs in south-west Britain and Ireland including the Channel Islands. Distributed from Britain southwards.

Cystoseira tamariscifolia (Hudson) Papenfuss

Description · Holdfast flattened, 20–25 mm in diameter. Stipe stout, cylindrical, branched profusely in an irregular fashion, often so much as to be almost indistinguishable. Bushy frond, 35–45 cm or more long, densely covered by awl-shaped spines, 3–4 mm long. Tufted, terminal reproductive bodies, distinct when mature, 5–10 mm long. Air bladders usually found at bases of reproductive bodies; typically only single bladder, but sometimes in twos or threes. Olive brown, blacker when dry, but iridescent blue and green when submerged. Colour may persist when removed from water. **Habitat & ecology** · Attached to rocks on lower shore and in shallow sublittoral situations; also in rock pools. **Similar species** · *C. baccata, C. foeniculacea,* and *C. granulata,* but these lack awl-like spines all over plant, and iridescence. *C. foeniculacea* has rough points all over branches resembling broken pieces of plant. *C. baccata* has reproductive bodies covered in delicate, spiny branchlets. Stem is short, giving off branches from bulbous knobs, and has irregularly scattered spine-like branchlets. Upper parts of branches also have long, oblong air bladders, sometimes in groups of 2–3.

Abundance & distribution
Frequent, locally common. Occurs on south and west coasts of Britain and Ireland. Distributed south to the Mediterranean.

Distinctive features

1. Frond strap-like, flattened, dichotomously branched.
2. Young plants, before frond growth, look like stalked buttons, gradually becoming concave on upper surface.

Distinctive features

1. Basal quarter of frond unbranched, then branching alternately.
2. Branches fork unevenly, dichotomously, or irregularly.
3. Reproductive bodies borne on branch tips.
4. Main branches may bear single air bladders.

Distinctive features

1. Frond covered with awl-shaped spines.
2. Reproductive bodies terminal, tufted, prominent when mature.
3. Air bladders, usually single, at bases of reproductive bodies.
4. Iridescent under water.

Halidrys siliquosa (Linnaeus) Lyngbye **Sea oak, pod weed**

Description · From the strong, flattened, cone-shaped holdfast branches ascend in a regular alternate fashion, giving the frond a zigzag appearance about its main axis. Branches also divide into alternate branchlets. Thallus stiff, rather flattened, 30–120 cm long. The numerous, seed-pod like air bladders are borne on short stalks at the ends of branchlets. Each bladder up to about 5 mm wide, 15–20 mm long, and marked by transverse bands corresponding to positions of the internal partitions that divide the complete bladder into 10–12 compartments. Long, ribbon-like structures resembling leaves may also occur. Colour typically a dull olive green to brownish green, or gingery-brown. **Habitat & ecology** · The plant grows on rocks under more sheltered conditions, usually in shallow water just below low tide level, though it can also be found in deeper mid- or lower-shore rock pools. The species is perennial. **Similar species** · Has the overall twiggy, bush-like appearance of *Cystoseira* species but the air bladders are distinctive.

Abundance & distribution
Frequent. Occurs all around Britain and Ireland. Distributed from Norway to Atlantic coasts of Spain and Portugal.

FAMILY **Sargassaceae**

Sargassum muticum (Yendo) Fensholt

Description · A fairly large wrack. This seaweed has a slender main stem which branches alternately. The branches bear small lance-shaped, leaf-like branchlets and spherical gas bladders, and smaller reproductive bodies held on short, slender stalks. It can grow to a length of over 1 m and tends to be greenish-brown to dark green. Is often unattached and may be found lying in rock pools. **Habitat & ecology** · Occurs in the mid- to low shore, often in rock pools where its growth may be prodigious. It is an introduced species from the Pacific and since its arrival in Britain it has spread to most southern coasts. Its spread further north is limited by low temperatures. May be regarded as a pest as it overgrows and chokes native species of plants and animals and fouls boat engine intakes, propellers, and fishermen's nets. It is spread when pieces break off. These are self-fertile and can release spores while floating along the coast.

Abundance & distribution
Common, locally abundant. On southern coasts of Britain and on the Atlantic coasts of France.

DIVISION **Rhodophyta** | CLASS **Rhodophyceae**
ORDER **Nemaliales,**

FAMILY **Gelidiaceae**

Gelidium pusillum (Stackhouse) Le Jolis

Description · Has a creeping root, attached to substrate by lateral rootlets. Erect fronds consist of cylindrical or slightly compressed main stems, up to 2 mm broad. Main stems unbranched or branched up to three times, oppositely, alternately, or radially. Numerous alternate or irregular branchlets, sometimes with flattened tips. Up to 15 cm long; size and complexity of branching highly variable, depending on position on shore. Overall outline irregular. Colour variable, black, purple, red, brown, or yellowish-green. **Habitat & ecology** · On rock and stones from mid- to low shore and in rock pools. Small plants may be found on upper shore. Found throughout year. Has been used as source of agar but this now less common because of small size. **Similar species** · *G. latifolium* has broad and flattened main stems and flattened branchlets. *G. sesquipedale* is often tufted, main branches parallel-sided, slightly flattened, often with hard or horny texture. Branchlets tend to be blunt ended. *Pterocladia capillacea* has fronds that are usually triangular in outline.

Abundance & distribution
Common. Distributed from central coast of Norway to Mediterranean and Cape Verde Islands. Also occurs in western Atlantic and Pacific Oceans.

Distinctive features

1. Holdfast a flattened cone.
2. Frond branches alternately.
3. Air bladders terminal on short stalks, resembling seed pods marked with transverse bands.

Distinctive features

1. Slender stem branching alternately.
2. Branchlets resembling lance-shaped leaves.
3. Spherical gas bladders and reproductive bodies on short stalks.

Distinctive features

1. Creeping root gives rise to unbranched or branched cylindrical stems.
2. Numerous cylindrical branchlets that may be flattened at ends.
3. Outline irregular.

FAMILY **Helminthocladiaceae**

Nemalion helminthoides (Velley in Withering) Batters
Sea noodle

Description · Up to about 40 cm long, the solid frond is cylindrical and somewhat worm-like, branching either from its base or dichotomously at irregular intervals. The branches taper towards their tips but are blunt-ending. The holdfast is tiny and disc-like. In colour the alga is a purplish- to brownish-red, to black. The texture is gelatinous or cartilaginous and often slimy to the touch. **Habitat & ecology** · Found on the mid-shore and lower, or in shallow subtidal situations, either on rocks and boulders or attached to limpets or barnacles. On fairly exposed shores, where it is most commonly found, it occurs during the summer and early autumn months.

Abundance & distribution
Locally common. Found all around Britain and Ireland. Distributed from middle Norway to Morocco, including the Mediterranean. Also found in the western Atlantic.

FAMILY **Chaetangiaceae**

Scinaia forcellata Bivona

Description · The frond, up to 10 cm tall, is typically tubular but may sometimes be flattened or compressed. The dichotomous or irregular branching is repeated, commencing close to the small, disc-like holdfast. There are not usually constrictions at the beginning of branches. Branches terminate in small, blunt forks. The alga, which is a dull red, or bright pinkish- or brownish-red, has a slimy feel. **Habitat & ecology** · A lower shore and shallow sublittoral species, found freely attached to rocks and boulders but generally only in pools or channels, especially where sand is present. **Similar species** · Resembles *S. turgida*, but this species has constrictions at the base of the branches and grows larger than *S. forcellata*.

Abundance & distribution
Locally common, albeit unobtrusive. Distributed around Britain and Ireland but may be absent from parts of the east coast of Britain. Distributed from southern Norway to Morocco.

FAMILY **Bonnemaisoniaceae**

Asparagopsis armata Harvey

Description · The delicate, slender frond of the gametophyte stage is up to 30 cm long and has a main stem that is bare in the lower part but branches irregularly further up. The holdfast looks like a network of small roots. Branches densely tufted, forming an elongated cone-like or feathery shape. These tufts are formed by small, spirally distributed, branchlets. As these are worn, some of the branches, instead of bearing branchlets, are covered with alternate barbs or thorns. Colour pinkish-red, yellowish-pink, or whitish-pink. The sporophyte (formerly known as *Falkenbergia rufolanosa*) forms tangled tufts of fine, pinkish-red filaments attached to other algae. **Habitat & ecology** · Possibly an immigrant from Australia, believed to have been introduced into European waters in about 1925. Found growing in shaded intertidal lower-shore rock pools and in shallow sublittoral situations where it may form extensive beds. The gametophyte is the sexually reproducing generation whilst the sporophytic form produces asexual spores which then grow into the gametophyte generation.

Abundance & distribution
Frequent, locally abundant. Gametophyte stage uncommon, often localised in Britain and Ireland; sporophyte more commonly encountered, though still not found on eastern coasts. Distributed south to the Mediterranean. Also found in the Pacific and Indian Oceans.

Distinctive features

1. Frond cylindrical, branching either from base or dichotomously at irregular intervals.
2. Branches tapering towards tips, but blunt ending.
3. Holdfast minute, disc-like.

Distinctive features

1. Frond typically cylindrical, or rather flattened, regular, repeated dichotomous branching.
2. Branching commences close to disc-like holdfast.
3. Branches end in small blunt forks.

Distinctive features

1. Main frond delicate, irregularly branched, bare at base.
2. Fronds have a feathery appearance.
3. Worn branches have alternate barb or thorn-like structures.

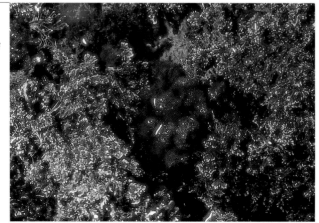

ORDER **Gigartinales**

FAMILY **Furcellariaceae**

Furcellaria lumbricalis (Hudson) Lamouroux

Description · Branched, entangled holdfast giving rise to stiff, cylindrical stems branched dichotomously. The stems and branches are slightly compressed at the dichotomies. Branches are increasingly shorter as they get nearer to their tips. The branches taper gradually and the tips are bifid and pointed except when they bear the pod-like reproductive bodies. The texture is cartilaginous and the colour a brownish-black. May exceed 30 cm in length. **Habitat & ecology** · Attached to rocks on the lower shore and in shallow subtidal waters to at least 12 m depth. Tolerant of some sand. Found all year round and takes 4–7 years to reach full size. **Similar species** · *Polyides rotundus* resembles it but may be distinguished by its fleshy, disc-like holdfast and the branches which are more completely cylindrical. *Gigartina pistillata* is similar but also has a disc-like holdfast. The branches also tend to be compressed in the upper reaches.

Abundance & distribution
Locally common. Occurs all around the British Isles and Ireland. Distributed from northern Russia to the Atlantic coast of France including the Baltic Sea, Iceland, and the Faeroes.

FAMILY **Rhodophyllidaceae**

Calliblepharis ciliata (Hudson) Kützing

Description · From the deeply branched, rhizoidal, holdfast the frond may grow directly, or may develop from a short stipe. The stipe (if present) is cylindrical and up to 1 cm long. The main frond is flat and broad, up to 15–30 cm long and 7 cm wide. It divides dichotomously or irregularly with wedge-shaped or ovate lobes. The margins of the frond, and sometimes the surfaces, are irregularly covered with short branchlets 4–5 mm long. Cartilaginous or leathery texture; dull purplish-red or dark red colour. **Habitat & ecology** · On rocks, boulders, or other algae sublittorally to 21 m depth. Also in rock pools from the mid-shore downwards. Can commonly be collected from masses of drift weed. Older plants may have their fronds encrusted with sessile invertebrates such as bryozoans. Found from spring to autumn. **Similar species** · May be confused with *C. jubata*, which has a narrower frond, longer fringing branchlets (up to 3 cm), and tends to live somewhat higher up the shore.

Abundance & distribution
Common. Occurs all around Ireland and on the southern and western coasts of Britain. Distributed south to Mauritania, including the Mediterranean.

Calliblepharis jubata (Gooding & Woodward) Kützing

Description · This species has a branched holdfast, and a cylindrical stipe up to 5 cm long. The main stem is flattened and up to 15 mm wide. It divides dichotomously or irregularly to form flattened, strap-like fronds that have similar but much smaller branches growing from their margins. The margins of the fronds are fringed with slender, pointed branchlets that also arise from the flat surfaces in older plants. The texture of this seaweed is cartilaginous and the colour is a dark reddish-brown. **Habitat & ecology** · A lower shore species that grows on rocks and other plants. Often found in rock pools. Also sublittoral but only to several metres depth. It may be washed up on the shore during spring months. **Similar species** · Closely resembles *C. ciliata*, but this species has broader fronds and smaller fringing branchlets. *C. jubata* may also be confused with *Palmaria palmata*, but this form has a disc-like holdfast.

Abundance & distribution
Locally common. Found all around Ireland and on south and west coasts of Britain. Distributed southwards to Mauritania including the Mediterranean.

Distinctive features

1. Holdfast a mass of root-like branches.
2. Stems cylindrical, regularly divided, successive branches shorter.
3. Tips of branches tapered, pointed, except during summer when bear pod-like reproductive bodies.

Distinctive features

1. Main frond flat, broad, irregularly branched.
2. Edges and flat surfaces of fronds with numerous short side branches.
3. Dull red colour.

Distinctive features

1. Fronds flattened, strap-like, dark reddish-brown.
2. Frond fringed with small, slender branchlets.
3. Rootlet-like holdfast.

FAMILY **Plocamiaceae**

Plocamium cartilagineum (Linnaeus) Dixon

Description · Frond up to 30 cm long, forming a tufted growth with tough main stems. Stems near their attachment tend to have few or no branches, whereas farther from the holdfast they branch alternately or irregularly. Between the main branches there may be small, up-curved branches growing from the main stem. Main branches may branch several more times but terminal branches have a characteristic comb-like appearance with small, pointed sub-branchlets only growing from one side of the tip. These give the plant a feathery appearance. Globular reproductive structures may occur all over the plant. The texture is cartilaginous, the colour translucent pinkish red to brownish-red, occasionally with a blue sheen. Plants may become bleached. **Habitat & ecology** · Typically found attached to rocks in shallow sublittoral situations to at least 30 m depth. It is not uncommonly found washed up on the shore. May also grow on the stipes of kelps. **Similar species** · Other species may appear similar but the branching pattern of *P. cartilagineum* is distinctive.

Abundance & distribution
Locally common. Occurs all around Britain and Ireland. Distributed from mid-Norway to Senegal, including the Mediterranean and Canary Islands.

FAMILY **Gracilariaceae**

Gracilaria verrucosa (Hudson) Papenfuss

Description · Up to 60 cm tall, with branched and bushy or long and stringy appearance. Several fronds usually grow from fleshy, disc-like holdfast. Branching usually begins near base of frond, may be very irregular, sometimes pinnate, unilateral, or dichotomous on same plant. Branches cylindrical, slender, 1–3 mm in diameter, often with short, very thin branchlets tapering at both ends. Reproductive bodies scattered over whole plant, as small knobbly or wart-like protuberances bulging from surfaces of main stems in summer and early autumn. Dark purplish-red or brown to green, sometimes bleached, often translucent. Texture quite elastic. **Habitat & ecology** · On rocks and stones mid-shore and sublittorally to depths of 15 m or more. Commonly occurs where sand covers rock surfaces. Tolerant of reduced salinities. **Similar species** · *G. bursa-pastoris* is fatter than *G. verrucosa*, fronds more compressed distinctly succulent, with brittle blades. *G. foliifera* has broad, compressed blade, divided di- or trichotomously with translucent, cartilaginous, brittle texture. Dull brownish- or purplish-red. *Cystoclonium purpureum* has branched holdfast. *Gigartina acicularis* can be similar but fronds usually compressed.

Abundance & distribution
Common. Occurs all around the Britain and Ireland. Distributed from Norway to South Africa, including the Baltic and Mediterranean Seas. Also western Atlantic, Indian and Pacific Oceans.

FAMILY **Gigartinaceae**

Chondrus crispus Stackhouse
Carragheen, Irish moss

Description · Holdfast disc-like, about 10 mm in diameter, from which narrow compressed stems grow and gradually expand to form flat, fan-like fronds. Fronds branch dichotomously up to 6–8 times, about 20 cm long. Form variable; fronds grow rapidly in width to give short-stalked, broad, fan-like appearance, in others frond only slightly widened and remains more or less constant in width throughout length. Typically deep reddish-purple, purple, or purplish-brown, but in strong sunlight frond tips or whole plant may be bleached greenish or yellowish-green. In water fronds, especially tips, often iridescent. **Similar species** · Resembles *Gigartina stellata*, but older examples have numerous short, stout papillae growing from margin of fronds, not found on *C. crispus*. *Phyllophora pseudocera-noides* similar but stipe usually cylindrical and long, blade short, widely expanded but much divided. *Gymnogongrus crenulatus* also often more branched; branching parallel-sided, never iridescent.

Abundance & distribution
Common. All around the British Isles and Ireland. Distributed from northern Russia to southern Spain including the Baltic Sea. Also the western Atlantic and Japan.

Distinctive features

1. Main stems tough, unbranched, or little branched towards bases.
2. Branching tufted, branches with branchlets whose terminal divisions are all on same side.
3. Globular reproductive bodies all over plant.

Distinctive features

1. Holdfast a fleshy disc.
2. Bushy or stringy stems with irregular branches usually with smaller branchlets.
3. Branches cylindrical, texture elastic.
4. Reproductive bodies like warty growths on stems.

Distinctive features

1. Fronds, especially tips, often brightly iridescent.
2. Deep reddish-purple to purple; frond tips or whole plant may turn greenish or greenish-yellow in strong sunlight.

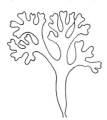

Gigartina stellata (Stackhouse in Withering) Batters
Carragheen moss, false carragheen moss

Description · Disc-like holdfast up to 5 cm across, giving rise to one or more fronds with short stipes that expand into strap-like fronds up to 8 mm broad and 17 cm tall. Fronds distinctly channelled or U-shaped in cross-section with thickened margins, dichotomously or, less frequently, irregularly branched. Fronds may be twisted and cartilaginous in texture and may be covered in scattered, warty, reproductive papillae. Brownish-red, purple, or black, sometimes greenish or apple green. Bleaching quite common. **Habitat & ecology** · On rock and stones, lower shore or sub-tidally. Sometimes common where there is exposure to wave action. Also under *Fucus* canopies where there is running water. Intolerant of mud or sand, easily damaged by the sun. **Similar species** · *G. acicularis*, but this has much narrower branches without inrolling. *G. pistillata* branches dichotomously with more cylindrical branches. Both species occur in south-west Britain and Ireland, southwards. *Chondrus crispus* is similar but margins of fronds not usually inrolled. Found with *G. stellata* and gathered with it as carragheen.

Abundance & distribution
Frequent. Found all around the British Isles and Ireland though may be scarce where habitat is lacking. Distributed from northern Russia to the Atlantic coast of Spain. Also found in the western Atlantic.

ORDER **Corallinales**

FAMILY **Corallinaceae** | SUBFAMILY **Corallinoidea**

Coralline algae have calcium carbonate incorporated in the thallus, giving them a chalky, hard texture. They form extensive turfs on the shore, especially in rock pools, and these provide a habitat for many other animals and plants. Some species live epiphytically on other plants.

Corallina elongata Ellis & Solander

Description · Crustose, chalky base, up to 15 cm wide, giving rise to densely tufted, branched, limp, calcareous fronds, up to 20 cm tall. Calcareous segments of main stems and branches ovoid or slightly triangular, nearly as wide as long. Branching very dense, branches divide pinnately into branchlets. Purplish-red to pinkish-red, with white calcareous deposits. When present, reproductive bodies form slightly swollen terminal segments, usually with small branches and a minute pore. **Habitat & ecology** · Attached to rock and boulders in mid- to lower-shore rock pools, or hanging down in sheltered and permanently wet crevices and gullies. Also in shallow sublittoral waters to at least 3 m depth.

Abundance & distribution
Locally, very common. Occurs in south-west Britain and Ireland. Distributed south to Senegal including the Mediterranean and Canary Islands.

Corallina officinalis Linnaeus

Description · Holdfast a hard calcareous crust, up to 7 cm in diameter, giving rise to several, almost cylindrical, segmented fronds. Segments calcareous, slightly longer than wide, with non-calcified joints, gradually becoming more compressed higher up plant and often slightly wider than lower down. Bottom half of plant little branched, but upper half branches profusely in single plane, giving fan-like shape. Branches stiff, erect. Grows 5–12 cm high, typically dull purple or pinkish-red to yellowish-pink, or pale lime green. Bleached or dried individuals white. **Habitat & ecology** · On rocks or in rock pools throughout littoral zone, and subtidally to at least 18 m. Important species, often forming dense turfs, providing habitat for many other animals and plants. Especially common in areas exposed to moderate or heavy wave action. Intolerant of drying out and individuals living near upper limit of distribution usually dwarfed and malformed. **Similar species** · *C. elongata*, but it is usually limp and reproductive bodies tend to be branched. *Haliptilon squamatum* has root-like holdfast and tends to branch dichotomously.

Abundance & distribution
Common, often abundant. Occurs all around British and Irish coasts. Distributed from northern Norway to West Africa, including the western Baltic and Mediterranean. Also occurs in western Atlantic.

Distinctive features

1. Disc-like holdfast.
2. Fronds strap-like, channelled or U-shaped in cross-section, margins thickened.
3. Often with wart-like protuberances.

Distinctive features

1. Densely tufted, calcareous algae with limp branches.
2. Segments of stems ovoid or triangular.
3. Reproductive bodies, when present, terminal, with horns.

Distinctive features

1. Frond calcareous and segmented, looking like a chain of beads.
2. Lower half of plant little branched, upper half profusely branched in single plane.

Jania rubens (Linnaeus) Lamouroux

Description · Minute, crustose, calcareous holdfast, usually hidden by rootlets or fronds. Fronds composed of narrow, cylindrical, calcareous segments reaching 2.5 cm height, with a chalky texture. Branching dichotomous and very dense, giving rise to fine, distinctly tufted plants, often together in large numbers. Reproductive bodies appear in spring; male bodies located on ends of branches and have a lanceolate shape, whereas female bodies are situated in forks of branches and resemble small urns. Pale greyish-pink or purplish-pink. **Habitat & ecology** · Extreme lower shore and sublittoral to 8 m or more depth. Grows on other seaweeds; especially on the brown alga, *Cladostephus verticillatus*, but also on *Cystoseira* species. It may live in rock pools. Occurs in a wide range of exposures, sometimes in dense turfs just below extreme low water. **Similar species** · Resembles *Corallina* species, and *Haliptilon squamatum*, but *J. rubens* has much finer and more densely branched fronds giving a tufted appearance. *Jania* is also epiphytic.

Abundance & distribution
Common. Found on the south coasts of Britain and Ireland, less abundant further north. Distributed from Norway to Cameroon, including the western Baltic and Mediterranean Seas. Also found in the west Atlantic.

FAMILY **Lithophylloideae**

Lithophyllum crouanii Foslie

Description · Calcareous, firmly attached, encrusting thallus typically with a circular outline, up to 15 cm diameter. Adjacent plants often grow into one another. Thallus 2–4 mm thick, flat or a bit lumpy. Margin thick and continuous. Reproductive bodies (conceptacles) circular, small, and flush with the surface, sometimes with a protruding central pore and often in dense groups. Reddish-purple with a whitish bloom; conceptacles pale in darker specimens. Colour bleaches with prolonged exposure to sunlight to greyish- or yellowish-pink. **Habitat & Ecology** · Low intertidal to sublittoral down to 50 m depth. Major contributor to crustose calcareous algal cover on rocky shores, especially in Scotland. Occurs at most exposures on rock, stones, and kelp holdfasts. **Similar species** · Resembles other species of crustose calcareous algae. Positive identification requires microscopic examination. This species overgrows *Titanoderma laminariae* and *Phytomatolithon lenormandii*, and is overgrown by *Phytomatolithon purpureum*, *Lithothamnion glaciale*, and *Lithophyllum incrustans*.

Abundance & distribution
Very common. Occurs throughout Britain and Ireland. Distributed from Arctic Russia to Spain.

Lithophyllum incrustans Philippi

Description · Encrusting, calcareous, weakly attached thallus, roughly circular outline continuous thick margin, up to 10 cm in diameter and 1 mm thick. Plant often degenerates and regenerates, so thickness can reach several millimetres. Surface flat, undulating, knobbly, or elaborate and complex. Where plants meet, slight or large ridges are raised. Texture chalky but soft. Matt pink or lavender, may be bleached by sun to pale greyish or turn deep purplish-brown in shady areas. Reproductive bodies, often grouped, appear as slightly sunken pores or raised circular structures, but when degenerated these can appear as small craters. **Habitat & ecology** · Best developed exposed on rocky shores. On rock and boulders, less often on mollusc shells. Also in shallow rock pools or margins of deep rock pools; often under algal canopies. Middle and lower shore, subtidally to at least 8 m.

Abundance & distribution
Very common. Occurs all around Britain and Ireland. Distributed from Norway to southern Spain and Mediterranean.

Distinctive features

1. Frond chalky and jointed.
2. Fronds branch dichotomously.
3. Often forms dense tufts.

Distinctive features

1. Encrusting, firmly attached calcareous alga.
2. Typically circular, up to 15 cm diameter.
3. Thallus 2–4 mm thick, flat or slightly lumpy; reddish-purple.

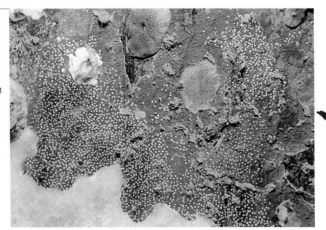

Distinctive features

1. Calcareous, thick, encrusting growth with thick margins.
2. Outline circular when young, irregular when old.
3. Surface smooth, undulating, knobbly, or very elaborate.
4. Pink to lavender, darker in shade, paler when bleached.

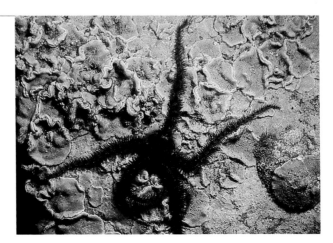

FAMILY **Melobesioideae**
Lithothamnion glaciale Kjellman

Description · Calcareous, encrusting or unattached. Encrusting form closely attached to substratum, circular when young, up to 20 cm in diameter, often coalescing with other plants as it grows. Margins thin, but plant grows to 4 mm thick. Thallus smooth, develops simple or branched cylindrical protuberances with blunt or pointed ends as it grows, reaching 15 mm long and 4 mm diameter. Unattached form consists of single branches, mass of branches, or knobbly, nodule-like structure. Matt red to dark pink or violet-pink, often with white speckles. Hard texture. **Habitat & ecology** · Lower shore and sublittoral to at least 34 m on rock, pebbles, and stabilised detritus. Often occurs in rock pools or water channels. Prefers sheltered habitats. Branches contribute to maerl beds.

Abundance & distribution
Common. Occurs in northern parts of Britain and Ireland. Distributed north to the Arctic. Also found in the western Atlantic and Pacific Oceans.

Mesophyllum lichenoides Ellis

Description · Encrusting calcareous thallus, often thin but commonly forms lobed or branched structures with free edges (unattached). Lobes convex, concave, or convoluted, resembling miniature bracket fungi. Several lobes or thalli, often attached centrally. Additional lobes and branches may develop from free margins and several plants may merge. Occasionally forms closely attached crusts. Texture smooth, occasionally warty but generally slightly glossy. Red, to purplish-brown or pink, in shaded areas. Margins of thalli usually pale yellow or cream-coloured and there may be pale concentric markings. Plants are up to 3 cm long and 2 cm broad. **Habitat & ecology** · Usually growing on *Corallina* species, occasionally on rock. Low-shore to shallow sublittoral habitats with some exposure to wave action. May envelope the host plant. It overgrows *Lithophyllum incrustans* and *Phytomatolithon purpureum*.

Abundance & distribution
Locally common. Distributed on the west and south-west coasts of Britain and Ireland. Distributed south to Mauritania, including the Mediterranean and Canary Islands.

Phytomatolithon calcareum (Pallas) Adey & McKibbin

Description · Encrusting, flat, calcareous thallus, or an unattached branched or nodular thallus. Unattached form consists of simple branches or branching systems of varying density with globular or flattened appearance, up to 7 cm diameter. Sometimes nodular. Individual branches delicate to robust, hard, cylindrical in cross-section or flattened, up to 6 mm in diameter. Surface smooth, mauvish-brown colour with white flaky areas and a matt texture. Dries to a pale red to reddish-grey. Reproductive bodies, swollen areas up to 0.5 mm in diameter, may occur in groups, near the tips of the branches. Encrusting form thin, smooth, or bumpy, with a matt texture. **Habitat & ecology** · Lower shore to shallow sublittoral, mainly as the unattached form. Along with *Lithothamnion coralloides* it is one of the main species found in maerl beds. **Similar species** · Resembles *Lithothamnion coralloides* but the branches tend to be thicker and harder with a chalky, matt texture rather than a slightly glossy appearance.

Abundance & distribution
Common. Found all around Britain and Ireland but mainly on south and west coasts and only as unattached plants. Distributed from southern Norway to the Mediterranean, including the Baltic Sea.

Distinctive features

1. Calcareous, encrusting or unattached.
2. Encrusting, firmly attached form, often with branching protuberances
3. Unattached form consists of single or massed branches, or nodules.

Distinctive features

1. Thin, encrusting, calcareous alga.
2. Margins often free, forming lobe-like or branch-like structures.
3. Reddish-brown to pink, often with pale yellow or cream margin.
4. Growing on or with *Corallina* species.

Distinctive features

1. Calcareous alga rarely forming an encrusting growth, usually forming unattached branching or nodular growths in maerl beds.
2. Mauvish-brown, with a matt texture.
3. Branches fairly hard and more than 1 mm thick.

Phytomatolithon purpureum (P. & H. Crouan) Woelkerling & Irvine

Description · Encrusting calcareous thallus, up to 4 mm thick, well attached. Outline circular or irregularly spreading, up to 20 cm diameter, often coalescing with other thalli, forming crests where they join. Margin thick, usually continuous, with strong ridges inside of edge. Surface flat or undulating, sometimes knobbly, generally smooth, may be with whitish flaky areas during summer. Dull pink with matt texture in summer, deep pinky-red and glossy in winter. Greenish when dry. Reproductive bodies form small pale rings with central pore or small sunken pits with raised rims. These become buried in thallus over time. **Habitat & ecology** · Growing on rock and stones, sometimes holdfasts and stipes of kelps. Low shore to sublittoral to at least 45 m. May form nodules in maerl beds. Occurs higher on shore in areas of strong wave action. Forms massive areas of bright pink crusts on low shore in winter.

Abundance & distribution
Very common. Occurs throughout British Isles and Ireland. Distributed from Arctic Russia to Morocco, including western Baltic Sea.

ORDER **Cryptonemiales**

FAMILY **Dumontiaceae**

Dilsea carnosa (Schmidel) Kuntze
Red rags

Description · Largest red seaweed, a short cylindrical stipe extends for up to 10 cm from small irregular base, then gradually expands to form tough, leathery, flat, spoon-shaped blade up to about 35–50 cm long and half as wide. Surface of frond smooth and shiny, with undivided margins, although those of older plants may be split from margin towards base and partially eroded. Typically opaque dark blood red, reddish-brown, or brick red, mature individuals sometimes having pale patches around margins. **Habitat & ecology** · On rocks and boulders at the ELWS, more commonly submerged in shallow situations to at least 24 m. **Similar species** · Small specimens resemble *Kallymenia microphylla*, though this only grows to about 5 cm tall. *Palmaria palmata* also similar but generally grows on other algae and its blades are dichotomously or irregularly divided into broad segments. *P. palmata* is edible but *D. carnosa* has a very poor food value, though it is eaten in some parts of Europe.

Abundance & distribution
Common. Occurs all around the British Isles and Ireland. Distributed from Arctic Russia and Spitsbergen to Portugal.

FAMILY **Kallymeniaceae**

Callophyllis laciniata (Hudson) Kützing

Description · Frond rather thick, flat, rapidly broadening and fan-shaped, up to about 15–25 cm long, with very short stipe growing from small, disc-like holdfast. Branching dichotomous or irregular, leading to frond being split into several bluntly tipped sections. Degree of splitting and overall shape quite variable. Margins often have curled proliferations. The texture is soft, cartilaginous. Colour an opaque but fairly bright pinkish-, brownish-, or purplish-red. In summer the reproductive bodies can appear either as minute, leaflet-like, structures scattered around the frond margin, or as tiny dots distributed over the whole of the frond surface. **Habitat & ecology** · Attached to rocks and stones in shallow water to at least 30 m depth. Also grows on other algae such as kelp stipes. Found throughout the year.

Abundance & distribution
Frequent. Occurs around Britain apart from the south-east and all around Ireland. Distributed from Norway and the Faeroes to Morocco, including the Mediterranean.

Distinctive features

1. Thick, encrusting, calcareous thallus.
2. Margin of thallus thick, with ridges inside of edge.
3. Surface flat, undulating, or knobbly.

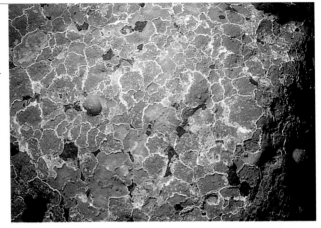

Distinctive features

1. Frond entire, broad, distinctly leathery, and with smooth shiny appearance.
2. Dark blood red colour.

Distinctive features

1. Frond thick, flat, growing from short stipe emerging from discoid holdfast.
2. Fronds branch dichotomously, branches blunt-tipped.
3. Opaque pinkish-, brownish-, or purplish-red.

ORDER **Palmariales**

FAMILY **Palmariaceae**

Palmaria palmata (Linnaeus) Kuntze
Dulse, dillisk, crannach

Description · Tough, fan-shaped and flattened frond 10–50 cm (rarely 1 m) long and up to 8 cm wide (rarely 16 cm). It grows directly from disc-like holdfast with no initial stem or stipe. Shape of plant very variable. Generally plants are divided dichotomously or palmately into broad blades. Older specimens, especially after they have been damaged, often have small, oval branchlets growing along frond margin. Younger parts of the alga more delicate than darker, tougher, and leathery older parts. Typically dark red to reddish-brown, with purplish tinge evident when submerged. Previously known as *Rhodymenia palmata*. **Habitat & ecology** · Middle to lower shore, growing epiphytically on other larger algae, especially the stipes of *Laminaria hyperborea*, or free-living attached to rocks and boulders. Edible either raw or cooked.

Abundance & distribution
Locally abundant. Occurs all around the coasts of Britain and Ireland. Distributed from Arctic Russia to Portugal including the Baltic. Also western Atlantic and Pacific oceans.

ORDER **Rhodymeniales**

FAMILY **Champiaceae**

Gastroclonium ovatum (Hudson) Papenfuss

Description · A striking alga, the frond is 5–15 cm tall, with rounded and cartilaginous main stems branching in an irregularly dichotomous fashion. There is a short stipe, usually no more than 10 mm long. Upper branches bear small oval to rounded, rather fleshy and firm, 'leaves' resembling pips or vesicles. These are translucent, sometimes divided by 3–4 septa, and may appear beaded. They become elongated when older. The holdfast is branched and small. The colour is a dark brown, purplish-red, occasionally greenish. **Habitat & ecology** · Attached to rock and boulders in rock pools and on the lower shore, particularly where there is some exposure to wave action. Also attached to plants, especially *Corallina* species. Occurs throughout the year. **Similar species** · *G. reflexum*, but the stipe is generally less than 5 mm long and hollow branches are always segmented and often bent.

Abundance & distribution
Uncommon. Distributed around the British Isles as far north as Orkney, and rare on the east coast. Occurs all around Ireland. Distributed south to Mauritania.

Lomentaria articulata (Hudson) Lyngbye

Description · Gregarious seaweed, attached by minute, discoidal holdfast. Fronds often tangled, making it hard to pick out individual plants. Tufted growths, with hollow stems and cylindrical or slightly flattened fronds, constricted at more or less regular intervals, with appearance of a chain of elongate beads or sausages. Main stems dichotomously branched; other branches may be opposite, alternate, or even whorled; branching only occurs at constrictions between adjacent 'segments' of stems. Commonly 3–8 cm tall, in some parts of British Isles individuals may attain 15–25 cm. Bright red, or pinkish- to brownish-red. **Habitat & ecology** · Occasionally on upper shore but more common at mid- and low-shore levels, and sublittorally to at least 18 m. On rock and other plants such as kelp stipes. Found all year. Frequently seen on seaward-facing surfaces of vertical or steeply sloping rocks. Although not large, can be fairly easily spotted by shiny or glistening beaded appearance. **Similar species** · *Chylocladia verticillata*, but this has more barrel-shaped segments. Terminal branchlets in *L. articulata* tend to be paired.

Abundance & distribution
Fairly common. Occurs on all British and Irish rocky shores. Distributed from middle Norway to Cameroon, including the Canary Islands, the Mediterranean and Black Seas.

Distinctive features

1. Frond grows directly from disc-like holdfast with no stipe.
2. Frond flattened, without midrib, very variable in width and shape.
3. Branches of frond branched in a roughly dichotomous manner.

Distinctive features

1. Main stems rounded, cartilaginous, branched in an irregularly dichotomous manner.
2. Distal branches bear small, rounded, pip-like fronds.
3. Holdfast small, branched.

Distinctive features

1. Fronds formed from repeatedly constricted stems and branches resembling chain of elongate beads or sausages.
2. Holdfast minute disc.
3. Main stems branch dichotomously.

FAMILY **Rhodymeniaceae**

Rhodymenia pseudopalmata (Lamouroux) Silva

Description · A small, delicate, and membranous plant, up to about 10 cm long. The short cylindrical stipe broadens into a flattened and rather fan-like frond which branches dichotomously or in a palmate fashion. The margins of the fronds generally lack peripheral leaflets. The holdfast is disc-like, the stipe up to about 1 cm long. The texture is cartilaginous and colour is typically purplish, pinkish, or brownish-red. **Habitat & ecology** · An epiphytic seaweed, typically found attached to the stipes of kelps on the lower shore or in shallow sublittoral situations to at least 17 m depth. The plant may also live freely attached to rocks and boulders. **Similar species** · Resembles *Palmaria palmata* but this species grows much larger than *R. pseudopalmata* and tends to have small branches or 'leaflets' growing from the margins of the main fronds. May be confused with some *Phyllophora* species.

Abundance & distribution
Uncommon. Found on south and west shores of Britain and Ireland. Distributed south to Morocco, including the Canary Islands and Azores.

ORDER **Ceramiales**

FAMILY **Ceramiaceae**

Ceramium species

Description · Delicate plants that appear tufted. Fronds are typically 2–30 cm tall, with dichotomously but unevenly branching main stems which, when examined under a hand lens, typically have a banded, segmented pattern. Side branches are arranged like those of the main stems, their paired terminal branchlets commonly curving inwards and looking like small pincers. **Habitat & ecology** · Either free-living, attached to rocks and boulders, or growing epiphytically on other algae, *Ceramium* species are found from the upper-middle to lower shores, and in shallow or deeper subtidal locations. **Similar species** · There are many species of *Ceramium*, and the very variable nature of several of them makes it extremely difficult to identify them with any degree of certainty. *C. rubrum* is probably the commonest species.

Abundance & distribution
Several species occur throughout much of Europe.

Halurus equisetifolius (Lightfoot) Kützing
Sea mare's-tail

Description · Fairly rigid frond, 7–25 cm tall, typically dark red or reddish-brown to rosy pink. Stiff main stem bearing numerous irregular branches, all of which have closely arranged whorls of small, up-curved, spike-like branchlets about 2 mm long, adjacent whorls overlapping each other and resembling *Equisetum* species (mare's tails) found on land. **Habitat & ecology** · Middle- and lower-shore species, attached to rock and boulders or in rock pools. Generally only found in spring and summer. **Similar species** · *Spondylothamnion multifidum* is similar, but has fewer whorls of branchlets that are well separated, not hiding stem. Locally common in southern Britain and Ireland, distributed southwards to Spain and Portugal. *Halurus flosculosus* has numerous delicate, dichotomously branched, thread-like filaments, forming dense tufts. Slimy, with pungent smell and pinkish-crimson (pigment released if immersed in fresh water). Tiny spherical reproductive bodies may be scattered over branches. Frequently occurs on all coasts of Britain and Ireland, distributed south to Atlantic coasts of Spain and France.

Abundance & distribution
Locally common. South-west Britain and Ireland. Distributed southwards to Atlantic coasts of north-west Europe.

Distinctive features

1. Stipe broadening into flattened, fan-like frond which branches dichotomously.
2. Frond margins lack peripheral leaflets.
3. Plant delicate and membranous.

Distinctive features

1. Main stems dichotomously, but unevenly, branched.
2. Tips of terminal branchlets typically incurved, resembling small pincers.
3. Stems show banded pattern of pigmentation under hand lens.

Distinctive features

1. Frond fairly rigid.
2. Main stem branched irregularly.
3. Branches bear closely arranged whorls of small, curved branchlets, successive whorls overlapping.

Ptilota gunneri Silva, Maggs & Irvine in Maggs & Hommersand

Description · The main stem is branched irregularly several times, but smooth. Branchlets and sub-branchlets, however, are oppositely branched. These branchlets are very closely branched, giving them a feathery or fern-like appearance. The subterminal branchlets are opaque. All branching is on the same plane. The plant grows to a length of about 20–30 cm and is a dark red or purplish-brown colour. **Habitat & ecology** · Grows on the lower shore, usually on other seaweeds such as the stipes of kelp species. **Similar species** · Closely resembles *Plumaria elegans*, but this species has fine branchlets along the main stems and the subterminal branchlets are translucent.

Abundance & distribution
Common. Found all around Britain and Ireland but more common in the north. Distributed northwards to Norway and Iceland.

FAMILY **Delesseriaceae**

Delesseria sanguinea (Hudson) Lamouroux
Sea beech

Description · Holdfast an irregularly shaped, thickened disc up to 1 cm in diameter. Cylindrical stipe begins to branch close to holdfast, giving rise to spirally arranged fronds which, when young, are lance-shaped with pointed tips, but become more rounded as they grow older. Fronds resemble beech leaves, with distinct midrib running full length that gives off pairs of lateral veins pointing forwards, with a wavy margin. Plant may grow to 40 cm and is crimson to bright pink. **Habitat & ecology** · Grows freely on rocks and boulders, and in rock pools, especially deep, shaded ones. Also grows epiphytically on stipes of other algae, especially *Laminaria hyperborea*. On the lower shore in deep shade or, more commonly, sublittorally to depths of 30 m or more. Large numbers may be washed ashore after a storm, though usually only a few grow in a locality. **Similar species** · Battered plants resemble *Phycodrys rubens*, but the fronds of this species have indented margins and look like oak leaves.

Abundance & distribution
Common. Occurs around the British Isles but scarce on the east coast of Britain. Distributed from Arctic Norway to Spain, occasionally including the Baltic Sea.

Drachiella spectabilis Ernst & Feldman

Description · Plant has a distinct stipe up to 1 cm long. This widens into a very thin, flattened, transparent frond up to 7 cm tall. There is no distinct midrib but the frond bears additional branched, filamentous attachment organs on its margins. The reproductive bodies may be visible on the plant surface as small outgrowths. The colour of *D. spectabilis* is deep purplish-red with a bright purplish-blue iridescence under water during spring and summer. **Habitat & ecology** · Grows subtidally on rock, often in kelp forests, to a depth of at least 30 m.

Abundance & distribution
Uncommon. Occurs on Atlantic coasts of Britain and Ireland.

Distinctive features

1. Branching in one plane.
2. Branchlets and sub-branchlets oppositely branched, giving a feathery or fern-like appearance.
3. Subterminal branchlets opaque.
4. Main stems smooth.

Distinctive features

1. Fronds leaf-like; distinct midrib, paired lateral veins, deeply ruffled margins.
2. Fronds lance-shaped, pointed tips when young, lance-shaped to oval when older.
3. Fronds spirally arranged.

Distinctive features

1. Very flattened frond.
2. Short stipe.
3. Filamentous attachment organs on frond.
4. Bright purplish-blue iridescence underwater.

Membranoptera alata (Hudson) Stackhouse

Description · Frond is 10–20 cm tall, in a single plane with a flat main stem. The midrib is distinct, often with pairs of veins running out from it (but branches and branchlets lack veins). Irregularly arranged dichotomous branches emerge from the edge of the frond, the branches tapering to end in rather pointed tips that are typically forked or bifid. The colour is a deep pinkish-crimson. The holdfast is small and disc-like. **Habitat & ecology** · Found on the mid-shore and lower, either freely attached to more shaded rocks and boulders or as an epiphyte on red or brown algae, especially in rock pools. Favours open coastal areas. **Similar species** · May be confused with *Cryptopleura ramosa*, *Hypoglossum woodwardi*, or *Apoglossum ruscifolium*. *C. ramosa* has distinctly broader fronds with more rounded tips, whilst the fronds of *H. woodwardi* are not obviously shallowly forked at their tips. In *A. ruscifolium* the fronds are broad, taper at each end and generally do not end in a fork.

Abundance & distribution
Very common. Found all around the British Isles and Ireland. Distributed from Norway to the Atlantic coasts of Spain and Portugal, including the Baltic, but not occurring in the Mediterranean.

Phycodrys rubens (Linnaeus) Batters

Description · The characteristic frond is very similar to an oak leaf in general appearance; 5–25 cm long, the tough main stem is several-branched, each branch forming a short stem bearing a 'leaf' with a distinct midrib from which opposite veins lead off towards the indented or toothed frond margin. Sometimes the margins of the 'leaves' are pointed. The holdfast is small and disc-like. The plant is a pale reddish- or pinkish-brown. **Habitat & ecology** · Free-living on rocks and boulders in shaded situations, or found epiphytically on the stipes of kelps on the lower shore. Individuals are often found stranded on the shore after storms. **Similar species** · The sea beech, *Delesseria sanguinea*, is somewhat similar in having a leaf-like frond with midrib and side veins, but can be distinguished from *P. rubens* by its entire or undivided frond margins.

Abundance & distribution
Locally common. Found all around the British Isles and Ireland. Distributed from the western Baltic Sea southwards to the Atlantic coasts of Spain and Portugal.

FAMILY **Dasyaceae**

Heterosiphonia plumosa (Ellis) Batters

Description · Has a flattened, feathery, or fern-like appearance. The frond is up to 15–20 cm long, with a tapering main stem that looks hairy. This branches irregularly or alternately producing lance-shaped or fern-like branches. The beginning of each branch is bare, but the rest has irregularly alternate branchlets, themselves with branchlets. Alternate side branches and branchlets are more slender than the main stem. Branches become shorter farther away from the base. The colour is a bright red to deep crimson. **Habitat & ecology** · An extreme lower shore to shallow subtidal species, free-living attached to rocks and boulders or growing as an epiphyte on other algae. Detached individuals may be stranded on the shore by receding tides. **Similar species** · Resembles *Brongniartella byssoides* but in this species the branches are closer together and the whole appearance is plume-like. The main stem is also not hairy.

Abundance & distribution
Locally common. This species is found around all coasts of Britain and Ireland. Distributed from the North Sea to Atlantic shores of Spain and Portugal.

Distinctive features

1. Frond with distinct midrib.
2. Growth in a single, flattened plane.
3. Branches irregularly dichotomous, tapering to end in forked tips.

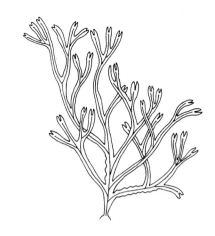

Distinctive features

1. Fronds leaf-like, very similar to oak leaves.
2. Main stem short, profusely branched.
3. 'Leaves' on branches with indented or toothed margins.

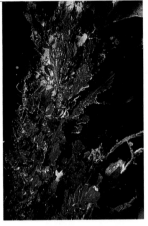

Distinctive features

1. Frond flattened, feathery, or fern-like.
2. Branches alternate or irregular.
3. Stem hairy.
4. Bright red to deep crimson.

FAMILY **Rhodomelaceae**

Halopitys incurvus (Hudson) Batters

Description · This alga has a ropy appearance and grows to 25 cm in height. The tough main stem branches irregularly to produce branches and numerous branchlets. Characteristically the branchlets only grow on one side of each branch and may appear paired, resembling a double toothed comb. Branches and branchlets curve upwards. The holdfast is formed by branched rootlets. The species is very dark red, often appearing blackish-brown or black. **Habitat & ecology** · Found on the lower shore growing on rocks and stones.

Abundance & distribution
Rare, but locally common. Found on south coasts of Britain and southwards.

Laurencia pinnatifida (Hudson) Lamouroux
Pepper dulse

Description · Holdfast stoloniferous but gives out extra tiny rootlets which reinforce attachment of plant. Fronds flattened and branch alternately in a single plane. Each branch subdivided into smaller branchlets, penultimate and terminal branchlets often being short, thick, and cartilaginous with rounded margins. Colour and shape vary considerably, depending upon environment. On the middle shore, where exposed to sunshine for a long period during low tide, plants may form yellowish-green, stunted, turf-like growth only a few centimetres high, but lower down are often dull red or purplish-brown. In shaded places may reach 20–30 cm in height. Has a pungent, unpleasant smell, and tastes peppery. **Habitat & ecology** · Forming extensive turfs on rocks and in crevices, mid-shore to low water springs. Not usually subtidal. Common on exposed to moderately sheltered shores. Erect plants develop from October, reaching maximum size February-May. **Similar species** · Resembles *L. obtusa*, although this is most often encountered growing epiphytically upon other algae. Its fronds are usually cylindrical with spiral branching.

Abundance & distribution
Common. Occurs on rocky shores all around the British Isles and Ireland. Distributed from Norway to the Mediterranean.

Odonthalia dentata (Linnaeus) Lyngbye

Description · Frond 7–30 cm long, flattened, tufted in appearance but with midrib only evident towards the base of plant. Main stems branch alternately or irregularly, branches similarly alternate. The branches are large, branchlets are quite stumpy. Margins of branches and branchlets with tooth-like serrations at their ends. Colour a dark or dusky reddish- or purplish-brown. **Habitat & ecology** · A lower-shore and shallow sublittoral species, usually found free-living attached to rocks and boulders, but occasionally occurs epiphytically on other seaweeds, such as kelps. Often grows in rock pools. **Similar species** · May resemble *Sphaerococcus coronopifolius*, but in this species the branches are fringed with very small branchlets.

Abundance & distribution
Common. Found all around Britain and Ireland but more common in the north. Distributed from northern Norway to northern France.

Distinctive features

1. Ropy appearance.
2. Branching, irregular branchlets only on one side of branches.

Distinctive features

1. Dull red, purplish-brown, almost black, olive green, or yellowish-green.
2. Stoloniferous holdfast; supplementary rootlets.
3. Frond flattened, only branching in one plane.
4. Texture cartilaginous.

Distinctive features

1. Frond flattened, alternately branched.
2. Midrib evident only towards base of alga.
3. Edges of branches and branchlets serrated or toothed.

Polysiphonia species

Description · Many species not well defined. Holdfast usually small, formed of rootlets that, when growing epiphytically, invade host plant tissues. Main stems usually rounded, often profusely branched dichotomously or alternately, giving bushy appearance to plant. Tips of branches appear segmented or jointed. Colour variable, depending upon species; *P. lanosa*, for example, is dark reddish-brown; *P. elongata* is a more yellowish-red. **Habitat & ecology** · About 30 species of free-living *Polysiphonia* occur, attached to rock, boulders, mollusc shells, or growing on a variety of intertidal and shallow sublittoral algae. *P. lanosa*, one of the most common species, forms tufted or bushy growths on the mid-shore wrack, *Ascophyllum nodosum*. Identification of many *Polysiphonia* species requires specialist knowledge. **Similar species** · *Rhodomela confervoides* is similar to *Polysiphonia*. It has spirally arranged branches that may be divided and covered with delicate, filamentous branchlets. Examination with hand lens will show that tips of branches do not have joints or segments shown by *Polysiphonia*.

Abundance & distribution
Depending upon the species, common and often locally abundant. Within European waters the genus has a range extending from the Baltic Sea southwards to the Mediterranean and on all intervening shores.

Rhodomela confervoides (Hudson) Silva

Description · Frond consists of cylindrical main stems bearing spirally arranged branches that may be divided and covered with delicate, filamentous branchlets. The alga, up to about 30 cm tall, generally has a cartilaginous texture but may, in spring, show softer areas of new growth. The holdfast is disc-like, the colour a reddish-brown. **Habitat & ecology** · Found on the lower shore to sublittoral depths of about 20 m, either freely attached to rocks and boulders or growing as an epiphyte on other algae. **Similar species** · May easily be confused with species of *Polysiphonia*, but careful examination with a hand lens shows that the tips of branches do not have the joints or segments which *Polysiphonia* does.

Abundance & distribution
Locally common. Found all around Britain and Ireland. Distributed from Norway and the Baltic Sea southwards to the Atlantic coasts of Spain and Portugal.

CLASS **Bangiophyceae** | ORDER **Bangiales**

FAMILY **Bangiaceae**

Porphyra umbilicalis (Linnaeus) Agardh
Purple laver, sloke, slake, black butter

Description · Growing singly or in tufts from a minute, disc-like holdfast. Frond (blade) shape very variable, but always membranous with soft, silky texture except that when dried out it resembles black plastic sheeting. Fronds typically 5–20 cm long but may reach 50–60 cm, often with folded or fluted appearance below which holdfast appears to be placed centrally. Younger, fresh plants green or dark rosy-red, even bright purple, but older specimens often olive green to dull brown or purplish-brown, whilst upper-shore examples uncovered by the tide for some time may be partially dried out and appear almost black and crispy. **Habitat & ecology** · Very adaptable and locally abundant, capable of living in wide range of conditions; most commonly found in mid- to upper-shore regions of more exposed coasts. On rocks and boulders, including those partially covered by sand. *Porphyra* species supposedly high in protein, and are rich in vitamins B and C. In some parts of Britain *P. umbilicalis* is known as 'Laver bread', and eaten after being washed in fresh water, boiled until tender, coated with oatmeal, and fried with bacon. **Similar species** · *P. leucosticta*, most commonly found as a mid-shore epiphyte on *Fucus* and other algae.

Abundance & distribution
Locally abundant. Found on all British and Irish coasts. Distributed from Norway to the Mediterranean, including the Baltic Sea. Also occurs in the western Atlantic.

Distinctive features

1. Holdfast consisting of branched 'rootlets'; this invades host tissues when the plants grow as epiphytes.
2. Stems rounded, branched alternately or dichotomously.

Distinctive features

1. Main stems cylindrical, bearing spirally arranged branches.
2. Branches often divided, covered with delicate, filamentous branchlets.
3. Holdfast disc-like.

Distinctive features

1. Holdfast a minute disc.
2. Frond an irregular, membranous, and gelatinous blade.
3. Colour dark reddish-purple, almost black when dry.

Angiosperms (flowering plants)

Very few angiosperms are adapted to living fully submerged in marine conditions. By far the greatest number, like lichens, are fully terrestrial, although several are tolerant of salt-water spray. In temperate latitudes only one group, the **seagrasses**, contains species that may be commonly found in shallow bays and along fairly sheltered shores.

FAMILIES **Posidoniaceae and Zosteraceae**

Zostera marina Linnaeus
Eel-grass, grass wrack

Description · The flat, dark or grass-green leaves are up to 1 m or more in length and 5–10 mm wide. The leaf bases, emerging from the rhizome, are not enclosed by a shaggy sheath. The end of the leaf is slightly notched, the vein pattern consisting of a distinct median longitudinal vein flanked by two close-set veins which turn inwards to meet each other close to the tip. The distance between the median vein and each pair of lateral veins is about twice that of the distance between each of the paired veins. Numerous flowers, which appear during the spring and summer, are inconspicuous and develop along one side of a short spike, similar to those seen on many terrestrial grasses. **Habitat & ecology** · A lower shore to shallow sublittoral seagrass, found in sheltered bays or estuaries growing in mud, sand or gravel. A disease wiped out large areas of this seagrass in the 1930s and it still has not recovered its former distribution. **Similar species** · *Z. nana* or *Z. noltii*, but both are smaller and have a different leaf vein pattern.

Abundance & distribution
Locally often forming extensive beds, with a distribution ranging from the Baltic Sea to Atlantic, Channel and North Sea coasts of northern Europe and into the Mediterranean. Its distribution around the British Isles tends to be somewhat patchy or sporadic.

Distinctive features

1. Leaves flat, dark green in colour.
2. Leaf bases not shaggy.
3. Leaf vein pattern consisting of distinct central vein flanked on either side by two close-set veins which curve inwards to meet each other at the notched leaf tip.

Animals (Kingdom Animalia)

Sponges

Phylum Porifera

This phylum contains the simplest types of multicellular invertebrates, whose body cells are organised into distinct layers but do not form either complex tissues or organs. Three grades of body form are recognised within the phylum, these being, in order of increasing complexity, the **asconoid**, **syconoid**, and **leuconoid**. The asconoid grade essentially consists of a simple sac externally covered by an outer cell wall (the **pinacoderm**) pierced by large numbers of small incurrent pores (**ostia**) lined by cells called **pinacocytes**. The inner lining layer of the asconoid sponge body (the **choanoderm**), separated from the pinacoderm by the **mesohyl**, contains flagellated cells (**choanocytes**). Beating of the flagella of these choanocytes creates currents that draw water into the main chamber of the sponge through the ostia. Water drawn into the body is filtered and then passed out of the main chamber through a single large excurrent aperture, the **osculum**. The whole arrangement of these components is known as an **aquiferous** system. Asconoid sponges may be solitary (**unitary**) or arranged into colonies (**modular**), colonial asconoids comprising a series of interlinked aquiferous systems which open via a single osculum. In syconoid sponges the body walls are folded and the choanoderm is situated in side pouches extending off the main chamber. In the most complex body form, the leuconoid grade, choanoderm-lined pouches are concentrated

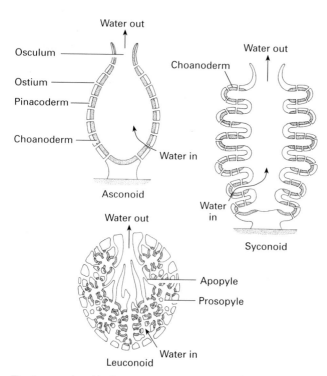

The three grades of body organisation among poriferans, showing the structures referred to in the text.

into separate chambers. Water entering through the ostia passes through pores (**prosopyles**) into the chambers, the excurrent water flow passing from these through an inner pore (the **apopyle**) to enter the main chamber which opens via one or more oscula.

Sponges are characteristically stiffened by a skeleton composed of small **spicules** of either calcium carbonate (**calcite**) or **silica**, though in one class the spicular skeleton may be reinforced or replaced by fibres of a tough, organic, collagenous substance called **spongin**. The higher classification of the phylum depends upon the nature of the skeleton and most sponge species are difficult to identify reliably without microscopic examination of their structure. There are three main classes:

Calcarea
Skeleton composed of calcareous (calcium carbonate) spicules. Marine only.

Hexactinellida (Triaxonida)
Skeleton composed of six-rayed siliceous spicules. Mainly deep water, marine only.

Demospongiae
Skeleton composed of siliceous (silica) spicules, which are either single-rayed (**monaxons**) or four-rayed (**tetraxons**); spongin fibres are also found in many species. A few species have no skeleton at all. Mostly marine, some freshwater species.

No members of the class Hexactinellida have yet been recorded from British coastal waters. The Demospongiae comprises by far the largest class of sponges, accounting for about 95% of the world species. A class known as the Sclerospongiae, the coralline sponges, has been generally abandoned and its members reassigned to the Calcarea and Demospongiae.

Most sponge species are **hermaphroditic** (male and female gametes produced within the same parent), though the two sexes may not occur at the same time. Spermatozoa are passed out of the body via the oscular water current to be taken up via the aquiferous system of neighbouring sponges. Fertilisation and the formation of embryos takes place in the mesohyl. Asexual reproduction occurs either by the regeneration of body fragments or via the development of specialised groups of cells called **gemmules**.

Further reading
Ackers, R. G., Moss, D., Picton, B. E., & Stone, S. M. K. (1985). *Sponges of the British Isles.* 4th edn. Marine Conservation Society, Ross-on-Wye.

Burton, M. (1963). *A revision of the classification of the calcareous sponges.* British Museum (Natural History), London.

Hartman, W. D. (1982). Porifera. In *Synopsis and classification of living organisms* (ed. P. Parker), Vol. 1, pp. 641–66. McGraw-Hill, New York.

CLASS Calcarea | SUBCLASS Calcinea

ORDER Clathrinida

FAMILY Clathrinidae

Clathrina coriacea (Montagu)

Description · This sponge grows as an irregularly shaped, encrusting sheet up to 1 cm thick and 25–30 mm or more across. The species is a dull greyish-white, sometimes with tints of yellow or pink. When examined closely it can be seen to be formed from a mass of thin-walled, branched, and interconnecting tubes which give a close, meshwork-like structure with a soft surface texture. The internal calcareous spicules typically possess three long rays. Neither oscula nor ostia (in and outflow openings) are visible to the naked eye. Previously known as *Leucosolenia coriacea*. **Habitat & ecology** · A lower-shore to shallow sublittoral species, found on clean rocks, usually on the undersurface of overhangs. **Similar species** · May easily be confused with the related *C. contorta*, but the colony of this form is smaller and has a coarser surface texture.

Abundance & distribution
A very common sponge. Found all around Britain and Ireland. Occurs on most northwestern European coasts, with a southerly range extending to the Mediterranean.

SUBCLASS Calcaronea | ORDER Leucosolenida

FAMILY Leucosoleniidae

Leucosolenia botryoides (Ellis & Solander)

Description · Delicate and small erect tubular growths, generally not or little branched, with a single large osculum at the end of each tube, which may be up to 2 cm tall. This sponge typically forms dense, moss-like clumps. The tubules grow from a profusely branched, root-like network of canals that stick to the surface of attachment. The colour is whitish, the surface texture soft. **Habitat & ecology** · Attached to algae or rock surfaces on the extreme lower shore and in shallow sublittoral situations. It is an annual species, the pelagic larva settling in summer. Breeding occurs in the autumn and again in the following summer. **Similar species** · Somewhat similar to the related *L. complicata*, with which it may be confused, but this species tends to be more compact and has lateral branches from main erect branches. It has a similar distribution to *L. botryoides*.

Abundance & distribution
Common. Occurs around all coasts of Britain and Ireland. Distributed from northern Norway and the western Baltic Sea to the Mediterranean coasts of Europe.

ORDER Sycettida

FAMILY Sycettidae

Sycon ciliatum (Fabricius)

Description · Shaped like a cylindrical vase or Grecian urn, and up to about 5 cm tall and 7.5 mm in width. The single large osculum forming the opening of the 'vase' is surrounded by a crown or fringe of stiff spines. The body of the vase itself, which has a rough or furry appearance, may seem to be attached by a slender stalk. The colour is a creamish-yellow to greyish-white. **Habitat & ecology** · Found attached to rocks and shells from the lower shore down to sublittoral depths of about 100 m. Also often found growing on other algae, such as kelp holdfasts or on fucoid or small red algae. Generally several individuals are found growing close to one another. **Similar species** · May easily be confused with *S. coronatum*, but this is typically a solitary form whereas *S. ciliatum* usually lives in groups of several individuals. According to some authorities the two species should be united as *S. ciliatum*.

Abundance & distribution
Fairly common. Found on all coasts of Britain and Ireland. Distributed south to the Mediterranean.

Distinctive features

1. Forms irregularly shaped, soft encrustations.
2. Close examination reveals a dense meshwork of thin-walled, branched, and interconnecting tubes.
3. Colour greyish-white, sometimes tinged pink or yellow.

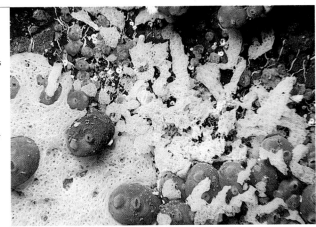

Distinctive features

1. Small, delicate, tubular sponge with few or no branches.
2. Tubules form dense, moss-like clumps growing from a root-like network of canals.
3. End of each tubule with oscular pore.

Distinctive features

1. Erect, vase- or Grecian urn-shaped, attached by distinct stalk.
2. Colour creamish-yellow to greyish-white.
3. Surface rough or furry.

FAMILY **Grantiidae**

Scypha compressa (Fabricius) **Purse sponge**

Description · A very easily identified sponge, characteristically forming flat, vase-shaped structures up to 2 cm tall and 1 cm wide, with a large osculum at the free end. It has no collar of spines around the osculum. The colour is greyish- or creamish-white. **Habitat & ecology** · Found on the lower shore and in shallow sublittoral situations, typically forming clumps on large brown seaweeds, among algal turfs, or attached to rocks. **Similar species** · Resembles *Sycon ciliatum* but this species has a margin of bristles around the osculum.

Abundance & distribution
One of the commonest of the north-western European sponges, with a widespread distribution extending from northern Norway southwards to the Gulf of St Malo.

Leuconia gossei (Bowerbank)

Description · This species can be encrusting or massive, usually with irregular ridges and mounds. It has large oscula that may be on short raised mounds. The sponge is rough to the touch and has a firm consistency. It is white or an off-white colour. **Habitat & ecology** · Grows on rocks on the low shore and subtidally. **Similar species** · *L. nivea* is a related species, but this forms sheet-like encrustations.

Abundance & distribution
Frequent. Distribution uncertain, but widespread in north-west Europe.

CLASS **Demospongiae** | SUBCLASS **Tetractinomorpha**

ORDER **Choristida**

FAMILY **Geodiidae**

Pachymatisma johnstonia (Bowerbank in Johnston) **Elephants ear sponge**

Description · A very distinctive species, forming grey or greyish-blue to violet large, irregular, firm mounds or plates with a solid consistency, up to 25–30 cm across and 25 cm high. The surface is smooth, with the large round oscula arranged in irregular lines. Oscula often have raised margins. The inner tissue, which is dull white in colour, contains both large and small siliceous spicules of several types. **Habitat & ecology** · A lower-shore and shallow sublittoral species found attached to rock and, often, on kelp holdfasts. Can be a conspicuous element of the benthic fauna. **Similar species** · Resembles *Dercitus bucklandi*.

Abundance & distribution
Widely distributed, locally very common. Found around all coasts of Britain and Ireland where suitable conditions exist. Distributed from Norway to Atlantic coasts of Spain.

Distinctive features

1. Forms flat, vase-shaped structures with a large, terminal, osculum.
2. Colour greyish- to creamish-white.
3. Often grows in clumps.

Distinctive features

1. Encrusting or massive, usually with irregular ridges and mounds.
2. Large oscula, sometimes raised on mounds.
3. Rough to the touch.

Distinctive features

1. Forms firm, solid mounds of greyish-blue to violet.
2. Surface smooth.
3. Oscula arranged in irregular lines.

FAMILY **Pachastrellidae**

Dercitus bucklandi (Bowerbank)

Description · Variable in form, either forming an encrusting growth or massive, with a fairly solid consistency, and up to 50 cm in diameter and 5 cm thick. Black or dark grey in colour. The smooth, even surface has irregularly scattered oscula of various sizes. **Habitat & ecology** · A sublittoral species, found growing on rocks and boulders. **Similar species** · Can be confused with *Pachymatisma johnstonia* but this species tends to form larger massive growths with its oscula in irregular lines.

Abundance & distribution
May be locally common. Distribution uncertain but probably extending to most north-west European coasts.

ORDER **Hadromerida**

FAMILY **Suberitidae**

Suberites carnosus (Johnston)

Description · Although sometimes forming an irregular mound, the most characteristic form of this sponge is as a smooth-surfaced sphere or globe, up to 15 cm across, yellowish-orange in colour. It is attached by a short stalk which may or may not be visible. The spherical form of the sponge usually possesses a single, large osculum through which the internal structure may be seen. This sponge is soft when expanded but firmer when contracted. **Habitat & ecology** · A shallow sublittoral species attached to rock or other hard substrata.

Abundance & distribution
Widespread and locally common. Found around most coasts of Britain and Ireland. Distribution uncertain but probably coasts of north-west Europe to the Mediterranean.

Suberites domuncula (Olivi)
Sea-orange, sulphur sponge

Description · A large orange to orange-yellow sponge, not uncommonly up to 15–30 cm in diameter, which may have a ball-like shape or appear as several joined mounds and spheres with an overall irregular shape. The oscula are large and distinct. It has a firm but elastic consistency, and the surface has a slightly rough texture. The sponge has a distinctive and pungent sulfurous smell. **Habitat & ecology** · Usually found in sublittoral habitats down to depths of about 200 m, less frequently on the lower shore. The sponge may grow on just about any hard surface, frequently occurring on whelk shells inhabited by hermit crabs which it may slowly dissolve to provide a secondary protective shelter for the crab. **Similar species** · May be confused with *Suberites carnosus* (p. 70), *Suberites ficus* (p. 72), or *Myxilla incrustans* (p. 84). Microscopic examination of the spicules may be necessary to certainly distinguish between these sponges.

Abundance & distribution
Fairly common. Found all around Britain and Ireland with a range extending to most coasts of the north-east Atlantic.

Distinctive features

1. Growth form either encrusting or massive, with a fairly solid consistency.
2. Colour dark grey or black.

Distinctive features

1. Typically forms large globe or sphere attached by short stalk.
2. Surface smooth, yellowish-orange.
3. Top of sphere with single large osculum.

Distinctive features

1. Often somewhat ball-shaped and large, it may consist of joined mounds and spheres, each with a single large osculum.
2. Fleshy and rough-surfaced to the touch.
3. Colour orange to orange-yellow.
4. Sulfurous smell.

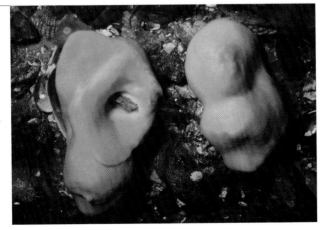

Suberites ficus (Esper)

Description · Somewhat variable in shape, this large sponge may be fig-like, but may also be irregularly spherical, lobed, or massive, and up to 30 cm across. The inner tissues are always yellow, but the rather rough surface may be red, orange, or grey. There is a single terminal oscular pore. It is most accurately identified by examination of its numerous spicule types. **Habitat & ecology** · Found growing on the lower shore and in shallow sublittoral waters on rocks and shells. Sometimes grows in cryptic habitats. **Similar species** · *S. domuncula* may appear similar. It is orange to orange-yellow, and a spherical or mound-like shape. It has large oscula and a distinctive pungent sulfurous smell. This sponge is often found on whelk shells inhabited by hermit crabs, sometimes completely dissolving the shell, though it may occur on any hard surface.

Abundance & distribution
Common, sometimes locally abundant. Found around all coasts of Britain and Ireland. Distribution uncertain but probably on most shores of the north-east Atlantic region.

Pseudosuberites sulphureus (Bowerbank)

Description · This sponge may form thin, irregular, encrusting patches up to 13 cm wide. The texture is firm. It is light to dark yellow. **Habitat & ecology** · Found on the low shore and subtidally growing on rock or other hard surfaces. May grow in very secluded habitats. **Similar species** · Resembles other species such as the encrusting form of *Suberites ficus*. Precise identification requires microscopic examination of the spicules.

Abundance & distribution
Frequent. Distribution uncertain but probably on most coasts of north-west Europe.

FAMILY **Polymastiidae**
Polymastia boletiformis (Lamarck)

Description · Growth form massive or cushion-like, firm in consistency and up to 10 cm in diameter. The upper surface bears numerous stout, tapering, flexible, cylindrical papillae that are typically about 2 cm tall but may reach 12 cm. The surfaces of the sponge are smooth. Oscula are located at the tops of the papillae. The colour varies from orange to yellow ochre, green, or dark grey. **Habitat & ecology** · A sublittoral epilithic species, growing on rocks and boulders, often on their upward-facing surfaces. **Similar species** · Resembles *P. mammillaris* but the base of this species is rough and the papillae more gently tapering than in *P. boletiformis*. The papillae of *P. mammillaris* tend to be paler in colour than the base.

Abundance & distribution
Locally common. Probably distributed around most north-west European coasts.

Distinctive features

1. Shaped like a fig, irregularly rounded, or massive.
2. Variable, red, orange, or grey, but inner tissues always yellow.
3. Single large, terminal, oscular pore.

Distinctive features

1. Thin and encrusting.
2. Yellow in colour.

Distinctive features

1. Upper surface of base with numerous papillae.
2. Oscula located at tips of papillae.
3. Orange, yellow ochre, green, or dark grey.

Polymastia mammillaris (Müller)

Description · This sponge forms a cushion-shaped mass, up to 12 cm across, with numerous papillae projecting from it. These papillae grow to 12 cm high, rounded or slightly compressed, slender and gently tapering. An osculum is usually present at the top of each papilla. The base of the sponge is firm in consistency and rough in texture. The papillae are flexible. The sponge is yellow, orange, pink, or grey and the papillae tend to be paler than the base, or even translucent. **Habitat & ecology** · A sublittoral epilithic species growing on rocks and boulders, tolerant enough of siltation to grow on upward-facing surfaces and may have its basal tissues silted over. **Similar species** · Resembles *P. boletiformis*, but in that species the sponge is entirely smooth, while the papillae are acutely tapering and the same colour as the base.

Abundance & distribution
Locally common, with a distribution extending to many north-west European coasts.

FAMILY **Clionidae**

Cliona celata Grant **Boring sponge**

Description · Often bright to deep yellow, sometimes with red coloration around oscular openings. Sponge surface is penetrated by numerous small holes, up to 3 mm across, with raised margins and through which small papillae protrude. Boring form is visible as yellow lobes (rounded tips of papillae) studding limestone or shells. Frequently develops into massive form, which is lobe-shaped and rounded, or forms thick ridges or plates. Massive form can reach 1 m across and 25 cm thick. **Habitat & ecology** · Occasionally on lower shore, more typically sublittoral to 100 m. Burrowing form bores into limestone rocks or bivalve shells such as *Ostrea*, *Pecten*, or *Venus*, where it fills a branching network of galleries. The massive, or mound, form develops when sponge has outgrown its habitat, or when it has completely filled crevices in non-calcareous rocks into which it cannot bore. Both forms occur on a variety of coasts, ranging from exposed open coasts to estuaries, sometimes to considerable depths. Can withstand sediment.

Abundance & distribution
Very common, locally abundant. Found all around Britain and Ireland. Distributed from Norway, Iceland, and the western Baltic Sea, to the Mediterranean.

FAMILY **Tethyidae**

Tethya aurantium (Pallas)

Description · An easily identifiable sponge, appearing like a large (up to about 10 cm diameter), firm sphere. The sphere has a short basal stalk which grows from a root-like mass but this may not be visible. The osculum is usually positioned near the apex of the sponge and is large and distinct. The surface of the sponge is covered in polygon-shaped protrusions, and the overall impression is of a golf-ball shape. Colour is a pale reddish-brown to golden brown, yellowish-orange, or yellow. Fine, web-like strands of tissue may be seen around the sponge. **Habitat & ecology** · Grows singly or in colonies on rocks, boulders, and stones in shallow sublittoral water to depths of about 130 m. It is often found in submarine caves but only rarely occurs in the extreme lower intertidal region. Often found on rock in kelp forests.

Abundance & distribution
Fairly common. Occurs all around Britain and Ireland. Distributed from Norway to the Mediterranean. Also reported from New Zealand.

Distinctive features

1. Upper surface of base with numerous, gently tapering, flexible, sub-cylindrical papillae.
2. Oscula at papillae tips.
3. Colour variable, papillae typically paler than basal tissues, sometimes translucent.

Distinctive features

1. Firm, covered in tubercles.
2. Contracts strongly out of water.
3. Typically deep yellow, may have red around oscular openings.

Distinctive features

1. Shaped like a large, firm sphere attached by a short stalk and root-like structures.
2. Single large apical osculum.

ORDER **Axinellida**

FAMILY **Axinellidae**

Axinella polypoides Schmidt

Description · Up to 50 cm tall, the branched shape varies from erect and pillar-like to somewhat fanned. There tend to be few branches and these are oval in cross-section. The surface is smooth and velvety, covered with oscula that are surrounded by radiating shallow surface grooves giving a star-like appearance. The colour is yellowish-orange to orangey-red. **Habitat & ecology** · Found growing in well-illuminated sublittoral locations on rock from 15–100 m depth. **Similar species** · May be confused with *A. verrucosa*, but this sponge is more branched and bush-like, with a knobbly surface appearance and brighter golden red colour.

Abundance & distribution
Sometimes locally common. Northern limit of distribution uncertain but found all around Ireland and on the west coast of Britain. Probably distributed from southern Norway to the Mediterranean (where it is common).

FAMILY **Raspailiidae**

Raspailia hispida (Montagu)

Description · This is a tree-like sponge, with long, slender, and mostly forked branches that may be somewhat flattened in cross-section. The branches are up to 13 cm long, the whole sponge 35 cm tall. The oscula are very small and not obvious. The whole sponge has a velvety or hairy surface. The colour is pale yellowish-brown or buff with a fairly soft, elastic consistency. **Habitat & ecology** · A sublittoral sponge found growing on rocks, boulders, and shells. **Similar species** · Resembles *R. ramosa*, with which it is often found, but the two sponges can be distinguished by their colour and nature of their branches.

Abundance & distribution
Common. Distribution is uncertain but it may be widespread on north-west European coasts.

Raspailia ramosa (Montagu)

Description · Tree-like or palmate growth form, with short, stout, and distinctly flattened and forked branches that have distinctly rounded tips. The branches reach about 2.5 cm long, the whole animal is up to 15 cm tall. Small oscula can be seen scattered over the surface, which is velvety or hairy. This species has a flexible consistency and the colour is a dark reddish-brown or dirty pale brown. **Habitat & ecology** · A sublittoral and epilithic sponge found growing on rocks and boulders. **Similar species** · Often occurs with *R. hispida* but differs from this species by the nature of its branches, smaller size, and colour.

Abundance & distribution
Locally common. Distribution uncertain but possibly widespread on European coasts.

Distinctive features

1. Erect, branching sponge.
2. Surface smooth and velvety.
3. Oscula with a star-shaped appearance.
4. Branches few, oval in cross-section.

Distinctive features

1. Growth form tree-like, with long, slender branches.
2. Branches mostly forked, occasionally rather flattened.
3. Surface velvety.

Distinctive features

1. Growth form tree-like, with stout, fan-shaped branches that have rounded tips.
2. Colour a dark reddish-brown.

SUBCLASS **Ceractinomorpha** | ORDER **Halichondrida**

FAMILY **Halichondriidae**

Ciocalypta penicillus (Bowerbank)

Description · Forms an encrusting, rough-surface cushion, up to about 10 cm across, from which highly characteristic pointed, conical projections or digits grow upwards. These projections are up to 5 mm thick and 5 cm tall, and firm but flexible to the touch. The cushion is brownish- or yellowish-white, the digits are often translucent. Frequently the encrusting cushion is covered with silt or sand, with only the digits visible. **Habitat & ecology** · This species is subtidal and typically found in clear waters with some exposure to wave action or tidal currents. It is usually attached to upward-facing rock surfaces covered in clean sand or gravel, sometimes with a layer of silt. **Similar species** · May be confused with *Polymastia mammillaris* but the morphology and translucent look of the digits are somewhat different.

Abundance & distribution
Common. Found on west and south coasts of Britain and Ireland. Distributed from Helgoland to the Mediterranean, including the Azores and Madeira.

Halichondria bowerbanki Burton

Description · Variable in appearance, growing as thin, irregular sheets, more solid mounds or, more commonly, forming massive growths giving rise to narrow, erect, finger-like processes that may be branching. This sponge is a pale yellow or yellowish-brown colour. Its consistency is soft and compressible, and it has a weak smell similar to that of *H. panicea*. **Habitat & ecology** · A lower-shore to shallow sublittoral species, but also often occurring in estuaries. It grows on rocks, algal holdfasts, worm tubes, and almost any other sedentary organism with a hard surface. **Similar species** · Very difficult to distinguish from the related *H. panicea*, which is more often greenish or orange and has a much stronger and distinct smell.

Abundance & distribution
Common. Occurs all around Britain and Ireland. Distribution uncertain but probably throughout much of the northeast Atlantic coastal region.

Halichondria panicea (Pallas) **Breadcrumb sponge**

Description · Forms irregular, soft growths as crust, mass, or clump of joined branches. Surface covered with large numbers of variably sized mounds on which oscula open. Surface texture wrinkly, or granular like breadcrumbs. Individual colonies reach 20–30 cm across and several centimetres thick but in ideal conditions this sponge can cover large areas, several metres across, forming a reef-like mass. Typically bright orange or deep reddish-orange in sheltered or sublittoral situations, green if living in well-illuminated habitats resulting from algae in tissues. Can also be whitish, yellowish, or brownish. **Habitat & ecology** · Rocks, boulders and stones, shells, or larger holdfasts of brown seaweeds, on lower shore to sublittoral situations. Occurs in estuaries. Orange-coloured form commonly found under rocky overhangs or in deep, narrow crevices. Green form covers rocks or boulders that are generally not shaded. Extensive reef-like areas, which this sponge may form, shelter a great diversity of invertebrate animals. **Similar species** · Easily confused with *H. bowerbanki*, which is usually pale yellow to yellowish-brown. This does not smell as strongly as *H. panicea*, is pliable, and will not break if bent. It does not occur in Mediterranean.

Abundance & distribution
Widespread and common, locally abundant. Found on most British and Irish rocky shores. Distribution extending from Norway and the western Baltic Sea to the Mediterranean.

Distinctive features

1. Encrusting cushion with conical, pointed projections extending to 5 cm tall.
2. Basal cushion often hidden by silt or sand.

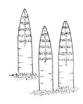

Distinctive features

1. Pale yellow to yellowish-brown.
2. Appearance variable: thin irregular sheets, solid mounds or, usually, flat, narrow, erect lobes that may branch.

Distinctive features

1. Often forms extensive areas of growth.
2. Numerous pores are obvious on raised mounds.
3. Colour bright orange in sublittoral or shaded intertidal situations, green in well-lit places.
4. Strong, rather acrid, kelp-like smell.

FAMILY **Hymeniacidonidae**

Hymeniacidon perleve (Montagu)

Description · This sponge sometimes forms a cushion-like shape with an uneven surface covered in small erect protrusions or papillae, though it may be smooth. Other examples may form thin encrusting sheets which are smooth to minutely tuberculate. Still others may appear as massive flanged growths, sometimes buried with only the tips of the flanges and oscular chimneys showing. The texture is firm but springy to the touch. The colour is highly variable. It may be a pinky orange, or dirty orange to brick-red. Intertidal specimens may be discoloured a dull greenish-orange by symbiotic algae. **Habitat & ecology** · This species is found on the lower shore and in shallow subtidal habitats. It grows on stones, rocks, on the carapaces of crabs, and on kelp species. On the shore it is usually found in damp areas shaded from the sun.

Abundance & distribution
Common. Found on all Irish coasts and all around Britain except for the east coast. Distributed from the Arctic to the Mediterranean.

ORDER **Haplosclerida**

FAMILY **Haliclonidae**

Haliclona oculata (Pallas)

Description · This sponge has a tree-like growth form, with rounded branches of 7 mm maximum diameter. The tips of the branches are rounded. Branches are often numerous but in sheltered conditions they may be few in number and somewhat flattened. The oscula are small but obvious. They have slightly raised margins and are frequently arranged in rows along the branches. This species grows to about 30 cm high. It has a tough but flexible consistency and may be pale brown, yellow, green, pinkish-red, or purple. **Habitat & ecology** · May occur on the lower shore but usually sublittoral growing on rock. Also found around the mouths of estuaries and is tolerant of silt. **Similar species** · Resembles *Axinella polypoides* but this species has flattened branches and the oscula tend to be more scattered.

Abundance & distribution
Common. Found all around Britain and Ireland. Distribution uncertain but probably throughout the north-east Atlantic.

FAMILY **Adociidae**

Adocia cineria (Grant)

Description · An encrusting sponge that forms thick, rounded, tubular, conical, or branch-like protuberances. The oscula (up to 2 mm wide) are located at the tops of these structures. Overall, individual sponges are irregular in shape, often lobe-shaped, and up to 3.5 cm high and 20 cm in width. The surface of the sponge appears quite smooth but is rough to the touch. The consistency is soft. The colour varies considerably and may be pure white, pale violet, red, deep purple, reddish-brown, brown, orange, or grey. **Habitat & ecology** · Occurs sublittorally growing on rock and large stones. May also be found in low-shore rock pools or amongst *Zostera* species (seagrasses).

Abundance & distribution
Frequent. Distribution uncertain. Found all around Ireland and on west and south-west coasts of Britain. Distributed south to the Atlantic coast of Spain.

Distinctive features

1. Cushion-like, massive, or encrusting sponge that is firm but springy to the touch.
2. Surface may be covered in small, erect protrusions.

Distinctive features

1. Tree-like growth form.
2. Branches usually with a rounded cross-section and rounded tips.
3. Oscula arranged along branches in irregular rows.

Distinctive features

1. Encrusting, irregular sponge.
2. Forms thick, rounded, tubular, conical, or branch-like protuber-ances.
3. Texture rough to touch but sponge is soft.

ORDER **Poecilosclerida**

FAMILY **Biemnidae**

Hemimycale columella (Bowerbank)

Description · Forms irregularly shaped thick sheets, up to about 1 cm thick, sometimes developed into low mounds. The surface has a character-istic honeycomb pattern of craters and ridges, with small holes situated in each crater. Larger oscula may be situated on raised chimneys. The colour is pale pinky-orange, yellow to orangey-brown, pink, or flesh. **Habitat & ecology** · A lower-shore and shallow sublittoral species, growing on hard surfaces. The sea-slug, *Discodoris planata*, may be found feeding on this sponge.

Abundance & distribution
Locally common. Mainly found on south-west coasts of Britain and Ireland. Distribution uncertain but probably from southern Norway to the Mediterranean, and the Azores.

FAMILY **Desmacidonidae**

Amphilectus fucorum (Esper)

Description · Somewhat variable in form, the most characteristic appearance of this rough-surfaced sponge is as slender, erect flexible lobes that are bright orange in colour and up to 10 cm long and 3 mm in diameter. It also forms thin, spreading sheets or more substantial mounds. The oscula are irregularly scattered on sheet and mound growths but appear in lines on the erect form. **Habitat & ecology** · A lower-shore to shallow sublittoral sponge found on rock and tubes of the polychaete *Sabella*. Also occurs on holdfasts of larger algae and among red seaweeds and may encrust hydroids. Similar to *Halichondria bowerbanki*, but this species tends to be yellowish and not as delicate as *Amphilectus*.

Abundance & distribution
Common. Found all around Britain and Ireland. Occurs throughout the north-east Atlantic region.

FAMILY **Myxillidae**

Myxilla fimbriata (Bowerbank)

Description · Up to 8 cm in diameter, this sponge forms cushion-like masses. The outline of individual sponges is irregular with an elastic consistency but variable firmness. The slightly roughened surface, with scattered oscula, is orange in life, but turns dark brown to black if preserved in alcohol. **Habitat & ecology** · A sublittoral species, found growing on rocks and boulders. **Similar species** · There are at least two other European species of *Myxilla* with which this form may be confused; specialist knowledge and microscopic examination of their internal structures are required for certain identification. *Suberites ficus* may also be similar in some of its growth forms.

Abundance & distribution
Locally common. Found on all British and Irish coasts. Distribution uncertain but probably throughout coasts of north-west Europe.

Distinctive features

1. Forms thick, irregularly shaped sheets or low mounds.
2. Surface with a honeycomb pattern of ridges and craters, with small hole in each crater.
3. Colour pale pinky-orange, pink, or orangey-brown.

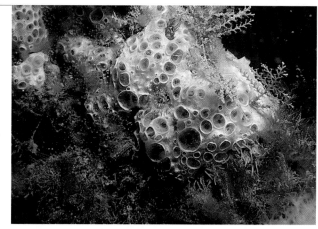

Distinctive features

1. Form variable: thin spreading sheets, distinct mounds, or slender, erect, flexible lobes.
2. Surface rough.
3. Bright orange.

Distinctive features

1. Rather elastic, variably firm, cushion-like growth.
2. Colour in life orange.

Myxilla incrustans (Johnston)

Description · Slimy to the touch when out of water. Typically forms thick, irregular crusts or massive growths, up to about 15 cm in width and 5 cm thick. Surface covered in pits, folds, furrows, and narrow channels, across which are web-like strands of tissue. The large oscula commonly appear like craters at the peaks of small volcanoes. The whole colony may have a conical shape in profile. Colour varies from a fairly bright orange or yellow to a dull yellowish-orange, or even pink or red. **Habitat & ecology** · A lower-shore to shallow sublittoral species usually growing in clear water. Generally attached to rocks but also found on hydroids or the carapaces of spider crabs. **Similar species** · Easily confused with yellow- or orange-coloured examples of *M. rosacea*, which is more commonly a distinct rose-red hue, or even with *Halichondria* species.

Abundance & distribution
Common. Found on all British and Irish coasts. Distribution uncertain but probably from Norway to Gibraltar.

FAMILY **Clathriidae**

Microciona atrasanguinea Bowerbank

Description · Forms thin but extensive sheets with an irregular outline, up to 20 cm across. The velvety surface is pitted and has networks of vessels radiating outwards from each osculum. The dark, blood-red colour is highly characteristic of the species. The skeleton is composed of spongin fibres among which are embedded both straight and curved spicules. **Habitat & ecology** · Found attached to rocks on the lower shore and in shallow sublittoral waters. The chromodorid sea-slug, *Rostanga rubra*, derives its red coloration by feeding on this form and species of *Ophlitaspongia*.

Abundance & distribution
Common. Found on all British and Irish coasts but possibly rare in South-East Britain. Distributed on most northeast Atlantic coasts but not occurring in the Mediterranean or North Sea.

ORDER **Dictyoceratida**

FAMILY **Dysideidae**

Dysidea fragilis (Montagu)

Description · Can be encrusting, or massive and lobe-shaped. Its surface is covered in small cone-like or pyramidal projections that give a distinctly spiky appearance. The oscula, which are scattered across the surface, are up to 5 mm in diameter and may be raised. The sponge may reach 30 cm across but in northern waters is often much smaller. The colour varies from brownish-, greenish-, or greyish-white to reddish-brown. It has a distinctive smell. **Habitat & ecology** · May be found on the low shore, particularly in crevices or rock pools. It also occurs subtidally on rock at shallow depths.

Abundance & distribution
Frequent. Distribution uncertain but probably occurs throughout much of the north-east Atlantic. Common in the Mediterranean.

Distinctive features

1. Grows in thick, irregular and slimy masses, covered in pits and mounds.
2. Oscula large, distinct, on top of volcano-shaped mounds.
3. Colour yellow or orange.

Distinctive features

1. Dark, blood-red colour.
2. Forms thin, irregularly shaped but extensive sheets.
3. Oscula surrounded by radiating network of vessels.

Distinctive features

1. Encrusting or massive.
2. Surface covered in conical or pyramidal projections, giving spiky appearance.
3. Scattered oscula to 5 mm diameter.

Anemones, corals, sea firs, jellyfishes, comb jellies, and sea gooseberries

Phylum Cnidaria

This phylum has evolved an extremely diverse range of body shapes, forms, and sizes and includes sea anemones, sea fans, sea firs, sea pens, corals, and jellyfishes. A fundamental feature of all of them, however, is that the body possesses only two cell layers (a **diploblastic** grade of organisation), the outer **ectoderm** and the inner **endoderm**, separated by an essentially structureless **mesogloea**. The mesogloea, depending upon the group concerned, may be a thin membrane with no cells, a thick, jelly-like layer, or a muscular, fibrous layer reinforced by cells derived from both the ecto- and endoderm.

Despite their diversity, two basic body forms can be recognised, the **polyp** and the **medusa**. The sessile polyp, at its simplest, is sac-like, with the single body cavity or gut (**coelenteron**) opening by a single mouth surrounded by one to several rings of **tentacles**. The tentacles are armed with stinging cells (**cnidocytes**) which contain **nematocysts**. These may be arranged singly or in groups, and are found on other parts of the body besides the tentacles. Nematocysts are small capsules containing a coiled thread that is explosively discharged when the nematocyst is triggered mechanically. The threads may be smooth or barbed, their length varying with species. Nematocysts are used in aggression and self-defence, as well as for catching and stunning prey. They possess **toxins** (poisons) which, in many cnidarians, are strong enough to inflict painful stings or, as with tropical sea wasps (box jellyfish), may be sufficiently powerful to be fatal to humans. The free-floating or swimming medusa is bell-shaped, with a central mouth located at the centre of the concave underside and variable numbers of tentacles hanging down from the margin of the bell.

Fundamentally, cnidarians possess two phases in their life-cycle, an asexual **polypoid** stage alternating with a sexually reproducing **medusoid** stage. Eggs and spermatozoa, shed by mature medusae, develop into a **planula** larva after fertilisation. The planula attaches to a suitable surface and then grows into a polyp which, in turn, buds asexually to form a colony. Specialised polyps in the colony subsequently bud-off medusae that break free to complete the life-cycle. Depending upon the group of cnidarians concerned, either the polypoid or the medusoid stage may be reduced or completely suppressed. Among the sea firs, for example, many species retain this basic alternation of stages, whilst others suppress the free-living medusoid stage, special polyps in the colony then either developing gonads for sexual reproduction or budding off medusae which remain attached to the colony. In anemones and corals the medusoid stage is entirely eliminated, internal gonads developing in the polyps and releasing their gametes into the coelenteron. The eggs are fertilised as they pass out of the polyp and then develop into a planula larva. Jellyfishes, on the other hand, represent advanced medusae, their polypoid stage being reduced to a single small **scyphistoma** that buds off (**strobilates**) sessile **ephyrae** which then develop directly into new medusae.

The systematics of the phylum Cnidaria is still controversial. At present it is generally considered to consist of four classes.

Anthozoa Regarded as the ancestral class. The medusoid stage is completely lacking. The group includes hard corals, anemones, soft corals, sea fans, sea pens, antipatharians, corals and tube anemones.

Hydrozoa These include the hydroids or sea firs and the siphonophores. The polypoid generation usually predominates and the medusoid stage may or may not exist. The siphonophores are unusual in being floating colonies of polyps and medusae.

Scyphozoa The jellyfishes. In this group the medusoid stage is dominant and the polypoid stage is small and inconspicuous, or completely lacking.

Cubozoa The box jellyfishes or sea wasps. A group of largely colourless medusae that only occur in tropical seas. The sting of many species is highly dangerous.

Further reading

Cornelius, P. F. S., Manuel, R. L., & Ryland, J. S. (1990). Cnidaria. In *The marine fauna of the British Isles and north-west Europe* (eds P. J. Hayward & J. S. Ryland), Vol. 1, pp. 101–80. Clarendon Press, Oxford.

Manuel, R. L. (1988). British Anthozoa. *Synopses of the British Fauna, New Series,* 18, 1–241.

Russell, F. S. (1970). *The medusae of the British Isles, II. Pelagic Scyphozoa, with a supplement to the first volume on hydromedusae.* Cambridge University Press, Cambridge.

Class Anthozoa (anemones, corals)

Anthozoans have no medusoid stage in their life-cycle. The cylindrical polyp body (**column**) is closed at its upper end by a transverse **oral disc**, from which hollow **tentacles** arise in concentric rings (**cycles**). The tentacles are characteristically armed with large numbers of nematocysts. The mouth is situated at the centre of the disc and opens into a throat or **actinopharynx** (a laterally flattened tube) with one or both ends modified to form ciliated grooves (**siphonoglyphs**) projecting into the body cavity (**coelenteron**). The coelenteron is subdivided by vertical, radially arranged **mesenteries** (ridge-like extensions of the inner body wall) whose free edges are developed into convoluted **mesenteric filaments**. Mesenteries are usually arranged in equal-sized pairs, those reaching the actinopharynx forming **perfect** mesenteries, those ending abruptly and not reaching it being **imperfect** mesenteries. The base of the column normally forms an **adhesive disc**, as in most solitary anemones, or is attached to a common basal tissue mass (**coenenchyme**), as in many colonial forms. The polyps are highly contractile and most can retract their tentacles into the body.

There are three subclasses, the **Octocorallia** (**Alcyonaria**), the **Hexacorallia** (**Zoantharia**) and the **Ceriantipatharia**.

Hexacorals (zoantharians) may be solitary, colonial, or in aggregations, their cylindrical polyps usually having their mesenteries

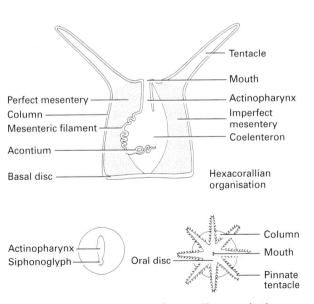

A typical anthozoan polyp, showing the main body structures. *Bottom left*: the actinopharynx with one margin developed into a siphonoglyph. *Bottom right*: an octocoral viewed from above, showing the eight pinnate tentacles.

organised into multiples of six. The top of the column commonly has a ring of sphincter muscles that are used to seal the polyp after it has retracted its tentacles and oral disc. One order within the group (the **Scleractinia**) possesses a calcified exoskeleton called a **corallum**. Around the British Isles the hexacorals are classified into four orders, the **Actiniaria** (anemones), **Corallimorpharia** (jewel anemones), **Scleractinia** (stony corals) and **Zoanthidea** (zoanthids). Some members of the group contain **zooxanthellae** (symbiotic photosynthetic unicellular algae) in their tissues.

All **anemones**, the largest of the hexacoral orders, are solitary, either attaching to an appropriate surface by their adhesive **basal disc** or using a rounded base (**physa**) to burrow into softer sediments. The column is usually very contractile. Its outer surface may be smooth or covered with hollow **verrucae**, flattened adhesive **suckers**, or solid **tubercles**. In some species tiny holes (**cinclides**) in the column wall indicate where stinging threads (**acontia**), originating on the mesenteries, may be ejected. The thicker lower part of the column (the **scapus**) may merge smoothly into the oral disc, or the column may be separated from the disc by a rim (**parapet**) and groove (**fosse**) succeeded by a thin-walled upper region (**capitulum**) immediately under the oral disc. In a few species a ring of hollow warts (**acrorhagi**) is located on either the parapet or the fosse. In most sea anemones the tentacles are arranged in multiples of six (**hexamerous symmetry**), the innermost two cycles containing 6 tentacles, the third cycle 12, the fourth cycle 24, and so on, although other numerical arrangements are found in some species. Depending upon the species, sea anemones may be hermaphroditic or possess separate sexes (**dioecious**). Gametes are fertilised externally, the zygote developing into a free-swimming **planula** larva. Most anemones can also reproduce asexually, either by **fission** (splitting) of the body into two, or by **pedal laceration** where part of the column becomes detached, rounds off and develops into a new polyp. In others, asexually formed miniature polyps are budded off inside the coelenteron and emerge through the mouth. Most sea anemones are actively carnivorous, using their nematocysts and tentacles to trap a wide range of fishes and invertebrates as food.

Stony coral (scleractinian) polyps are similar to actiniarians in morphology but have no siphonoglyphs in their actinopharynx. They live in a calcareous (**aragonitic**) exoskeleton, either solitary (the exoskeleton is then called a **corallum**) or in colonies (exoskeletons of polyps termed **corallites**) joined by a common calcified **coenosteum**. Within the calcified skeleton, septa (**sclerosepta**) are deposited as ridges between the mesenteries. The living polyp tissues can be retracted between the sclerosepta.

Zoanthids may be solitary or colonial. The polyps are short and cylindrical, occurring singly or in groups joined by a creeping **stolon**, a basal mat of canals lined by endodermal tissue, or an encrusting sheet of coenenchyme. Although the polyps have no exoskeleton, their columns may be stiffened or supported by sand grains. The single siphonoglyph of the mouth is regarded as ventral. Around the oral disc the tentacles are arranged in two cycles. Most species of zoanthids contain symbiotic **zooxanthellae**.

Jewel anemones form a small order in which the short tentacles often end in knobs (**capitate** tentacles). Corallimorpharians, which are either solitary or weakly colonial, have no calcified skeleton.

Octocorals are entirely colonial, the polyps (**zooids**) having eight pinnate tentacles arranged in a single cycle. Each zooid consists of a retractile terminal **anthocodium** and a basal, more skeletised, **anthostele** into which the anthocodium is withdrawn. The actinopharynx has a single siphonoglyph. Most octocorals possess internal calcareous **sclerites** or **spicules**, others have a rod-like **skeletal axis**. The coelenteric cavities of the zooids are interconnected by endodermally lined channels called **solenia**. The subclass contains the soft corals, sea fans, and sea pens.

The subclass **Ceriantipatharia** forms a group of anthozoans that have complete mesenteries but very weak musculature. There are generally six primary mesenteries but additional mesenteries may arise from the single siphonoglyph. The two orders of the group are the **Antipatharia** and the **Ceriantharia**. Genetic studies have shown that these two orders are highly divergent and some taxonomists regard them as entirely separate groups. Antipatharians include the black or thorny corals. They have a tree-like or dendritic shape, like gorgonians, and are generally restricted to deep waters or tropical seas. Some antipatharians are harvested for jewellery. Ceriantharians (tube anemones) are large, solitary anemones that construct felt-like tubes composed of mucus, nematocysts, and mud in soft sediments, buried to the level of the oral disc. The oral disc and tentacles are expanded at the surface of the sediment and are all that can be seen of the animals. The column, which in some species may be as long as 1 m, is posteriorly (basally) tapered with a central pore. The mouth, which possesses a single siphonoglyph conventionally designated as the dorsal side, is surrounded by short **labial tentacles**. Three or four cycles of longer **marginal tentacles** are located around the rim of the oral disc. In the coelenteron the mesenteries are coupled but not arranged in pairs. A distinctive type of nematocyst, called a **ptychocyst**, is found in tube anemones. The pelagic larva, an **arachnactis** larva, develops tentacles and mesenteries before settling.

SUBCLASS **Hexacorallia** | ORDER **Actiniaria** |
SUBORDER **Nynantheae**

FAMILY **Actiniidae**

Actinia equina (Linnaeus) **Beadlet anemone**

Description · 5–7 cm tall and 6 cm in diameter when fully expanded, often smaller. Column smooth, oral disc bearing about 192 rapidly retractile tentacles in 5–6 rows. Tentacles may reach 2 cm when extended. Outside tentacles a circle of 24 (occasionally 48) hollow warts normally evident. Usually blue, may vary to white, red, pink, rich pale lilac, or violet blue. At low tide anemone resembles firm, pyramidal, jelly-like mass with no external evidence of tentacles. Column typically shades of crimson, but can be paler, greenish- or yellowish-brown, or olive. Pallid forms may be lilac, pink, pale green, straw-coloured or nearly colourless. Foot often a different colour to column: grey tinged with green, blue, or pink. **Habitat & ecology** · Extremely common from mid-shore to sublittoral depths of about 8–10 m, attached to rocks and boulders, in crevices, below rocky overhangs, or in rock pools. Found on extremely exposed to very sheltered shores; withstands wide ranges of salinity and temperature. Local populations clonal; members of different clones strongly antagonistic towards each other. Young are budded internally and brooded. **Similar species** · *A. fragacea*, but this is distinguished by large spots on column.

Abundance & distribution Extremely common on most British rocky shores. Range

Actinia fragacea Tugwell **Strawberry anemone**

Description · Column up to 10 cm diameter, smooth, oral disc bearing about 192 rapidly retractile tentacles in 5–6 rows. Column usually crimson or dark reddish-brown with green spots. Disc and tentacles crimson to dark reddish-brown and unmarked. Species possesses 24 or 48 hollow warts on the outside of the tentacles as in *A. equina*. Colours of *A. fragacea* variable, may be very rich or dull and weak. Green spots also vary in size, shape, and density and the hollow warts may be pale blue, whitish, pink, or red. The foot of the anemone may be marked with crimson radial lines. **Habitat & ecology** · This species is frequently encountered in the south-west of the United Kingdom on rocky shores. It generally occurs lower on the shore than *A. equina*, though the two species often occur together. *A. fragacea* is thought to be oviparous as opposed to brooding its young. **Similar species** · *A. fragacea* has green spots on its column, distinguishing it from *A. equina*.

Abundance & distribution Common in south-west England. Distribution uncertain but possibly similar to *A. equina*. North-east Atlantic region from Norway to the Mediterranean and West Africa.

Anemonia viridis (Forskål) **Snakelocks anemone**

Description · A very distinctive anemone; the long, typically greenish tentacles rarely retract completely. Up to 200 tentacles irregularly arranged around oral disc, characteristically appearing as writhing mass. Tentacles may be up to 15 cm long and are brown or grey to bright green. Tips of tentacles usually tinged an obvious pinkish or purplish, and base may be scarlet. The dull brown to grey, smooth-surfaced column, to 13 cm in diameter and 5 cm tall, not always easily seen beneath crown of tentacles and often spread out at its base. **Habitat & ecology** · Lower shore and sublittorally down to 20 m. Has preference for well-illuminated situations and green colour comes from presence of symbiotic algae, zooxanthellae, in the tissues. Typically attached to rocks, boulders, and other hard surfaces but also found living on larger seaweeds. It also occurs higher on the shore in rock pools or crevices. This anemone is oviparous (produces eggs) or reproduces by fission. The spider crab, *Inachus phalangium*, may be found associated with it.

Abundance & distribution Common on rocky shores on west coast of Britain but absent from the southern part of the North Sea and eastern region of the English Channel. Range is from the Atlantic, northern North Sea, and western Channel coasts of northern

extends from the White Sea to the west coast of Africa, Canary Islands, Cape Verde Islands, and Mediterranean.

Distinctive features

1. Ring of 24 blue hollow warts around outside of tentacles.
2. No spots on column.

Distinctive features

1. Ring of 24 blue hollow warts around the outside of the tentacles
2. Green spots on column.

Europe into the Mediterranean, Madeira, and the Canary Islands.

Distinctive features

1. Mass of up to 200 tentacles rarely retract fully.
2. A sticky sensation can be felt when a finger is drawn through the tentacles.
3. Tentacles are typically greenish, usually with pinkish or purplish tips.

Anthopleura ballii (Cocks)

Description · Fairly large anemone, up to 10 cm tall. Column trumpet-shaped when fully expanded; may appear translucent. Sometimes looks low and broad. Column has up to 96 longitudinal rows of small warts, each with red spot in centre. Disc circular and broad, with wide space between mouth and tentacles. Five cycles of stout tentacles, tapering to blunt point, and up to about 3 cm long. Up to 96 tentacles (arranged 6, 6, 12, 24, 48). Column generally yellowish, orange, or rose towards base, with fine red flecks, changing to grey or brown or even pale yellow to colourless further up, and finally sometimes to brown with a greenish tinge below margin. Dark brown area with cream spots around mouth. Tentacles generally brown towards bases, paler near tips. Two pale transverse bars may be visible on tentacles along with cream-coloured flecks. Paler parts of tentacles greenish (sometimes vivid) or pale yellow, pink, or grey. **Habitat & ecology** · Generally intertidal, beneath seaweed or in cracks in pools, also under stones or in holes in chalky areas. Like *Anemonia viridis*, may contain zooxanthellae. **Similar species** · Resembles *Anthopleura thallia*, but this is smaller, often with debris attached to column, and tends to occur in pools and crevices on very exposed shores.

Abundance & distribution
Locally common. Found in south-west Britain and Ireland. Elsewhere distributed from the Atlantic coast of France to the Mediterranean.

Bunodactis verrucosa (Pennant)

Description · To about 3 cm tall. Column pillar-like, slightly wider above and coloured pink, lilac, grey or brownish, marked with longitudinal rows of spots. Large, conspicuous white warts form six rows. A further 18 rows are grey, while 24 are of smaller white or grey warts. When anemone contracted these warts give it appearance of a sea urchin test without its spines. Oral disc dull green around mouth to dark grey further out. May have grey radial lines bounded on either side by red line. Lips of mouth yellowish-grey, mouth marked on each side with magenta spot. Tentacles, in four cycles: 6, 6, 12, 24, stout and blunt. On oral side tentacles are purplish-grey, darkest along midline with median row of pale oval spots varying in strength. These spots may give tentacles a barred appearance. **Habitat & ecology** · Generally intertidal in wide range of habitats, but particularly in rock pools or cracks and crevices, especially with *Corallina* species. May occur in sand attached to rock or a stone under surface. Broods its young like *Actinia equina* and may be gregarious.

Abundance & distribution
Occurs on south-west coast of Britain, Irish Sea, and Ireland. Also found south to the Mediterranean. May be locally common.

Urticina eques (Gosse)

Description · Large anemone; tentacles and oral disc may reach 30 cm across. Often attaches loosely to substratum. Column shape variable, but higher than wide and marked with inconspicuous white warts that may be barely visible. Column rarely encrusted with foreign matter; varies from pale straw, white, pale grey to deep crimson, brownish-orange, or lavender. May be marked with spots, streaks, and blotches of orange, scarlet, or crimson. Tentacles large (up to 6 cm long and 1 cm in diameter at base), arranged in up to five cycles, in multiples of 10 (10, 10, 20, 40, 80). They are stout, blunt, and may be white, colourless, or various shades of yellow, red, or purple/lilac, sometimes banded. Oral disc colour varies but often pale pink becoming brownish towards mouth, and may be marked by conspicuous crimson radial stripes. **Habitat & ecology** · Usually subtidal to at least 400 m, but occasionally found at low water spring tide level. Reproduces sexually. **Similar species** · Resembles *U. felina* but much larger and often more active. It is also more loosely attached to substratum and usually does not have debris attached to column.

Abundance & distribution
Found all around Britain but not in the Channel. Occurs in Norway, Iceland, and Sweden and into the Arctic circle. Widespread, locally common.

Distinctive features

1. Trumpet-shaped column.
2. Wide space between mouth and tentacles.
3. Rows of warts on column, each with a red spot.

Distinctive features

1. Pink/lilac/grey column with longitudinal rows of white and grey warts.
2. Resembles the shell of an urchin without spines when contracted.

Distinctive features

1. Large size.
2. Large stout tentacles arranged in multiples of 10.
3. Usually without debris attached to column.
4. Column usually smooth.

Urticina felina (Linnaeus) **Dahlia anemone**

Description · Column usually short and squat, maximum diameter 10 cm. Column colour highly variable, often dull or dark and almost invariably encrusted with fragments of shells, gravel, and various other debris that stick to conspicuous warts. Background colour may be marked with splashes of crimson, varies from shades of brown or green to dull yellow, orange, or even pale blue. Oral disc round, may be shades of grey, blue-grey, crimson, white, or even colourless, often marked with conspicuous crimson radial stripes which can be flanked by cream or brownish-yellow stripes. Tentacles arranged as for *U. eques* but the last cycle is incomplete. Tentacles short, stout, and blunt, often banded. **Habitat & ecology** · Found intertidally in crevices or pools, usually low shore but occasionally reaches MSL in deep pools. Sometimes covers itself in gravel. Occurs subtidally to 100 m. Reproduces sexually. **Similar species** · Resembles *U. eques* but is smaller, more firmly attached to substrate, and with column often covered in debris.

Abundance & distribution
Found on all coasts of Britain and Ireland. Distributed from the Arctic to the Bay of Biscay. Common below neap low tide level.

FAMILY **Aiptasiidae**

Aiptasia mutabilis (Gravenhorst)

Description · The base is sucker-like and adhesive. The column, up to 20 cm tall, is trumpet shaped, smooth, and a yellowish-brown colour, sometimes with a blue or violet tinge that may result from zooxanthellae. The disc may be marked with bluish or greenish lines. There are about 100 long, robust, whitish tentacles which are not readily retractable. The tentacles may spread to 15 cm wide. **Habitat & ecology** · An extreme lower-shore and shallow sublittoral species, found on rocks, in crevices, or on large algal holdfasts. On the shore it is usually found under rocky overhangs or in pools. In the Mediterranean this species is preyed upon by the aeolid sea-slug, *Spurilla neapolitana*.

Abundance & distribution
Locally common in south-west Britain and Channel Islands. Distributed south to the Mediterranean.

FAMILY **Metridiidae**

Metridium senile (Linnaeus) **Plumose anemone**

Description · An extremely beautiful anemone when fully expanded. Smooth-surfaced column, lacking both warts and verrucae, possesses numerous tiny holes through which stinging threads can be ejected. Base adhesive, may reach a height of 8–50 cm. Below crown of tentacles distinct collar may be present, and oral disc distinctly lobed. Long tentacles, more translucent than column, so numerous (up to about 200) and densely distributed that they have characteristic plume-like or fluffy appearance. Commonest variety, *M. senile* variety *dianthus*, the largest: grows from 20–50 cm tall. Variety *pallidum* smaller, with maximum diameter of some 25 mm. Colour very variable, but white, cream, orange, pinky-brown, or brown are amongst commonest. Column may appear striped. **Habitat & ecology** · Attached to rocks, boulders, piers, wrecks, and other hard surfaces from extreme lower shore to sublittoral depths of about 100 m. Variety *dianthus* often found in shallow sublittoral situations growing in dense clonal aggregations. Is oviparous but reproduces asexually usually by pedal laceration.

Abundance & distribution
Common on most British coasts, with a distribution ranging from the Mediterranean to Norway, including Iceland, Faroes, Channel and North Sea.

Distinctive features

1. Column encrusted in debris.
2. Short and squat anemone.
3. Tentacles arranged in multiples of ten.

Distinctive features

1. Robust, long whitish tentacles, not easily retracted.
2. Column trumpet-shaped, tall, smooth, yellowish-brown, sometimes bluish or violet.

Distinctive features

1. Tentacles numerous, crowded, and with a distinctly fluffy appearance.
2. Column smooth.
3. Colour variable, often pink, white, brown, cream, or orange.
4. Oral disc lobed.

FAMILY Sagartiidae
Actinothoe sphyrodeta (Gosse)

Description · Small, reaching 3 cm in height with diameter of base up to
1 cm. Column pillar-like when extended, high and narrow. Column often
smooth and a dull, uneven, greyish-white. It may appear striped with
alternate stripes of opaque and more translucent white, or may also tend
towards dull blue, green, brown, or yellow. Transparent dots may be visible
on upper part of column. Base often wider than column. This species often
appears flower-like with up to 100 pure white tentacles irregularly arranged
in five cycles with part of a sixth. Tentacles tend to have darker markings
around base. Oral disc may be white or greyish-white, or brilliant orange,
dull or pale orange, or yellow. This species may eject fine stinging threads if
disturbed. **Habitat & ecology** · Low on shores, especially on rock
overhangs or in caves. Also found under stones, in pools, or in kelp
holdfasts. Common sublittorally down to 50 m. Often occurs in large
numbers. Is oviparous but may reproduce asexually by fission. **Similar
species** · Distinguished from similar varieties of *Sagartia elegans* by lack of
suckers on column.

Abundance & Distribution
Locally common in southwest
England and southwest Ireland
and occurs in the Channel
Islands, southern North Sea,
and Atlantic coast of France.
Distributed from Shetland to
the Bay of Biscay.

Cereus pedunculatus (Pennant)
Daisy anemone

Description · The firmly adhesive base gives rise to a trumpet-shaped,
orange to buff-grey column which, at its upper end, is 3–12 cm in diameter
and fringed with enormous numbers (500–1000) short and brightly
patterned tentacles. The oral disc, fringed by the tentacles, often has a
puckered appearance and is usually brown with darker markings,
sometimes rather beautifully patterned with light or dark brown dots.
Cinclides (small holes through which stinging threads may be extruded) are
present on the upper part of the column, which also bears numerous pale
grey suckers to which debris is frequently stuck. **Habitat & ecology** ·
Found on rocky coasts from the middle-shore to shallow sublittoral
situations, typically anchored deeply in clean rock pool crevices, or on
stones and shells buried in mud or sand, sometimes also occurring in
estuaries. Individuals buried in softer substrata are usually found with only
their oral disc expanded at the sediment surface.

Abundance & distribution
Sometimes found locally in
large numbers. Distributed
from west and south Atlantic
coasts of Britain and Ireland
(as far north as Scottish
Borders) south to Channel
coasts and Mediterranean.
Reported from North Sea, but

Sagartia ornata (Holdsworth)

Description · Small, up to 1.6 cm high, base relatively wide, up to 1.5 cm
diameter. Column smooth when extended, usually dark olive green (may be
dark brown or orangey-brown) with slightly paler longitudinal lines. May
be irregular paler areas on middle and upper parts of column (suckers or
cinclides). Lower part of column may be sheathed in mucus and detritus.
Oral disc surrounded by yellowish-green, then very dark green ring, then
greyish-green area where tentacles are attached. Radial lines pale yellowish-
grey near mouth, edged with green. Moving out to tentacles, radial lines
change to pale translucent green. Between these colours is a pale cream spot

(12 in all around oral disc). There are also finer, dark green radial lines with
a spot near mouth. Tentacles relatively long, blunt, slender, in 5–6 cycles: 6,
6, 12, 24, etc. Primary and secondary tentacles mid-green with brown tinge
to tip and four pale transverse bars. Tertiary tentacles have four bars and
two triangular pale marks near base (forming B-shape). Tentacles often pale
salmon around base. Both oral disc and tentacles may be pale; tentacles
may be unmarked and white or orange. **Habitat & ecology** · Common
intertidally, especially in crevices, kelp holdfasts, on *Ascophyllum* and
Zostera, on and under stones and shells, and in rock pools. Tolerates

brackish conditions in
estuaries. Also occurs
subtidally. Broods young,
produced asexually by budding
inside column.

Abundance & distribution
Found on all British coasts and
occurs from Iceland and
Norway to the Mediterranean.

Distinctive features

1. Flower-like appearance.
2. Pure white tentacles.
3. Smooth column (no suckers).

its occurrence there is unconfirmed.

Distinctive features

1. Body shaped like a tall trumpet, with short tentacles forming a fringe at the upper end.
2. Column smooth, with cinclides present near top of column.
3. Upper part of column with numerous pale grey suckers, often with debris attached.

Distinctive features

1. Small anemone with greenish to olive green column with paler stripes.
2. Central part of oral disc tinged with yellow.
3. Ring of 12 white spots on disc.

Sagartia elegans (Dalyell)

Description · Strongly adhesive base, 3–4 cm in diameter, up to about 6 cm tall and widest at top. Column reddish-brown, covered with small, wart-like suckers. At top of column ring of up to 200 tentacles, each up to about 15 mm long, surrounds oral disc in which mouth centrally placed; when fully expanded tentacles may have spread of about 6 cm. There are five distinct colour varieties: *S. elegans* variety *aurantiaca* has orange tentacles (not illustrated); variety *miniata* has both tentacles and oral disc clearly patterned, usually in shades of brown (a); variety *venusta* has orange oral disc and white tentacles (b); variety *nivea* has white oral disc and tentacles (c); variety *rosea* has pink, rose red, or magenta tentacles and orange or dull white oral disc (d). When irritated the anemone ejects sticky white threads. **Habitat & ecology** · Found on exposed to sheltered rocky shores, in rock pools, under rock overhangs, or in crevices, from the lower shore to sublittoral depths of about 50 m. Reproduces by pedal laceration.

Abundance & distribution
Fairly common on British rocky shores, the distribution ranges from the Atlantic, North Sea, and Channel coasts of northern Europe into the Mediterranean.

(a)

Sagartia troglodytes (Price in Johnston)

Description · Moderately sized, very variable in coloration, often speckled. Column smooth and pillar-like when extended, to 15 cm tall, base much wider than column. Column usually yellowish-drab, paler below and greyish towards top but may be flesh coloured becoming yellowish-brown above; dull drab below, darker above; cream below, greenish-olive above; pale grey below, dark greenish-grey above. Lower part of column may be striped with paler lines and pale spots (suckers). Oral disc can be almost any colour from white to black though often yellowish-grey around mouth and dark blackish-grey towards edge. Disc often marked with radial stripes (6–24 depending on size) on which pale spot occurs near mouth. About 190 tentacles of moderate length, arranged in six cycles: 6, 6, 12, 24, 48, 96. Tentacles slender, blunt, marked with four pale bars and median, longitudinal, dark grey stripe interrupted by pale bars. At base of tentacles a black bar abutting a white B-shaped mark outlined in black. May be tinge of buff, orange, or pinkish-orange near base of tentacles. Tentacles may be patternless and completely pale, or bright orange or white, occasionally tinged pale lilac, rose to reddish-purple, or violet. **Similar species** · Resembles *S. elegans* but in that species inner tentacles often do not form

two cycles of 6 but an inner cycle, frequently of uneven number (7–14). *S. elegans* usually attaches to hard surfaces such as rocks rather than buried objects. *S. elegans* emits stinging threads more readily than *S. troglodytes*.

Abundance & distribution
Found on all coasts of Britain.

Distinctive features

1. Column covered with wart-like suckers.
2. Tall and slender, widest across the oral disc.
3. Column reddish-brown, tentacles and oral disc of various colours.

(c)

(d)

Distributed from Iceland and Faeroes to Mediterranean.

Distinctive features

1. Even number of tentacles, up to about 190.
2. Often attached to buried object in sand or mud.
3. B-shaped spot at base of tentacles.

Sagartiogeton laceratus (Dalyell)

Description · Small anemone, reaching 2–3 cm in height. Column very flat and wrinkled when retracted but forms slender translucent pillar when expanded. Ring of small, dark, or translucent spots visible just below margin. Column pale buff-grey in lower part with 12 narrow, cream-coloured stripes running up column with darker yellowish areas between. Column may vary with tones of reddish-, pinkish-, or yellowish- to orangey-brown. May be loose covering of mucous and sediment particles near base. Disc perfectly circular but small compared to tentacles, and orange to yellowish-grey. Tentacles arranged in 4–5 cycles, up to 3 cm long, and slender, tapering to fine point. Tentacles have dark base and may be marked with opaque double bar near base and double median purplish-brown line along oral side. **Habitat & ecology** · Shallow subtidal waters on hard substrates, including *Turritella* shells or the tubes of fan worms or sea squirts. It reproduces asexually by pedal laceration so that the tentacles are often not arranged in multiples of six in their cycles.

Abundance & distribution
Frequent on all British and Irish coasts. Distribution is from northern Norway to the Atlantic coast of France.

Sagartiogeton undatus (Müller)

Description · Moderately sized, reaching height of 12 cm and diameter of 6 cm. Remarkably flat when contracted. Column appears elongate when expanded and lacks suckers. Oral disc wider than column; mouth large. Up to 200 long, slender tentacles. Column colour variable but usually striped with alternating dark and light colours. Dark stripes vary from dark grey or brown to lilac-grey, pinkish, or buff. Upper column dull red, salmon pink, buff, or light brown to yellowish-brown, dark brown, or grey. Often dark spots (cinclides) on upper part of column just below margin. Oral disc generally grey or brown sometimes with delicate patterns of darker or lighter spots. Tentacles usually have two distinctive dark longitudinal stripes. **Habitat & ecology** · Subtidal, but also on lower shore. Generally found attached to stones or shells buried in sand or mud. Also occurs in crevices or holes in rocks, on shells of various molluscs such as *Ostrea edulis* or on crab carapaces. Oviparous. **Similar species** · *Sagartia troglodytes* and *Cereus pedunculatus*, but both these have suckers and *C. pedunculatus* has many more tentacles.

Abundance & distribution
Frequent around all coasts of Britain and Ireland. Distribution uncertain but probably from Norway to the Atlantic coasts of France, Spain, and Portugal, and the Mediterranean and Black Seas.

FAMILY **Hormathiidae**

Adamsia carciniopados (Otto) **Cloak anemone**

Description · Moderately sized, body up to 5–7 cm diameter when unattached to a shell. Base expanded to form two wings that wrap around shell occupied by hermit crab. Elliptical oral disc and rest of column lie beneath body of hermit crab. Up to roughly 500 tentacles, arranged in 7–8 cycles. Oral disc and tentacles usually white or cream, sometimes with white or lilac tinge. Anemone column beneath hermit crab usually white whilst parts that wrap around top of hermit crab are brownish, yellowish-brown, light orange, reddish-brown, or tawny brown, often with purplish or lilac tinge. Upper parts of anemone usually marked with magenta spots. Occasionally individuals will be completely white or white with pink spots. Anemone may or may not wrap around entire shell occupied by crab depending on relative size of shell and anemone. **Habitat & ecology** · Has a commensal relationship with hermit crab, *Pagurus prideauxi*, to extent that anemone rarely encountered unattached to shell occupied by it. Anemone can even secrete a chitinous extension to crab's shell, negating necessity for crab to change shells as it grows (a hazardous operation). Anemone may eject stinging threads if disturbed. Oviparous.

Abundance & distribution
Generally occurs sublittorally but occasionally found at low water spring tide level. Distributed from Norway to the Mediterranean. May be locally common.

Distinctive features

1. Small slender anemone.
2. Ring of dark or translucent spots beneath margin.
3. Tentacles long compared to body.
4. Irregular base and number of tentacles because of reproduction by pedal laceration.

Distinctive features

1. Moderately sized anemone with slender delicate tentacles.
2. Often attached to stones or shells buried in sand or mud.
3. Tentacles often with two dark longitudinal stripes.

Distinctive features

1. Single anemone wrapped around shell occupied by hermit crab.
2. Parts of anemone wrapped around shell usually brown with pink spots.

Calliactis parasitica (Couch) **'Parasitic' anemone**

Description · Up to 8–10 cm tall, 5 cm in width, with firm, stiff, and pillar-like column when retracted. Column has strongly adhesive base and lower part has small holes, often visible as pale spots surrounded by darker ring. These are cinclides, through which long stinging threads may be ejected. Oral disc surrounded by up to about 700 slender translucent greyish-yellow, cream, or straw-coloured tentacles. Background colour of anemone may be uneven pale yellow, white, cream, pale brown, or buff with broad bands or stripes of darker colour (drab brown, purplish-pink, or reddish) broken into spots. **Habitat & ecology** · Often found attached to the shells of *Buccinum undatum* or other gastropods inhabited by hermit crab, *Pagurus bernhardus*, sometimes with several anemones growing on single shell. May also be found attached to claws or carapace of *Maja* or *Carcinus*, growing on rocks, empty shells, or muddy or mixed sediments at sublittoral depths of 3–100 m. Occasionally intertidal. Relationship with hermit crabs symbiotic rather than parasitic, for anemone affords protection to crab from potential predators, at same time benefiting from feeding activity of crab.

Abundance & distribution
Fairly common on some British coasts, with a distribution extending from the Channel, Irish Sea, and western Ireland. Atlantic coasts of northern Europe into the Mediterranean.

FAMILY **Haloclavidae**

Peachia cylindrica (Reid)

Description · Burrowing species with a worm-like column, base not adhesive. When fully contracted animal may not be recognised as an anemone, but when fully extended and protruding above surface of substrate in which it is living the 12 (occasionally other numbers) tentacles encircling oral disc are distinct. Tentacles, which may have a span up to 15 cm, are almost translucent pale brown but marked with very character-istic W-shaped white patterns, more distinctly so nearer mouth. In normal extension column is often 6–10 cm long and 2 cm in diameter, but fully stretched individuals may have length of 20–25 cm. Column translucent pinkish-brown, with 12 fine lines extending along its length, sometimes with darker markings. **Habitat & ecology** · Burrows in mud, muddy sand, or mixed shell and gravel near the extreme low water level of shores, to sublittoral depths of about 50 m. The anemone is difficult to watch, because it rapidly contracts below the sediment surface at the slightest disturbance.

Abundance & distribution
Common off the British coast but difficult to find because of its burrowing habits. Distribution of this anemone extends from Atlantic, Channel, North Sea, and Ireland to the Mediterranean.

ORDER **Scleractinia**

FAMILY **Dendrophylliidae**

Balanophyllia regia Gosse
Scarlet-and-gold star coral

Description · A solitary coral living in a spongy, porous corallum about 1 cm in diameter but not quite as tall. The polyp is brightly coloured red or orange or yellow-orange, with about 48 translucent gold or yellow speckled tentacles that spread to a diameter of about 2.5 cm. **Habitat & ecology** · Found on the extreme lower shore or subtidally attached to rocks, often in caves or in areas exposed to considerable water movement.

Abundance & distribution
Rare, locally common. Found in south Wales and south-western England. Distributed south to Morocco and the Canary Islands, including the Mediterranean.

Distinctive features

1. Typically lives on the shells of common whelk, *Buccinum undatum*, occupied by hermit crabs.
2. Enormous numbers (up to 700) of slender tentacles.
3. Column pale yellowish-brown with longitudinal dark stripes, tentacles translucent greyish-yellow, cream, or straw coloured.

Distinctive features

1. Burrowing habit.
2. Usually 12 fully retractile tentacles.

Distinctive features

1. Solitary polyps growing in a spongy, porous, walled corallum.
2. Column of polyp a brilliant red or orange.
3. 48 translucent tentacles speckled in gold or yellow.

FAMILY **Caryophylliidae**

Caryophyllia smithii Stokes and Broderip
Devonshire cup coral

Description · A very characteristic solitary coral species, identifiable by its 80 or so club-ended translucent tentacles. The solid, calcified corallum has smooth-edged projecting septa. The polyps are variably green, brown, white, or pink, often with lips of contrasting colours. The corallum may be up to 1.5 cm in diameter and about as tall. **Habitat & ecology** · Found attached to rocks and shells from extreme low water spring tide level to sublittoral depths of about 100 m. The small but very distinctive barnacle, *Megatrema* (*Boscia*) *anglicum*, is usually found singly or in groups of 3–4, as an epizooite, at the edge of the corallum. **Similar species** · Two other species may be confused with this form, *Balanophyllia regia* and *C. clavus*; the latter form is now thought by some authorities to be synonymous with *C. smithii*. *Balanophyllia* has a brilliant scarlet-orange body and gold-flecked transparent tentacles which lack the terminal knobs.

Abundance & distribution
Sometimes locally common, found on south and west coasts of Britain and Ireland, north to the northern Hebrides, south to the Mediterranean.

ORDER **Zoanthidea**

FAMILY **Epizoanthidae**

Epizoanthus couchii (Johnston)

Description · A colonial species, the slender polyps are 10–15 mm tall and about 5 mm in diameter. They grow from a thin, sheet-like, encrusting layer of tissue, which is itself often hidden by being overgrown by other encrusting organisms. The outer surface of the polyp column has the appearance and texture of fine sand. Around the mouth there are up to 35 thin, slender tentacles about 5 mm long when extended, each ending in a small white knob. **Habitat & ecology** · Found living on rocks, stones, pebbles, or shells from extreme low water spring tide level to deep sublittoral situations.

Abundance & distribution
A rather inconspicuous though not uncommon species, with a distribution restricted to the south and west coasts of the British Isles and north-western France.

FAMILY **Parazoanthidae**

Parazoanthus axinellae (Schmidt)

Description · Colonial, with stolons (tissue growth linking polyps) as thin lamellae joining polyps which are up to 1–2 cm tall and brilliantly coloured orange to yellow. Each polyp bears two concentric oral circlets of golden yellow tentacles; in total there are 26–36 tentacles. **Habitat & ecology** · On cave walls and other rocky faces, or attached to sponges, shells, corals, worm tubes, or sea squirts in sublittoral depths of about 6–100 m. Quite commonly found encrusting the skeleton of larger sea fans. **Similar species** · Resembles *P. anguicomus*, with which it may be confused, but with smaller polyps bearing slightly fewer tentacles. Paler coloured individuals may also be confused with *Epizoanthus* species.

Abundance & distribution
Locally sometimes fairly common, the distribution extends from the Mediterranean northwards to Atlantic coasts of north-western Europe as far north as Bardsey Island, North Wales.

Distinctive features

1. A solitary species living in a calcified basal medium.
2. Tentacles translucent, ending in distinct club-shaped swellings.

Distinctive features

1. Slender polyps grow from a thin, encrusting sheet of coenenchyme, which is often hidden by other encrusting organisms.
2. Column of polyps often with fine, sandy textured surface.
3. Colonial.

Distinctive features

1. Polyps brilliantly coloured orange to yellow.
2. 26–36 golden yellow tentacles on oral disc, arranged in two concentric circlets.

ORDER **Corallimorpharia**

FAMILY **Corallimorphidae**

Corynactis viridis Allman **Jewel anemone**

Description · A brightly coloured, reddish, pinkish, or greenish solitary species, typically occurring in dense clumps. If maintained in an aquarium after collection the colours usually fade. Rather squat in shape, up to about 1 cm tall and a similar diameter, the expanded oral disc and tentacles may be up to 2.5 cm across. The base of the column is broad and adhesive. Oral tentacles are arranged in three concentric circlets. The mouth is situated at the top of a minute cone. **Habitat & ecology** · Lower shore and sublittoral to depths of about 100 m on rocky coasts.

Abundance & distribution Often locally abundant beneath outcropping rocky overhangs, found on southern and western coasts of England, as far north as Scotland, and Ireland, and southwards to the Mediterranean.

SUBCLASS **Octocorallia** | ORDER **Gorgonacea**

FAMILY **Plexauridae**

Eunicella verrucosa (Pallas) **Sea fan**

Description · A very distinctive colonial species branching at all levels but only in a single plane. Up to 30 cm tall, the soft pink outer tissue encloses a brown horny skeletal support. The pink or white polyps are small, up to 3 mm across when fully expanded, and situated in slight swellings on the surface. Polyps living towards the tips of the colony are typically arranged in two rows. **Habitat & ecology** · Sublittoral, attached by its holdfast to rocks and boulders or vertical rocky faces, usually not shallower than 10–15 m and may extend to depths of 200 m or more. A sea slug, *Tritonia nilsodhneri*, may be found among its branches. This species is coloured and shaped to resemble the surface of *Eunicella* and is therefore very hard to spot.

Abundance & distribution Range extends from the western parts of the English Channel and south-west Ireland, north to west Scotland and southwards to the Mediterranean and north-west Africa. Not common.

ORDER **Pennatulacea** | SUBORDER **Subsessiliflorae**

FAMILY **Pennatulidae**

Pennatula phosphorea Linnaeus **Phosphorescent sea pen**

Description · Forms a distinctive, feather-like colony up to 20–40 cm tall. The comparatively slender, fleshy, red central column bears narrow branches arranged in an almost flat plane, the branches carrying the white polyps which, when expanded, are about 1 mm long. Branches only extend from the upper half to two-thirds of the central stem. When mechanically stimulated the colony may flash phosphorescently. **Habitat & ecology** · Sublittoral from 20 m down, growing in sand and clay sediments.

Abundance & distribution May be locally common, with a range extending from the western Baltic southwards to North Sea, Atlantic, and Mediterranean coasts of north-west Europe.

Distinctive features

1. Brightly coloured red, pink, or green in the wild.
2. Oral tentacles arranged in three circlets.
3. Body shape rather squat, about as tall as wide.

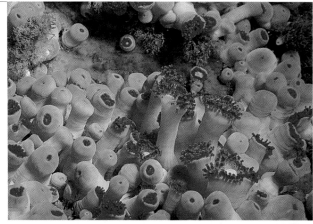

Distinctive features

1. Branched at all levels but only in a single plane.
2. Outer surface soft and pink.
3. Polyps pink or white, those near tips of branches arranged in two rows.

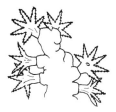

Distinctive features

1. Red, fleshy central column with side branches arranged in single plane.
2. White polyps on branches.
3. At night flashes phosphorescently when disturbed.

FAMILY Virgulariidae
Virgularia mirabilis (Müller)

Description · Up to about 20 cm tall, occasionally reaching 50 cm, the very slender central column has a small, swollen anchor and carries the polyp-bearing, slender side branches for its full height. Polyps are arranged into groups of 3–8. The whole animal has a delicate, feathery appearance with a creamy-yellow colour. **Habitat & ecology** · Sublittoral, found in muddy sediments at depths of about 10–30 m and more. In softer mud it forms a permanent tube into which it withdraws when disturbed. **Similar species** · *Funiculina quadrangularis* is superficially similar, but this has a stem with a square cross-section and grows up to 2 m long.

Abundance & distribution
Locally common. this sea pen is found on all British muddy coasts and has a distribution extending south to the Mediterranean.

ORDER Alcyonacea

FAMILY Alcyoniidae
Alcyonium digitatum Linnaeus
Dead-man's fingers

Description · This colonial soft coral, which may grow to a height of about 20 cm, has a thick, fleshy, irregular shape. The polyps, which make up the colony, are evenly distributed over the surface but only emerge when they are feeding. The colonies are commonly a whitish or dull orange colour, but some individuals may have a yellowish or pale brown tinge. **Habitat & ecology** · Found sublittorally to depths of about 50 m attached to rocks or on shells or stones; intertidally, where they occur on the lower shore, they are most commonly found in rock pools or dangling down from the undersurface of horizontal clefts and rocky overhangs. The sea slug, *Tritonia hombergi*, may be found feeding on the polyps of *A. digitatum*.

Abundance & distribution
Widely distributed and common around the British Isles, it has a range extending from Iceland to the Bay of Biscay, but is not found in the Mediterranean.

Alcyonium glomeratum (Hassall)

Description · Slender, fleshy lobes up to 30 cm long. Polyps are always white, but the fleshy matrix in which they are embedded is variously deep red to yellow. **Habitat & ecology** · A shallow sublittoral species living on rocky coasts, typically in more shaded situations where it is sheltered from strong water currents. **Similar species** · Easily confused with *A. digitatum* but has slenderer lobes.

Abundance & distribution
Sometimes locally quite common, this species is found on south and western coasts of the British Isles and southwards into the Bay of Biscay.

Distinctive features

1. Central column slender, entire colony with a delicate, feathery appearance.
2. Polyp-bearing side branches extend full height of central column.

Distinctive features

1. Fleshy, finger-like lobes.

Distinctive features

1. White polyps embedded in red to yellow fleshy matrix.
2. Fleshy lobes slender, up to 30 cm long.

Alcyonium hibernicum Renouf

Description · Forms lobe-like or finger-like fleshy colonies. These are superficially similar to other *Alcyonium* species but generally much smaller, reaching a maximum height of 30 mm when contracted. Colony colour is generally light to dark pink in Atlantic specimens and various shades of pink to red in Mediterranean specimens. **Habitat & ecology** · Generally occurs in shallow subtidal waters attached to shaded vertical and overhanging rock surfaces. It asexually produces planula larvae from an ovum without fertilization. **Similar species** · Much taxonomic confusion exists within this group, but recent genetic studies have shown that *A. hibernicum* is separate from a similar small species called *A. coralloides*. *A. coralloides*, too, is found on vertical or overhanging rock surfaces but also on the skeletons of dead sea fans. Colonies have a greater tendency to be thinly encrusting and show a greater variation in colour, ranging from deep red through various shades of pink, yellow, and white. *A. coralloides* is distributed from coasts of Brittany in France to the Mediterranean.

Abundance & distribution
Uncommon throughout British Isles and Ireland. Elsewhere distributed along the Atlantic coasts of France, Spain, and Portugal and parts of the north-west Mediterranean.

ORDER **Stolonifera**

FAMILY **Clavulariidae**

Sarcodictyon roseum (Philippi)

Description · This animal forms narrow stolons along the substrate. At close intervals a polyp, up to 10 mm high, is located. The stolon may be branched and overgrown by other organisms. The stolon is deep pink, red, yellowish, or even colourless. The polyps are bright white. When retracted the polyps are marked by swellings on the stolon. The organism is very difficult to spot in this state. **Habitat & ecology** · Grows on rocks, dead corals, and shells from the low shore to offshore. It is small and difficult to see, and therefore easy to miss. **Similar species** · The only superficially similar species is *Alcyonium coralloides* (see *A. hibernicum*), but this species tends to form encrusting sheets or finger-like colonies.

Abundance & distribution
Common on all coasts of Britain. Distributed from Britain south to the Mediterranean.

SUBCLASS **Ceriantipatharia** | ORDER **Ceriantharia**

FAMILY **Cerianthidae**

Cerianthus lloydii Gosse

Description · Polyps large and cylindrical, up to 15–20 cm tall, the oral end surrounded by about 60–70 outer brownish tentacles which are up to 4–5 cm long and cannot be withdrawn; there are similar numbers of inner tentacles. The column is yellowish in colour. Only the oral disc and tentacles are visible at the surface of the substrate in which the species lives. **Habitat & ecology** · Constructs thick, felt-like tubes in soft substrata such as fine silty or muddy sand on the extreme lower shore, and sublittorally to depths of about 35 m.

Abundance & distribution
Locally sometimes quite common, the distribution of this burrowing anemone extends from the island of Spitzbergen southwards around all north-western European coasts to the Bay of Biscay.

Distinctive features

1. Lobe- or finger-like colonies.
2. Fleshy consistency.
3. Small size.

Distinctive features

1. Narrow, creeping stolons.
2. Closely spaced polyps, bright white when open.
3. Polyps appear as swellings on the stolon when retracted.

Distinctive features

1. Large, cylindrical column surrounded by two rows of non-retractile tentacles; about 60–70 in each row.

Class Hydrozoa
(sea firs)

Hydrozoans typically exhibit alternating sessile polypoid and free-swimming medusoid stages in their life-cycle, though in some forms the medusoid stage is greatly reduced and not free. The polyp or **hydroid** stage may be solitary or colonial. It consists of a basal part, the **hydrorhiza**, which may be encrusting, a fibrous mass of tubes, or developed into **stolons**, and an erect stem (**hydrocaulus**), which in many species is branched (branches are called **hydrocladia**). The whole organism is externally covered by a **chitinous** exoskeleton (**perisarc**) enclosing a hollow **coenosarc** containing the shared, colonial **coelenteron**.

Polyps (**hydranths**) are budded off from the coenosarc. The order **Hydroida** contains two suborders:

Athecata Hydranths not enclosed by hydrothecae; polyps solitary or colonial, normally sessile except for the family **Velellidae**, whose members are planktonic. The medusae (**anthomedusae**) are tall, bell-shaped, and carry the gonads on their manubrium.

Thecata Each hydranth enclosed by a cup-shaped growth of the perisarc called a **hydrotheca**, which may or may not be carried on a stalk (**pedicel**); gonophores in obvious gonothecae. Medusae (**leptomedusae**) are

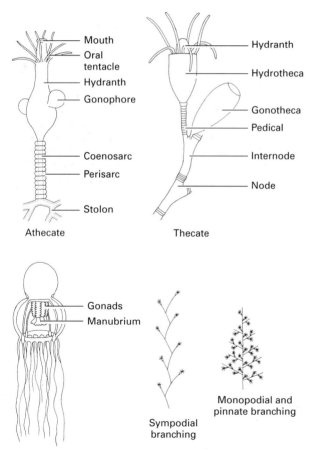

The structure of athecate and thecate hydroids. *Bottom left*: a typical hydroid anthomedusa. *Bottom middle and right*: two of the branching patterns typical of the class.

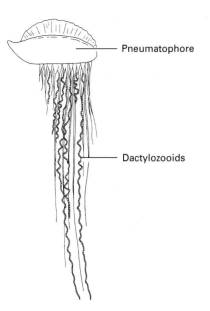

Pneumatophore

Dactylozooids

Physalia physalis, showing the general appearance of a complete individual.

saucer-shaped or hemispherical, usually with marginal tentacles which sometimes alternate with statocysts (balancing organs); the gonads are situated on the radial canals.

Many hydroids possess **polymorphic hydranths** (different forms), including **gastrozooids** (feeding hydranths), and **blastostyles**, often enclosed in special hydrothecae called **gonothecae**, which are responsible for budding

off the sexually reproducing medusoid stage of the colony; the blastostyle and gonotheca together are often called the **gonangium**.

The order **Siphonophora** comprises floating or free-swimming colonial hydrozoans composed of several different polyps (zooids), each specialised for certain functions. These include feeding zooids, stinging zooids, reproductive zooids, and fishing zooids. The zooids hang down in dense clusters below a float (**pneumatophore**) or swimming bell, and are budded from a stem or **siphosome**. The medusoid stage in the life-cycle remains attached to the colony. In some species the fishing zooids (**dactylozooids**) may trail from the float for several tens of metres and are armed with enormous numbers of very powerful nematocysts that can inflict a painful and dangerous sting.

Most siphonophores are pelagic and oceanic, reaching coastal waters only when blown in by strong winds. Only one species, a member of the family **Physaliidae**, is regularly found on western European shores; when stranded on the shore usually only the pneumatophore is found. Other species of siphonophores have been observed in the sea, off western coasts of Europe. Some authors treat the siphonophores as a subclass of the Hydrozoa, in which case the suborders used in the present text are raised to the status of orders.

ORDER **Hydroida** | SUBORDER **Athecata**

FAMILY **Tubulariidae**

Tubularia indivisa Linnaeus

Description · Colonial hydroid with erect stems that rarely branch and are often joined at base and tightly plaited together, growing from a tangled mass of 'roots'. Stems are up to 18–20 cm tall, may be longitudinally striated and pale yellow. Tips of stems are hollow and enclosed by a chitinous perisarc. Terminal polyps or hydranths are pink and possess two rings of tentacles; oral ring, around polyp mouth, consists of about 40 erect tentacles, whereas aboral ring comprises about 30 longer, flexible, white tentacles. Reproductive bodies, when present, hang down from polyps like small bunches of grapes. **Habitat & ecology** · Sometimes found in lower shore rock pools, more often attached to hard surfaces such as rocks or wrecks in sublittoral situations. **Similar species** · *T. larynx* is very similar but tends to be smaller. Stems not joined and has fewer tentacles on hydranth. Other athecatous hydroids, such as *Eudendrium rameum* and *Ectopleura dumartieri* may be confused with *T. indivisa* and careful examination is needed for identification.

Abundance & distribution
Widespread and fairly common, but unobtrusive, on all British rocky coasts, with a range extending from Norway, through the North Sea and Channel coasts of northern Europe.

FAMILY **Velellidae**

Velella velella (Linnaeus) **Jack-by-the-wind-sailor**

Description · This remarkable animal has appearance of a stiff jelly-like oval disc with distinctive 'sail' arising from middle. Suspended below disc is large central feeding polyp with mouth. There are numerous tentacles round fringe of disc, with stinging cells to capture prey. Between mouth and tentacles are polyps that bud off male and female medusae. Overall, colony translucent blue to deep blue. Animal grows to about 10 cm along longest axis. **Habitat & ecology** · Pleustonic (simultaneously inhabits air and water); lives on ocean surfaces, preying on small plankton. Remarkable life history: male and female medusae budded off from main colony and release eggs and sperm. Fertilised eggs sink and develop into Conaria larvae, which are dispersed by deep-sea currents. At late stage of development these larvae develop gas bladders and float back to surface to form 'adult' colony. *V. vellela* is preyed upon by purple sea snail, *Janthina janthina*. These may consume entire colony, leaving only chitinous float and sail, which may be colonised by other animals.

Abundance & distribution
Rare. Occasionally seen washed up in large numbers on west coasts of Britain and Ireland following westerly gales. Occurs as far north as the Faeroes.

FAMILY **Corynidae**

Coryne pusilla Pallas

Description · A colonial, but straggly looking hydroid. The curved stems, each branching irregularly two or three times, grow from a creeping network of 'roots' to a height of about 10–25 mm. The pink, elongate and cylindrical polyps, carried on the ends of each branch, possess about 25–30 distinctly club-shaped and irregularly distributed short tentacles. During the summer months the large spherical reproductive bodies are distributed between the tentacles. The skeleton covering the stems has a distinct, close-ringed appearance. **Habitat & ecology** · Lower-shore intertidal as an epizooite on large brown seaweeds, or in deeper sublittoral situations growing freely on rocky surfaces.

Abundance & distribution
Fairly common on most British rocky shores, the range of this species extends from northern Norway, through the North Sea and Channel coasts of northern Europe into the Mediterranean and southwards to the Cape Verde islands.

Distinctive features

1. Colonial, with erect stems bearing terminal pink polyps with two rings of tentacles.
2. Reproductive bodies resemble small bunches of grapes hanging down from polyps.

Distinctive features

1. Flat, oval jelly disc.
2. Sail arises from the middle of the disc.

Distinctive features

1. Colonial but straggly, with creeping 'roots' and irregularly branching stems.
2. Pink, cylindrical polyps have distinctly club-shaped tentacles.

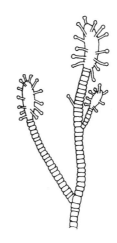

FAMILY **Clavidae**

Clava multicornis (Forskål)

Description · A fairly distinctive colonial species. Erect unbranched stems, reaching 2–3 cm tall, grow from an open network of root-like extensions. The terminal polyps, which cannot be retracted into skeletal cups, are distinctly pink and elongate and have tapering tentacles scattered over their distal surface. The rose-red reproductive bodies form clustered groups in a ring below the tentacles during spring and summer. **Habitat & ecology** · Common as an epizooite growing on the reproductive bodies of the brown seaweed *Ascophyllum nodosum*, but sometimes found on larger species of *Fucus* and, less frequently, growing on mid- to lower-shore stones or in rock pools in sheltered to fairly exposed conditions. **Similar species** · Several other athecatous hydroids occur in similar habitats, but the pink, elongate polyps of this species, with their scattered tentacles, are usually sufficient to identify it. A related species, *C. squamata*, has a densely packed 'rooting' network, and stems reaching a height of 2.5 cm with crowded groups of club-shaped, rather than elongate, polyps.

Abundance & distribution
Fairly common on most British rocky shores, with a distribution extending from northern Norway, the Atlantic, North Sea, and Channel coasts of northern Europe and into the Mediterranean.

FAMILY **Bougainvilliidae**

Bougainvillia ramosa (Van Beneden)

Description · Stolon forms encrusting and branched mat, from which erect stems may attain height of 5–10 cm. Perisarc, which does not surround terminal polyps, pale yellowish-brown. Stems are little branched, but branches emerge in loose spiral series. Polyps conical shape, with 12–20 pale and slender tentacles. Reproductive structures grow on short stalks at bases of polyps; they may appear singly or in clusters. Free-swimming medusoid stage, liberated from reproductive bodies, has rounded bell shape and is up to about 4 mm tall with four marginal groups of 4–9 tentacles. Mouth stalk and ripe gonads of medusa greenish-brown. **Habitat & ecology** · Attached to stones, rocks, algae, or other hydroids on lower shore, to sublittoral depths of about 30 m. **Similar species** · The polyp (hydroid generation) may be confused with *Hydractinia echinata*, but this hydroid is typically shorter (1.5 cm), grows on shells inhabited by hermit crabs, and has polyps with upper and lower circles of eight tentacles each, lower tentacles being shorter than upper.

Abundance & distribution
Common throughout much of its range, which extends from the western Baltic Sea to Atlantic, Channel, and North Sea coasts of northern Europe and into the Mediterranean.

FAMILY **Pandeidae**

Neoturris pileata (Forskål)

Description · This species is only known from the medusoid generation. The umbrella is an elongate bell shape of a diameter up to 25 mm at the base. The edge of the umbrella is fringed with 60–90 hollow and smooth tentacles, up to 80 mm in length. These have a large, laterally compressed bulb shape where they attach at the base. The stomach, which can be seen within the umbrella, is flask-shaped; its length varies greatly but never extends beyond the margin of the umbrella. **Habitat & ecology** · This is the medusoid form of an unknown polyp stage, though it may be the deep-water species *Leukartiara abyssi*. It appears in May and may be seen floating in Atlantic waters up to September. Many other small medusoid forms of hydroids are seen in waters around Britain but their identification requires specialist expertise.

Abundance & distribution
Rarely recorded around Britain and limited mainly to west and north coasts. This species is distributed in the northern and mid-Atlantic, but not in Arctic seas. It has also been recorded from the Philippines.

Distinctive features

1. Colonial, stems unbranched.
2. Terminal polyps pink in colour, with tapering tentacles scattered over distal end.
3. Polyps non-retractile, elongate.

Distinctive features

1. Polyps non-retractile.
2. Stolon branching, stems little branched but in a loose spiral series.
3. Polyps long and conical.

Distinctive features

1. Medusa.
2. Umbrella has an elongated bell shape.
3. Margin of umbrella with 60–90 tentacles with bulbous attachment points.

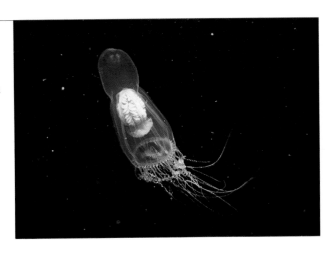

SUBORDER **Thecata**

FAMILY **Campanulariidae**

Obelia geniculata (Linnaeus)

Description · A distinctive and colonial hydroid, with creeping and fairly straight stolon from which erect stems grow to height of about 4–5 cm. Stems normally widely spaced and with characteristic zigzag appearance, polyps developing alternately from each branching node. Chitinous reddish-brown perisarc, which encases hollow stems, extends around polyps as bell-shaped and smooth-edged cup; when disturbed, polyps withdraw into cups and may not be visible. Reproductive structures, evident during summer, erect and club-shaped, growing from axils of cups enclosing polyps. **Habitat & ecology** · Typically lives as epizooite on middle and lower shore algae, particularly *Fucus serratus* and species of kelps, but also growing on seaweeds in shallow sublittoral situations. **Similar species** · Related species in northern Europe include at least three *Obelia*. Zigzag branching of *O. geniculata* (a) should easily distinguish it from *O. longissima* (b) and *O. dichotoma* (c). *O. bidentata* sometimes slightly zigzag but tends to have paired lateral branches; it grows to 15 cm tall.

Abundance & distribution
Very common and abundant on most British coasts, with an almost cosmopolitan distribution which includes the Baltic Sea, Atlantic, Channel, and North Sea coasts of northern Europe, and the Mediterranean.

FAMILY **Haleciidae**

Halecium halecinum (Linnaeus)
Herring-bone hydroid

Description · The best-known species of *Halecium*; colonial, up to 25 cm tall, stiff, and regularly feather-shaped. Several stems may grow from a fibrous attachment point. Each main stem bears equally spaced, parallel, alternating branches on which polyps are surrounded by funnel-like cups; several cups may become superimposed. Polyps much larger than, and thus protrude beyond, their cups. Gonothecae, on upper sides of branches, are dimorphic; males oval-shaped, females oblong. **Habitat & ecology** · Attaches to stones, shells, and hard worm tubes (such as those of *Chaetopterus*) in shallow sublittoral situations and deeper. Closely related species may grow on other hydroids. Sea slugs such as *Doto fragilis* may be found living on *Halecium* species.

Abundance & distribution
Widespread, often locally common, the distribution of *H. halecinum* extends from Norway, to Atlantic coasts of north-west Europe, the Mediterranean, and South Africa. Some related species appear almost cosmopolitan.

FAMILY **Sertulariidae**

Dynamena pumila (Linnaeus)

Description · Forms stiff, erect, and usually unbranched stems up to 3 cm tall, growing from long, creeping, and branched stolons. Funnel-like cups enclosing the polyps are cowl- or hood-shaped; polyps occur in opposite pairs on the main stem, which is widest at the base of each pair of polyps. About two-thirds of each cup lie close against the main stem, the distal third typically curving out sharply. The oval-shaped and basally tapered gonothecae are positioned at the base of the cups. **Habitat & ecology** · Found growing in dense populations on seaweeds (particularly species of *Fucus* and *Laminaria*) and rocks from mid-shore levels to shallow sublittoral situations. **Similar species** · Although the commonest and most familiar of the thecate hydroids, there are several other species with which this form may easily be confused.

Abundance & distribution
Often locally very common and abundant, especially in British and Irish waters, the species has a distribution extending from the Arctic shores of Norway south to Atlantic coasts of France. It is less common on the most exposed rocky shores.

Distinctive features

1. Polyps grow on zigzag, branching stems.
2. Polyps develop on alternate sides of stem.
3. Polyps surrounded by chitinous, bell-shaped extensions of skeleton.

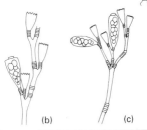

(a)

(b)   (c)

Distinctive features

1. Stems single, with equally spaced, parallel, alternating branches bearing polyps.
2. Polyps larger than, and protruding from, their surrounding funnel-like cups.

Distinctive features

1. Polyps paired, opposite, on main stem.
2. Main stem widest at base of each pair of polyps.

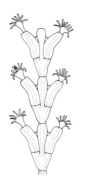

Hydrallmania falcata (Linnaeus)

Description · A very tall hydroid with main stems forming an elongate spiral up to 50 cm in height. The colonies arise from a basal stolon. The lateral branches are arranged in a spiral fashion, with regular pinnate side branches. There are tube-like cups in rows of 4–10 along the branches with a short gap between. The reproductive gonothecae are an elongated egg shape with a short stalk. **Habitat & ecology** · This species is usually found subtidally at 20–100 m depth. It grows on stones, shells, and other hard substrates, sometimes in sandy areas.

Abundance & distribution
Common around all coasts of Britain. Distributed from the Arctic to Portugal and south-west Spain.

Sertularia cupressina Linnaeus **Whiteweed**

Description · Colonial, the tall (up to 45–50 cm) slender stems grow from creeping 'roots' and branch alternately, branches themselves bearing branchlets. The colony overall has a long, feathery appearance. Polyps are arranged in two rows, and reproductive bodies grow from the branchlets. Tubular cups, tapering towards an out-turned opening where the rim carries one or two long, sharp teeth. Gonothecae are slender and cigar-shaped, tapering at both ends, with a short stalk. Colonies are typically pink or white in colour. **Habitat & ecology** · Found growing on bivalve shells, such as *Aequipecten opercularis*, stones, or other hydroids, occasionally attached to crabs, and also occurs in shallow to quite deep water. In shallow conditions it may grow on sand. Young sea slugs of the species *Dendronotus frondosus* eat it. It is also often dried, dyed, and used decoratively, as in flower arrangements. European communities are sometimes commercially harvested for export to the USA.

Abundance & distribution
Sometimes locally common, particularly in sheltered bays where it may form dense beds. The distribution extends from the western Baltic Sea southwards to North Sea, English Channel, and Atlantic coasts of north-west Europe.

FAMILY **Plumulariidae**

Nemertesia antennina (Linnaeus) **Sea beard**

Description · This colonial hydroid forms clusters of up to 50 stiff, thick, erect, and unbranched stems up to 25 cm tall. Stems grow from a matted filamentous base of rootlets which effectively form a holdfast. Stems bear bundles of 6–10 short whorled branches, which are incurved and widest at their bases, and carry polyps contained in smooth-rimmed cups. The reproductive polyps and their short-stalked and egg-shaped gonothecae are located in the angle between the main stem and its branches. The colonies have a yellowish colour and horny texture. Previously known as *Antennularia antennina*. **Habitat & ecology** · A colonial species, typically found attached to secure surfaces, such as stones, pebbles, or empty shells in shallow sublittoral and deeper situations, it also occurs where sandy sediments accumulate. The sea slug, *Doto pinnatifida*, is often found living on it.

Abundance & distribution
Common. The distribution of this hydroid extends from Icelandic and northern Norwegian coasts southwards to the Mediterranean and north-west Africa. It is common on most British coasts.

Distinctive features

1. Tall hydroid with main stem forming an elongate spiral.
2. Side branches spirally arranged and pinnate.
3. Tube-like cups, in rows of 4–10.

Distinctive features

1. Colony consists of long, slender stems with alternate branches bearing branchlets.
2. Tubular cups, out-turned rim with two long, sharp teeth.

Distinctive features

1. Main stems stiff, erect, unbranched.
2. Stems bear whorled branches in groups of 6–10.
3. Edges of funnel-like cups smooth-rimmed.

Nemertesia ramosa (Lamouroux)

Description · A colonial species like other members of the genus, the thick main stems, up to 15 cm tall, divide and subdivide irregularly; they develop from a 'holdfast' composed of very matted fibres. The long, outwardly curved, branches emerging from the main stems are hairy, close-set, and organised into whorls. The cups are small and vase-like, separated from each other by only a single joint. Pear-shaped gonothecae face inwards towards the main stem. **Habitat & ecology** · Similar to that described for *N. antennina*.

Abundance & distribution
Very similar to *N. antennina*.

Kirchenpaueria pinnata (Linnaeus)

Description · This hydroid usually appears as clusters of plume-like growth arising from a small, branched, root-like attachment. The stems are straight to slightly zigzagged. Gently curved, parallel branches are arranged alternately on either side of the stem in a pinnate arrangement. Usually up to 6 cm high, though may grow to 10 cm or more. **Habitat & ecology** · Occurs on a wide variety of substrates, including shells, algae, seagrass, and artificial structures such as wood pilings. It is found on the lower shore and subtidally to at least 100 m depth. *K. pinnata* reproduces in early spring to late summer and the larvae are brooded within the reproductive polyps. **Similar species** · Resembles *Plumularia setacea*. This is pale to dark yellowish-brown and characteristically the length of the stem between the attachment points of the branches is alternately short and long. The rarer species, *K. similis*, is very similar to *K. pinnata* and microscopic examination is required to separate them.

Abundance & distribution
Common around all coasts of Britain and Ireland. Distributed from Iceland and the Faeroes to the Mediterranean and South Africa. Not present in the Black Sea and found only in the Skagerrak and in the Kattegat as far as Copenhagen.

FAMILY **Aglaopheniidae**
Aglaophenia pluma (Linnaeus)

Description · Colonial, forming feathery or plume-like growths, typically composed of erect single shoots up to 8 cm long; some colonies may branch dichotomously and reach 15 cm. Minute, cup-shaped structures surrounding polyps, arranged in single series along upper surface of branches. Reproductive bodies located near main stem at bases of branches. These are pod-like, with up to ten per stem. They have 5–8 ribs. Colour honey yellow to brownish-yellow. **Habitat & ecology** · Lower shore to shallow sublittoral, found attached to hard substrates, growing on brown seaweeds such as *Halidrys*, *Sargassum*, or kelps, or on mollusc shells. **Similar species** · About 13 European species of aglaopheniids are known, including 11 species of *Aglaophenia*. Individual species are often difficult to distinguish and careful examination of specimens is required. European examples include *A. harpago*, *A. kirchenpaueri*, and *A. tubulifera*. *A. acacia* is distributed from western Scotland to Canary Islands and is distinguishable by its growth form in which the plumes arise from the stem in opposite pairs.

Abundance & distribution
May be locally common, but the difficulty in reliably distinguishing between *Aglaophenia* species leads to uncertainty over their abundance. *A. pluma* occurs from western Scotland southwards as far as South Africa, including the

Distinctive features

1. Main stems irregularly divided and subdivided.
2. Branches of main stem close-set and arranged into whorls.
3. Cups separated by only a single joint.

Distinctive features

1. Forms clusters of plume-like growths up to 10 cm high.
2. Stem straight to slightly zigzagged.
3. Branches alternate on either side of stem, parallel and gently curved.

Mediterranean. The species may be cosmopolitan.

Distinctive features

1. Colonies erect, shape typically feathery or regularly pinnate.
2. Polyps surrounded by short cups with two deeply toothed rims.
3. Pod-like reproductive structures located near the main stem.

ORDER **Siphonophora** | SUBORDER **Physonectae**

FAMILY **Apolemiidae**

Apolemia uvaria (Leseur)

Description · A very unusual form of gelatinous zooplankton. This animal has a small float (that does not float at the surface) attached to a contractile stem that is usually held horizontally in the water and may be helically coiled. Pairs of polyps are suspended along the stem with 5–6 tentacles between each pair. These form a curtain-like net and the whole structure may be up to 20 m long. **Habitat & ecology** · Physonectid siphonophores are an unusual group of animals often found in the deep waters of the oceans. *Apolemia* is planktonic and deploys its net-like array of tentacles to capture other gelatinous animals such as salps, ctenophores, and hydroid medusae, which it consumes. In turn *Apolemia* is known to form part of the diet of certain marine turtles. These animals are extremely delicate.

Abundance & distribution Rarely recorded in British waters but is a species associated with Atlantic oceanic water and therefore most likely to be encountered on west coasts. Distributed in the Atlantic as far south as South Africa.

SUBORDER **Cystonectae**

FAMILY **Physaliidae**

Physalia physalis (Linnaeus)
Portuguese man-of-war

Description · A very distinctive species, easily identified by its purplish or silvery-blue float, which has a reddish tinge. The float is up to 30 cm long and 10 cm wide, with a distinctive pleated crest extending longitudinally on its upper surface. Below the float different types of polyps are suspended on extremely long, trailing tentacles; the fishing and defensive polyps may extend for several tens of metres and are armed with enormous numbers of stinging nematocysts, whereas the feeding and reproductive polyps are shorter. The sting of the nematocysts can be extremely dangerous to humans. **Habitat & ecology** · A surface-dwelling species, fairly common in open oceanic waters but may be driven into coastal regions by onshore gales, even becoming stranded on the shore by receding tides. Those washed ashore may be so damaged that only their float is found.

Abundance & distribution A fairly common species with a worldwide distribution, usually found in northern European waters after being blown in by south-westerly gales.

Class Scyphozoa (jellyfishes)

The polypoid stage in the life-cycle is either totally suppressed or reduced to a scyphistoma. The upper side of the bell is called the **aboral** (or **exumbrellar**) surface, the lower the **oral** (or **umbrellar**) surface. The mouth is usually located at the end of a short, tubular, umbrellar extension termed the **manubrium**, which may be fringed with arms or tentacles. The coelenteron is subdivided into four **perradial pouches** by **septa** (**interradii**), which give the animals a **tetraradial** symmetry. From each perradial pouch a canal extends outwards to connect with a **marginal ring canal**. The rim of the bell bears nematocyst-armed tentacles and, often,

small **statocysts** (sensory balancing organs). Within European coastal waters three orders are commonly found, although a fourth (primarily oceanic in habit) may sometimes be blown into inshore areas. The orders are:
Stauromedusae Secondarily sessile scyphozoans which live attached upside-down, the aboral surface of their bell developing a short stalk with an adhesive basal disc. The bell has eight marginal lobes (arms), each bearing a cluster of short, knobbly-ending tentacles.
Coronatae Primarily oceanic; the bell is divided into two lobes by an obvious groove orientated parallel to the margin, which bears tentacles alternating with sensory organs. The bell rim is deeply scalloped.

Distinctive features

1. Long, gelatinous animal.
2. Forms a curtain-like array of polyps and tentacles that may be helically coiled.

Distinctive features

1. Oval, crested float.
2. Long, dangling fishing and other types of polyps hang below the float.
3. Extremely dangerous sting.

Semaeostomeae Bell generally deep, with scalloped or lobed margins which bear tentacles either in groups or in a single, evenly spaced series. The manubrium is usually four-lobed and often highly frilled. Some species are capable of inflicting a painful sting.

Rhizostomeae Large and solidly built jellyfish; the rim of the bell is smooth, without tentacles. The manubrium has eight arms, each subdivided into numerous frilled mouths. All rhizostomeans are **microphagous** (feed on small, particulate material), employing mucus to catch their food.

Scyphozoan structure. *Top*: *Rhizostoma octopus*. *Bottom*: an oral view, showing the basic tetraradial symmetry of the group.

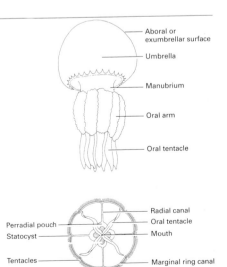

- Aboral or exumbrellar surface
- Umbrella
- Manubrium
- Oral arm
- Oral tentacle

Perradial pouch
Statocyst
- Radial canal
- Oral tentacle
- Mouth
Tentacles
- Marginal ring canal

ORDER **Stauromedusae**

FAMILY **Eleutherocarpidae**

Haliclystus auricula (Rathke) **Stalked jellyfish**

Description · This species resembles an inverted, funnel-shaped bell, attached to the substrate by a stout stalk. There are eight short arms, joined almost for their entire length by a membrane. At the tip of each arm is a tuft of 60–100 small tentacles. Between each arm, lying midway along the membrane, is an oval-shaped, inverted arm with a dorsal groove. The body is translucent and very variable in colour, from grey to green, yellow, brown, red, or purple. Grows up to 2 cm high and 3 cm in diameter.
Habitat & ecology · Occurs on the lower shore and in the shallow subtidal. It is usually found attached to algae or the blades of seagrasses such as *Zostera* species. Stalked jellyfish develop directly from the scyphistoma (asexual replicative) stage of the jellyfish which in turn develops from a planula larva. **Similar species** · There are six other species of stalked jellyfish in the UK, several of which superficially resemble *H. auricula*.

Abundance & distribution
Frequently encountered around all coasts of Britain and Ireland. Distributed throughout the north Atlantic but rare in the North Sea and western Baltic.

ORDER **Semaeostomeae**

FAMILY **Pelagiidae**

Chrysaora hysoscella (Linnaeus)
Compass jellyfish

Description · The rather flattened and saucer-shaped bell or umbrella is up to 30 cm in diameter. The edges of the bell are developed into 32 lobes and bear 24 tentacles, arranged in eight groups of three which alternate with eight sensory organs. The four frilly oral arms are longer than the bell tentacles. The colour is typically a yellowish-white marked by 16 inverted, V-shaped, brownish bands radiating from the top of the bell. **Habitat & ecology** · A pelagic species. It has an immobile, asexual reproductive stage in its life-cycle, with budding off small free-living medusae occurring during the winter months. Adult jellyfish feed on arrow worms, sea gooseberries, smaller jellyfish, and fish. **Similar species** · Although it may be confused with the common jellyfish, *Aurelia aurita*, when stranded on the shore, the V-shaped markings on the upper surface of the bell make it quite distinctive when swimming.

Abundance & distribution
Mainly found in coastal waters of the Atlantic, English Channel, and North Sea areas of north-west Europe, particularly during months of July to September. This jellyfish has been recorded from Norway southwards to West Africa and throughout the Mediterranean.

FAMILY **Cyaneidae**

Cyanea capillata (Linnaeus)
Lion's mane jellyfish

Description · A large, dark brick-red to yellowish jellyfish, with a saucer-shaped umbrella or bell which may reach a diameter of 2 m but is more commonly about 50 cm across. The margins of the bell are lobed. There are more than 65 tentacles in each of the eight groups attached to the sub-umbrellar surface. The manubrium bears four thick, frilled, and folded arms, and the stomach pouches are branched. The lion's mane jellyfish can sting severely; tentacles may become detached in the water, becoming a particular nuisance to divers and swimmers. **Habitat & ecology** · A carnivorous, pelagic jellyfish, feeding on a range of planktonic organisms including small fish. It is sometimes stranded on the shore by falling tides. The asexual reproductive stage buds off small free-living medusae during April and May. **Similar species** · Resembles *C. lamarckii*.

Abundance & distribution
A circumpolar, oceanic species. Distributed in north-west Europe from the north-east Atlantic and Arctic waters to the western Baltic Sea, the northern part of the North Sea, and the Irish Sea. Occasionally found as far south as the English Channel.

Distinctive features

1. Resembles an inverted, funnel-shaped umbrella.
2. Attached to substrate by a stalk.
3. Eight arms with tufts of tentacles on the tips.

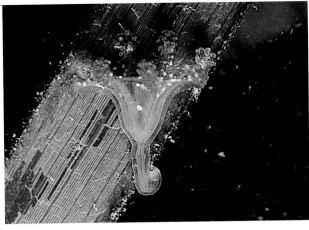

Distinctive features

1. Bell rather flattened saucer shape.
2. Bell edge developed into 32 lobes.
3. Yellowish-white, marked with 16 V-shaped, brownish bands.

Distinctive features

1. Sub-umbrellar tentacles in dense groups.
2. Manubrium with four thick, frilled, folded arms.
3. May inflict severe sting.

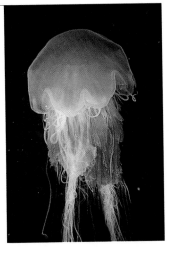

FAMILY **Ulmaridae**

Aurelia aurita (Linnaeus)
Common jellyfish, moon jellyfish

Description · An easily recognisable and common European jellyfish, the saucer-shaped bell is up to 25–40 cm in diameter, transparent but with a faint bluish-white tint and fringed with short, marginal tentacles. The four purplish-blue and horseshoe-shaped gonads are easily distinguished through the upper surface of the bell. Underneath, the feeding tentacles are large, obvious, and distinctly frilly in appearance. **Habitat & ecology** · A pelagic species, forming breeding aggregations during the late summer months, after which it migrates using the sun as a compass. Onshore gales fairly commonly leave individuals stranded by the falling tide, either in larger rock pools or on the shore surface.

Abundance & distribution
Common in surface and shallow offshore waters, with a distribution extending from northern Norway and the Baltic sea to Atlantic, North Sea, and Channel regions of northern Europe, and into the Mediterranean and Black Seas.

ORDER **Rhizostomeae**

FAMILY **Rhizostomidae**

Rhizostoma octopus (Linnaeus)

Description · A large jellyfish, the domed bell or umbrella has a solid appearance and is up to 1 m in diameter. The edge of the bell is developed into 96 small, marginal, typically blue-violet lobes; the rest of the bell is pale blue, whitish, or yellowish. Beneath the bell the eight oral arms are fused, with a frilly appearance because of their numerous subdivisions. Each oral arm, which may be bluish, reddish, or yellowish, ends in a smooth and somewhat club-shaped oral tentacle. Mature males have blue gonads, whereas those of ripe females are reddish-brown. **Habitat & ecology** · Occurs in coastal waters or stranded on the shore or in rock pools by receding tides after being blown inshore by surface winds. It swarms during late summer months and usually over-winters in deeper waters. *Hyperia galba*, a large crustacean with enormous greenish eyes, is commonly found in the gastric or gonad pouches of this jellyfish.

Abundance & distribution
Pelagic, common in open waters all year. Distributed from western Baltic Sea to Atlantic, North Sea, and Channel coasts of northern Europe, and Mediterranean. Mediterranean *R. pulmo* is probably a variant of *R. octopus* rather than a distinct species.

Phylum Ctenophora (comb jellies, sea gooseberries)

A few benthic (bottom-dwelling) species are known, but most **ctenophores** are pelagic in habit. Typically somewhat egg-shaped, a few species are elongate and ribbon-like. At one time included with the Cnidaria in the phylum Coelenterata, ctenophores differ from cnidarians in several ways. The body is delicate, transparent, and comprised of two thin cellular layers separated by a thick, often iridescent or luminous, jelly-like material which forms the bulk of the animal. The animals are primarily **radially symmetrical** but have a **secondary bilateral symmetry**.

Their most characteristic feature is the presence of eight longitudinal series of **swimming combs**, each being composed of transverse rows of **cilia** fused into small plates. It is the beating of these ciliary plates, with their rhythmic up-and-down movement, which gives the animals a shimmering appearance as they swim. The mouth is located at the bottom of the body and opens into a series of digestive canals; these canals open by one or two small pores at the opposite end. In **tentaculate** ctenophores (class **Tentaculata**) a pair of long, **extensile tentacles**, armed with sticky cells, can be protruded through pits on either side of the body and trailed along like fishing lines to trap prey

Distinctive features

1. Bell or umbrella saucer-shaped.
2. Four purplish-blue gonad rings visible through upper surface of bell.
3. Bell fringed by small marginal tentacles.

Distinctive features

1. Bell or umbrella solid and domed.
2. Eight fused oral arms.
3. Margin of bell with 96 lobes.

(surface plankton). Other ctenophores (class **Nuda**) lack these tentacles.

Further reading

Harbison, G. R. & Madin, L. P. (1982). Ctenophora. In *Synopsis and classification of living organisms* (ed. P. Parker), Vol. 1, pp. 707–15. McGraw-Hill, New York.

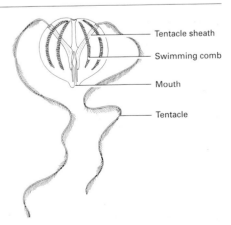

— Tentacle sheath

— Swimming comb

— Mouth

— Tentacle

The main structures of a ctenophore.

CLASS **Tentaculata** | ORDER **Cydippida**

FAMILY **Pleurobrachiidae**

Pleurobrachia pileus (Müller) **Sea gooseberry**

Description · The body is a firm, round to oval shape, up to 2–3 cm long, marked with eight distinct swimming combs that extend from the apex but do not quite reach the base, where the mouth is situated. The two long feathery tentacles, which are retractile and have filiform side branches, may trail up to 14 cm behind the body and are used for catching prey. The bodies of these animals are almost completely colourless and transparent, but the gut typically has a whitish-orange tinge to it and is clearly visible through the body surface. At night the animals may emit light. **Habitat & ecology** · Basically a pelagic species, individuals, or occasionally shoals comprising many specimens, may be found in rock pools after being stranded by falling tides, particularly during the summer months. Young individuals are often caught in tow-nets.

Abundance & distribution
Common in open water, not infrequently found in rock pools on the shore. The distribution of this species extends from the Baltic Sea to Atlantic, North Sea, and Channel coasts, the waters of northern Europe, and into the Mediterranean.

ORDER **Lobata**

FAMILY **Bolinopsidae**

Bolinopsis infundibulum (Müller)

Description · The largest ctenophore likely to be seen in northern European coastal waters, this species can grow to a length of 10–15 cm. A delicate animal with an elongated oval shape, it has four long and four short swimming combs of cilia, which do not reach to the end of the body. The lower part of the body is formed by a pair of large distinctive oral lobes. The body is more or less transparent. **Habitat & ecology** · Pelagic. Possibly common off western coasts during the summer. It feeds by swimming through the water mouth-first, with eggs, copepods, and other plankton being directed towards special grooves and then to the mouth by the oral lobes. In turn *Bolinopsis* may be preyed upon by another ctenophore called *Beroe*, or by fish such as cod. **Similar species** · Resembles *Beroe*, but this species lacks the oral lobes of *B. infundibulum*.

Abundance & distribution
Frequent in coastal waters in northern Europe. Common in the North Atlantic.

Distinctive features

1. Two long, feathery tentacles.
2. Pale orange gut.
3. Body round to oval, with distinct rows of combs extending from apex.

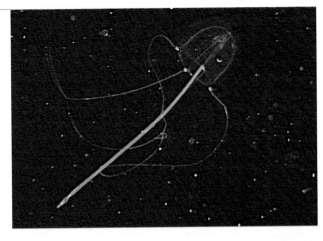

Distinctive features

1. Elongated oval shape.
2. Four long and four short rows of cilia.
3. A pair of large oral lobes.
4. Transparent.

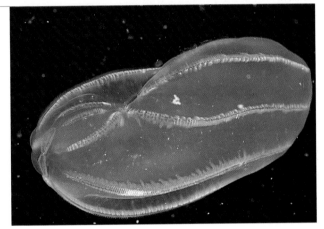

Non-segmented worms

Phylum Platyhelminthes (flatworms)

The systematics of this phylum is under continuous review because of new data arising from studies of the morphology and genetic relationships between members of the group. Here we adopt the systematic organisation presented in Brusca & Brusca (1990), but interested readers should consult the latest scientific literature for up-to-date information.

The Platyhelminthes contain four classes, the **Turbellaria**, **Monogenea**, **Trematoda**, and **Cestoda**. All except the Turbellaria are parasitic (flukes and tapeworms), whereas the Turbellaria comprise the free-living flatworms, of which a small number are found in marine habitats.

Turbellarian flatworms are typically bilaterally symmetrical, unsegmented, and dorsoventrally flattened, with a gut opening via a single ventral aperture, the **pharynx**, which is often protruded for feeding. The gut itself is often deeply and profusely branched. There is a distinct head (**cephalisation**), which frequently bears sensory **eyespots** and **tentacles**. The body surface in turbellarians is

CLASS **Turbellaria** | ORDER **Tricladida**

FAMILY **Procerodidae**
Procerodes littoralis (Oersted)

Description · A small species, up to about 5 mm long, the body is rather oval in shape but narrows somewhat in front, the head bearing a pair of triangular tentacles with a small black eyespot at the base of each. When actively crawling over hard surfaces the tentacles may be extended, giving the head a horned appearance. Typically an overall dull brown, although the head may be fringed with whitish-brown markings. **Habitat & ecology** · Found on the upper and middle shore under stones, usually close to freshwater outflows discharging on to the beach.

Abundance & distribution
Not uncommon but difficult to find because of its small size, this flatworm has a distribution which extends from the Baltic Sea to Atlantic, North Sea, and Channel coasts of northern Europe.

ORDER **Polycladida** | SUBORDER **Cotylea**

FAMILY **Euryleptidae**
Prostheceraeus vittatus (Montagu)
Candy-striped flatworm

Description · Up to 3 cm or more long, the distinctly flat and leaf-shaped body tapers posteriorly to a point and often has its lateral margins folded upwards and inrolled. The blunt head bears a pair of distinct tentacles. The general colour is off-white to creamish-pink, marked with irregularly shaped slender, longitudinal reddish-brown stripes. **Habitat & ecology** · Found under stones partially embedded in muddy sediments, mid- and lower shore, or crawling freely on rocks and seaweeds in shallow subtidal waters.

Abundance & distribution
Perhaps locally common but unobtrusive, found in the North Sea, English Channel, and Atlantic coasts of France, Spain, Portugal, and possibly Mediterranean.

ciliated, unlike that of the parasitic classes, and movement is achieved by **ciliary gliding**. Changes in body shape and direction of movement are controlled by muscle activity. All species are **hermaphroditic**, with complex reproductive systems, development from the fertilised eggs usually being direct, but a few polyclads possess a larval stage. **Excretion** and possibly **osmoregulation** are carried out by unicellular **protonephridia** or **flame cells**. There is no body cavity, the bulk of the animal consisting of a heterogeneous, semi-liquid, packing tissue (**parenchyma**). Turbellarians are active carnivores, feeding on small animals or carrion.

The class Turbellaria contains ten orders,

each of which includes marine species. In a few groups the animals are small and entirely interstitial in their habits, but others may be quite large, and a few, especially in the exclusively marine order **Polycladida**, are strikingly marked with vivid colour patterns.

Further reading

Ball, I. R. & Reynoldson, T. B. (1981). British planarians. *Synopses of the British Fauna, New Series*, **19**, 1–141.

Brusca, R. C, & Brusca, G. J. (1990). *Invertebrates*. Sinuer Associates, Sunderland, Massachusetts.

Crezée, M. (1982). Turbellaria. In *Synopsis and classification of living organisms* (ed. P. Parker), Vol. 1, pp. 718–40. McGraw-Hill, New York.

Prudhoe, S. (1982). British polyclad turbellarians. *Synopses of the British Fauna, New Series*, **26**, 1–77.

Distinctive features

1. Two triangular tentacles on head.
2. Small black eyespot at each tentacle base.
3. Overall dull brown, head sometimes fringed whitish-brown.

Distinctive features

1. Body flattened, leaf-shaped; tail pointed.
2. Head with pair of distinct tentacles.
3. Pinkish-cream; irregularly shaped, longitudinal brown stripes.

Phylum Nematoda (roundworms)

One of the largest invertebrate phyla, with probably more than 12 000 described species worldwide, though this is most likely only a fraction of the existing species. **Nematoda** are found in every conceivable type of habitat on land and in fresh, brackish, and marine waters. They are the most diverse group of animals in the deep-sea bed. Most free-living marine nematodes are small and slender, with both ends of their body pointed; individuals are rarely more than a few millimetres long and may be much less than one millimetre in diameter. The body surface is covered by a cuticle, beneath which is a layer of longitudinal muscles; nematodes completely lack circular muscles. The gut opens by an anterior **mouth**, but the posterior anus is often subterminal and many species possess a slender, curled, post-anal **tail**. Sensory **papillae** or **setae** (bristles) are usually located at either end of the body but may also occur almost anywhere along its length. Although the identification of nematodes is extremely difficult and requires specialist knowledge, their generally stiff and transparent or translucent appearance, and characteristic sinusoidal thrashing movement, allows them to be easily distinguished from other marine worms.

Marine nematodes may be free-living or parasitic, the former being especially abundant in fine intertidal sediments (mud and fine sand), or in and among the holdfasts of seaweeds.

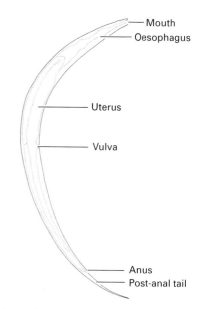

Some of the parts of a typical nematode worm

Further reading

Maggenti, A. R. (1982). Nemata. In *Synopsis and classification of living organisms* (ed. P. Parker), Vol. 1, pp. 879–929. McGraw-Hill, New York.

Platt, H. M. & Warwick, R. M. (1983). Freeliving marine nematodes. Part 1, British enoplids. *Synopses of the British Fauna, New Series*, **28**, 1–307.

Phylum Nemertea (ribbon worms)

Nemertea are typically long, slender, bilaterally symmetrical, soft-bodied worms with a ciliated epidermal surface. Most are capable of extreme contraction and elongation of their bodies, which, depending upon the species, may only be a few millimetres long or up to 30 m or more in the case of *Lineus longissimus*. Some of the dorsoventrally flattened forms may be 6–8 mm or more wide, whilst the members of one small subclass, **Bdellonemertea**, are leech-like with a posterior ventral sucker. Pelagic nemerteans are often comparatively short relative to their width, several species possessing **cephalic tentacles** and **caudal fins**. The main features of

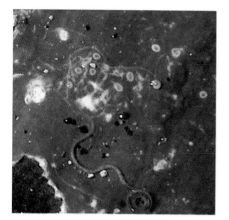

nemerteans are that they possess a characteristic protrusible **proboscis**, housed when retracted in a tubular, fluid-filled, chamber (the **rhynchocoel**) extending above the gut. They also have a gut with separate **mouth** and **anus** and a well-developed **blood system**. Most nemertean species are marine, though a few forms are known from freshwater and terrestrial habitats. Marine species are mainly benthic in their habits, though one group (the pelagic **Polystilifera**) swim or float only in deep-water oceanic regions, rarely being encountered close to land.

Although many species possess very characteristic and striking colour patterns, others do not and, within the phylum as a whole, their classification and identification depends upon the use of **histological** procedures to study their internal morphology. This generally makes the worms difficult to identify. The phylum is divided into two classes, **Anopla** and **Enopla**, each containing two subclasses. In the **Anopla** the mouth is below or posterior to the brain, the proboscis has no **stylet** armature, and the longitudinal nerve cords are embedded in body-wall layers. The two subclasses are:

Palaeonemertea Outermost body-wall muscle layer circular, longitudinal nerve cords either external to the muscle layers or embedded in longitudinal layer. Entirely marine and benthic.

Heteronemertea Body wall musculature in three layers, outer and inner longitudinal, middle circular, the longitudinal nerve cords being located just outside the circular musculature. Mostly marine and benthic, a few freshwater species are known and one, possibly an endoparasite, in echiuroids.

In **Enopla** the mouth is anterior to the brain and usually shares a common opening with the proboscis. The proboscis is usually armed with one or several **stylets**, and the longitudinal nerve cords are internal to the body wall musculature. The Enopla are subdivided into:

Hoplonemertea Body worm-like, gut straight, proboscis armed with stylets, no posterior ventral sucker. Two orders.

Monostilifera Proboscis armature consisting of a single, needle-like, central **stylet** carried on a cylindrical **basis**. Mostly marine and benthic, but with some freshwater species known; all the terrestrial nemerteans belong in this order.

Polystilifera Proboscis armature consisting of a pad- or shield-like basis carrying several small **stylets**. Two suborders.

    Reptantia: marine, benthic polystiliferans.
    Pelagica: marine pelagic polystiliferans.

Bdellonemertea Body leech-like, with posterior **ventral sucker**, proboscis not armed, gut sinuous. The few bdellonemertean species known are entirely marine **entocommensals** living in the mantle cavity of bivalve molluscs.

Further reading

Gibson, R. (1972). *Nemerteans.* Hutchinson, London.

Gibson, R. (1994). Nemertea (2nd edn). *Synopses of the British Fauna, New Series*, **24**, 1–224.

Gibson, R. & Knight-Jones, E. W. (1990). Platyhelminthes, Nematoda, and Nemertea. In *The marine fauna of the British Isles and North-West Europe* (eds P. J. Hayward & J. S. Ryland), Vol. 1, pp. 181–200. Clarendon Press, Oxford.

CLASS **Anopla** | SUBCLASS **Palaeonemertea**

FAMILY **Tubulanidae**

Tubulanus annulatus (Montagu)
Football-jersey worm

Strikingly marked nemertean, 75 cm or more long but rarely over 3–4 mm wide unless strongly contracted. General colour vivid brick-red, orangey-red, or bright brownish-red, paler ventrally; mid-dorsal and lateral longitudinal white stripes, transverse white rings. Mid-dorsal stripe in front extends on to rounded cephalic lobe, ending in T-shaped transverse band close behind snout tip. Lateral stripes do not extend as far forwards as cephalic lobe. Apart from first two or three, irregularly spaced, transverse bands, bands arranged more or less equidistantly along body length.
Habitat & ecology · Occasionally found on lower shore under stones or boulders, on sand or mud, or entangled amongst kelp holdfasts; more common sublittorally to 40 m or more on gravel, stones, mud, fine sand, shelly sand, or among scallops.

Abundance & distribution
Not uncommon sublittorally, but with unobtrusive habits. Has wide distribution in northern hemisphere and recorded from Pacific coast of North America eastwards to Atlantic, North Sea, and Mediterranean coasts of Europe.

SUBCLASS **Heteronemertea**

FAMILY **Lineidae**

(a)

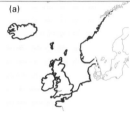

Lineus and *Ramphogordius* species

Description · *Lineus* species are amongst the most common nemerteans found on northern European shores. All of them have a long, slender body of variable length, depending on the species. The head is spatulate and always has a pair of lateral, longitudinal slits. Most species have tiny, usually black, eyes along the anterior lateral margins of the head. The tail usually tapers to a pointed or blunt end without a terminal cirrus. The different species can be recognised thus:

(b)

(a) *Lineus bilineatus* (Renier)

Body up to 50 cm long. The head lacks eyes. The colour of the body is reddish-brown, sometimes paler ventrally, with two distinctive longitudinal, narrow white stripes that run the entire length of the body.

(b) *Lineus longissimus* (Gunnerus)

Body can be extremely long; specimens of 10–15 m are not uncommon and over 30 m has been recorded. Young specimens are smaller. The width of the body may be 1–10 mm depending upon the degree of contraction. The colour ranges from a dark olive brown or rich chocolate brown in smaller examples to dark blackish-brown or purplish-black in larger individuals. The beating of the epidermal cilia often causes a purplish iridescence. The body may appear to be longitudinally streaked with pale lines, especially on the anterior dorsal surface. Ventrally the colour may be slightly paler than the dorsal. The head is rather rectangular in shape, often appearing slightly notched at its pale tip, and bears 10–40 deep-set and inconspicuous small reddish-brown or black eyes on each side.

(c)

(c) *Lineus ruber* (Müller)

This species is mostly less than 7–8 cm long. The bluntly rounded head has 0–7 small brown or black eyes along each dorsolateral margin, positioned just above the lateral head furrows. The animal is typically a light to dark reddish-brown, paler ventrally, with the brain lobes showing dorsally as pinkish-red patches at the rear of the head. Some specimens may have a violet, greenish-red or yellowish-brown hue, and in sexually mature individuals the gonads appear as whitish lateral spots throughout the intestinal region of the body.

(d)

Distinctive features

1. Mid-dorsal and lateral, longitudinal white stripes and transverse bands on background of red.
2. Anterior end distinctly lobed.

Distinctive features

1. Body long and slender.
2. Head with a pair of lateral, longitudinal slits.
3. Tail simple.

(a)

Lineus longissimus

(b)

(d) *Lineus viridis* (Müller)

Very similar to *L. ruber*. It is also typically up to 7–8 cm long, occasionally reaching 13 cm and 1–3 mm wide. The head bears 0–9 small black ocelli along each side of the head. The body is characteristically dark olive green to greenish-black in colour, less often a pale green, mature adults frequently being marked with slender, pale 'rings' arranged at more or less regular intervals along the body. There is also a species of nemertean that is indistinguishable from *L. ruber* or *L. viridis* in body shape but which can only be distinguished from them genetically.

(e) *Ramphogordius sanguineus* (Rathke)

This is a slender nemertean, up to 10–20 cm long. On the head there are 4–6 pairs of eyes which are more evenly distributed than in *L. ruber*. The mouth always starts some distance behind the end of the head slits. The colour varies from a bright reddish-brown to dull yellowish-brown, usually paler on the underside and in the posterior regions. Dark specimens can appear deep purplish-red or even greyish-black. This species coils spirally if disturbed.

Habitat & ecology · *L. ruber, L. viridis*, and *R. sanguineus* occur intertidally from the upper middle shore, downwards, in muddy sand or sand, most frequently under stones or rock. They may also occur in algal holdfasts, amongst mussels, or on estuarine muds. *R. sanguineus* seems to be tolerant of reduced oxygen conditions and may also be found in lagoons. *L. bilineatus* is found on lower middle-shore to sublittoral situations in shelly gravel, muddy sand, or clean fine sand, amongst coralline algae in rockpools, between the holdfasts of kelps, on mussel or oyster shells, or amongst the tubes of polychaete worms. *L. longissimus* can be found on the extreme lower shore coiled into writhing knots beneath boulders or rocks on muddy sand, in rock crevices or fissures, entangled amongst kelp holdfasts or in rock pools. It is much more common sublittorally on mud, sand, stone, or shell sediments. When handled, this nemertean secretes copious volumes of thick whitish mucus which has a characteristic pungent odour.

(e)

Abundance & distribution
L. ruber, L. viridis, and *R. sanguineus* are all frequently found and often locally common. *L. bilineatus* is also common but less widespread than the previous three species. *L. longissimus* is widespread but it is rare that more than a few are ever found at one locality. *R. sanguineus* has a more or less cosmopolitan distribution, but off the coasts of northern Europe is found from the coasts of Sweden and the North Sea, southwards to the Mediterranean. *L. ruber* and *L. viridis* are found from the Arctic to the Mediterranean, including the Baltic Sea. *L. ruber* may also occur in the southern hemisphere. *L. longissimus* occurs from Iceland and Norway to the Atlantic coasts of Spain. *L. bilineatus* has a similar distribution but only occurs as far south as the Channel.

CLASS Enopla | SUBCLASS Hoplonemertea

FAMILY Amphiporidae

Amphiporus lactifloreus (Johnston)

Description · One of commonest British nemerteans. Up to 25–35 mm long, exceptionally 10–12 cm, and 1–3 mm wide. Body rounded, slender, gradually tapering towards blunt, pointed tail. Head, bearing anterior and posterior groups of eyes on either side, bluntly oval, slightly pointed or spatulate, depending upon degree of contraction. Colour varies, depending on gut contents and state of sexual maturation. Immature individuals typically dull pink or dirty white, with paler head, tail, and lateral margins; brain lobes show as dark pink or reddish patches at rear of head. Gonads of mature females orange to dark red, those of ripe males light brownish-grey to creamish-grey. Gut contents may impart brownish, greenish, or greyish hue to intestinal region. Individuals with dark brown to black head are most probably infected with the sporozoan parasite *Haplosporidium malacobdellae*.

Abundance & distribution
Widely distributed around the British Isles, often locally very common. Recorded from Atlantic and Arctic coasts of North America north of Cape Cod, and eastwards to Atlantic, North Sea, and Channel coasts of northern Europe, and in the Mediterranean.

(c)

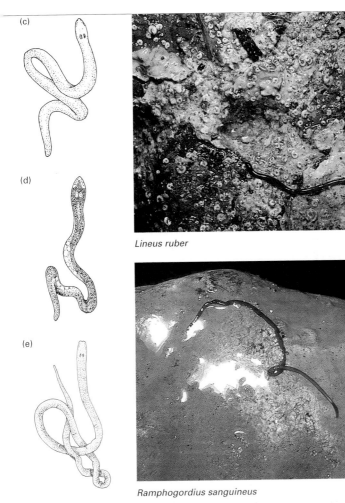

Lineus ruber

(d)

(e)

Ramphogordius sanguineus

Distinctive features

1. Eyes arranged in anterior and posterior groups on either side of head.
2. General colour dull pink to dirty white.

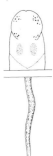

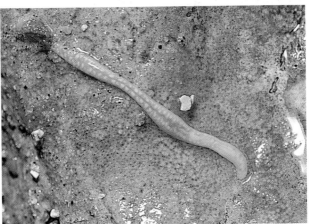

Phylum Sipuncula (peanut worms)

The cylindrical, coelomate body is unsegmented but may bear various **papillae**, **hooks**, and **shields**. The posteriorly tapering portion forms the **trunk**, into which the narrow and retractable **introvert** can be withdrawn. The **mouth** is located at the end of the introvert and surrounded by a frilled **disc** that may be divided into short **tentacles**. The long, U-shaped coiled **gut** opens dorsally near the front end at the **anus**, on either side of which there are usually two **excretory pores**. Dorsal to the mouth, situated above the **brain**, is a sensory structure, the **nuchal organ**. In a number of species some of the tentacles encircling the mouth form a horseshoe-shaped arc around the nuchal organ. The sexes are usually separate and fertilisation typically external, most species have a planktonic **trochophore** larva. At least one species is hermaphroditic and two reproduce asexually by fission.

Sipunculans live in softer sediments, feeding mainly on detritus (**detritivorous**) deposited in the upper layers of muddy sand. They are also found in mud or sand-filled cracks and crevices in rocks, within softer rocks or coral, or underneath turfs or encrustations of calcareous algae. The members of the phylum are very homogeneous in their anatomy, the two recognised classes being:

Sipunculidea Tentacles mainly surrounding the mouth, although a few dorsally may form an arc around the nuchal organ.

Phascolosomatidea All tentacles dorsal to mouth, forming horseshoe-shaped arc around nuchal organ.

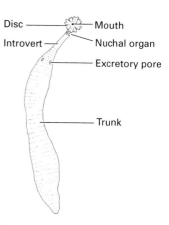

The typical appearance of a sipunculan.

Several species of sipunculids are common in north-west Europe but they tend to live in burrows either in muddy sand or gravel, or in sediment-filled crevices. One species, *Phascolion strombi* (Montagu) is often found in mollusc shells or polychaete tubes. Occasionally sipunculids are found underneath rocks and stones lying in an exposed burrow in muddy sand.

Further reading

Gibbs, P. E. (1977). British sipunculans. *Synopsis of the British Fauna, New Series*, **12**, 1–35.
Gibbs, P. E. & Cutler, E. B. (1987). A classification of the phylum Sipuncula. *Bulletin of the British Museum (Natural History) Zoology*, **52**, 43–58.
Knight-Jones, E. W. & Ryland, J. S. (1990). Priapulida, Sipuncula, Echiura, Pogonophora, and Entoprocta. In *The marine fauna of the British Isles and North-West Europe* (eds P. J. Hayward & J. S. Ryland), Vol. 1, pp. 307–21. Clarendon Press, Oxford.

Phylum Echiura (acorn worms)

The plump, pear-shaped, or elongated cylindrical and **unsegmented** body possesses a characteristic slender, **inrolled** anterior **proboscis,** which is long, soft, mobile, retractile, and contains the brain. The proboscis, which may differ in colour from the rest of the body, is often the only part of the animal visible on the surface of substrate, stretched out from the burrow opening. It is very easily damaged or broken off from the body. The ventral surface of the proboscis, which in some types is forked (**bifurcate**) at its tip, forms a shallow, ciliated **groove** or furrow which transports **mucus** and trapped **detritus** to the ventral mouth, enclosed by the proboscis base. The **gut,** very much longer than the body, follows a highly convoluted route through the body to end at the terminal posterior **anus.** Close behind the mouth, on the underside of the body, there is usually a pair of **chitinous hooks** and one or more **excretory pores.** Echiuroids are coelomate, with a fluid-filled body (**coelomic**) cavity. It is possible that echiuroids are ancestrally related to annelid worms, because most possess at least one pair of **chaetae** and some have a **trochophore** larva in their life-cycle.

Echiuroids feed on small invertebrates and organic deposits (detritus) which they trap with their proboscis mucus. The classification of the phylum includes three orders, one of which, the Echiuroinea, is known to have representatives in north-west European waters. This order has two families:

Bonelliidae Females plumply pear-shaped, males reduced (**dwarf**) and **parasitic** on the females. Proboscis may be truncate or bifurcated.

Echiuridae Males and females similar in size. Proboscis never bifurcated.

Several species occur in north-west Europe, many of them living in burrows in sand or muddy sand. These burrows may have spoke-shaped markings around them caused by the proboscis moving around the burrow entrance. The proboscis may be seen stretched

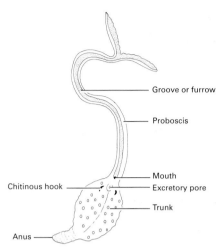

Drawing of an echiuran with its bifurcate proboscis extended.

out on the surface of the seabed, especially the long, green, truncate proboscis of *Maxmuelleria lankesteri* (Herdman) (photo this page). The dark green bifurcated proboscis of *Bonellia viridis* Rolando may be visible projecting from rock crevices, sometimes in intertidal rock pools. Positive identification of many echiuroids requires specialist knowledge and dissection and examination of the internal structure of the body.

Further reading

Knight-Jones, E. W. & Ryland, J. S. (1990). Priapulida, Sipuncula, Echiura, Pogonophora, and Entoprocta. In *The marine fauna of the British Isles and North-West Europe* (eds P. J. Hayward & J. S. Ryland), Vol. 1, pp. 307–21. Clarendon Press, Oxford.

Maxmuelleria lankesteri

Segmented worms

Phylum Annelida

A large phylum, the **Annelida** or 'true' worms comprise about 15 000 described living species. Annelids typically possess a long, cylindrical body composed of serially repeated segments externally recognisable by the intersegmental **annular** constrictions; annelids are both **coelomate** and **segmented**. The first segment, the **prostomium**, is above and in front of the mouth and both houses the brain and usually bears sensory structures such as eyes and antennae. The second segment (the **buccal segment** or **peristomium**) encloses the mouth. The gut is comparatively simple, extending as a straight tube from the mouth to the final segment of the body, the **pygidium**, on which the anus opens. Between the peristomium and pygidium the body consists of a variable number of serially repeated segments, depending upon the species, each of which contains a set of body structures and organs similar to those of all the other segments. Segmentation is usually externally distinguishable by pores, as well as projecting **chaetae** or **parapodia**, many of which are employed for movement. Burrowing, crawling, or swimming movement by annelids is achieved by the two body-wall muscle layers, circular and longitudinal, alternately contracting and relaxing against the fluid-filled **coelomic cavity** (which provides an efficient **hydrostatic skeleton**) to cause elongation or contraction of the body regions. Effectively, peristaltic waves of muscular activity move along the body, projecting chaetae or parapodia which grip the sediment or push against the water, providing the **locomotory** force.

A few annelids grow to lengths of more than 1 m, some are less than a few millimetres long, but most as adults are about 1–15 cm in length. Growing worms add new segments from just in front of the pygidium.

A diverse group of invertebrates, found in all habitats, there are three major classes, the **Hirudinea** (leeches), **Oligochaeta** (earthworms), and **Polychaeta** (bristle worms). A fourth class is also recognised, the **Myzostomaria**; this is a small group of disc-like worms, thought to have evolved from polychaete-like ancestors, living as **commensals** or **parasites** on echinoderms. Polychaetes, the largest of the annelid classes, are entirely aquatic in habit and regarded as representing the basic annelid body form. A typical segment bears on each side well-developed fleshy lobes (the **parapodium**) housing **chitinous** bristles (**chaetae**). The head of most polychaetes possesses a variety of sensory appendages which, in filter-feeding tube-dwelling species, may be developed into a conspicuous **fan-like** structure which is often the only part of the animal visible above the substrate in which its tube is burrowed. In many polychaetes the anterior portion of the body forms a '**thoracic**' region, both more complex in structure and stouter than the posterior 'abdomen'. Oligochaetes and leeches lack parapodia, and also have smooth heads with no sensory appendages. Leeches also have no chaetae, whereas oligochaetes generally have fewer and smaller chaetae than polychaetes. Locomotion by leeches may be either a '**looping**' movement, achieved by alternately attaching and releasing anterior and posterior suckers, or **swimming** by undulating their flattened bodies in a dorsoventral plane. In oligochaetes and leeches part of the body (the **saddle**) is modified for reproduction; this saddle may be permanent, may develop only during the breeding period, or may be externally invisible.

Further reading

George, J. D. & Hartmann-Schröder, G. (1985). Polychaetes: British Amphinomida, Spintherida and Eunicida. *Synopses of the British Fauna, New Series*, **32**, 1-221.

Giere, O. & Pfannkuche, O. (1982). Biology and ecology of marine Oligochaeta, a review. *Oceanography and Marine Biology Annual Review*, **20**, 173–308.

Knight-Jones, P. (1983). Contributions to the taxonomy of Sabellidae (Polychaeta). *Zoological Journal of the Linnean Society*, **79**, 245–95.

Knight-Jones, P. & Knight-Jones, E. W. (1977). Taxonomy and ecology of British Spirorbidae (Polychaeta). *Journal of the Marine Biological Association of the United Kingdom*, **57**, 453–99.

Nelson-Smith, A., Knight-Jones, P., & Knight-Jones, E. W. (1990). Annelida. In *The marine fauna of the British Isles and North-West Europe* (eds P. J. Hayward & J. S. Ryland), Vol. 1, pp. 201–306. Clarendon Press, Oxford.

Pleijel, F. & Dales, R. P. (1991). Polychaetes: British Phyllodocoideans, Typhloscolecoideans and Tomopteroideans. In *Synopses of the British Fauna No. 45* (eds D. M. Kermack & R. S. K. Barnes). UBS/Dr W. Backhuys, Oegstgeest, The Netherlands.

Class Polychaeta

The largest annelid class, the **polychaetes** exhibit a wide range of body forms. The basic body plan, however, consists of a head formed from the **prostomium** and several highly modified anterior segments fused together, bearing a variety of specialised **sensory** and other structures such as **eyes, eyespots, antennae, palps, jaws, ciliated flaps,** and **tentacular cirri.** The palps normally flank the mouth, antennae (either singly or in pairs) occur on the top or sides of the head, and the tentacles often appear as several pairs immediately behind the head. There may also be ciliated dorsal **nuchal organs,** of various shapes and functions, passing back from the rear edge of the prostomium. The first portion of the gut (**pharynx**) is often muscular, **eversible** (protrusible), armed with opposable **chitinous jaws** and **teeth,** and functions as a **proboscis** for food capture. Behind the head the body consists of a variable number of essentially similar segments, the number depending upon the species concerned and the age of the individual. Most have lateral, locomotory, fleshy outgrowths (**parapodia**), which may, sometimes, be modified for respiration. Several different component structures, the nature of which can be important for identification, make up each parapodium. The parapodial lobes surround one or more bundles of **chaetae** (**setae**), a complete parapodium consisting of two parts, the dorsal **notopod** and the ventral **neuropod,** although one or the other may be missing. Notopods and neuropods may be very similar,

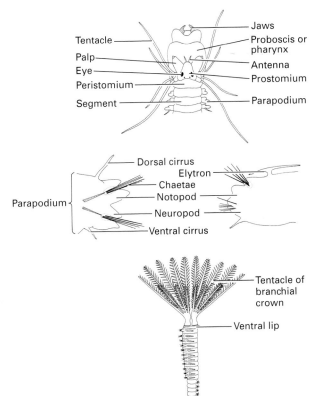

Some of the main features of polychaete annelids. *Top*: the various structures at the anterior end of a nereid. *Middle*: two variants of polychaete parapodia. *Bottom*: the tentacular branchial crown of a tube-dwelling polychaete

each containing bundles of chaetae which may be paddle-, spear-, or needle-like in shape and are often used as simple 'legs' or 'paddles'. Each **parapodial lobe** may also possess a long or short, tubular or conical, fleshy **cirrus**, the **dorsal cirrus** typically being above the notopodial chaetae, the **ventral cirrus** below the neuropodial chaetae. Cirri, usually dorsally, may be modified to form **gills**, **tentacles**, or **protective scales**. Some of the segments may completely lack chaetae and are said to be **achaetous**; the remaining segments with chaetae form the **chaetigers**. In actively swimming or crawling polychaete groups, segments are usually obvious and prominent, although their number may not be externally discernible because each may be marked by transverse superficial annulations. The sexes are usually separate, with external fertilisation, and there is commonly a pelagic larval stage in the life-cycle.

The class is so diverse in its body form, habits, and ecology that it cannot be easily classified into orders and this has led to a great deal of debate regarding the systematics of the group. For the purposes of this book we adopt the classification of Pleijel & Dales (1991) but the reader should be aware that other schemes exist. At least 30 families have representatives living in north-west European waters. The basic body plan, described above, is very much modified in the different groups. Very broadly,

the polychaetes can be divided into two ecological categories, the freely living, active predatory forms (the **Errantia**), and those which are sedentary and either burrowing or tube-dwelling (the **Sedentaria** or **Tubicola**). In both these groups examples can be found which do not ideally fit the typical body form. Errant polychaetes generally resemble the basic polychaete form already described, whereas those that burrow into or through sands and muds tend to have a rounded or conical head and smaller parapods, as well as shorter, stouter, and hooked chaetae. Many of these burrowing forms retain a protrusible proboscis (pharynx) but use it as an anchor within the substrate to pull themselves forwards, or else engulf the sediment through which they are moving and digest out any organic material contained therein. The more sedentary burrowing polychaetes often cover themselves with **mucus**, to which sand grains, detritus, or small stones may become attached. Other Sedentaria make a permanent burrow for themselves in softer sediments, or even in rock, or build a strong **tube** composed either of sand grains cemented together or of **calcite** (calcium carbonate). Sedentary polychaetes often have their bodies divisible into anterior and posterior **thoracic** and **abdominal** regions respectively. Their parapods also tend to be small but elaborate, with notopods similar to those of errant polychaetes but neuropods

ORDER **Phyllodocida** | SUPERFAMILY **Aphroditoidea**

FAMILY **Aphroditidae**, SUBFAMILY **Aphroditinae**
Aphrodita aculeata (Linnaeus)
Sea mouse

Description · A large and distinctive polychaete, up to 10–20 cm long and 2–3.5 cm wide, easy to identify because of the dense mat of dark grey to greyish-brown fine chaetae covering the dorsal scales and surface of the head. At the anterior end there is a single pair of horn-like palps. Along either side of the oval body stiff blackish bristles and cirri, slanted obliquely backwards, emerge from the dorsal mat or felt, whilst the body margins are fringed with fine golden brown, blue, or green iridescent chaetae. Ventrally the approximately 40 segments, brownish-yellow in colour, are distinct and give the flattened surface the appearance of a deeply ridged shoe sole.
Habitat & ecology · Rarely found intertidally unless stranded, the sea mouse lives on clean or muddy sand in shallow to moderately deep sublittoral situations.

Abundance & distribution
Uncommon. Found all around the British Isles and Ireland. Distributed throughout the north-east Atlantic area including the western Baltic Sea, south to the Mediterranean.

modified to form a **torus** (a pair of swollen ridges extending down the side of each segment and enclosing **uncini**, a stack of small plates with toothed outer margins). Notopodial chaetae are used for movement within the tubes, but the uncini, when pressed against the inner tube walls, anchor or lock the worms securely in place. Sedentary polychaetes have overcome the potential problems of respiration, food acquisition, and excretion in several ways. Some have evolved a series of widely spreading mobile tentacles that they use for **detritus** collection, others irrigate their tubes and filter out suspended matter which includes organic food material. Gills, which may look like small, tufted bushes or bunches of longer filaments, often coloured reddish from the **haemoglobin** in their blood, tend to be located close to the head. In the most specialised Sedentaria, the fan worms, however, a stiff, feathery crown of ciliated tentacles (the **branchial crown**) is carried on the head, the ciliary water currents drawn through it being used for filtering food from suspension, respiration, and the elimination of metabolic wastes.

Within the Polychaeta the sexes are usually separate, though some tubeworms are hermaphroditic. Paler coloured or transparent species may exhibit chromatic sexual **dimorphism**, the male and female gametes being differently coloured. Eggs and spermatozoa are commonly shed separately into the sea water, where external fertilisation occurs, but in some families elaborate devices have evolved that increase the chances of successful breeding. Such devices often result in an increase in swimming efficiency during the reproductive period, sexually ripe individuals swimming to the water surface and congregating (**swarming**) before releasing their gametes. Perhaps the most advanced form of this behaviour is found in species where the posterior few body segments alone become modified for swimming (called **epitokes**), these then breaking free from the remainder of the body to swarm. Epitoke formation is a feature, for example, of several members of the family **Syllidae**. Swarming is often highly coordinated and precisely timed. Other species may bud off posteriorly a chain of sexually mature individuals (**stolons**) which, when released, swarm for breeding purposes.

Distinctive features

1. Body distinctly oval in shape.
2. Dorsal surface mostly covered with dense mat of fine, felt-like greyish-brown mat of chaetae.
3. Body fringed with green, blue or golden iridescent chaetae.
4. Ventral surface like ridged sole of a shoe.

FAMILY **Polynoidae** | SUBFAMILY **Polynoinae**

Lepidonotus clava (Montagu)

Description · Up to about 3 cm long, body more or less equal width throughout and dorsoventrally flattened. Dorsally 12 pairs of round scales borne on alternate parapodia. These overlap each other in young individuals but not in older worms, when middle of back almost uncovered and last two segments exposed. First few scales tend to be warty, but most are smooth and none fringed. Scales dark brown, with central whitish blotch surrounded by reddish and yellowish marbling. Chaetae, present on 26 segments, organised into two groups on each parapodium. Each of these also bears curved cirrus and posterior end of body has pair of short cirri. Head, partially obscured from above; two pairs of eyes, three antennae, pair of long pointed palps, and three pairs of lateral tentacular cirri. **Habitat & ecology** · Lower shore intertidal, typically found beneath rocks, boulders, and stones. **Similar species** · Other scale worms, such as *L. squamatus*, but in this species scales overlap covering entire dorsal surface of body. *Lagisca extenuata* has 15 pairs of scales and distinct tail region comprising 8–9 segments not covered by scales.

Abundance & distribution
Common. Found in the southern North Sea, Channel, Irish Sea, and western Scotland, and southern and western Ireland. Distributed south to the Mediterranean.

SUPERFAMILY **Phyllodocoidea**

FAMILY **Phyllodocidae**

Eulalia viridis (Linnaeus) **Greenleaf worm**

Description · Distinctive bright grass-green to dark green colour, sometimes with black dorsal patches, body up to 5–15 cm long with 60–200 segments. On either side at rear of head are four long, fairly stout, green tentacular cirri, plus single shorter dorsal fifth antenna situated between two distinct black eyes. Tip of head has four short, anteriorly directed antennae. Parapodia of each segment bear large, dorsal, elongate-triangular, rather pointed, dorsal cirri and small, oval, ventral cirri. **Habitat & ecology** · Occasionally as high as mid-shore, more frequently lower shore or shallow sublittoral situations on rock, in rock crevices, or amongst kelp holdfasts. Individuals not uncommonly found crawling on rock surface when uncovered by tide. Its roughly marble-sized, gelatinous, green egg masses often found attached to rocks or seaweeds, or on sand, in lower shore zone. **Similar species** · *E. bilineata* somewhat similar but usually smaller, marked with pair of irregular darker lines along its dorsal surface, has oval rather than pointed dorsal cirri, and is paler green. *E. pusilla* is much smaller offshore species that tends to be more brownish.

Abundance & distribution
Very common. Found all around Britain and Ireland. Distributed from Norway to Mediterranean and throughout northern hemisphere.

Phyllodoce lamelligera Johnston

Description · Large, slender polychaete. Compressed body up to 60 cm long, with 300–400 segments. Head (prostomium) elongate, truncated cone shape with four short, conical antennae and two black eyes. At rear of head four pairs of slender tentacular cirri, the moderately long posterior pair reaching back to body segments 6–8. Protrusible proboscis, hexagonal in section, lacks jaws but is both longitudinally and transversely ridged and its opening is encircled by 16 papillae. Parapodia bear conspicuous, asymmetrical, lance- or elongate heart-shaped, olive green to brownish-yellow dorsal cirri or paddles. Body greenish or bluish with metallic blue iridescence. Younger specimens may be yellowish, especially along the midline of the body. Two short anal cirri. **Habitat & ecology** · Under rocks and boulders, lower shore to sublittoral, often among kelps. **Similar species** · May be confused with *P. laminosa*, but this form may be even longer, has shorter and more pointed parapodial paddles, and is a very dark green with paler green or brown cross-banding.

Abundance & distribution
Locally common. Found on south and west coasts of Britain and Ireland. Distributed south to the Mediterranean. It also occurs in the Pacific Ocean.

Distinctive features

1. Dorsal surface almost completely covered by 12 pairs of dark brown round scales.
2. Scales with central whitish patch.
3. Last two segments on body not covered by scales.

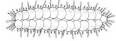

Distinctive features

1. Overall colour bright to dark green.
2. Four pairs of long but fairly stout tentacles.

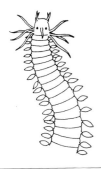

Distinctive features

1. Head truncate, cone shape; four short antennae, two black eyes.
2. Four pairs of slender tentacular cirri at rear of head.
3. Body greenish or bluish with metallic blue iridescence.

Pirakia punctifera Johnston

Description · This paddle worm, also known as *Eumida punctifera*, has a fairly stout body 6–15 cm long. The head bears four pairs of moderately long but stout tentacles and a fifth antenna arising from a dark patch situated between the eyes. Parapodia are developed into broad, heart-shaped paddles that are blotched brown in their centre and have pointed tips. The animals are greenish or yellowish, with one or two bands of darker spots across the upper surface of each segment. Mature females tend to be more orange and males whitish. The proboscis, when protruded, is long and covered with large numbers of small papillae. **Habitat & ecology** · A lower-shore and sublittoral species, typically found beneath stones and boulders, in kelp holdfasts, or in muddy or shelly gravel. **Similar species** · There are several but they tend to be smaller than *P. punctifera* and have different colour patterns.

Abundance & distribution
Locally fairly common. Found on the Channel and south-west coasts of Britain and around Ireland. Distributed south to the Adriatic Sea.

SUPERFAMILY **Glyceroidea**

FAMILY **Glyceridae**

Glycera species

(a)

Description · Elongate, narrow worms, rounded in cross-section with numerous segments. The head is small, elongate, conical, and has four minute antennae at the tip. The robust, protrusible proboscis has four large teeth arranged in a cross. Several species in the region. *G. tridactyla* is up to 10 cm long, with 14–18 annulations making up the head. It is iridescent pink with non-retractile finger-like gills along the body. *G. alba* is up to 7.5 cm long, with 8–10 annulations making up the head. It is milky white, also with non-retractile gills. *G. gigantea* is up to 35 cm long with 12–14 annulations making up the head. It is greyish with a pinkish anterior region and has retractile globular gills. *G. rouxi* is up to 20 cm long, reddish and has retractile finger-like gills. *G. capitata* lacks gills. **Habitat & ecology** · Active, carnivorous worms, generally found in clean sand from low shore to shallow sublittoral. When swimming they throw the body into spiral undulations and may tightly coil if disturbed. Large specimens may give a painful bite.

Abundance & distribution
Common. *G. gigantea* and *G. tridactyla*: (a) south and west coasts of Britain, all around Ireland, south to the Mediterranean. *G. alba* and *G. rouxi*: (b) most British and Irish coasts, south to the Mediterranean. *G. capitata*: Arctic to the Atlantic coasts of Spain and Portugal.

SUPERFAMILY **Nereidoidea**

FAMILY **Syllidae**

Myrianida pinnigera (Montagu)

Description · A small polychaete, 1.5–3 cm long, but distinctly coloured in being white with large red, orange, or yellow patches dorsally on about every third or fourth segment. The anterior-most patch extends over several segments. On the head there are four distinct black eyes. The middle antenna, upper tentacles, and dorsal cirri are long and flattened, shaped rather like an elongate, narrow, leaf. There are three pairs of tentacles on the head, the most posterior pair being the longest. During the breeding period the worm may appear twice as long as normal because it may trail up to 30 stolons behind it. **Habitat & ecology** · Breeding in this species is achieved by budding off a train of small individuals (stolons) posteriorly. When these are released they swarm before releasing the gametes.

Abundance & distribution
Not common. Found in south-west Britain. Distributed south on Atlantic coasts of France, Spain, and Portugal, and the Mediterranean.

Distinctive features

1. Head with fifth antenna extending from dark patch between eyes.
2. Head with four pairs of fairly long but stout tentacles.

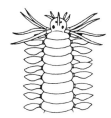

Distinctive features

1. Elongate, narrow body with numerous segments.
2. Anterior end elongate, conical, with four tiny antennae at end.
3. Large proboscis with four teeth, readily protrusible.

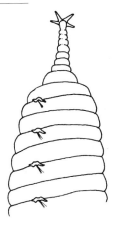

Distinctive features

1. Colour white, marked dorsally by patches of yellow, orange or red on every third or fourth segment.

FAMILY **Nereidae**

Nereis and *Perinereis* species

Description · Slender, elongate polychaetes of a medium to large size. The head typically has two ovoid palps, each with a terminal knob. Between these is a pair of short antennae, and on the dorsal surface of the head two pairs of eyes. These worms have a robust proboscis armed with a pair of large chitinous jaws at the end and covered with a scattering of smaller teeth. On the sides and behind the head are four pairs of large tentacles. Each segment has parapodia with dorsal and ventral cirri and a dorsal and two ventral bundles of chaetae. These give these worms a distinctly bristly appearance. There is a pair of anal cirri. These species are very difficult to distinguish from one another.

(a) *Nereis diversicolor* Müller

Known as the rag worm, this has a rather flabby, flattened body with a distinctive blood vessel visible along the dorsal surface. It grows to about 12 cm long and is a greenish, yellowish, or orange colour. Its antennae are shorter than the palps and the tentacles are about as long as the body is wide.

(b) *Perinereis cultrifera* (Grube)

Also known as the rag worm, is very similar to the preceding species but grows larger (25 cm) and, when the proboscis is protruded, two curved, dark chitinous ridges can be seen on it.

(c) *Nereis pelagica* Linnaeus

Similar to *N. diversicolor* in having a prominent dorsal blood vessel. This species grows to about 21 cm long and the body is smooth and cylindrical, rather than flattened, tapering only towards the end. The colour is golden or bronze often with a metallic, greenish sheen.

(d) *Nereis fucata* (Savigny)

This worm grows to 20 cm. Its very long parapodia give it a flattened appearance. The antennae are as long as the palps but the tentacles are shorter than the body width. The overall colour is pink or yellowish, often with white lines on either side of the dorsal blood vessel.

(e) *Nereis irrorata* (Malmgren)

This species reaches 30 cm; it is broad at the front of the body but then becomes slender and flattened. The tentacles are longer than the width of the body, the final pair of tentacles being particularly long. This worm is brick red with scattered grey and white spots.

(f) *Nereis longissima* (Johnston)

This is a particularly long species, up to 50 cm, with antennae shorter than the palps and tentacles shorter than the width of the body. It is blue-grey or pink.

(g) *Nereis virens* (Sars)

The king rag worm, this very large species grows up to 30 cm long with a bulky body. The antennae are shorter than the palps and the tentacles are about as wide as the body, except the last pair, which are longer. The dorsal flaps of the parapodia of this species are especially large giving the edges of the body a frilled appearance.

Habitat & ecology · Most nereids produce a mucous tube in which they live. *N. diversicolor* is probably the commonest species, living intertidally, often where the sand is blackened and often in estuaries. *N. virens* shares a similar type of habitat, though is not as widespread in its occurrence. *N. longissima* also has a similar habitat though it is found lower on the shore or subtidally. *N. irrorata* and *P. cultrifera* generally have tubes in sediment within rock crevices, under rocks, or in *Zostera* beds. *N. pelagica* is found

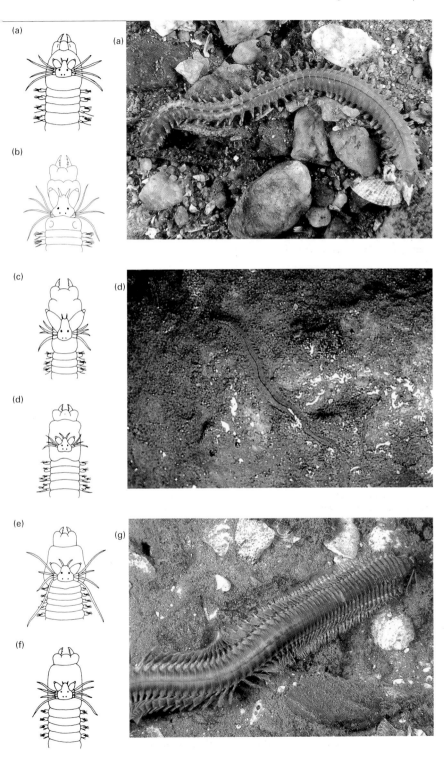

on the low shore or subtidally in algae, kelp holdfasts, or in mussel beds. *N. fucata* unusually occupies whelk shells in which hermit crabs are living. Most nereids are predators and the chitinous jaws on the proboscis of larger specimens can be used to inflict a nasty bite.

(g)

Abundance & distribution
Common. *N. diversicolor*, *N. fucata*, and *P. cultrifera* are found all around Britain and Ireland and are distributed from Norway to the Mediterranean. *N. pelagica* is found all around Britain and Ireland and is distributed from the Arctic to the

---

SUPERFAMILY **Nephtyoidea** | FAMILY **Nephtyidae**

Nephtys caeca Fabricius

Description · Large: 15–25 cm long. Body has 90–150 segments bearing distinctly bilobed parapodia with a very small dorsal, and conical ventral, cirrus except for first segment, on which dorsal and ventral cirri nearly as long as antennae. A gill is located between two groups of well-developed yellowish chaetae on each side of parapodia in first few segments. Head has four small antennae at anterior corners, and pair of tiny eyes. Proboscis, when protruded, covered with large numbers of similar-sized papillae. Tail has long single filament or thread. Generally pearly-grey, with tinges of blue, brown, or reddish-brown. **Habitat & ecology** · Middle shore to shallow sublittoral situations, sometimes amongst stones and rocks, more usually burrowing in clean or muddy sand. Appears to have varied range of foods but probably mostly carnivorous. When disturbed may try to swim with a characteristic side-to-side wriggling motion.

Abundance & distribution
Common. Found all around Britain and Ireland. Distributed from Arctic to Atlantic coasts of Spain, including western Mediterranean.

ORDER **Spionida** | SUPERFAMILY **Spionidea**

FAMILY **Spionidae**

Scolelepis squamata (Müller)

Description · Slender, up to 5–8 cm long, with about 200 chaetae-bearing segments. Narrow, elongate, conical head bears two distinct eyes and pair of long, mobile pointed palps which are coiled up into spirals when animal is disturbed. Palps fragile, easily broken off. Pair of small gills present on almost every segment of body, commencing at second. Dorsal part of parapod on each of these segments also extended upwards and partially over dorsal body surface. Small anal funnel has scalloped margin. Typically greenish-blue, females tending to be more distinctly green and males paler; mid-dorsal blood vessel distinct and bright red. Blood vessels also evident in palps and gills. **Habitat & ecology** · Typically lives in exposed sandy or muddy sand beaches in lower half of tidal range. May cover itself with loose sheath of sand-grains adhering to mucus. Swims actively when disturbed, with a spiral coiling motion.

Abundance & distribution
Very common. Found all around Britain and Ireland. Distributed throughout the north-east Atlantic to the Mediterranean.

(g)

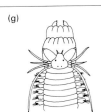

Mediterranean. *N. longissima* and *N. virens* are found all around Britain and Ireland and distributed from Norway to the Atlantic coasts of Spain and Portugal. *N. irrorata* is found in south-west Britain and southwards to the Mediterranean.

Distinctive features

1. Slender, bristly, elongate worms of medium to large size.
2. Head has a pair of ovoid palps between which is a pair of antennae.
3. Four eyes on head and four pairs of tentacles on and behind head.
4. Protrusible proboscis with large, chitinous jaws.

Distinctive features

1. Proboscis when protruded covered with numerous, similar-sized papillae.
2. Both dorsal and ventral parapodial cirri of first segment about as long as antennae.

Distinctive features

1. Head narrow, elongate and conical.
2. Two distinct eyes.
3. Single pair of very long, mobile palps, which coil spirally; easily broken off.

SUPERFAMILY **Chaetopteroidea**

FAMILY **Chaetopteridae**

Chaetopterus variopedatus (Renier)

Description · Large and comparatively bulky, though fragile. Body up to 25 cm long and 2.5 cm wide. Anteriorly a distinct large and funnel-shaped mouth, with two long, pointed palps. Approximately first nine segments bear chaetae. Obvious 'mid-body' region consists of five wide, elongate segments. On these segments upper portions of parapodia modified in sequence to form pair of 'wings'. These support mucus bag in which worm lives. There is also a cup-like structure that rolls mucous bag up and final three segments bearing ventral flap- or fan-like paddles that circulate water through burrow. Throughout remaining length of body parapodia are bristled but ventrally formed into sucker-like structures. Generally yellowish- or greenish-white, although sexually mature females have distinct pinkish tinge; mid-body region typically has segments with luminescent bluish tinge. **Habitat & ecology** · Found at extreme low water spring tide levels and sublittorally to deeper waters, this polychaete lives in a U-shaped parchment-like tube, which may be 40 cm or more in total length, buried in mud or sand. Both ends of the tube are somewhat

narrowed and may protrude slightly above the sediment surface.

Abundance & distribution Uncommon. Found all around Britain and Ireland. Distributed from North Sea to the Mediterranean; possibly cosmopolitan.

Phyllochaetopterus anglicus Potts

Description · Very slender, up to 4 cm long. Head has semicircular or slit-like mouth, a pair of short antennae and a pair of long palps or tentacles. These are often spiralled or rolled up. Anterior part of worm, with 10–18 segments, rather flattened with spear-shaped chaetae. Middle part of body comprises 7–24 segments in which dorsal part of parapodia has a bilobed flap. Posterior region made up of simpler short segments. Colour yellow with reddish markings on anterior part of body and sometimes a greenish hue to posterior region. The worms occupy a tough, translucent tube that is often attached to rock by the posterior end. Tubes may be branched and are often annulated. **Habitat & ecology** · This animal occupies its tube, attached to rock from the lower shore to the shallow sublittoral. The middle body segments are covered in cilia and these generate a feeding current of water. Sometimes these tubes will occur in very high densities.

Abundance & distribution Common, locally abundant. Found in the Irish Sea, south-west Britain, and Ireland. Distributed south to the Mediterranean.

SUPERFAMILY **Cirratuloidea**

FAMILY **Cirratulidae**

Cirratulus cirratus (Müller)

Description · Up to 12 cm long, this worm has a slender body composed of about 100–130 segments. The blunt head is indistinct, but bears on either side of its hind border a row of 4–8 large eyes. Parapodia have dorsal and ventral groups of chaetae, whilst from almost every segment a long, slender gill filament, red or yellowish in colour, emerges from the dorsolateral surface. The first segment appears to be subdivided into three rings; on the last two of these there are two groups of 2–8 thread-like tentacles. The body of the worm is orange, brown, or reddish in colour. **Habitat & ecology** · Typically found beneath stones and boulders partially embedded in mud or muddy sand, less commonly occupying rock crevices and cracks, especially when these have trapped finer sediment particles. **Similar species** · May be confused with *C. filiformis*, but this species is greenish-brown, much slenderer, and has no eyes on its pointed head.

Abundance & distribution Common. Found around all coasts of Britain and Ireland. Distributed from the North Sea to the Mediterranean.

Distinctive features

1. Lives in U-shaped, parchment-like tube.
2. Body with three distinct regions.
3. Head with large terminal mouth and two elongate palps.

Distinctive features

1. Slender worm occupying translucent, yellowish tube.
2. Head with pair of short antennae and pair of long spiralled or rolled palps.

Distinctive features

1. Head blunt, indistinct, with 4–8 large eyes each side.
2. For most of body length long red or yellowish gill filaments emerge from dorsal surface.

ORDER **Capitellida**

FAMILY **Capitellidae**

Capitella capitata (Fabricius)

Description · The body, 2–10 cm long when resting, is very contractile and extensile. With 90 or more segments bearing tufts of small chaetae, the anterior end is distinctly pointed, without tentacles or antennae, but has two small eyes on the ventral surface. Posterior portion of the body gradually tapers to end in a blunt, slightly bifurcated, tip. The more or less distinct anterior part consists of nine segments, longer than those of the remaining body; on the dorsal surface of the last two segments of this region there is a genital pore which, in males, is surrounded by spines organised into the shape of a cross, in females forming an elongate swelling. The worms are typically a reddish-purple. **Habitat & ecology** · A lower-shore to shallow sublittoral species, usually found under pebbles or small stones in muddy sand, frequently under moderate to heavy organically polluted conditions. May be one of the dominant animal species in polluted sediments.

Abundance & distribution
Locally abundant. Found all around Britain and Ireland. Distributed from Arctic to Mediterranean including western Baltic Sea. This species encompasses a complex of closely related, remarkably similar forms, and apparently

FAMILY **Arenicolidae**

Arenicola species **Lug worm, lug**

Description · Two main species of lug worms in northern European waters, the blow lug, *Arenicola marina* (Linnaeus) and the black lug, *Arenicola defodiens* Cadman & Nelson-Smith. Neither has eyes nor tentacles. Average lengths 11 cm in the blow lug, 18 cm in the black lug. Body with three distinct regions. Anterior part of six swollen segments bearing tufts of chaetae or bristles but no gills, followed by 13 segments, each formed into five narrow rings. Each segment with a pair of reddish dorsolateral gills close to the chaetae. In black lug gills are pinnate with more, longer main stems and thin membranes between side branches, in blow lug gills dendritic with fewer, shorter stems and no membranes. Third region abruptly narrow, segments with neither gills nor bristles. Black lug typically black or dark yellow, rarely brown, blow lug pink, green, dark brown or black. **Habitat & ecology** · Both species burrow in clean or muddy sand, black lug on lower shore, more exposed beaches, blow lug on mid-shore, less exposed areas.

Abundance & distribution
Locally often very abundant. The distribution of the black lug worm is uncertain but is found from south Wales to Lancashire and in the Firth of Forth. The blow lug is found around all coasts of Britain and Ireland. It is distributed from

ORDER **Oweniida**

FAMILY **Oweniidae**

Owenia fusiformis Delle Chiaje

Description · Body cylindrical up to 10 cm long, with only 20–30 segments. The head is capped by a membranous crown subdivided into six frilled lobes, the trilobed mouth being located terminally within the crown. The body colour is greenish-yellow with pale bands; the crown is suffused with red. **Habitat & ecology** · The worm lives in a membranous tube, with overlapping shell fragments or sand grains stuck to its surface, in sand or muddy sand from the lower parts of fairly sheltered shores to shallow sublittoral situations. The upper part of the tube normally protrudes above the sediment surface. This species may occur in huge numbers. The mollusc, *Acteon tornatilis*, is known to feed on this and other species of tube-dwelling polychaetes.

Abundance & distribution
Common, locally abundant. Found all around Britain and Ireland. Distributed from Norway to the Mediterranean. The species is probably cosmopolitan and is also found in the Indian and Pacific Oceans.

enjoys an almost cosmopolitan distribution in the northern hemisphere.

Distinctive features

1. Head with neither tentacles nor antennae.
2. Without external gills or other obvious appendages.
3. Head pointed, with two ventral eyes.

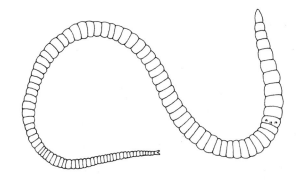

the Arctic to the Mediterranean including the western Baltic.

Distinctive features

1. Body with three distinct regions.
2. Anterior region six swollen segments without gills but with bristles.
3. Middle body with 13 segments bearing paired gills.
4. Posterior region not swollen, gills and bristles absent.

Distinctive features

1. Body cylindrical, with 20–30 segments.
2. Head with membranous crown of six frilled lobes.
3. Tube membranous, with sand grains and shell fragments stuck to its outer surface.

ORDER **Terebellida**

FAMILY **Sabellariidae**

Sabellaria alveolata (Linnaeus)
Honeycomb worm

Description · Body 3–4 cm long, head bearing circular crown of three
concentric rings of spines, those of outer ring somewhat comb-like, blunt-
faced, and cut into about five teeth. Mouth fringed by numerous feeding
tentacles, behind which are two short palps. Most body segments bear
distinct, finger-like gills, pointing dorsally. Body ends in long, tube-like tail,
which lacks gills and parapodia, is indistinctly segmented, and bent
forwards along underside of body. Reddish or violet-white. Occupies strong
tube made of sand grains cemented with mucus. Tube attached to solid
surface, usually other *Sabellaria* tubes, throughout length. **Habitat &
ecology** · Lower shore and shallow sublittoral colonial species, found on
rocks in tubes. Often colonies of tubes, which commonly overgrow rocks or
other hard structures to which attached, are so dense that their openings
form a distinctive honeycomb reef (a). These colonies, especially prone to
mechanical damage, are raised above surrounding substrate and classed as a
type of reef, forming habitat for other animals. **Similar species** ·
Somewhat resembles *S. spinulosa* but crown of this is horseshoe-shaped
and tubes tend to be separated rather than forming dense colonies (b).

Abundance & distribution
Common, locally abundant.
Distribution of this southern
species extends northwards on
British coasts to Firth of Clyde
(on west) and Berwick (on
east), southwards to Atlantic
coasts of Ireland and Europe,
and into Mediterranean.

FAMILY **Terebellidae**

Eupolymnia nebulosa (Montagu)

Description · The body of this worm is 5–15 cm long with an anterior
region of 17 segments that bear chaetae. The swollen head lobe, carrying
numerous long, mobile feeding tentacles which can shorten but not retract,
forms a collar with numerous small, dark eyespots, whilst close behind the
head there are three pairs of bushy, much-branched gills. The colour is
orangey-grey, pale red, pink, or pale brown, covered all over with white
spots. The gills are a bright red or orange, also sometimes with white spots.
The feeding tentacles are pink or whitish with chalky white markings or
rings. **Habitat & ecology** · A lower-shore and shallow sublittoral species,
found living in sandy tubes which lack a fringe around their opening,
attached to the underside of old shells, stones, or boulders, or in crevices.
Often only the tentacles are seen creeping over the substrate. **Similar
species** · Closely resembles *E. nesidensis*, but this form is smaller, with a
firm body not spotted in white.

Abundance & distribution
Locally common. Found
around most of Britain and
Ireland. Distributed from
Norway to the Mediterranean.
Also found in the Red Sea,
Arabian Gulf, and Indian and
Pacific Oceans.

Distinctive features

1. Head with a circular crown of three concentric rings of spines.
2. Most body segments with distinct, dorsally pointing, finger-like gills.
3. Densely colonial in tubes made of cemented sand grains, tube openings giving a honeycomb appearance.

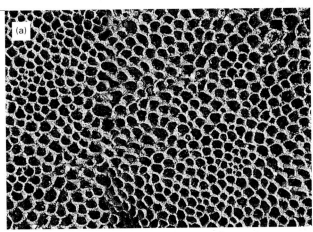

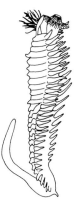

Distinctive feature

1. Swollen head lobe bearing numerous long, mobile tentacles.
2. Head lobe forms collar with numerous tiny, dark eyespots.
3. Three pairs of bushy red or orange gills behind head.

Lanice conchilega (Pallas)
Sand mason

Description · Body up to 30 cm long. Mouth-bearing head segment possesses long white or cream feeding tentacles, the bases of which are enclosed by a pair of triangular lobes. The tentacles can be shortened but not completely retracted. There are three pairs of blood-red branching gills situated close behind the head. In total the body has 150–300 segments; the swollen anterior portion consists of 17 segments, seven having chaetae; the remainder of the body is thin and fragile with rectangular, flap-like parapodia. The worm is yellowish, greenish, pink, or brown. It forms a tube of cemented sand grains, bits of shell, or tiny stone fragments. The end of the tube is divided into smaller tubes and may appear ragged. **Habitat & ecology** · Found from the mid-shore downwards, typically on fairly exposed sandy beaches. The very characteristic sand-grain covered, tough tubes, with a frayed or split upper end, typically project 2–3 cm above the surface of the sediment.

Abundance & distribution
Locally abundant. Found all around Britain and Ireland. Distributed from the Arctic to the Mediterranean.

ORDER **Sabellida**

FAMILY **Sabellidae**

Bispira volutacornis (Montagu)

Description · Body to about 10 cm long or more and 1 cm in width. When expanded the head is crowned by two interlocking semicircular whorls of about 200 ciliated feeding tentacles up to 3 cm high. Below the tentacles is a distinct, but incomplete collar, being separated on the dorsal midline. The body, mostly hidden in its tube, consists of about 60 or more segments, most bearing chaetae, with the ventral surface slightly flattened. Tentacles pale yellowish, brownish, or whitish, rarely with a violet tinge; the body brown, purplish-brown, or greenish. The tube is wrinkled, short, membranous, and supple, grey and externally covered with mud at its opening but elsewhere colourless and transparent and rather horny at its posterior end. **Habitat & ecology** · Found attached to the shaded undersides or overhangs of rocks and boulders, protruding from rock crevices, or in rock pools. Sometimes found on the lower shore, more usually in shallow to deeper sublittoral waters. Several individuals often occur together.

Abundance & distribution
Locally common. Found all around Britain and Ireland but probably more common in the south. Distributed from western Norway to the Mediterranean.

Myxicola infundibulum (Renier)

Description · The posteriorly tapering body is up to 20 cm long but if disturbed contracts strongly into its thick, carrot-shaped, gelatinous, and transparent tube, which has outer layers stained greyish-brown. The crown is bilobed but joined to form a single funnel, formed of about 60–80 feeding tentacles which, for most of their length, are joined by a web but have their triangular, purplish-brown tips free. The brownish-yellow body has eight thoracic and more than 100 abdominal segments, each of which bear chaetae and is subdivided into two annulations. **Habitat & ecology** · Lower shore and sublittoral, often in estuarine muds. **Similar species** · *M. sarsi* is very similar but smaller, found in fine muddy sand, and has a more northerly distribution, not being found south of the Isle of Man or north-east England.

Abundance & distribution
Locally common. In Britain only from the coasts of south-west England and south-west Wales. Distributed south to the Mediterranean and the Azores.

Distinctive features

1. Head with numerous white or cream tentacles.
2. Three pairs of branched, blood-red gills behind head.
3. Tube made of fairly coarse sand grains, shell and stone fragments.

Distinctive features

1. Crown of two inter-locking whorls of about 200 whitish tentacles.
2. Membranous tube transparent, colourless except at its opening.

Distinctive features

1. Tentacular crown looks like a funnel with only tips of tentacles free.
2. Tube thick, tapered, gelatinous, transparent but outer surface stained greyish-brown.

Sabella pavonina Savigny **Peacock worm**

Description · Slender body, 25–30 cm long, up to 5 mm wide, bearing up to about 100 tentacular gills grouped in two semicircles, one larger than the other, forming crown. This is usually pale creamy-yellow or occasionally dull red, often banded with brown or reddish-brown. Membranous tube of these worms is composed of muco-silt with a smooth, rubbery texture. Typically stands erect up to 10 cm above the sediment. When worm retracts, end of tube collapses, forming slit-like aperture. **Habitat & ecology** · Lives in muddy sand at or below low water level, sometimes in seagrass beds. Reaches largest size in sheltered areas with rich food supply, and tends to be smaller in areas exposed to strong currents. **Similar species** · *S. spallanzanii*, but larger, up to 30 cm high. Tentacles of crown are arranged in two groups, one forming a semicircle, the other involuted to form two or more whorls or open spirals. Found in Channel Islands to Mediterranean, including Azores and Canaries.

Abundance & distribution Common, locally abundant. Found all around Britain and Ireland. Distributed from northern Norway, Iceland, and the Faeroes to South Africa including the Mediterranean.

FAMILY **Serpulidae**

Filograna implexa Berkeley

Description · A small worm that inhabits delicate, translucent white tubes on which occasional growth rings may be visible. These usually form an interwoven network. The worm reaches about 4 mm long, with about 30 segments and eight small pinnate tentacles. One tentacle on each side has a tiny, cup-shaped, pale yellow operculum (used for sealing tube when worm withdraws). The overall colour is pink, with pink, white, or colourless tentacles. **Habitat & ecology** · May be found on the lower shore, and more usually subtidally encrusting rocks, corals, and bryozoans such as *Pentapora* species. Also inhabits kelp holdfasts. **Similar species** · It may be confused with *Salmacina dysteri* but this species lacks the cup-shaped opercula on the tentacles.

Abundance & distribution Locally abundant. Found in south-west and western Britain and Ireland. Distributed from Norway southwards to the Mediterranean. Distribution uncertain but probably cosmopolitan.

Pomatoceros lamarcki (Quatrefages) **Keel worm**

Description · Tube-dwelling worm about 25 mm long with body comprising 80–100 chaetae-bearing segments. Head bears two gills, whilst operculum (used to close the tube opening when the worm is retracted) is a solid cup-shaped calcareous plug flanked on either side by fleshy protrusion from opercular stalk. There may or may not be an eccentrically positioned spine on the top of the operculum. Body and crown of very variable colour but nearly always bright. Calcareous tubes in which the animals live are 3–5 mm wide, triangular in cross-section with an obvious single median and less distinct lateral longitudinal ridges, sinuous, smooth-surfaced and dirty white in colour, with the median ridge ending above the opening in a sharp projecting spine. **Habitat & ecology** · A lower shore tube worm, often gregarious. Cements its tubes to rocks, boulders, or almost any other hard and secure object. **Similar species** · *P. triqueter*, which is mostly sublittoral. Its calcareous tube has only a single longitudinal ridge and a shallow, saucer-like operculum.

Abundance & distribution Very common, locally abundant. Found on all coasts of Britain and Ireland. Distributed from Norway to the Mediterranean.

Distinctive features

1. Tube worm with two groups of banded tentacular gills, resembling single crown when fully distended.
2. Tube erect, smooth, rubbery; made of mud particles.

Distinctive features

1. Inhabits fine interwoven, translucent white tubes.
2. Small worm with up to eight pinnate tentacles in feeding crown.
3. One tentacle each side with cup-shaped operculum.

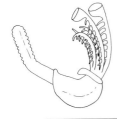

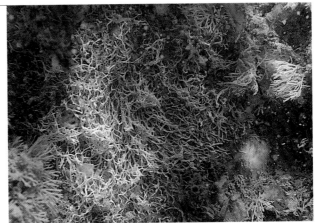

Distinctive features

1. Whitish calcareous tube, sinuous, with obvious single median ridge ending at opening by sharp projecting spine and lateral longitudinal ridges.
2. Calcareous operculum solid, cup-shaped.
3. Head with two gills, brightly but variably coloured.

Pomatoceros triqueter (Linnaeus)

Description · Body up to about 2.5 cm long, with 80–100 segments
bearing chaetae, anteriorly ending in solid, saucer-shaped, calcareous plug
or operculum (a modified tentacle) used to seal tube opening when animal
withdrawn. Ampulla (terminal portion of operculum) shallowly dish-
shaped, its distal part often conical but with or without projections.
Calcareous tube in which animal lives has only single median ridge.
Anterior (protruded) end of worm with crown of filamentous gills. Colour
very variable: body red, brown, green, or yellowish; gills red, brown, yellow,
and white, or blue and white. **Habitat & ecology** · Mainly sublittoral,
occasionally found on extreme lower shore, attached to rocks and boulders.
It lives in a chalky, calcareous and, in section, triangular-shaped tube, which
is irregularly sinuous in shape, posteriorly tapering, and ventrally adhered
to rocky surfaces for its full length. **Similar species** · Very similar to *P.
lamarcki*, although in this species the ampulla is cup-shaped and the tube
possesses a distinct median keel and, in adult individuals, a pair of lateral
vestigial ridges.

Abundance & distribution
Very common, locally
abundant. Found on all coasts
of Britain and Ireland.
Distributed from Norway to the
Mediterranean.

Salmacina dysteri (Huxley)

Description · This species is about 4 mm long with about 30 body
segments. The posterior portion of body is about twice as long as anterior.
The head has eight pink tentacles, each bearing a white, pink, or colourless
crown. The almost translucent whitish tubes have a delicate construction.
Habitat & ecology · Typically found attached to pebbles or shells, the
tubes of this gregarious species usually form an interwoven, branched
complex in which a system of cavities permits easy water circulation. Lower
shore to sublittoral. **Similar species** · Is almost identical to the closely
related *Filograna implexa*, although the two forms are usually listed as
separate species; the only major difference is that *Salmacina* does not have
cup-shaped chitinous opercula at the tips of two of the tentacles, as found
in *Filograna*.

Abundance & distribution
Common, locally very
abundant. Found all around
Britain and Ireland. Distributed
from Norway to Mediterranean
coasts of Europe.

Serpula vermicularis Linnaeus

Description · The pale yellow to brick red slender body, 5–7 cm long,
comprises about 200 chaetae-bearing segments. On the head the two gills
each consists of 30–40 filaments, united at their base. The tentacular crown
is banded in red, pink, and white. The calcareous operculum is shaped like
a stalked but solid funnel, slightly concave at its end and with 20–40 or
more radial furrows or grooves which look like small rounded teeth. The
cylindrical tube of this species, about 5 mm in diameter, is anchored at its
base but often otherwise remains unattached. It is pinkish to pale red and
has occasional thickened rings and longitudinal ridges. Tubes of different
individuals may be twisted amongst each other, sometimes to the extent
that they form distinctive masses. **Habitat & ecology** · A lower-shore and
shallow sublittoral species, attached to stones, rocks, boulders, and old
mollusc shells, often in sheltered conditions.

Abundance & distribution
Common, locally abundant.
Found on south and west coasts
of Britain and all around
Ireland. Distributed from
Norway to the Mediterranean.
Probably cosmopolitan.

Distinctive features

1. Tube calcareous, irregularly sinuous, with only a single, median ridge.
2. End of operculum (ampulla) shallowly dish-shaped.

Distinctive features

1. Worms live in delicate, translucent, whitish tubes.
2. Head bearing eight pink tentacles, without cup-shaped chitinous opercula.

Distinctive features

1. Operculum shaped like a solid trumpet-mouth.
2. Tentacular crown banded in white, pink. and red.
3. Tubes with longitudinal ridges.

FAMILY **Spirorbidae**

Spirorbis spirorbis (Linnaeus)

Description · This small, tube-dwelling polychaete inhabits a sinistrally coiled (left-handed), smooth, white, calcareous tube about 3–4 mm in overall diameter, with a prominent flange spreading over attachment surface. Worm up to 3–3.5 mm long, consists of 21–35 chaetae-bearing segments, three of which are thoracic, and head bearing two gills, each composed of 4–5 small, transparent filaments. Operculum comparatively large and usually distinct, ending in oblique calcareous plate. Long known as *S. borealis* and still often listed erroneously under this name. **Habitat & ecology** · Typically found attached to fronds of lower-shore brown seaweed *Fucus serratus*, it also lives on kelps or on basal parts of *Himanthalia* in shallow sublittoral situations. **Similar species** · Among other species with which *S. spirorbis* may be confused are *S. corallinae*, which lives attached to red alga *Corallina officinalis*, *S. rupestris*, which lives attached to rocks encrusted with calcareous red algae, and *S. tridentatus*, which is found on rocks, stones, and shells in sheltered gullies and pools. Several other species of polychaete inhabit similar tubes, often on other types of substrate.

Abundance & distribution
Abundant. Found on all coasts of Britain and Ireland. Distributed from northern Norway to the Channel.

Class Oligochaeta

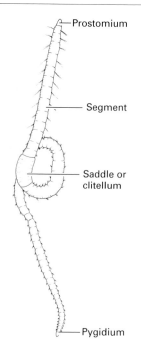

Oligochaetes, typified by the well-known earthworms, are also found in aquatic habitats. Many aquatic marine species are very small and extremely difficult to identify, though they may fairly easily be found under rotting seaweed on the strand-line or in richly organic estuarine muds. Marine and estuarine oligochaetes generally have a simple conical head, sometimes with eyespots but no appendages. The **prostomium** may be extended some distance in front of the mouth. The body is typically long, cylindrical, and slender, with a large number of segments, each of which bears four bundles of **chaetae**, two situated dorsolaterally, two ventrolaterally. The number of chaetae is smaller than that found in polychaetes. Individual chaetae are very variable in size and shape; in the dorsolateral bundles found in many members of the families **Naididae** and **Tubificidae**, for example, they are long and slender (**hair chaetae**), whereas in others they are flatter and somewhat curved or scimitar-like (**sigmoid**

Prostomium

Segment

Saddle or clitellum

Pygidium

Some of the external features of an oligochaete

Distinctive features

1. Lives in small, white, coiled, calcareous tube.
2. Head with two gills, composed of 4–5 transparent filaments.
3. Operculum ends in oblique calcareous plate.

chaetae). Often the tips of the chaetae are forked or toothed. All oligochaetes are **hermaphroditic**, with paired male and female reproductive organs opening separately on the ventral body surface. Cross-fertilisation is normal, spermatozoa sometimes being stored for long periods of time in a pair of special sacs (**spermathecae**). The segments bearing the reproductive organs are sometimes thicker in diameter than those of the remainder of the body, forming a **saddle** or **clitellum** which often secretes a **cocoon** into which the sexual gametes are discharged during breeding. The position of the male and female **genital pores** and **spermathecal pores** can often be used to distinguish between oligochaete families but are usually hard to find and require microscopic examination. Many aquatic oligochaetes reproduce asexually; naidids, for example, bud off chains of daughter individuals, whilst tubificids, at least under artificial conditions, undergo **fission** (the body breaks up into a number of fragments, each of which then develops into a new worm).

Marine oligochaetes are not a well studied group, and some species which can be found living at the strand-line, under rotting vegetation, appear perfectly capable of surviving under fully terrestrial conditions. Other species normally found in freshwater are clearly tolerant of varying salinity levels for they may also be common in estuarine muds, or occur intertidally where freshwater run-offs cross beaches and where they will be subject to more saline conditions during high tide. Within north-west European waters three major families are known. These are the **Enchytraeidae** (pot worms), **Naididae** (naidids), and **Tubificidae** (sludge worms).

Insects, crabs, barnacles, shrimps, and sea spiders

Phylum Arthropoda

A large and varied group of invertebrates characterised by a number of features, the most obvious of which is a bilaterally symmetrical and **segmented** body. Each segment primitively has a pair of jointed appendages but many arthropod groups have a strong tendency towards specialisation of certain groups of segments of the body, known as **tagmosis**. Thus specialised regions, such as the head, thorax, and abdomen may be called **tagmata**. The **cuticle** of arthropods forms a **chitinous exoskeleton** that in some groups is heavily **calcified**. This means that arthropods have to go through a process of **moulting** or **ecdysis** in order to grow. The body cavity or **coelom** in arthropods is reduced to parts of the reproductive and excretory systems. The body cavity is open and called a **haemocoel**. The haemocoel is effectively a blood-filled chamber in which the organs are in direct contact with the body fluid. There is still a muscular dorsal blood vessel that functions as a **heart**. The gut in arthropods has a mouth and anus, and the nervous system is similar to that of annelids in consisting of a **dorsal brain** and paired **ventral nerve cords**. Arthropods have a pair of **compound eyes** and a number of simple **median eyes**, though in some groups these have become reduced or lost.

There has been much debate about the systematics of the phylum. There are opposing views as to whether or not it is **monophyletic** (all members arising from a distant common ancestor). Here we take the view that the phylum is monophyletic and therefore the main arthropod groups are treated as subphyla rather than phyla in their own right.

Subphylum Uniramia

In uniramians the body is divided into a distinct **cephalon** or head region and a **trunk** that may or may not be specialised into tagmata. There are four pairs of cephalic

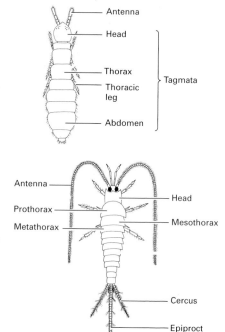

The external parts of a collembolan (*top*) and an apterygote insect (*bottom*).

appendages, one pair of preoral antennae, and three pairs of postoral appendages. Three classes are the **Myriapoda**, in which the trunk is elongate and consists of homogenous segments, the **Collembola** (springtails), and the **Insecta**, in which the trunk is divided into thorax and abdomen.

A subclass of the **Myriapoda**, the **Chilopoda** (centipedes) are long, flattened, predatory arthropods with a large number of body segments, each possessing a single pair of legs. Each segment is composed of a dorsal tergite, a ventral sternite, and several lateral pleurites. Tergites are often divided transversely. The head bears eyes and a pair of long antennae. Intertidal and supralittoral centipedes belong in the order **Geophilomorpha**, a group of mainly fully terrestrial burrowing species.

Most **collembolans** live in moist soils on land, though a few are found intertidally. The body, usually covered with bristles (**setae**) or sometimes scales of different types, is subdivided into three regions (**tagmata**): head, a thorax of three segments, and an abdomen of six. The paired antennae on the head mostly have four segments, their lengths varying between species. Groups of 1–8 eyes (**ocelli**) are situated on each side of the head, and in many forms a **post-antennal organ** is situated between the antennae and eyes. A ventral extension of the head capsule forms a pouch in which the **mouth-parts** are located. Each of the thoracic segments bears a pair of legs that end in claws, typically with teeth on them. On the underside of the first abdominal segment a bilobed **ventral tube** is used for attachment to the substrate, whilst the fourth segment often has a **furcula** (**springing organ**) from which the group gets its common name of springtails.

The sexes are separate, eggs being laid singly or in batches. Often there are 5–7 immature stages in the life-cycle. The diet of collembolans is predominantly decaying organic matter (**saprophagous**), though some terrestrial species feed on soil nematodes.

In **insects** the body, covered by a thickened **cuticle**, is composed of three segmented regions (**tagmata**): head, thorax, and abdomen, with the segments showing various degrees of fusion. In the head all six segments are fully fused, but the thorax comprises three distinct segments termed, from front to back, **prothorax**, **mesothorax**, and **metathorax**, and the number of abdominal segments is variable. Each segment typically has a dorsal **tergum**, a ventral **sternum** and, on each side, a **pleuron**; in some forms these are divided into a number of **sclerites**. The head possesses a single pair of **antennae**, paired **mandibles** and **maxillae** and a single **labium** formed by partial fusion of the second maxillae. There are typically three pairs of thoracic legs. Most insects possess one or two pairs of **wings** on the meso- and/or metathorax, but one subclass which has never developed wings (the **Apterygota**) includes the order **Thysanura** (**bristle-tails**). Winged insects, or those which have secondarily lost their wings, comprise the subclass **Pterygota**. Insects lay eggs which in most groups develop into larvae, but in the Apterygota the eggs hatch directly into miniature, sexually immature, adults.

Bristle-tails are amongst the most primitive Apterygota, with elongate, spindle-shaped bodies that are widest towards the front. The antennae on the head are slender and thread-like, and the terminal abdominal segment bears a median slender tail (**epiproct**) which is flanked on each side by two equally long **cerci**.

Further reading

Blower, J. G. (1985). Millipedes. *Synopses of the British Fauna, New Series*, **35**, 1-242.

Elliot, P., King, P. E., Morgan, C. I., Pugh, P. J. A., Smith, A. and Wheeler, S. L. A. (1990). Chelicerata, Uniramia, and Tardigrada. In *The marine fauna of the British Isles and North-West Europe* (eds P. J. Hayward & J. S. Ryland), Vol. 1, pp. 553–627. Clarendon Press, Oxford.

SUPERCLASS **Hexapoda** | CLASS **Collembola** | ORDER **Podurida**

FAMILY **Neanuridae**

Anurida maritima (Guerin)

Description · This small, wingless, insect-like animal is up to about 3 mm long, and a blackish-blue to slate blue colour. The head possesses a pair of small black eyes and a single pair of short antennae. The thorax bears three pairs of legs, and the plump, segmented abdomen is broad towards its hind end. The body is covered with short hairs. Previously known as *Lipura maritima*.

Habitat & ecology · Found intertidally on the upper shore, crawling on rocks or seaweeds, or floating on the surface film of rock pools. Although small, its habit of forming groups on the surface of rock pools makes it quite easy to find. During high tidal periods it shelters in rocky crevices. **Similar species** · *Anuridella marina* is somewhat similar to *A. maritima* but smaller, only about 1–2 mm long, and a fairly bright yellowish-white. Less common than *A. maritima*, it occurs on west coasts of Britain and Ireland, and is distributed south to the Mediterranean.

Abundance & distribution
Common, locally abundant. Found around all coasts of Britain and Ireland. Distributed from the North Sea south to the Mediterranean.

Subphylum Crustacea

With more than 30 000 species known worldwide, the **Crustacea** show enormous diversity in structure, adaptation, and development. Although most species are marine, occurring in all habitats from the abyssal depths to the supralittoral levels of the shore, terrestrial and freshwater forms are by no means uncommon. The basic crustacean body consists of segments (**somites**) arranged into distinct regions, the **head**, **thorax**, and **abdomen**, with a tailpiece, the **telson**. A number of the anterior thoracic somites, typically two, may in some groups be fused with the head, and a fold derived from the head reaches posteriorly to cover most or all of the thorax as a distinct **carapace**. The organisation of the abdomen also varies considerably, depending upon the group, and it is often greatly reduced. The **exoskeleton** of crustaceans is basically composed of **chitin** but reinforced with **calcium carbonate** to give it rigidity. Growth necessitates periodic moulting (**ecdysis**) of the exoskeleton, this being under **hormonal** control and involving resorption of calcium salts from the old exoskeleton which are then deposited in the newly formed chitinous shell. Each body segment, except for the head, primitively bears a single pair of **biramous** (forked or two-branched) appendages, though the head has three pairs (called either the **antennule**, **antenna**, and **mandibles**, or **antenna 1**, **antenna 2**, and **mandibles**). The appendages of the two

anterior thoracic somites are modified for use as accessory feeding structures and comprise the **maxillule** (**maxilla 1**) and **maxilla** (**maxilla 2**). The remaining thoracic appendages (**pereopods**), together with those of the abdomen (**pleopods**), are widely modified in the different groups of the phylum. Pereopods are usually modified for walking or swimming, but are sometimes **chelate** (bear claws) and then used for feeding or aggression. Pleopods are mostly used for reproduction, locomotion, and brooding.

A biramous crustacean limb has two segmented **rami**, comprising the external **exopodite** and the internal **endopodite**, both of which arise from a **peduncle** consisting of two **articles** (parts), the **coxa** and **basis**. The peduncle of the limbs in all crustacean groups is followed successively by an **ischium**, **merus**, **carpus**, **propodus**, and terminal **dactyl**. The simple biramous type of limb is retained by some primitive crustacean groups, but in most the exopodite is developed as the major functional part, whilst the endopodite is reduced, lost, or modified for some specific purpose such as respiration, feeding, or cleaning. In a number of more advanced crustacean groups additional respiratory structures, **podobranchs** and **pleurobranchs**, are associated with the thoracic limbs.

Except for sessile barnacles (subclass **Cirripedia**), which are mostly hermaphroditic, crustaceans generally possess separate sexes. Fertilised eggs hatch into a larva, the **nauplius**.

Distinctive features

1. Segmented body with six legs but no wings.
2. Blackish-blue colour.
3. Body covered with short hairs.

In many crustacean groups this is the first free-swimming stage in the life-cycle, but in more advanced groups it and subsequent developmental stages (**instars**) may be brooded by the parent and a later larval form, the **zoea**, is often the first swimming stage. Moulting occurs between each instar.

Crustaceans range in size from less than 0.5 mm to more than 1 m. In consequence of the enormous morphological diversity distinguishable throughout the phylum, their classification and taxonomy are complex and subject to considerable debate, with no uniformly accepted system. For the purposes of the present book we adopt the classification system of Brusca & Brusca (1990) in which the subphylum Crustacea is divided into five classes: **Remepedia**, **Cephalocarida**, **Branchiopoda**, **Maxillopoda**, and **Malacostraca**. The Maxillopoda contains the subclasses **Ostracoda**, **Copepoda**, and **Cirripedia** which are treated as separate classes in many other classification schemes. Malacostracan crustaceans constitute by far the largest group, with more than 19 000 described species, and the classification within this class alone is exceedingly complicated.

Further reading

Athersuch, J. & Horne, D. J. (1984). A review of some European genera of the family Loxoconchidae (Crustacea: Ostracoda). *Zoological Journal of the Linnean Society*, **81**, 1–22.

Brusca, R. C. and Brusca, G. J. (1990). *Invertebrates* Sinauer Associates. Sunderland, Massachusetts.

Fincham, A. A. & Wickins, J. F. (1976). Identification of commercial prawns and shrimps. *British Museum (Natural History) Publications*, **779**, 1–7.

Gotto, R. V. (1979). The association of copepods with marine invertebrates. *Advances in Marine Biology*, **16**, 1–109.

Holdich, D. M. & Jones, J. A. (1983). Tanaids. *Synopses of the British Fauna, New Series*, **2**, 7, 1–98.

Ingle, R. W. (1983). Shallow-water crabs. *Synopses of the British Fauna, New Series*, **25**, 1–206.

Isaac, M. J. & Moyse, J. (1990). Crustacea I: Entomostraca. In *The marine fauna of the British Isles and North-West Europe* (eds P. J. Hayward & J. S. Ryland), Vol. 1, pp. 322–61. Clarendon Press, Oxford.

Isaac, M. J., Makings, P., Naylor, E., Smalden, G. and Withers, R. G. (1990). Crustacea II: Malacostraca Peracarida.. In *The marine fauna of the British Isles and north-west Europe* (eds P. J. Hayward & J. S. Ryland), Vol. 1, pp. 362–488. Clarendon Press, Oxford.

Jones, N. S. (1976). British cumaceans. *Synopses of the British Fauna, New Series*, **27**, 1–66.

Lincoln, R. J. (1979). *British marine Amphipoda: Gammaridea*. British Museum (Natural History), London.

Mauchline, J. (1980). The biology of mysids and euphausids. *Advances in Marine Biology*, **18**, 1–677.

Moyse, J. & Smaldon, G. (1990). Crustacea III: Malacostraca Eucarida. In *The marine fauna of the British Isles and North-West Europe* (eds P. J. Hayward & J. S. Ryland), Vol. 1, pp. 489–552. Clarendon Press, Oxford.

Naylor, E. (1972). British marine isopods. *Synopses of the British Fauna, New Series*, **3**, 1-86.

Smaldon, G. (1979). British coastal shrimps and prawns. *Synopses of the British Fauna, New Series*, **15**, 1–142.

Class Maxillopoda

The subclass **Ostracoda** comprises mostly very small crustaceans, rarely more than 1 mm in length. In general they resemble a tiny kidney bean with legs, for they are covered by a **bivalved carapace**, forming part of the exoskeleton, into which the body can be completely withdrawn. The two halves of the carapace are closed by an **adductor muscle** attached to the centre of each valve. At moulting the valves are shed, as well as the remaining exoskeletal parts. The body of ostracods is much modified and mostly has few external signs of segmentation. They possess 5–7 pairs of appendages, typically these comprising two pairs of **antennae** and a pair of **mandibles** arising from an indistinctly defined head, with the first thoracic limbs modified as a pair of **maxillae** (**maxilla 1**), the second thoracic limbs (appendage 5) either forming **maxillae 2** or the first pair of walking legs, whilst the remaining two pairs of limbs are always **thoracic walking legs**. There are no abdominal limbs, but the body posteriorly terminates in an unpaired **caudal furca** which may be in front of or behind the anus.

Although more than 150 European species of Ostracoda are known, their minute size makes them easily overlooked. They are often abundant among algae, between sessile invertebrates, under rocks, or on the surface of soft sediments, and are widespread in marine, brackish, and freshwater habitats. Most marine species are benthic, either crawling on or burrowing into the substrate, but some swim freely and a few are planktonic.

After the Malacostraca, the subclass **Copepoda** comprises the second largest crustacean group, with about 10 000 species being known worldwide. Most are small, less than about 2 mm long, with slender, spindle-shaped, and more or less distinctly segmented bodies formed into a **head** or **cephalosome**, the **thorax** or **postcephalic trunk**, and the postgenital **abdomen**. The cephalosome consists of five cephalic somites or segments and one of the thoracic somites. The thorax consists of the second to sixth thoracic somites, each with a pair of biramous swimming legs and the genital or seventh thoracic somite. Following this are four postgenital abdominal somites. Commensal and parasitic copepods have a highly modified body form. The head bears two pairs of **antennae**, which are usually well developed and used either for locomotion or grasping (**prehension**). Mouth-parts comprise paired **mandibles, maxillae 1, maxillae 2,** and **maxillipeds**. The mandibles frequently possess a **palp** and are often **biramous**. There are six thoracic segments, the first usually being fused with the head, and five abdominal segments, some of which are almost always fused. The thoracic limbs are small, and there are none on the abdomen. The terminal abdominal

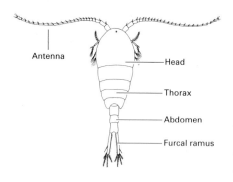

Antenna
Head
Thorax
Abdomen
Furcal ramus

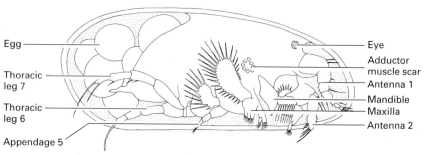

Egg
Thoracic leg 7
Thoracic leg 6
Appendage 5
Eye
Adductor muscle scar
Antenna 1
Mandible
Maxilla
Antenna 2

The main features of copepod (*top*) and ostracod (*bottom*) crustaceans.

segment bears a pair of short or very long furcal rami which are typically bristly (**setose**). During their reproductive period female copepods are easily identified by the large single or paired, sometimes brightly coloured, egg sacs carried below or on either side of the abdomen.

The subclass is divided into two infraclasses, the **Progymnoplea** and the **Neocopepoda**, which are distinguished by the form of body tagmosis. The Progymnoplea consists of the genus *Platycopia*, a group of small, free-living copepods that occur above the seabed in shallow seas such as the North Sea. The other two genera are only found in caves. Nine neocopepod orders are recognised. Members of the orders **Calanoida** and **Cyclopoida** are both abundant and very important members of the zooplankton, whilst members of the order **Harpacticoida** are common in or on soft sediments or in silty areas of many marine habitats. Many groups of copepods, with the exception of the orders Calanoida and **Misophrioida**, contain commensal or parasitic species and some orders are exclusively parasitic, the modifications to their adult morphology making them almost unrecognisable as copepods. Those species parasitic on fishes are better known than those infesting invertebrates. In general the identification of copepods is difficult and requires both microscopic examination and specialist knowledge.

The main order of the subclass **Cirripedia**, the **Thoracica**, is the largest within the class **Maxillopoda** and encompasses all the true barnacles. Adult barnacles possess a highly modified body (**prosoma**), with six pairs of biramous thoracic limbs (**cirri**) and three pairs of head appendages (two pairs of **maxillae** and the **mandibles**). The first two pairs of thoracic cirri are often modified to function as **maxillipeds**, the remainder are long and feathery (**setose**), forming a curved, fan-like net which is actively swept through the water to filter out suspended particulate material. The order Thoracica contains three suborders, two of them, the **Balanomorpha** and **Verrucomorpha**, commonly being referred to as acorn barnacles, the third, the **Lepadomorpha**, comprising the stalked or goose barnacles.

Acorn barnacles have their body enclosed by calcareous **wall plates**; these consist of a dorsal **carina**, a ventral **rostrum**, and paired lateral plates (**carinolaterals** and **rostrolaterals**). In some species the number of wall plates is reduced, in others there may be additional accessory plates. Adults are attached directly to any suitable secure surface, such as rocks or mollusc shells, by a cuticular or calcified **base**, their plates forming a low conical shape with an opening at the top which is closed by **opercular plates**; there are only two plates in the family **Verrucidae**, the shell opening being to one side, but four in the families **Balanidae** and **Chthamalidae**, where the opercular plates form paired **terga** (at the carinal end of the opening) and **scuta** (at the rostral end). These plates form two door-like flaps which open to allow the cirri to emerge; each consists of one **tergum** and one **scutum**, hinged together where they meet in the midline and edged by a flexible **tergoscutal flap** that is sometimes brightly coloured. In lepadomorph barnacles the body and plates form a **capitulum** which is attached to the substrate by a fleshy stalk or **peduncle**. The peduncle houses the ovary and may or may not be armoured with plates.

Most barnacles are hermaphroditic, with internal fertilisation and the eggs hatching into a free-swimming **nauplius** larva, which has three pairs of appendages. Nauplii grow and feed as zooplankton, then moulting to form a **cyprid** larval stage that has a bivalve **carapace**, six pairs of swimming limbs, and an obvious pair of antennae. The antennae are used for exploring the substrate prior to settlement, which is followed by **metamorphosis** into the adult stage. As it is the cyprid carapace that develops into the wall plates of the adult, the 'acorn' comprises part of the exoskeleton. Uniquely among crustaceans, barnacles do not shed all of their exoskeleton when they moult but shed only the flexible covering of the prosoma and appendages, not the wall plates.

Some barnacles, such as members of the order **Rhizocephala**, are not recognisable as such as adults, although they have the typical naupliid and cyprid larval stages in their life-cycle. Adults typically infest crabs or hermit crabs and possess highly modified bodies.

SUBCLASS **Cirripedia** | ORDER **Thoracica** | SUBORDER **Lepadomorpha**

FAMILY **Scalpellidae**

Scalpellum scalpellum (Linnaeus)

Description · This barnacle has a peduncle or stalk up to 2–2.5 cm long, thick and stiff, and covered by large numbers of small, overlapping plates arranged in transverse rows. Attached to the stalk is a distinctively shaped capitulum, somewhat trapezoid with a pointed or beaked tip. It is about 2.5–3 cm long and composed of 13 roughly triangular plates; these comprise six pairs of lateral plates, variously aligned, and a single elongate carinal plate with an obvious median ridge. **Habitat & ecology** · A sublittoral species, found at depths of 10–500 m or more, permanently attached to rocks, boulders, shells, hydroids, erect bryozoans, etc. **Similar species** · Resembles smaller, *Pollicipes pollicipes*, which is found on the lower shore and in shallower sublittoral situations. It can be distinguished by the short, broad capitulum, and the short length of the stalk (much shorter than the capitulum).

Abundance & distribution
Locally uncommon. Found on the west coasts of Britain and Ireland. Distributed from Iceland and Norway to the Mediterranean, Azores, and West Africa.

FAMILY **Lepadidae**

Lepas anatifera Linnaeus **Common goose barnacle**

Description · This barnacle consists of a flexible stalk 4–85 cm long, flexible and contractile. When contracted partially or wholly, this stalk is wrinkled. It is purplish- to greyish-brown in colour. Attached to the stalk is the roughly oblong capitulum (enclosed cavity with most of the body parts). This is up to 4–5 cm long with five large, smooth, and translucent white calcareous plates, often with a tinge of blue-grey, separated by dark reddish-brown to black skin. **Habitat & ecology** · Naturally pelagic, growing in colonies on large or small floating objects such as driftwood, bottles, etc. Usually found after westerly gales, and is the commonest species of goose barnacle washed up on British shores. **Similar species** · There are several other species of *Lepas* which may be mistaken for this form, particularly *L. anserifera*, but they are usually less commonly found stranded on European shores.

Abundance & distribution
Cosmopolitan in warmer seas, its abundance depends on size of floating object to which colony is attached, but may run to thousands of specimens. Rarely stranded on North Sea shores; more common on south and west shores of British Isles or Atlantic European coasts.

SUBORDER **Verrucomorpha**

FAMILY **Verrucidae**

Verruca stroemia (Müller)

Description · Very small barnacle, up to 5 mm in diameter, flat and irregular in shape. Shell with four very differently sized plates, two derived from plates of the shell aperture (one tergal, one scutal), the other two mostly regarded as equivalent to carinal and rostral plates of other barnacles. All four plates have radiating crests that interlock at the sutures between plates and are marked with heavy grooves and striations. The outline is irregularly rounded or square. The operculum of the shell opening consists of only a single flat plate. The tergoscutal flaps bordering the open aperture are pink or red, the base is uncalcified. **Habitat & ecology** · Found on the lower shore to sublittoral depths of 500 m or more, attached to rocks, boulders, shells, algal holdfasts, or almost any suitable surface, or in rock crevices.

Abundance & distribution
Common, locally abundant, though sometimes overlooked because of its small size. Found all around Britain and Ireland. Distributed from Iceland and Arctic Norway to the Mediterranean.

Distinctive features

1. Capitulum of 13 plates, six pairs of laterals, and single carinal with distinct median ridge.
2. Peduncle short, stiff, covered by transverse rows of small, overlapping plates.

Distinctive features

1. Capitulum with five whitish plates separated by dark reddish-brown to black skin.
2. Plates often tinged blue-grey.
3. Peduncle or stalk contractile, flexible.

Distinctive features

1. Flat, irregularly shaped shell made of four differently sized plates.
2. Shell opening with single, flat plate.
3. Open shell bordered by pink or red tergoscutal flaps.

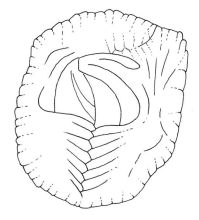

Balanomorph barnacles

One of the most important space-occupying organisms on the rocky shores of northern Europe. They become increasingly dominant on exposed shores, replacing intertidal, canopy-forming, algae such as fucoids at the most exposed locations. On shores of intermediate exposure barnacles are involved in a complex system of patch dynamics. Fucoid algae, limpets, or barnacles inhabit different areas on the shore, creating a patch mosaic that changes over a period of years. These changes are regulated through predation by animals such as dogwhelks and seabirds, disturbance from storm events, natural variability in the recruitment of larvae of barnacles and limpets and the spores of algae, and competition between the space-occupying sessile animals and plants. Moving further south in Europe, the influence of canopy-forming algae on shores decreases and barnacles become more dominant.

The identification of these barnacles is difficult, as they can vary in shape according to the degree of crowding from other barnacles, but may be aided by examination of the colour of the tergoscutal flaps beneath the plates of the shell opening. Barnacles may open their apertures to reveal the colour of these flaps if splashed with a little seawater.

SUBORDER **Balanomorpha**

FAMILY **Chthamalidae**

Chthamalus montagui Southward

Description · Small barnacles, about 6–10 mm in diameter, with a low conical shape and irregular, slightly crenellate outline. The opening is kite-shaped and the tergal plates are less than half the length of the scutal, and join close to one edge of the shell. The shell has six solid, coarsely ridged plates, the anterior slightly larger than the posterior, but the surface is often so corroded that sutures between plates are indistinguishable. The shell is brownish or greyish, the tergoscutal flaps blue with brown and black markings. **Habitat & ecology** · Upper shore, attached to rocks on moderately exposed shores, occasionally found at low water neap tide level. Breeds during summer. **Similar species** · Adult *C. stellatus* have oval or circular opening and the tergoscutal flaps are bright blue with orange and black markings.

Abundance & distribution · Locally common. (a) *C. montagui* found on south and west coasts of British Isles but also reported from Irish Sea and, becoming increasingly less common, southwards to Mediterranean. *C. stellatus* (b) has similar distribution but is rare in Irish Sea.

FAMILY **Balanidae**

Balanus balanus (Linnaeus)

Description · Large barnacles, up to 2.5–3 cm in diameter, with a very irregular outline and opening that is pointed in front but rounded at the rear. The wall has six plates, the front and rear plates being very similar in size. The plates are thick and heavily ridged, white or with a brownish tinge. The anterior scutal plates of the shell aperture have prominent ridges, the terga are sharply pointed. The flaps between the scuta and terga have a yellow edge and are striped brown and white. The shell base is calcified. **Habitat & ecology** · Intertidal on lower shore to sublittoral depths of several hundred metres, attached to rocks, boulders, stones, and shells. Also found on hulls of ships and boats. **Similar species** · Several other barnacle species have a crenellate shape to their shell edge, but that of *B. balanus* is both very irregular and crenellate. The shape of the shell aperture in other forms is also either diamond-shaped or broadly oval.

Abundance & distribution
Common, locally abundant. Found all around the British Isles and Ireland except for Cornwall. Distributed from Arctic Norway and Iceland to the British Isles.

469

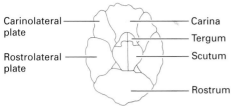

An acorn barnacle viewed from above, showing the pattern of plates making up the wall and the four plates that close the shell opening.

Distinctive features

1. Low, conical-shaped shell with six coarsely ridged plates.
2. Opening kite-shaped, tergal plates and scutal plates join close to one end of shell.
3. Tergoscutal flaps blue with brown and black markings.

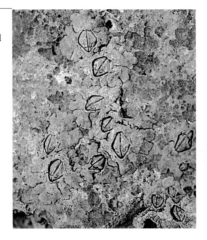

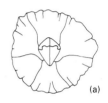

(a)

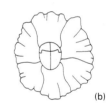

(b)

Distinctive features

1. Shell composed of six thick and heavily ridged plates; front and rear plates very similar in size.
2. Shell opening pointed at front, rounded at rear.
3. Shell outline very irregular.

Balanus crenatus Bruguière

Description · Moderately sized, up to 2 cm in diameter. Conical shape when growing alone but taller and more columnar when densely crowded. Shell aperture roughly diamond-shaped. Shell has six white plates, typically smooth in young individuals but irregularly ribbed in adults. Front and rear plates obviously dissimilar in size. Tergoscutal flaps edged in turn with yellow, brown, and yellow stripes. Calcareous shell base ridged with radiating lines. **Habitat & ecology** · Lower shore and shallow sublittoral, attached to rocks and boulders, small stones, old shells, ship hulls, and almost any artificial structure. Often on or underneath algae, especially *Fucus serratus*. **Similar species** · In densely crowded populations *B. crenatus* (a) may be confused with other barnacles because its features are obscured. The introduced *B. amphitrite* is similar but has thin, pearly white or grey plates marked with several dark brown or purple stripes. Tergoscutal flaps white with black or purple spots (b). Estuarine *B. improvisus* resembles *B. amphitrite*, but shell plates not striped (c). Tergoscutal flaps spotted with pale purple and white.

Abundance & distribution
Very common, locally abundant. Found all around Britain and Ireland but may be scarce on the east coast of Britain. Distributed from Arctic coasts to Bordeaux in the Bay of Biscay.

Balanus perforatus Bruguière

Description · Large barnacles, typically volcano-shaped and up to 3–5 cm in diameter and in height, with a simple, circular outline and small oval opening in which the tergal and scutal plates are deeply located. The wall has six plates, but the sutures between adjacent plates are often obscure. The plates are strong and finely ribbed, variously coloured dull purple to pink or white, in part striped, but becoming a dull grey colour when eroded. The tergoscutal flaps are brown or purplish with patches of blue and white. The shell base is porous and calcareous. **Habitat & ecology** · Found on almost any suitable hard surface, from ships and artificial structures to rocks and boulders, at mid-shore levels to shallow sublittoral situations. **Similar species** · Although there are several other European species of barnacles, the classic conical shape and coloration of *B. perforatus* usually distinguish it easily from other forms.

Abundance & distribution
Common, locally abundant. Found in south-west Britain. Distributed south to West Africa, including the Mediterranean.

Elminius modestus Darwin

Description · Small, only about 5–10 mm in diameter, with low conical shape, irregular rounded outline, and fairly large, diamond-shaped opening. Wall has four symmetrically placed and notched plates that are smooth in young individuals but become coarsely ridged with age. Shells opalescent greyish-white in young examples, becoming dull greyish-brown in older and corroded shells. Tergoscutal flaps white, with central brownish-orange spot. Barnacle base calcareous. **Habitat & ecology** · Upper-middle shore to shallow sublittoral, found attached to variety of surfaces, such as algae, rocks, boulders, shells, ship hulls, dock walls, and pier pilings. Particularly common under estuarine conditions or on open coasts subject to freshwater drainage. Fast growing, it matures early and breeds throughout year. Peak settlement of planktonic larvae occurs between late spring and autumn. Is an immigrant to European waters, being introduced from its native New Zealand during World War II. A competitor for space with *Semibalanus balanoides*, *Balanus improvisus*, and *B. crenatus*. *E. modestus* has displaced *B. improvisus* from several estuaries in UK.

Abundance & distribution
Locally common, sometimes abundant. Found on south, west, and east coasts of Britain. Also found on north coasts of France and in northern Spain. Its range is probably still extending but is limited by low temperatures in the north.

Distinctive features

1. Shell of six white plates, front and rear different in size, smooth in juveniles, irregularly ribbed in adults.
2. Shell opening diamond-shaped.
3. Shell outline very variable, depending upon density of population.

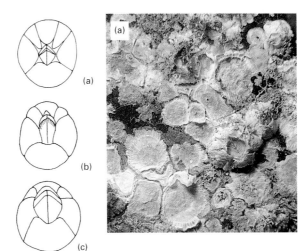

Distinctive features

1. Volcano-shaped shell composed of six plates, sutures between adjacent plates often indistinct.
2. Shell opening small, oval, deeply sunk at apex of shells.

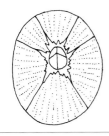

Distinctive features

1. Shell composed of four symmetrically placed plates.
2. Shell opening fairly large and diamond-shaped.

Megatrema anglicum (Leach)

Description · A very small barnacle only found on the coral *Caryophyllia smithii*. It has a cup-shaped base and a conical top giving the whole shell a vase-like shape. There are no sutures but the shell is marked with longitudinal striations. The shell opening is small and laterally compressed with the scutal and tergal plates deeply set. The diameter at the base is about 6 mm. **Habitat & ecology** · This species is always found growing in groups of a few individuals on the stony parts of the Devonshire cup coral. It is subtidal and has been found to depths of about 50 m.

Abundance & distribution
Frequent. Found on south and west coasts of Britain. Distributed south to West Africa. Also reported from the Pacific.

Semibalanus balanoides (Linnaeus)

Description · Mostly small, about 5–10 mm in diameter, rarely up to 15 mm, with a very variable shape ranging from tall and tubular when crowded to low and conical when solitary. Outline round to oval with an irregular margin. There are six white, cream, or greyish-brown shell plates; anterior plate distinctly smaller than posterior and flanked on each side by a narrow anterolateral plate. Shell opening relatively large and diamond-shaped. Scutal plates have squared projections that fit into corresponding notches in tergal plates. Tergoscutal flaps white, with brown spot on their central groove. Basis uncalcified and cuticular. **Habitat & ecology** · Mid-shore intertidal, attached to rocks, boulders, shells, or any suitable surface including artificial structures. Less often found sublittorally. Distributed around mid-tide level on moderately sheltered shores, but found further up shore as exposure increases. Isolated specimens usually fairly easy to identify, but in crowded populations many characteristic features may be hidden and it may then be confused with other barnacle species which form dense communities.

Abundance & distribution
Common, locally very abundant. Occurs on all British and Irish coasts. Distributed from Arctic Norway to Spain.

Class Malacostraca

The largest of the crustacean classes, with more than 20 000 species known from marine, freshwater, and terrestrial habitats, **malacostracans** possess **compound eyes**, two pairs of usually well-developed **antennae** (the first pair typically biramous), and a fused head and thorax generally covered by a **carapace**. Primitively the **head** consists of five segments, the thorax (**pereon**) eight, and the abdomen (**pleon**) six, rarely seven. The head and pereon may be fused. Both the thoracic and abdominal segments bear basically biramous appendages although in many groups they are modified, reduced, or completely lost. The first three pairs of thoracic appendages are used in feeding, the remaining five pairs are typically developed as walking legs (**pereopods**). The abdominal appendages (**pleopods** and **uropods**) are variously modified for swimming, reproduction, or respiration.

Among all the crustaceans, the Malacostraca exhibit the widest range of adaptive, morphological, ecological, and functional diversity, and are often both common and widespread in marine habitats. Most are particle-feeding scavengers, but some filter-feed on plankton and others are actively carnivorous. The classification of the Malacostraca is complex. There are two recognised subclasses, the **Phyllocarida** and the **Eumalacostraca**.

A primitive group of malacostracans, most

Distinctive features

1. A small, vase-shaped barnacle.
2. Always growing on the coral *Caryophyllia smithii*.

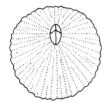

Distinctive features

1. Shell made of six plates, anterior plate obviously smaller than posterior.
2. Scutal plates with squared projection that fits notch in tergal plates.

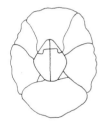

phyllocarids are known only as fossils. Only one order, the **Leptostraca**, contains living representatives, with about ten described species. Leptostracans are comparatively small, rather shrimp-like crustaceans, with their thorax and part of the abdomen enclosed in a large, bivalved **carapace** hinged along the mid-dorsal line. An **adductor muscle** attaches the carapace to the head region, the head being covered by a dorsal **rostral plate** which is hinged and moveable. Anteriorly **antennae** extend from under the carapace, those of the male possessing a slender **antennal flagellum** almost as long as the body. The eight thoracic segments each possess a pair of biramous leaf- or plate-shaped limbs which are either used for swimming and feeding or, in females, may be modified for egg brooding. The abdomen consists of seven segments, all but the last bearing appendages which are either **biramous** and well-developed (segments 1–4), or reduced and **uniramous** (segments 5 and 6). The abdomen ends posteriorly in a pair of long **furcal rami**.

The only leptostracan species commonly found in British waters, *Nebalia bipes* (Fabricius) (family **Nebaliidae**), occurs intertidally in rock pools and shallow sublittoral situations, often abundantly, under stones, in rotting algae, or in shaded rock pools. The sexes exhibit anatomical **sexual dimorphism** in that the carapace and furcal rami of the male are proportionately longer than those of the female, and whereas **antenna 2** in males reaches back virtually to the end of the body, in females it is shorter than the length of the carapace. Up to 12 mm long, they are light to dark brown or greenish, and possess large, stalked red eyes. *N. bipes* is distributed from northern Norway and Iceland to the Mediterranean. A similar species, *N. typhlops* (Sars) occurs in deep water to the west of Britain and Ireland. It lacks obvious eyes.

Superorder Eucarida

This superorder of the subclass Eumalacostraca encompasses the best known of all the malacostracan groups, including forms such as crabs, prawns, shrimps, and lobsters. In all, the thorax is dorsally fused to a rigid carapace which shows no external signs of segmentation. Eggs are typically brooded by the female, attached to the abdominal appendages. The eggs hatch into **post-naupliar** larvae which then pass through a series of larval stages (**instars**) before undergoing the final metamorphosis into the adult form.

The largest group of eucaridan malacostracans, the order **Decapoda**, contains a variety of body forms and structures so great that the classification of decapods is very complex. In all, the thoracic segments are dorsally fused to a carapace that extends on either side as a fold to form the **branchial chambers** enclosing the **gills**. Water circulation through the branchial chambers is achieved by rhythmic beating of the **scaphognathites**, the large modified **endopodites** of the **maxillae**. There are five pairs of thoracic limbs, the first pair usually ending in **chelae** (claws) and termed **chelipeds**. There are also typically five pairs of biramous abdominal limbs (**pleopods**), usually used for swimming or, in the females of some groups, for brooding the eggs.

Decapods are often divided into two suborders on the basis of the adult mode of locomotion; the **Natantia** comprises the swimming decapods, the **Reptantia** the walking decapods. A more natural classification is achieved, however, on the basis of morphological and reproductive features, by recognising the suborders **Dendrobranchiata**

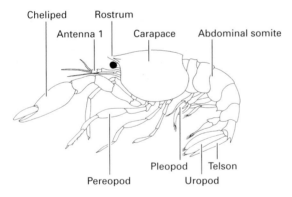

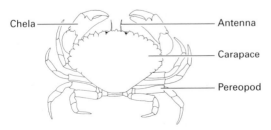

The main external features of natantic (*top*) and reptantic (*bottom*) decapod crustaceans.

(with branched gills and eggs not being brooded by the females but hatching into a planktonic **nauplius** larva) and **Pleocyemata** (with unbranched gills and eggs being brooded by the females, hatching into a planktonic **zoea** larva). The Dendrobranchiata contains a single **infraorder**, the **Periaeidea**, whereas the Pleocyemata comprises seven infraorders (including the **Caridea, Thalassinidea, Astacidea, Palinura, Anomura** and **Brachyura**), of which four together are equivalent to the Reptantia, the remaining three (plus the dendrobranchiate Periaeidea) corresponding to the Natantia.

Suborder Pleocyemata

Caridean prawns and shrimps, and other natantic decapods, typically have an elongate body, sometimes bilaterally compressed, divided into a **cephalothorax** and **abdomen**, usually with a terminal posterior **telson** forming, with the **uropods**, a distinctive **tail-fan**. The **carapace** in many groups has a prominent anterior **rostrum** projecting forwards between the stalked eyes and two pairs of antennae. The rostrum may be toothed or smooth, long (as in most prawns) or short (as in shrimps). The first pair of antennae (or **antennules**) in most groups bears a **biramous** flagellum, but in the prawn family Palaemonidae the flagellum is **triramous** (three-branched). The first two or three pairs of thoracic limbs are usually clawed (**chelate**). The **mouth-parts** consist of a pair of **mandibles**, two pairs of **maxillae**, and three pairs of **maxillipeds**, the maxillipeds representing modifications of the first three pairs of thoracic limbs although the third pair is typically the least modified. There are five pairs of **pereopods** (thoracic limbs) used for locomotion, the anterior two or three pairs ending in a **chela** (claw) and being used for feeding, defence, and offence. Each abdominal segment bears a pair of **biramous pleopods** which beat rhythmically and are used for swimming. The sixth pleopods are both flattened and expanded, forming **uropods** which form a part of the tail-fan.

The sexes are separate, eggs being carried by the females attached to long bristles (**setae**) developed on the abdominal pleopods. The eggs hatch into a planktonic **zoea** larva which passes through several further larval stages before attaining the adult form.

Most carideans are marine, frequently being found in intertidal or shallow sublittoral situations, often much deeper, though brackish-water, fresh water, and estuarine species are common. Several species are of commercial importance as a shellfish food. In north-west European waters representatives of seven families are commonly encountered, including the **Alpheidae** (which resemble small lobsters), **Crangonidae** (shrimps), **Hippolytidae** (humpback prawns), two prawn families (**Palaemonidae, Pandalidae**), and the **Pasiphaeidae** and **Processidae**.

Thalassinids are a group of mud and ghost shrimps that live in deep burrows in mud or sand, or in coral rubble. They generally have a dorsoventrally flattened abdomen, a well developed tail and a smooth, laterally compressed carapace. The first two pairs of pereopods are chelate and the first pair is often enlarged. The relationships both within the group and between it and other decapod groups are uncertain and they are sometimes grouped with the Anomura. A few species are common in European waters but are rarely seen as they live deep within burrows. They include the genera *Callianassa* and *Upogebia*.

Astacideans (lobsters) often possess a heavy, strong exoskeleton. The **carapace** is elongate, cylindrical or slightly flattened, but not fused ventrally. Its surface possesses a transverse groove (**post-cervical groove**) and oblique grooves (**branchiocardiac grooves**) which meet dorsally. The first three pairs of thoracic limbs are **chelate** (clawed), the **chelae** on the first pair of limbs being characteristically enlarged and massive to form powerful claws. The abdomen is usually elongate, cylindrical or compressed, and usually ends in a well-developed **tail-fan**.

In European waters members of the family **Nephropidae**, including the common lobster, and Norway lobster or scampi, are commercially important and well-known.

Palinurans (spiny lobsters and crawfish) typically possess a heavily armoured exoskeleton. The **carapace** is broad, somewhat flattened, and rectangular or almost cylindrical, its lateral margins in many forms being well-defined and covered with numerous **spines** or **teeth**. Spines are also found over many parts of the abdomen and on the larger limbs. There is normally no **rostrum**. The **pereopods** (thoracic limbs) are either all without claws, or the first four pairs or all five possess **chelae**. The edge of the carapace above the eyes is often deeply indented (**orbital indentations**), though the eyes are sometimes reduced. In many members of the family **Palinuridae** the **peduncle** of **antenna 2** is massively enlarged, thick, and spiny, with a long, stout flagellum. In the family **Scyllaridae** all five pairs of **pereopods** are similar and without **chelae**, the first antennae are slender and short, and the second antennae are much modified, with no flagellum, and look like broad, flat plates. The **tail-fan** is often wide and strong, and used for rapid swimming during escape.

Palinurans are characteristically found subtidally in shallower inshore waters, on coarse sandy or gravelly sediments, or under rocks and boulders. In north-west European waters species of Palinuridae and Scyllaridae are often common, whereas representatives of a third family, **Polychelidae**, are less often encountered as they live in the deep sea.

Anomuran decapods (hermit crabs, porcelain crabs, and squat lobsters) possess a very variable body form but, in all, the **carapace** is not fused with the ventral part of the exoskeleton in front of the mouth. The first **pereopods** (thoracic limbs) are typically large and bear claws, but the fifth thoracic limbs tend to be small, reduced, and hidden. The last thoracic segment is free from the carapace.

With about nine anomuran families represented in north-west European waters, the three best known are:

Paguridae (hermit crabs) Body adapted for living in gastropod shells, carapace is reduced, abdomen is soft and asymmetrically twisted or coiled to fit the internal contours of the shell inhabited. **Pleopods** (abdominal limbs) are mostly missing, except in females where those on the left side of the abdomen are retained for holding the developing eggs. In both sexes the last left **pereopod** (thoracic limb) is retained and modified as a **hook** for anchoring the animal inside its shell. More

than 20 species of hermit crabs are recorded from European coasts, typically in intertidal to sublittoral situations and often aggregated in large numbers, especially in mid- to lower-shore rock pools.

Galatheidae (squat lobsters) Dorso-ventrally flattened, elongate, and somewhat oval when viewed from above, with a lightly calcified carapace which is longer than it is wide and bears obvious transverse **sutures**. The **carapace** and limbs may be spiny. The abdomen is tightly tucked under the thorax (**reflexed**). The eyes tend to be large and distinct, and the eye sockets have a spiny **rostrum** on their outer margins. The **chelipeds** are mostly much longer than the carapace, with long and slender **chelae**; some species can give a vicious and painful nip. There are about ten European species, usually found from the lower shore to sublittoral depths under boulders or on coarse substrates. This group is relatively common in the deep sea.

Porcellanidae (porcelain crabs) Carapace small, almost circular, abdomen thin and flattened, **flexed** beneath the thorax. The first pair of **pereopods** is enlarged and armed with large claws (**chelate**), the fifth pereopods are small, thin and held tucked away inside the **branchial chamber**. The **antennae** tend to be long and slender. Both of the common European species are suspension feeders, found living on the lower shore or sublittorally on rocky or coarse gravelly sediments, or attached to bushy and erect hydroid or bryozoan colonies.

True crabs belong to the infraorder **Brachyura** and are mainly bottom-dwelling, walking decapods found living intertidally or sublittorally, although some species can swim actively. They are usually strongly built, with a heavy exoskeleton. The **carapace** is dorsoven-trally flattened, mostly with sharpened rims, and fused to the ventral exoskeleton below the mouth. The shape of the carapace is often a useful aid to species identification. **Antennae** are usually short. The **abdomen** is reduced and **flexed** forwards underneath the carapace. The first pair of **pereopods** often bear large, strong **chelae**, the remaining pairs of pereopods being variously developed but typically ending in claw-like joints; in swimming forms they may be flattened, hair-fringed, and paddle-shaped. All brachyurans lack a **tail-fan**.

With representatives of at least 13 families known from European waters, the better-known species belong in one or another of the following:

Leucosiidae (nut crabs) Small, carapace diamond-shaped and knobbly, eyestalks very short. About ten European species but many more live in deeper, offshore waters.

Majidae (spider crabs) Pereopods (thoracic limbs) long or extremely long and slender, the first pair **chelate** (bearing claws) but typically shorter than the remaining legs. Carapace oval or pear-shaped, usually with spines and often with sharp **rostral projections** between the long-stalked **eyes**. Many smaller-sized species move sluggishly and are found among algae or hydroids, pieces of which they often attach to their bodies for **camouflage**. About 20 European species.

Corystidae (masked crabs) Burrowing crabs with an elongated carapace and long, hairy antennae that interlock to form an inhalant tube when buried.

Atelecyclidae Carapace round and smooth, typically with numerous sharp, marginal teeth and fringed with long, dense **setae**. Chelipeds rather short but strong.

Cancridae Carapace wide, oval, lobed on frontal and lateral margins (pie-crust effect), chelae usually powerfully developed. This family includes the commercially important edible crab.

Portunidae This family includes the common shore crab and swimming crabs, with paddle-shaped **dactyls** (terminal segment) on the fifth pair of **pereopods**. Carapace broader than long, typically with conspicuous **anterolateral teeth** and 3–5 sharp to blunt teeth between the eyes. Some of the portunid species are extremely aggressive and can give a painful nip with their chelae. Sixteen common European species.

Xanthidae Heavy-bodied crabs, with a broadly oval **carapace, anterolateral teeth** not usually well developed. **Frontal** region of carapace between the eyes straight, convex, or vaguely lobed. **Chelae** typically large, powerful. About eight common European species.

Goneplacidae (rectangular crabs) Crabs with a rectangular carapace and very long chelipeds.

Pinnotheridae (pea crabs) Small, soft-bodied, found living **commensally** in the **branchial chambers** of larger bivalve molluscs or in large, solitary ascidians. Carapace mostly smooth and rounded with no anterolateral teeth and a straight or smoothly convex frontal region between the eyes. Pea crabs have complex life-cycles involving **intermediate hosts**. Two fairly common European species.

INFRAORDER **Caridea**

FAMILY **Palaemonidae**

Palaemon elegans Rathke

Description · Up to 6.3 cm long, carapace and abdominal surfaces are usually marked by irregular slender brown or yellowish-brown bands. Rostrum is either almost straight or slightly curved upwards, with 7–9 dorsal and three (rarely two or four) ventral teeth. Two or three of dorsal rostral spines are located behind eye sockets. Previously known as *Leander squilla*. **Habitat & ecology** · Rarely found sublittorally, far more typically intertidal on rocky shores in pools. **Similar species** · Several other species of European prawns with which this form may be confused; usually distinguishable by shape, size, and tooth pattern on rostrum, but some overlap in teeth number between species occurs. *P. serratus* particularly similar but grows to over 11 cm long, with relatively long, distinctly upwardly curved rostrum, and may have red-brown bands on its body. *P. longirostris* also larger and generally found in estuaries. It has tiny reddish chromatophores on the body. *P. adspersus* grows to about 7 cm long and is yellowish-grey with distinctive pigment spots on lower half of rostrum.

Abundance & distribution
May be locally common, with distribution extending from Baltic and south-west Norway to North Sea, English Channel, Atlantic, and Mediterranean coasts of Europe, south to Azores and east to Black Sea.

Palaemon serratus (Pennant)

Description · A moderately sized shrimp growing to a maximum length of 11 cm. The rostrum is curved upwards, usually with a bifid tip and with 6–7 dorsal and 4–5 ventral teeth. Two of the dorsal teeth are behind the level of the eyes. The telson has two pairs of lateral spines. The colour is variable, overall greyish or brownish with brownish-red bands of pigment. These are oblique or horizontal on the carapace and vertical on the abdominal segments. Between these bands are spots of reddish pigment. There are also red spots on the rostrum. **Habitat & ecology** · Intertidal on rocky shores in rock pools, or amongst algae on the lower shore. Also found in *Zostera* beds and in the lower reaches of estuaries. Occurs subtidally to 40 m depth. **Similar species** · Other *Palaemon* species are similar but the shape of the rostrum is distinctive.

Abundance & distribution
Frequent. Occurs off the south, south-west, and west coasts of Britain, and the south, south-west, south-east, and west coasts of Ireland. Distributed from Denmark to Mauritania, including the Mediterranean and Black Seas.

FAMILY **Pandalidae**

Pandalus montagui Leach **Pink shrimp**

Description · A large shrimp, growing up to 16 cm in length. The body is semi-translucent with patches of red on the carapace and abdominal segments. The carapace has a long, upturned rostrum with 10–12 small spines that reach from behind the eyes to halfway along the rostrum. There are also up to 7 larger spines on the lower edge of the rostrum. On the carapace just below the eye there is a small spine. This species has long, slender legs. **Habitat & ecology** · Found at depths of 5–230 m. This species is commercially fished in the UK. **Similar species** · There are several other similar species of shrimp in northern Europe. These are typically smaller than *P. montagui* and usually have different numbers of spines on the rostrum. They include *P. borealis*, *P. propinquus*, and *Dichelopandalus bonnieri*.

Abundance & distribution
Common on all British coasts. Distributed from Norway, Iceland, and Greenland to the English Channel.

Distinctive features

1. Rostrum straight or slightly up-curved, with 7–9 dorsal teeth, 2–3 of which are situated behind the eye sockets.
2. Ventral margin of rostrum with three (rarely two or four) ventral teeth.
3. Dorsal surface marked with slender, irregular yellowish-brown or brown bands.

Distinctive features

1. Moderately sized shrimp with an upturned rostrum ending in a bifid tip.
2. Telson with two pairs of lateral spines.

Distinctive features

1. Large shrimp.
2. Long, upturned rostrum.
3. 10–12 small spines on upper surface of rostrum.
4. Up to seven spines on lower surface of rostrum.

FAMILY **Crangonidae**

Crangon crangon (Linnaeus) **Brown shrimp**

Description · Body up to 9 cm long, typically an almost transparent mottled grey or brown colour, with main antennae almost as long as body. Near front of carapace is a single central and one pair of lateral spines pointing forwards; the rostrum between eyes reduced to a small tooth. Carapace about one-quarter of total length. First two pairs of thoracic legs bear claws, the first pair much larger than second. The third and fourth legs are longest. Also known as *C. vulgaris*. **Habitat & ecology** · Occurs on the lower shore and in shallow sublittoral situations on fine, muddy sand and gravel; it is also found in estuaries and is an important commercial species. **Similar species** · There are several other members of the family Crangonidae, to which the brown shrimp belongs, with which it may be confused. The shape of the carapace and its spine pattern are important in distinguishing between species. The species *C. allmanni* has a deep, mid-dorsal longitudinal groove on the sixth abdominal segment.

Abundance & distribution
Locally common and often abundant, the distribution extends from the Baltic to North Sea, English Channel, Atlantic, and Mediterranean coasts of Europe.

INFRAORDER **Thalassinidea**

FAMILY **Callianassidae**

Callianassa subterranea (Montagu)

Description · Prawn-like crustacean, up to 4 cm long, with a minute rostrum and small eyes. The first pair of walking legs are hairy but dissimilar in size, one claw being larger than the other; the tips of the claws are barely crossed. The remaining four pairs of walking legs are slender and hairy, their tips sometimes being flattened. The slender abdomen is often curled forwards under the thorax. Colour varies from pale purplish-brown or white to pale reddish or bluish-green. **Habitat & ecology** · Lives burrowed in muddy sand from the extreme lower shore to sublittoral depths of about 20 m. **Similar species** · *C. tyrrhena* is larger and whitish with blue or pink spots, occasionally greyish-green. The tips of its chelipeds are crossed. *Upogebia* species have a rostrum and the claws are equal in size. *U. stellata* is commonest, yellowish-white, often spotted orange. Other burrowing shrimps include *Axius stirhynchus*, *Calocaris macandreae*, and *Jaxea nocturna*, which has enormous claws compared to body size.

Abundance & distribution
May be locally common, occurring on south coasts of the British Isles, to the Bay of Biscay and Iberian Peninsula, and probably also into the Mediterranean.

INFRAORDER **Astacidea**

FAMILY **Nephropidae**

Homarus gammarus (Linnaeus) **Common lobster**

Description · Length variable; larger specimens may reach 50 cm, and lengths of 1 m and weights of more than 5 kg have been recorded. Carapace and abdomen slightly granular, generally lack spines or ridges, dark blue-black dorsally, often with paler coalescing yellowish or orange patches ventrally. Main antennae as long as body, rostrum short and spiny. Claws on first pair of walking legs massive, right one usually being somewhat larger than left. Second and third walking legs end in small pincers. **Habitat & ecology** · A prized and valuable commercial species, in the wild occurring on lower-shore to sublittoral depths of about 60 m, in holes or larger crevices in rocks, or occupying deep tunnels excavated in soft sediments beneath rocks. Aggressive and solitary; claws powerful enough to be harmful to man. Breeds once a year after 5 years of age, females brooding eggs for about 9 months. Some commercial shell-fisheries culture lobsters. Exploitation for food has led to it becoming less common than it was.

Abundance & distribution
Locally common, though their solitary habit precludes them from being abundant. Distributed from the Lofoten Islands to western Baltic, North Sea, English Channel, Atlantic, and Mediterranean coasts of Europe, south to north-west Africa and east to the Black Sea.

Distinctive features

1. Main antennae almost as long as body.
2. Carapace about one-quarter of body length, with single dorsal and paired lateral, forward-pointing spines near its front.

Distinctive features

1. Prawn-like shape, with minute rostrum and small eyes.
2. First pair of walking legs and claws dissimilar in size, tips of claws barely crossed.

Distinctive features

1. Carapace and abdomen slightly granular but lacking spines or ridges.
2. Rostrum short and spiny.
3. Claws large, powerful, right claw larger than left.

Nephrops norvegicus (Linnaeus)
Norway lobster, scampi, Dublin Bay prawn, langoustine

Description · Up to 24 cm long and pale orange in colour, the rostrum at the front of the carapace is long and spiny. The long, slender claws have characteristic longitudinal, spiny ridges. The eyes are very large, intensely black, and kidney-shaped. At the rear of the abdomen the paired uropods and single telson typically form a rather broad and flattened tail-fan whose posterior margins are clad with dense, short bristles. **Habitat & ecology** · Entirely sublittoral, mostly found at depths of 200–800 m, occasionally as shallow as 20 m, in extensive shallow and branching burrows which it builds in flatter, softer sediments such as fine or silty mud. An important seafood species which, in many areas of its range, has been seriously overfished commercially. The rare British fish, Fries' goby, *Lesueurigobius friesii*, shares the burrows of *N. norvegicus*.

Abundance & distribution
Locally both common and abundant, with a distribution extending from the Mediterranean and Morocco northwards to Atlantic, English Channel, and North Sea coasts of Europe, Norway, and Iceland.

INFRAORDER **Palinura**

FAMILY **Palinuridae**

Palinurus elephas (Fabricius)
Common crawfish, spiny lobster, langouste

Description · This large crayfish, up to 30–50 cm long, has no claws on any of its walking legs except in females, which have small pincers on fifth pair of legs. Reddish-brown carapace marked with yellowish spots, its sharp, anteriorly projecting spines can inflict wounds unless the animals are handled carefully; abdominal segments also sharply spined. Second antennae distinctly longer than body, first pair of walking legs obviously stouter than remaining legs. Previously known as *P. vulgaris*. **Habitat & ecology** · Found in shallow situations and to depths of 70 m or more, in crevices or under and among rocks and boulders, occasionally on more stony ground. Breeds during September and October, the reddish eggs being brooded by the female. A highly prized shellfish delicacy in many parts of Europe. **Similar species** · *P. mauretanicus*, but in this species first walking legs are a similar thickness to remaining legs and carapace has two more-or-less distinct mid-dorsal rows of spines.

Abundance & distribution
Locally common in regions where it has not been overfished, the distribution ranges from south and west coasts of the British Isles and Ireland to the Mediterranean and Azores.

INFRAORDER **Anomura**

FAMILY **Paguridae**

Pagurus bernhardus (Linnaeus)
Common hermit crab

Description · Carapace up to 35–40 mm long, body up to 100 mm. Carapace greyish-red, claws reddish-brown. First pair of walking legs bears large, coarsely granulated or toothed claws, right claw larger than left. Claws on second and third walking legs spiny, fourth and fifth walking legs greatly reduced. Previously known as *Eupagurus bernhardus*. **Habitat & ecology** · Intertidally in rock pools and sublittorally to 140–150 m, occasionally deeper, on rocky or sandy bottoms in almost any suitable gastropod shell. Intertidal specimens, commonly found in littorinid or dog whelk shells, usually smaller than sublittoral examples which frequently inhabit shells of *Buccinum undatum*. Common commensals of hermit crab include sponge *Suberites domuncula*, anemone *Calliactis parasitica*, or hydroid *Hydractinia echinata* growing on outer shell surface, polychaete *Nereis fucata* which shares crab's shell, or the shell-less barnacle, *Trypetesa lampas*, which bores into the shell. Crab often infested with parasites, such as rhizocephalan barnacle, *Clistosaccus paguri*. **Similar species** · There are several other hermit crab species with which this form may be confused.

Abundance & distribution
Locally both common and abundant, with a wide distribution extending from the Atlantic coast of North America to Iceland, Norway, and the western Baltic southwards to North Sea, English Channel, and Atlantic coasts of Europe as far as Portugal.

Distinctive features

1. Claws long, slender, with longitudinal spiny ridges.
2. Distinct tail-fan formed from telson and two pairs of uropods.

Distinctive features

1. Second antennae distinctly longer than body.
2. Walking legs without claws, except for fifth pair of legs in females.

Distinctive features

1. First pair of walking legs with large, coarsely granulate or toothed claws, right claw larger than left.

Pagurus prideauxi Leach

Description · Muddy reddish-brown and paler spotted carapace, which does not extend as rostrum between eyes, is up to about 14 mm long; body some 60 mm in length. Claws salmon-pink, larger right one being almost hairless but evenly covered with granules. Eye stalks stubby, short, white with a pale orange band close behind large eyes. Once known as *Eupagurus prideauxi*. **Habitat & ecology** · Extreme lower shore to sublittoral depths of about 40 m, although recorded from as deep as 400 m, on gravel, sand, or mud, occupying small gastropod shells. Shells inhabited by adults often have cloak anemone, *Adamsia carciniopados* (previously called *A. palliata*), living on their surface. **Similar species** · Somewhat resembles, but smaller than, *P. bernhardus*; this species has two prominent longitudinal rows of tubercles on right chela as well as scattering of tubercles. *P. cuanensis* also very similar; tends to be reddish-brown with dark spots and white markings, and reddish legs. Chelae densely covered with hairs and conical tubercles, particularly along midline. This species can be common and is distributed from Norway to South Africa, including Mediterranean.

Abundance & distribution
Locally very common, often abundant, with a distribution ranging from Norway to all western European coasts, the Mediterranean, and southwards to the Cape Verde Islands.

FAMILY **Galatheidae** | SUBFAMILY **Galatheinae**

Galathea dispersa Bate

Description · Body up to 45 mm long; the pointed rostrum is hairy and has four distinct spines on either side. The first walking legs, as long as the body, are hairy and bear similarly sized claws. Colour variable: yellowish, a dull orange, or red, often patterned with red and white spots, but never with blue markings. Each abdominal segment has three transverse grooves, the middle one being the deepest. **Habitat & ecology** · Occasionally found on the extreme lower shore, mostly sublittoral at depths of 10–500 m, among boulders and rocks or with coralline algae. Females carry their eggs during the spring months. **Similar species** · May be mistaken for other species such as *G. squamifera*.

Abundance & distribution
May be locally common. Found all around Britain and Ireland. Distributed from Norway and southern Iceland to the Mediterranean, including Madeira and the Canary Islands.

Galathea intermedia Lilljeborg

Description · A small, squat lobster. The body is only about 18 mm long, with a narrow, bluntly pointed, rostrum with four small, bluntly rounded spines on each side; the rostrum is not hairy. The basal joint of the first antennae possess two large spines, rather than three as in other galatheids. The first walking legs, as long as the body, are slightly hairy and bear similar-sized claws. Mostly salmon-pink or salmon-red. **Habitat & ecology** · A shallow sublittoral species, mostly found down to depths of 15–20 m, occasionally slightly deeper, among rocks and boulders. The two spines on the basal segment of the first antennae enable this species to be identified accurately, but require a hand lens or microscopic examination to be distinguished.

Abundance & distribution
Locally common and often abundant, with a range extending from Norway to North Sea, English Channel, Atlantic and Mediterranean coasts of Europe south to Dakar in West Africa.

Distinctive features

1. Right claw on first pair of walking legs larger than left, almost hairless, covered with granules.
2. Claws salmon-pink.
3. Carapace between eyes not forming rostrum.

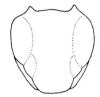

Distinctive features

1. Rostrum pointed, hairy, with four spines each side.
2. Abdominal segments with deep transverse furrow or groove flanked by shallower parallel grooves.

Distinctive features

1. Rostrum narrow, pointed, not hairy, with fine teeth or spines on each side.
2. Basal joint of first antennae with two spines.

Galathea squamifera Leach

Description · Up to about 65 mm long, about half taken up by the carapace. The triangular and pointed rostrum has four spines on either side, the most posterior spine being obviously smaller than the others. The first walking legs, about 1.5 times as long as the body, lack spines but are covered with close-set, scale-like tubercles and bear long, similar-sized claws. Generally a dark chestnut brown with a greenish tinge and red tips to the spines; younger individuals are more reddish. **Habitat & ecology** · Found beneath rocks and boulders, or in rock pools on the extreme lower levels of rocky beaches, and sublittorally to depths of about 30–70 m. This is the most common of the European squat lobsters, females carrying their eggs during late winter and spring. The species is a filter-feeder on suspended detritus. **Similar species** · May be confused with *G. dispersa* but is generally larger, darker-coloured, and lacks white spots.

Abundance & distribution
Locally both common and abundant. Distribution extends from Norway to all European coasts, including the Mediterranean, and south to the Azores.

Galathea strigosa (Linnaeus)

Description · A large species, up to 9 cm long. The rostrum is covered with fringed scales, has a long terminal or apical spine, and three spines on either side. The segments of the first walking legs are densely covered with sharp spines; the similar-sized claws are less spiny. The colour is diagnostic for the species, the carapace being covered with bright red patches and bands of vivid blue. **Habitat & ecology** · Sometimes found on gravel or under rocks and boulders, or in permanent rock pools, on the extreme lower shore, more usually sublittoral and offshore to depths of 600 m.

Abundance & distribution
Very common and locally abundant. Distribution extends from North Cape and Scandinavia to all European coasts, including the Mediterranean, south to the Canary Islands and east to the Red Sea.

Munida rugosa (Fabricius)
Long-clawed squat lobster

Description · The carapace, including the long, sharply pointed rostrum, is about 3 cm long, the total length up to 6 cm when the abdomen is extended. The posterior margin of the carapace bears a few spines, the base of the rostrum has a shorter spine on each side. Pinkish-yellow, with the carapace margins and transverse grooves reddish, and red spines. The claw-bearing legs (chelipeds) are very long, at least twice the body length, with long and delicate pincers. The antennae are about three-quarters the length of the chelipeds. The largest of the shallow-water squat lobsters in European waters. **Habitat & ecology** · Found from extreme low water to 150 m, on sand or other soft sediments, or on stony bottoms. **Similar species** · Similar to *M. tenuimana*, this form is yellowish-brown and lives in deeper water, to depths of about 1000 m.

Abundance & distribution
Locally fairly common, with a distribution extending from Norway to Atlantic, English Channel, North Sea, and Mediterranean coasts of Europe, and south to Madeira.

Distinctive features

1. Rostrum triangular, pointed, with four spines on each side.
2. Claws on first walking legs similarly sized, covered in close-set tubercles.

Distinctive features

1. Rostrum pointed, covered with fringed scales, with three spines each side.
2. Carapace coloured with bright red patches and vivid blue bands.

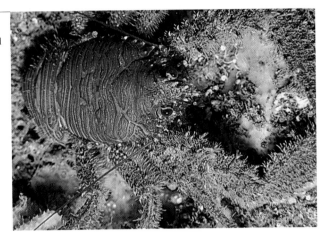

Distinctive features

1. Rostrum ends in long, sharp spine flanked by single shorter spine on each side.
2. Claw-bearing legs twice as long as body.

FAMILY **Porcellanidae**

Pisidia longicornis (Linnaeus)
Long-clawed porcelain crab

Description · Up to 1 cm long, the olive-brown, olive green, or dark reddish brown to maroon carapace is almost circular except for three bluntly pointed lobes between the deep-set eyes. The whole animal is smooth and hairless. The claws are unequal in size, with the right claw larger; the pincers are slightly twisted and meet only at their tips. The antennae are long and slender. The last pair of walking legs is very slender and held tucked under the carapace, so that at first glance the crabs appear to have only four pairs of legs. **Habitat & ecology** · Found on the lower shore intertidally and to sublittoral depths of 100 m, living on rocky or gravelly bottoms, among the bryozoan *Pentapora foliacea*, or in large hydroid clumps. Porcelain crabs are suspension feeders.

Abundance & distribution
Locally both common and abundant, occurring on all European coasts from Norway to the Mediterranean and southwards to the Canary Islands and Angola in West Africa.

Porcellana platycheles (Pennant)
Broad-clawed porcelain crab

Description · Carapace nearly circular, flat and smooth, up to about 1.5 cm long and very crab-like in appearance, although porcelain crabs are not true crabs but more closely related to squat lobsters and hermit crabs. Antennae very long, slender, claws on first walking legs wide, flat and strong, unequal in size, and densely fringed with long hairs. The remaining legs are also densely hairy, though the fifth pair is slender and tucked under the carapace. The colour is greyish-brown above, a dirty yellowish-white below. **Habitat & ecology** · An intertidal species, found under rocks and boulders on muddy and gravelly sediments. Females reproduce during their second year, carrying their eggs during spring and summer.

Abundance & distribution
Locally both very common and abundant, with a distribution extending from the Shetland Islands southwards to North Sea, English Channel, Atlantic, and Mediterranean shores of Europe, and to the Canary Islands.

INFRAORDER **Brachyura**

FAMILY **Leucosiidae**

Ebalia granulosa Milne Edwards

Description · Carapace rounded diamond-shape, truncated, shallowly notched both in front and at rear, at most about 11 mm long. Lateral (branchial) regions of carapace slightly prominent, similar swelling occurring towards front in cardiac region. Eyestalks very short, the two black eyes recessed into carapace. Claws (chelipeds) broad and strong, with longitudinal ridges on merus and carpus (two segments bearing claws). Remaining eight limbs bear strong spines. In males abdominal segments 3–5 fused, in females segments 4–6. Generally pale yellowish-brown with two spots on carapace. **Habitat & ecology** · Found on sublittoral coarse substrata throughout continental shelf regions and into deeper waters. **Similar species** · Closely resembles *E. tumefacta* but in this species branchial regions are strongly inflated and posterior part of carapace only has shallow notch. This species is reddish or yellowish, often spotted red or marked with brown, black, orange, or red. Very common around British Isles and Ireland, and distributed from Norway to Africa but not found in Mediterranean. Other *Ebalia* species tend to be covered in tubercles, especially on chelae.

Abundance & distribution
Rare, found occasionally off the Atlantic coasts of Britain and Ireland and extending southwards to the Mediterranean.

Distinctive features

1. Carapace almost circular, three blunt lobes between eyes.
2. Body smooth, hairless.
3. Right claw larger than left; pincers slightly twisted, meeting only at tips.

Distinctive features

1. Carapace almost circular, flat, smooth.
2. Claws on first walking legs wide, flat, densely fringed with hairs.
3. Remaining legs strongly hairy.

Distinctive features

1. Carapace rounded diamond shape, shallowly notched and truncate in front and rear.
2. Eyes deeply recessed into carapace.
3. Two segments of front legs bear claws with longi-tudinal ridges.
4. Pale yellowish-brown.

FAMILY **Majidae** | SUBFAMILY **Oregoninae**
Hyas araneus (Linnaeus)
Great spider crab

Description · Carapace somewhat roundly triangular or pear-shaped, posteriorly rounded, up to 11 cm long, slightly domed, and covered with bristles and tubercles. The two close-set, rostral spines form an anteriorly notched, triangular rostrum. Behind the eyes there is a large, flat spine on each side of the body. The first pair of legs bear claws, the right claw being slightly larger than the left. The carapace is a dull red to brown dorsally, and dirty white ventrally, but is often covered with hydroids, sponges, or seaweeds. **Habitat & ecology** · Found among rocks and boulders, or on coarse sand or gravel, sometimes among seaweed, from the lower shore to depths of about 50 m sublittorally.

Abundance & distribution
Sometimes locally common, the distribution extends from the English Channel to North Sea, north-east Atlantic, and Baltic coasts of Europe, and to northern Norway, Spitzbergen, and Iceland. It is also found off Greenland and North America.

SUBFAMILY **Inachinae**
Inachus dorsettensis (Pennant)
Scorpion spider crab

Description · Carapace light brown or grey with reddish spots, pear-shaped, up to 3 cm long and 2.7 cm wide, with the spines of the short rostrum separated by a U-shaped cleft. The surface of the carapace is regularly patterned with spines, with an obvious transverse row of four near the front. Behind the short-stalked eyes there is a sharp spine (post-orbital spine) on each side of the carapace. **Habitat & ecology** · Found sublittorally at depths of 6–100 m on stones, sand, or mud. **Similar species** · Very similar to *I. phalangium*, but the rostral spines in this species curve inwards and are not separated by a cleft.

Abundance & distribution
Locally common, with a range extending from South Africa northwards to the Mediterranean and Atlantic, English Channel, and North Sea coasts as far as Norway.

Macropodia tenuirostris (Leach)

Description · Carapace triangular, up to 19 mm long; rostrum very elongated to form a point longer than three peduncle segments of antennae. Towards front of carapace three large tubercles form triangle, with three additional tubercles occurring farther back. Anterolateral carapace margin angled, with a spine some distance behind eye. Main antennae longer than rostrum. Eyestalks long but cannot be retracted. First pair of walking legs, bearing weakly developed claws, short but compara-tively stout, whereas all other legs extremely long and slender. Reddish-brown to yellowish-red, often masked by encrusting organisms. **Habitat & ecology** · On shore at extreme low water mark down to more than 160 m depth. Often found on coarse ground or amongst seaweeds. **Similar species** · There are several other spider crabs, such as *M. deflexa*, in which each anterolateral edge of carapace bears at least one distinct spine. However, *M. deflexa* often has distinctly down-curved rostrum and more tubercles on carapace. *M. deflexa* carapace also generally slenderer than other *Macropodia* species and up to 30 mm long. *M. rostrata*, long-legged spider crab, also locally common. This has sharply angled anterolateral edge to each side of carapace but these are not produced into spines. *M. linaresi* has double spine either side of carapace in anterolateral position.

Abundance & distribution
Common around all coasts of Britain. Range extends from the Faeroes to Portugal.

Distinctive features

1. Carapace slightly domed, pear-shaped, or roundly triangular.
2. Carapace covered with bristles and tubercles.
3. Rostral spines close-set, rostrum appearing triangular.

Distinctive features

1. Carapace pear-shaped, rostral spines separated by U-shaped cleft.
2. Dorsal carapace surface patterned with spines.
3. Single sharp spine each side of carapace just behind eyes.

Distinctive features

1. Carapace triangular.
2. Rostral spines joined; rostrum longer than third peduncle of antennae.
3. Spine on margin of front half of carapace.
4. First legs relatively stout, short, with weak claws.

SUBFAMILY **Majinae**

Maja squinado (Herbst)
Common spider crab, spiny spider crab

Description · The carapace is pear-shaped, lateral margins fringed with spines, rounded posterior margin without spines. Up to 20 cm long and 15 cm wide, the claws may be up to 45 cm long. Variably whitish, yellowish, reddish-brown, or red, larger individuals often partially camouflage themselves by attaching seaweeds or hydroids to the carapace or legs. The rostrum is formed from two, thick horns. The eyes can be fully retracted into their orbits. Also known as *Maia squinado*. **Habitat & ecology ·** Sometimes found in deep pools on the lower shore, usually sublittoral to about 50 m depth, on coarse sand and mixed substrata. The species is edible and commercially important in some European countries. While breeding (late summer), animals may aggregate in piles of 20 or more individuals close to the shore. **Similar species ·** *M. verrucosa*, which is smaller with rostral spines outwardly curved. The stone crab, *Lithodes maja*, a superficially similar northern species, has fifth pair of walking legs very small hidden beneath carapace.

Abundance & distribution
Locally both common and abundant, the distribution extends from the southern North Sea to west and south-west coasts of the British Isles, the Bay of Biscay and Iberian Peninsula, the Mediterranean, and south to the Cape Verde Islands.

SUBFAMILY **Pisinae**

Eurynome aspersa (Pennant)

Description · A short-legged spider crab. Carapace roughly oval, longer (1.7 cm) than it is wide (1.3 cm), covered with large, irregular, warty growths among which is a tightly fused group just anterior to centre and loosely fused group towards rear and along posterior margin. Front of carapace extended into two long rostral horns separated by V-shaped cleft. Eyestalks short; sides of carapace bear large, variably sized triangular spines. Light reddish- to greyish-brown, often with hint of greyish-blue. **Habitat & ecology ·** Sublittoral, mostly at depths of 12–40 m but sometimes deeper or shallower, on mixed stony, shell, and sand sediments. **Similar species ·** *E. spinosa*, but it lacks fused group of warty outgrowths along posterior margin. *Pisa tetraodon* and *P. armata* similar shape to *E. aspersa* but body is not covered in irregular warty growths; instead it has much less dense scattering of tubercles. Both these species also have four forwardly directed large spines on anterior margin of carapace between eyes. *P. tetraodon* also has five spines after eyes along lateral margins of carapace. *P. armata* only two. *P. tetraodon* can be locally common and is distributed

from southwest coasts of Britain and Ireland to Mediterranean.

Abundance & distribution
Locally common; range extends from West Africa and Mediterranean to all European coasts as far north as Norway.

FAMILY **Corystidae**

Corystes cassivelaunus (Pennant)
Masked crab

Description · Carapace roughly elongate oval, up to 4 cm long, slightly more than half as wide, with four teeth on each side, of which the second is the largest. Colour pale red, brownish-yellow, or yellowish-white, often with a faint pattern reminiscent of a face. Between the eyes there are two close-set, central, blunt teeth flanked by two very small, knob-like teeth. The antennae, which are extremely long and hairy, are held together throughout their length. The first walking legs are comparatively slender, twice the length of the carapace in males, about equal to the carapace length in females. **Habitat & ecology ·** Found on the extreme lower shore and sublittorally to depths of about 90 m, usually buried in sand or other soft sediments and using its long antennae like a tube to allow surface water to reach the gills. The crab feeds on invertebrates burrowing into the substrate in which it lives.

Abundance & distribution
Frequent to locally abundant on all coasts of Britain and Ireland. Distribution extends from Norway to Portugal, including the Mediterranean.

Distinctive features

1. Carapace pear-shaped; posterior margin lacks spines, lateral edges fringed with spines.
2. Claws typically more than twice body length.
3. Rostrum with two stout horns.

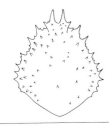

Distinctive features

1. Carapace roughly oval, slightly longer than wide, front extended as pair of long rostral horns separated by V-shaped cleft.
2. Sides of carapace with variably sized triangular teeth.
3. Carapace surface warty, with fused group of warts near centre and loose group of warts near hind margin.

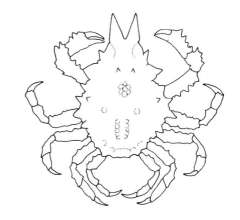

Distinctive features

1. Carapace elongate oval, four teeth on each side.
2. Antennae extremely long, hairy.
3. First walking legs as long as carapace (females), or twice as long (males).

FAMILY **Atelecyclidae**

Atelecyclus rotundatus (Olivi)
Circular crab

Description · Up to 3–4 cm long, the reddish-brown carapace is almost circular in outline and has a toothed margin; there are three teeth between the eyes, the middle one longer than the other two, and 9–11 teeth on either anterolateral edge outside the eyes. The first pair of walking legs is massive but with comparatively small, similarly sized, black-tipped claws. The carapace and legs are lightly clad in brown hairs. **Habitat & ecology** · An entirely sublittoral species, found on sand and gravel at depths of 12–300 m. **Similar species** · The carapace of *A. undecimdentatus* is both broader and has coarser granulations. It is rare. *Thia scutellata* is also similar but the front of the carapace lacks teeth.

Abundance & distribution
May be locally common, with a distribution extending from Norway to South Africa, including all western European coasts but not the Mediterranean.

FAMILY **Cancridae**

Cancer pagurus Linnaeus **Edible crab**

Description · Carapace oval, reddish-brown, commonly up to 9 cm long and 15 cm wide, but widths of 25 cm have been recorded. The margin of the carapace is characteristically crimped with 10–11 rounded anterolateral lobes outside the eyes (like a piecrust), with five small, blunt teeth between the eyes. Claws massive, similarly sized, and black-tipped. **Habitat & ecology** · The most commercially important crab species of western Europe, occurring between mid-tide levels and sublittoral depths of 100 m or more, typically on rocky substrata but also on mixed, coarse sediments or muddy sand. Smaller juveniles are often found under rocks and boulders, or in rock pools on the lower shore. Females migrate inshore during late spring to moult and mate, moving offshore again in late summer.

Abundance & distribution
Common and often abundant, found throughout western Europe from northern Norway southwards, in the Mediterranean, and south to West Africa.

FAMILY **Portunidae** | SUBFAMILY **Polybiinae**

Liocarcinus depurator (Linnaeus)
Harbour crab, swimming crab

Description · The trapezoid carapace is up to 4 cm long, 5.1 cm wide, and reddish-brown in colour. The oval dactyl (paddle) which forms the terminal portion of the last legs is characteristically violet. Between the eyes there are three bluntly rounded teeth on the edge of the carapace, with five sharp teeth on each anterolateral edge. The upper carapace surface has short, transverse rows of hairs. Previously known as *Macropipus depurator*. **Habitat & ecology** · Found on the extreme lower shore and sublittorally to depths of 450 m, on soft, sandy, and mixed muddy sand sediments. **Similar species** · There are several similarly shaped crab species but the violet paddles on the last legs of this species usually confirm its identification.

Abundance & distribution
Locally very common, with a distribution extending from Norway to North Sea, English Channel, Atlantic, and Mediterranean coasts of Europe south to West Africa.

Distinctive features

1. Reddish-brown carapace, almost circular.
2. Margin of carapace with 3 teeth between eyes, 9–11 anterolateral teeth outside eyes.
3. Claws black-tipped.

Distinctive features

1. Oval reddish-brown carapace, piecrust margin.
2. Claws massive, black-tipped.
3. Five small, blunt teeth on carapace rim between eyes.

Distinctive features

1. Carapace trapezoid, dorsally covered by short, transverse rows of hairs.
2. Paddle of last legs oval, violet in colour.

Necora puber (Linnaeus)
Velvet swimming crab, velvet fiddler, witch crab, devil crab

Description · Carapace rather flat, 5–6.5 cm long and about 6.6 cm wide. Its front margin between the red eyes bears up to about ten narrow and unequal teeth; the anterolateral margins have five sharp, anteriorly pointing teeth. The chelipeds are slender, with rows of tubercles forming ridges on the subterminal segment (the propodus). Dorsal surface of carapace blue, masked by brown velvety texture, with red prominences. The segments of the hind legs are flattened, fringed with hairs and rather oval; they are used in swimming. **Habitat & ecology** · A lower-shore to shallow sublittoral species, sometimes as deep as 70 m, on rocky and stony substrata and under boulders. In some areas of Europe the species is fished commercially for food. It can move rapidly and is often very aggressive when threatened; the claws can inflict a painful nip.

Abundance & distribution
Widespread and locally both common and abundant. Distribution ranges from west Norway to North Sea, English Channel, Atlantic, Mediterranean, and Black Sea coasts of Europe south to West Africa.

SUBFAMILY **Carcininae**

Carcinus maenas (Linnaeus)
Common shore crab, green crab

Description · Carapace up to 5.5–6 cm long, 7–7.5 cm wide, rather trapezoid in shape, with three bluntly rounded teeth between the eyes and five sharp teeth on each anterolateral margin outside the eyes, carapace sharply tapering behind these teeth. Carapace colour is very variable, ranging from almost white or speckled as a juvenile to dark green, mottled greyish-green, or brownish as an adult; the middle upper surface of the carapace often has a triangular death's-head or other strong pattern. The undersurface is usually yellowish-green, the legs sometimes green or brick red. **Habitat & ecology** · Found intertidally and to sublittoral depths of about 200 m, occurring in almost any type of habitat from estuarine muds, salt marshes, rock pools, and sand to rocky shores under boulders and rocks or among algae. The parasitic barnacle, *Sacculina carcini*, is often found infesting the green crab, particularly sublittoral specimens.

Abundance & distribution
Very common and abundant, with a very widespread distribution that extends to all European coasts including the Mediterranean, south to West Africa, north to Iceland, and north-east North America and the Indo-west Pacific.

Portumnus latipes (Pennant)

Description · This small crab has a rounded, heart-shaped carapace up to about 2 cm long. There are three bluntly pointed teeth on the carapace between the eyes, the middle one being slightly longer than the other two. There are five lateral teeth on the carapace, the fourth one notably small. The claws are slightly different in size and the upper part of the pincers hairy. The ends of the posterior legs are distinctly flattened. The crab is reddish with whitish markings. **Habitat & ecology** · Occurs on the extreme low shore and sublittorally to 150 m. Usually found in sandy areas.

Abundance & distribution
Common. Found on all British coasts, except the north, and all around Ireland. Distributed southwards to North Africa.

Distinctive features

1. Carapace rather flat, as wide as long or slightly wider.
2. Edge of carapace between red eyes with about ten narrow, unequal teeth.
3. Claws slender, penultimate segment ridged with tubercles.

Distinctive features

1. Carapace trapezoid, sharply tapering from about halfway back.
2. Edge of carapace with three blunt teeth between eyes, five sharp teeth outside eyes.

Distinctive features

1. Small crab with heart-shaped carapace.
2. Three bluntly pointed teeth between the eyes, the middle one longest.
3. Five lateral teeth on carapace, the fourth one small.

FAMILY **Xanthidae**

Xantho incisus Leach

Description · The carapace is trapezoid-shaped, up to 2 cm long but about twice as wide. Its dark brown surface is covered in smoothly rounded knobs. The anterolateral margins of the carapace bear five indistinct teeth outside the eyes, whereas between the eyes the margin is almost straight but with a slight indentation. The black-tipped claws, whose carpal segments lack spines and tubercles, are large and strong. **Habitat & ecology** · A lower-shore species also found sublittorally to depths of about 40 m, typically occurring on rocky substrates or beneath rocks and boulders on coarse sediments. **Similar species** · *X. pilipes* is very similar but the tips of the chelae are brown rather than black and the teeth along the edges of the carapace are fringed with hairs. This species may be locally abundant and is distributed from Norway to West Africa, including south and west coasts of Britain and Ireland, and the Mediterranean.

Abundance & distribution
Sometimes locally common, with a distribution extending from Atlantic coasts of England and Ireland to the Mediterranean, and southwards to the Cape Verde and Canary Islands, and the Azores.

FAMILY **Goneplacidae**

Goneplax rhomboides (Linnaeus)
Angular crab

Description · Carapace transversely rectangular, wider than it is long and with a large, distinct spine at each front corner, a short way behind which is a smaller spine on each side. In males the carapace is typically up to 3.4 cm wide and 2 cm long, in females about half these dimensions. The rim of the carapace between the eyes is straight, the eyestalks are long, thick, and retractile. In males the first walking legs are up to 4–5 times the length of the carapace, slender, and bear narrow, sharply pointed, and bluntly toothed claws, the outer of which is black. These legs are shorter in females. The carapace is typically a reddish-yellow, often more yellowish in the posterior half. **Habitat & ecology** · Found sublittorally at depths of about 5–100 m, living in complex, branching burrows dug in muddy sand.

Abundance & distribution
Locally common and may be abundant. Found on all suitable British coasts, with a distribution extending south to the Mediterranean and South Africa.

Superorder Peracarida

Peracaridan malacostracans generally possess no or only a weakly developed carapace, though their thoracic segments are usually distinct. Females brood their eggs in a chamber, called a **marsupium**, formed from a series of plates derived from the coxal segments of the **pereopods** (thoracic limbs). The life-cycle has no larval stages, the eggs hatching directly into immature adults. Most groups of peracaridans are either filter-feeders or **detritivores** (feed on detritus). Within the British Isles representatives of five orders are commonly found, these being the **Mysidacea**,

Amphipoda, Cumacea, Isopoda, and Tanaidacea.

Opossum shrimps (**Mysidacea**) are small, shrimp-like peracaridan malacostracans, rarely more than 3 cm long. The body is typically more or less cylindrical and essentially retains the primitive organisation for the class in comprising six fused **head** segments, eight **thoracic**, and six **abdominal** segments; the abdomen is flexible and generally accounts for more than half the overall length of the body. The head is often fused with the anterior thoracic segments to form a **cephalothorax**. The **carapace** is thin but large, covering the head and most of the thorax dorsally and laterally, but is not attached to the last three

Distinctive features

1. Carapace trapezoid-shaped.

2. Carapace margin between eyes almost straight, outside eyes with five indistinct teeth.

3. Strong claws black-tipped.

Distinctive features

1. Carapace rectangular, wider than long; obvious large spine at each front corner.

2. Front carapace edge between eyes straight.

3. Eyes on long, thick, retractile stalks.

thoracic segments. At its front the carapace bears a small, untoothed rostrum which in some forms may be almost indistinguishable. On the head two conspicuous, dark, compound **eyes**, composed of numerous **ommatidia**, are carried on movable eyestalks. The head appendages consist of paired **antennae 1** and **2**, **mandibles**, and **maxillae 1** and **2**. The biramous antennae are well-developed, the flattened exopodite forming an **antennal scale**. Antenna 1 has a basal **protopod** composed of three distinct segments forming the **peduncle**, which bears two long **annulated flagellae**, whilst antenna 2 has a single long flagellum. In adult males a third **setose** (bristly) **appendix masculina** also extends from the peduncle. The thoracic appendages are biramous and feathery, their simple **endopodites** serving for manipulating food or walking, their fringed **exopodites** being used for swimming. The endopodites of the first two or three pairs of thoracic appendages are modified as **maxillipeds**. None of the thoracic appendages is ever **chelate** (clawed). Each of the abdominal segments bears a posterior pair of appendages, the abdomen ending in a **telson** which is wider at its base than at its tip. The posterior end of the body bears a distinct tail-fan formed from the telson and the paired **uropods** of the sixth abdominal segment. These biramous uropods have lost most of their segmentation, instead appearing as a

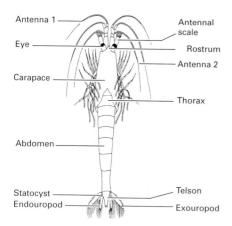

A mysid crustacean.

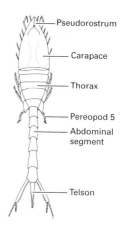

A cumacean crustacean.

single flattened blade; the endopodal and exopodal parts of the uropods are known, respectively, as **endouropods** and **exouropods**. The base of each endouropod is swollen and houses a distinct **statocyst** (balancing organ), this being one of the most characteristic features of mysids as a group.

The sexes are separate. Females possess a large ventral pouch (**marsupium**) for holding the eggs and developing young, which are released as small immature adults; there is no separate larval form in the life-cycle. It is the marsupium which gives the order its common name of opossum shrimps. Most mysids are colourless, and transparent or translucent, though some are distinctly red or green. They are generally distinguished by differences in the size, shape, and spine form of the antennal scales and telson. With about 40 species in northern European waters, they are widespread at shallow depths (to 20 m), but species diversity increases markedly at greater depths. They tend not to be common intertidally, although they may move onto sandy or muddy shores with the incoming tide, especially at night. Mysids are typically found swimming slowly close to the bottom, often in their greatest numbers just below low tide level.

Cumaceans are small peracarid malacostracans with **bilaterally compressed** bodies and a distinctively shaped **carapace** that covers only the head and first few thoracic segments, with which it is fused. The lateral margins of the

carapace are formed into folds which enclose the anterior appendages, these consisting of one or two pairs of **maxillae** and three pairs of **maxillipeds**. The anterior margin of the carapace is also developed into two **pseudorostral lobes** which together comprise a **pseudorostrum**. The single eye is located just behind the pseudorostrum. The much slenderer posterior portion of the body consists of five thoracic and six elongate abdominal segments, the abdomen posteriorly ending in a **telson**. In both sexes the thorax bears five pairs of **pereopods**, whereas up to five pairs of abdominal appendages (**pleopods**) only occur in males. Females can also be distinguished by their very small **antenna 2**; in males this has a very long, slender **flagellum** which extends for about half the body length. **Sexual dimorphism** is often quite marked in cumacean species: apart from the differences already mentioned, both the shape and surface sculpturing of the carapace may differ between the sexes.

Cumaceans may be found intertidally or in shallow sublittoral situations, typically in or on fine to coarse sands, muddy sands, or gravels. About 100 European species are known, with representatives of three families (**Bodotriidae, Nannastacidae, Pseudocumatidae**) commonly occurring in British waters.

Tanaids are small, dorsoventrally compressed or elongate, cylindrical, peracaridan malacostracans that somewhat

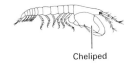

Cheliped

A tanaid crustacean.

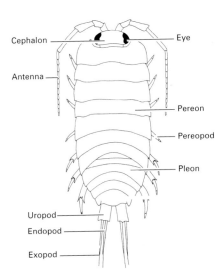

Ligia oceanica, showing the main external features of an isopod crustacean.

resemble **isopods** but from which they can be distinguished by their large claw-like second **pereopods**, called **chelipeds**. The reduced **carapace** covers only the **cephalothorax** (formed from fusion of the head and first two thoracic segments). The lateral margins of the carapace are folded and enclose a **branchial chamber**, and the front edge of the carapace may be extended as a **rostrum**. Eyes are found in some species. The chelipeds, which end in small pincers, are succeeded by six pairs of walking **pereopods**, which are usually very similar to each other, and five abdominal segments (fused in some species) bearing small **pleopods** modified for swimming (**swimmerets**); swimmerets are missing from the females of some species. The sixth abdominal segment is fused with the **telson** to form a **pleotelson**, which bears a single pair of **uniramous** or **biramous uropods**. Sexual dimorphism in the group is often marked. Females have a ventral **marsupium** in which they brood their eggs, the young being released as advanced juveniles called **mancas**.

Tanaids are intertidal to sublittoral burrowers or tube-builders in silty and muddy substrata, or occur under stones, in crevices, or among red algae such as *Corallina* and *Laurencia*. There are at least 40 north-west European species, with eight occurring in intertidal habitats around the British Isles, but their small size makes them unobtrusive and easily overlooked. Species diversity among tanaids increases markedly at depths of more than 200 m. Members of five families are found in British waters, the **Apseudidae**, **Leptognathiidae, Nototanaidae, Paratanaidae**, and **Tanaidae**.

Often somewhat similar to woodlice, **isopods** typically possess dorsoventrally flattened bodies comprising a head (**cephalon**), a thorax (**pereon**) of seven segments, and an abdomen (**pleon**) of six segments, with no carapace. The head has two prominent **eyes**, which are never carried on

stalks, and two pairs of antennae. The first thoracic segment, rarely also the second, is fused with the head, its appendages being modified as **maxillipeds**. The remaining thoracic segments bear more or less similar **uniramous pereopods** used for walking. The **coxopodites** (one of the two **peduncle articles** or segments) may be expanded to form **coxal plates** that are visible from above. Part or all of the abdomen may be fused with the telson to form a **pleotelson**, although the abdomen typically bears five pairs of **biramous pleopods**, which usually have a respiratory function, and a pair of uniramous or biramous **uropods**.

Isopod sexes are separate, eggs brooded by the females hatching as juveniles which grow to their adult size via a series of moults. In a few species sexual dimorphism is marked. The Isopoda form a large class, with about 10 000 known living species divided into nine suborders, found on land or in marine and freshwater habitats; about 200 marine species occur in European waters, from at least 18 families. There are also several highly specialised parasitic species. Marine isopods are found from the upper-shore levels downwards into the sublittoral, among barnacles, bryozoans, hydroids, or other sessile invertebrates, in rock crevices, attached to

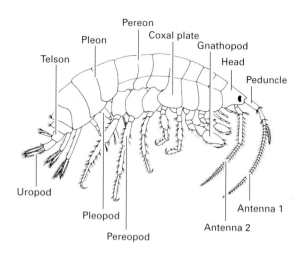

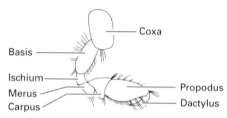

Top: the main external features of an amphipod crustacean. *Bottom*: the seven parts of a thoracic appendage.

seaweeds, under stones and boulders, or in sandy sediments. Species of the family **Idoteidae** are often seen attached to *Ascophyllum* and other fucoids on the midshore, whilst the very common and rapidly moving sea slater (family **Ligiidae**) is frequently found in large numbers under boulders or in crevices near high water mark. Not all isopods, however, are easily identifiable, for remarkably similar-looking species may live in totally different microhabitats.

Although the body morphology may vary considerably, **amphipods** typically possess bilaterally compressed, often rather arched, bodies comprising a head fused with the first thoracic segment, seven discernible thoracic segments, and six abdominal segments. The head bears six pairs of appendages: **antennae 1** and **2**, **mandibles**, **maxillae 1** and **2**, and **maxillipeds**. Antenna 1 has a stalk (**peduncle**) composed of three segments (**articles**) carrying a variably sized **flagellum**, and

sometimes a smaller **accessory flagellum**; antenna 2 has a five-articled peduncle carrying a flagellum which varies in size between species and sometimes between sexes of the same species. Each of the visible thoracic segments possesses a pair of **uniramous** appendages, of which the first one or two pairs are almost always modified as **gnathopods** (bearing small claws or pincers). Each thoracic appendage (**pereopod**) is formed of seven segments; commencing at the body these are in turn the **coxa**, **basis**, **ischium**, **merus**, **carpus**, **propodus**, and **dactylus**. The shape, length, and general form of the pereopods and their component segments are of taxonomic significance. Of the six abdominal segments, the first three comprise the **pleosome** and carry **biramous pleopods** used for jumping, the last three form the **urosome** and bear **uniramous** or **biramous uropods** employed for swimming. The abdominal region ends in a **telson** attached dorsally to the last urosomal

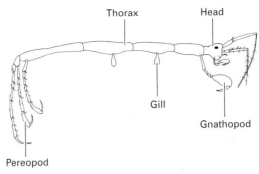

A caprellid amphipod, showing the main external features.

segment. The thoracic and abdominal segments in amphipods are often less easy to distinguish than in isopods.

Sexes are separate, females possessing a ventral brood pouch. Examples from three major suborders are found in north-west Europe, in freshwater or marine habitats.

In the two suborders, **Gammaridea** and **Hyperiidea**, the thorax and abdomen are distinct, the head is not fused with the first thoracic segment, and the abdomen bears both pleopods and uropods. They also possess more than three pairs of gills and 4–5 pairs of brood lamellae (carried on the thoracic segments). These two suborders can be distinguished by the following features:

Gammaridea (sandhoppers) Benthic habits, eyes of variable size, occasionally missing, but never occupying most of the head. Maxillipeds with palps. Coxae typically present and comparatively large. Basic body shape bilaterally compressed, curved towards ventral side.

Hyperiidea Pelagic habits, with very large eyes occupying most of the head. Maxillipeds with no palps. Coxae small or absent. Body more rounded than compressed.

The widest morphological variation from the basic amphipod form described above is found in the suborder **Caprellidea**.

Caprellidea (skeleton shrimps) Bodies long and cylindrical, the number and type of appendages reduced. Head immovably fused to first two thoracic segments but first thoracic segment distinct and bearing first pair of gnathopods. Thorax (**mesosome**) with three pairs of terminal pereopods. Abdomen (**metasome**) usually very reduced, with neither pleopods nor uropods. Two or three pairs of gills. Two pairs of **brood lamellae**.

ORDER Isopoda | SUBORDER Flabellifera

FAMILY Limnoriidae

Limnoria lignorum (Rathke) **Gribble**

Description · Somewhat like a small woodlouse, only about 35 mm long. Both pairs of antennae on the head are short. The general shape of body is an elongate rectangle with rounded corners and slightly convex sides. On the fifth abdominal segment there is a short but distinct dorsal longitudinal ridge. The pleotelson is broad and rounded, with the two branched uropods situated one on each side at the rear. The colour is greenish-brown. **Habitat & ecology** · A low-shore or shallow sublittoral species which bores into soft and waterlogged wood, particularly pier pilings, where it can be a nuisance. **Similar species** · There are a few other species of *Limnoria* with which this form may be confused. *L. tripunctata* is a warmer water species that has three tubercles on the pleotelson. *L. quadripunctata* has four tubercles on the pleotelson and may be found in slightly drier conditions than *L. lignorum*.

Abundance & distribution
Common. Found all around Britain and Ireland. Distributed from the western Baltic and Norway to France. Also occurs on both Atlantic and Pacific seaboards of North America to 40° S.

FAMILY Sphaeromatidae

Lekanesphaera rugicauda (Leach)

Description · Stout oval body, which can be rolled into a ball. Pleotelson is tapered, with posterior margin nearly straight and dorsally covered in small tubercles. Outer branch of posterior appendages (uropods) is smooth. There is a pair of eyes in anterolateral position. Colour greyish, maximum size about 1 cm. **Habitat & ecology** · Occurs intertidally from the high shore to mid-shore levels. Usually lives in sheltered areas such as estuaries or salt marshes. Found under stones, shells, and driftwood, also burrows and lives in crevices. **Similar species** · *Sphaeroma serratum* has a smooth pleotelson and the uropods are serrated. It is a pale green to greyish-green colour and grows to a length of 1.2 cm. It is found from southern and western coasts of Britain and Ireland and is distributed south to the Mediterranean. *L. hookeri* has two longitudinal rows of tubercles on the pleotelson. *L. levii* has slight serrations on the uropods. There are also several similar-looking species of *Dynamene*, *Camecopea*, and *Cymodoce*.

Abundance & distribution
Very common. Found on all coasts of Britain and Ireland. Distributed from south-east Sweden to the Bay of Biscay.

SUBORDER Valvifera

FAMILY Idoteidae

Idotea baltica (Pallas)

Description · Body elongate oblong-oval shape. Dorsoventrally flattened. Males up to 3 cm long, females slightly smaller. The final body segment, the pleotelson, has a three-toothed posterior margin, with the central tooth being larger than the lateral, which may be missing in small specimens. Antennae flexible, about a quarter of the body length. The colour ranges from uniform brown to green, but there are often small white patches or streaks along the dorsal surface. Females normally darker than males. **Habitat & ecology** · Primarily a shallow sublittoral species but not uncommonly washed up on shore attached to stranded seaweeds. It may also sometimes be found living on algae on the lower shore. **Similar species** · Resembles *I. metallica*, but this has a very squared pleotelson with three indistinct, small, rounded teeth. *I. emarginata* is also similar but the pleotelson is squarish, becoming concave with the corners bluntly pointed. *I. linearis* is slenderer and grows to 4 cm long. The posterior edge of the pleotelson is more concave.

Abundance & distribution
Common, locally abundant. Found all around Britain and Ireland. Distributed from northern Norway to the Mediterranean and Black Sea, including the Baltic.

Distinctive features

1. Elongate rectangular shape, slightly convex margins.
2. Two pairs of short antennae.
3. Telson broad, rounded; branched uropods at each posterior corner.

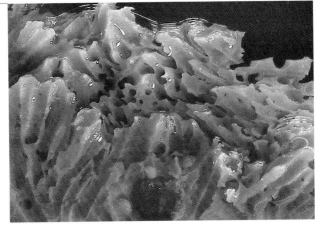

Distinctive features

1. Body broadly oval, curls into ball when disturbed.
2. Pleotelson tapered, posterior edge straight, covered in small tubercles.
3. Outer edge of uropod untoothed.

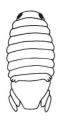

Distinctive features

1. Body elongate oblong-oval shape, dorsoventrally flattened.
2. Rear margin of telson with three points or teeth.
3. Brown to green, with mid-dorsal white markings.

Idotea granulosa Rathke

Description · Body an elongate oval shape, narrowing sharply posteriorly, dorsoventrally flattened. Males are up to 2 cm long and females up to 1.3 cm. Antennae usually less than one-fifth body length. Posterior margins of pleotelson taper sharply to end in long, distinct, median blunt point. Either side of median point pleotelson is concave. Colour depends upon alga animal is living on, but may be red, green, or brown, occasionally with longitudinal white markings. **Habitat & ecology** · Intertidal, found on all but most exposed rocky shores, living on algae; larger specimens typically associated with *Ascophyllum* or *Fucus*, smaller individuals with *Cladophora* or *Polysiphonia*. **Similar species** · *I. neglecta* broader, and median tooth of pleotelson less pronounced. *I. pelagica* typical of exposed shores; smaller than *I. granulosa*; pleotelson rounded, with very short, blunt, median tooth. Tends to be purplish-brown, with white diamond-shaped patches or longitudinal stripes. *I. chelipes* smaller; pleotelson with nearly parallel sides and very small median tooth. Lives in sheltered situations, especially lagoons or estuaries.

Abundance & distribution
Common. Found all around Britain and Ireland. Distributed from Arctic Norway to northern France, including the Baltic.

SUBORDER Asellota

FAMILY Janiridae

Jaera nordmanni (Rathke)

Description · Body dorsoventrally flattened, shaped like a broadly oval woodlouse that is widest across the middle region, laterally fringed with dense bristles. The transversely rectangular head has a pair of small black eyes set quite close to the midline. Females up to about 3.5 mm long, males about 4.5 mm. The pleotelson is oval, with a deep median notch and a pair of short uropods extending posteriorly. Typically slate to bluish-grey or black. **Habitat & ecology** · A mid- to upper-shore species, very tolerant of reduced salinities, found under stones and boulders on coarse sand or gravel, typically where freshwater run-off crosses the shore. **Similar species** · May be confused with *J. albifrons*, but *J. nordmanni* has a more distinctly oval body more densely fringed with bristles, and is also usually paler in colour. *J. hopeana* tends to be broader with a very shallow notch in the pleotelson. There are several other similar European species of *Jaera*.

Abundance & distribution
Common, locally abundant. Found on the south and west coasts of Britain and all around Ireland. Distributed south to the Mediterranean and Azores.

SUBORDER Oniscoidea

FAMILY Ligiidae

Ligia oceanica (Linnaeus)
Sea slater

Description · A large, woodlouse-like isopod up to 3 cm long. The dorsoventrally flattened body posteriorly ends in a pair of long spines or uropods whose basis or peduncle extends well beyond the end of the telson, each basis bearing two long, slender, and almost equal-sized branches. The transversely lozenge-shaped head has a large black eye at each lateral margin. The colour is typically grey or greyish-green, younger individuals being pale brown, often mottled black. **Habitat & ecology** · An upper-shore species found beneath boulders and rocks, in crevices or caves, on quays and groynes, almost anywhere above high water level where it is damp and affords shelter during the day. The sea slater usually emerges at dusk, when it may be found in huge numbers foraging for food. Other species of *Ligia* are found in southern Europe.

Abundance & distribution
Common, locally abundant. Found all around Britain and Ireland. Distributed from Norway to Spain, including Iceland, the Faeroes, and the southern Baltic.

Distinctive features

1. Body elongate, dorso-ventrally flattened, slightly oval.
2. Rear margin of telson sharply tapered, ending in long, blunt point.
3. Brown, red, or green, sometimes with white markings.

Distinctive features

1. Body broadly oval, flattened, widest in mid-body region.
2. Telson oval, with deep median notch and two short, posteriorly projecting, uropods.
3. Lateral body margins in both sexes densely fringed with bristles.

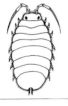

Distinctive features

1. Like a large, flattened woodlouse.
2. Posterior end with pair of long, forked uropods.
3. Black eyes at margin of transversely lozenge-shaped head.

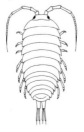

ORDER **Amphipoda** | SUBORDER **Gammaridea**

FAMILY **Gammaridae**

Gammarus locusta (Linnaeus)

Description · A large amphipod, up to 3 cm or more long, with an angular head bearing two pairs of long antennae, the first of which has a short sub-branch. The eyes are large, kidney-shaped, and black. The abdomen bears three pairs of long swimming limbs and three shorter pairs of jumping appendages. The urosome (the last three segments of the body) is strongly convex, with obvious angular dorsal humps, and carries dense tufts of setae and spines. The colour is brownish to greenish. Despite being a common species, specialist knowledge and microscopic examination may be needed to confirm its identification. **Habitat & ecology** · Found intertidally and in shallow sublittoral situations to about 30 m depth, under stones and boulders, or among dense beds of seaweeds. **Similar species** · May be confused with other gammarids, of which there are at least 16 European species.

Abundance & distribution
Common, locally abundant. Found on all coasts of Britain and Ireland. Distributed from Norway and Iceland to the Atlantic coasts of Portugal.

FAMILY **Dexaminidae**

Tritaeta gibbosa (Bate)

Description · A small species, up to 6 mm long, but easily identified by its small, rectangular coxal plates, long, split telson, and distinct dorsal tooth on the first urosome segment. The eyes are large and a round-oval shape. In males the lower antennae are longer than the upper, but in females both are of similar length. The two pairs of gnathopods, used for grasping, are small, and the three pairs of uropods are branched, with the third uropods twice as long as the second. The colour is whitish with brown patches. **Habitat & ecology** · Lives in intertidal and subtidal habitats to a depth of 150 m, among algae but especially with sponges and tunicates.

Abundance & distribution
Locally common. Found around Britain and Ireland but probably absent from the eastern Channel and southern North Sea. Distributed from Norway to Senegal, including the Mediterranean, Black Sea, and Azores.

FAMILY **Ischyroceridae**

Jassa falcata (Montagu)

Description · Body 8–12 mm long, slender and depressed. Head with pair of small, rounded eyes. Upper antennae about half as long as, and distinctly slenderer than, lower and have no side branch. Both first and second thoracic legs end in joint bent back to form pincer-like claw, that on second legs being larger and varying in shape with sex. Greyish with reddish-brown markings, though these may vary through red, black, or green depending upon habitat. Telson small and triangular, with two setae on either side of tip. **Habitat & ecology** · Found in tubes, which it builds, from mid-shore to shallow sublittoral situations, often on seaweeds or among hydroids, stones or boulders, in kelp holdfasts or on artificial structures such as ships and buoys. Not uncommonly significant as a fouling species and tubes may build up sufficiently to block water-pipes and ducts running from power stations into sea. **Similar species** · Closely resembles other members of genus, particularly *J. marmorata*. Microscopic examination often needed to confirm species.

Abundance & distribution
Common, locally abundant. Found all around Britain and Ireland. Distributed from the North Sea to the Mediterranean. Also found in the Pacific and Indian Oceans and regarded as cosmopolitan in temperate and warm to temperate waters.

Distinctive features

1. Head angular, with pair of kidney-shaped black eyes.
2. Two pairs of long antennae.
3. Last three segments of body (urosome) strongly convex.

Distinctive features

1. Coxal plates rectangular.
2. Telson long and split.
3. First urosome segment has distinct dorsal tooth.

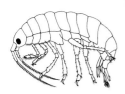

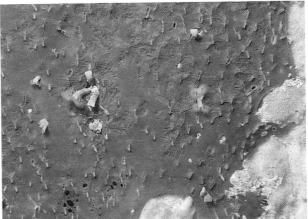

Distinctive features

1. Upper antennae slenderer than, and half length of, lower antennae.
2. First and second thoracic legs end in pincer-like claws.
3. Telson small, triangular, with two setae on each side of tip.

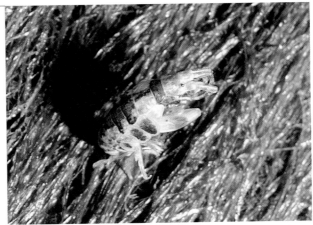

SUBORDER **Caprellidea**

FAMILY **Caprellidae**

Caprella linearis (Linnaeus)
Ghost shrimp

Description · The slender, somewhat cylindrical, body of caprellids has fewer appendages than other amphipods. Male *Caprella linearis*, reaching lengths of 20–22 mm, are somewhat larger than females, which at most are only about 14 mm long. The bulbous head bears two pairs of unbranched antennae, the upper about twice as long as the lower, whose undersurface is clad in paired rows of long setae. Dorsally the body surface is generally smooth, but may have pairs of tiny tubercles on some segments. The second gnathopod is larger than the first. The animal has a habit of grasping the substratum with its posterior appendages and arching the rest of the body into the overlying water. **Habitat & ecology** · A lower-shore and shallow sublittoral species, mainly found clinging to hydroid cnidarians and other sessile organisms by means of their posterior pereopods, but occasionally seen free-swimming.

Abundance & distribution
Often common but unobtrusive. Found around all coasts of Britain and Ireland. Distributed from southern Norway and the western Baltic to the Atlantic coasts of Spain and Portugal.

Phylum Pycnogonida

Pycnogonids have a very characteristic flat, and usually distinctly segmented body with eight pairs of legs. The head (**cephalon**), which is fused with the first **trunk** segment, is anteriorly developed into a cylindrical or bulbous **proboscis** with the mouth at its tip. On the dorsal surface of the cephalon two forward-facing and two backward-facing **eyes** are carried on a **tubercle**, other head appendages including a pair of slender sensory **palps**, a pair of **chelifores** which end in claws (**chelae**) used for feeding and, in many species, a pair of long, slender **ovigers** that are used for holding the eggs against the ventral body surface. Females typically carry eggs on the **femur** segments of their legs. Each trunk

segment has a distinct process on either side of which the eight long legs articulate. Both the ovaries and digestive system extend into the legs, which are used for walking and swimming. At the hind end an unsegmented **abdomen** or **anal process**, with the anus at its end, extends from the last trunk segment. The pycnogonids are considered by some to be a class of the arthropods.

Intertidal and shallow water pycnogonids are often quite numerous but slow moving, and unobtrusive because they are small. In the deep sea and in Antarctica pycnogonids grow to a much larger size. In northern European coastal waters they are found most commonly on bushy red algae encrusted with bryozoans, or among tufts of hydroids or bryozoans on which they feed **suctorially**. Among the British

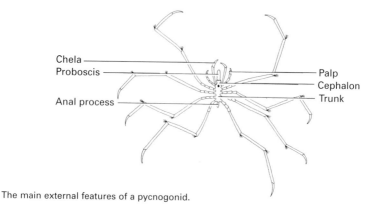

Chela
Proboscis
Anal process
Palp
Cephalon
Trunk

The main external features of a pycnogonid.

Distinctive features

1. Slender, cylindrical, flexible body.
2. Upper antennae on bulbous head about twice as long as lower.

families, containing about 20 species in all, members of the **Nymphonidae** and **Pycnogonidae** are found on most rocky shores.

Further reading

Elliot, P., King, P. E., Morgan, C. I., Pugh, P. J. A., Smith, A. and Wheeler, S. L. A. (1990). Chelicerata, Uniramia, and Tardigrada. In *The marine fauna of the British Isles and north-west Europe* (eds P. J. Hayward & J. S. Ryland), Vol. 1, pp. 553–627. Clarendon Press, Oxford.

King, P. E. (1974). British sea spiders. *Synopses of the British Fauna, New Series*, **5**, 1–68.

King, P. E. (1986). A revised key to the adults of littoral pycnogonids in the British Isles. *Field Studies*, **6**, 493–516.

FAMILY **Nymphonidae**

Nymphon gracile Leach

Description · Body slender, smooth, about 4–8 mm long, sometimes larger, with relatively short anterior proboscis, twice as long as wide, and bearing on each side a pair of pincer-like chelicerae (feeding appendages). Four pairs of slender walking legs, 3–4 times as long as body. Also a pair of much shorter 'legs', the ovigers; although these occur in both sexes, the male uses them to carry eggs after they are laid by the female. Colour typically translucent with pinkish gut. **Habitat & ecology** · A shallow water species, not uncommonly found on lower shore during summer, slowly creeping among bryozoans, hydroids, or sea anemones on which it feeds suctorially. The ovigers are used to carry the eggs and clean the body. Therefore when a male is carrying eggs it may become fouled with sessile organisms such as hydroids. **Similar species** · May easily be confused with other species in genus, such as *N. rubrum*, *N. hirtum*, or *N. brevirostre*. *N. hirtum* is notably hairy. Microscopic examination required to distinguish between these species reliably.

Abundance & distribution
Locally common but unobtrusive. Found on the west coasts of Britain and Ireland. Distributed from western Norway southwards to Morocco, including the Mediterranean.

FAMILY **Pycnogonidae**

Pycnogonum littorale (Strøm)

Description · Body stout, up to 5 mm long and mostly covered in tubercles. The four pairs of walking legs are thick, curved, have a 'segmented' appearance, and end in strongly curved claws. Anteriorly the proboscis is sharply tapered, stout, and conical, the head bearing neither palps nor chelicerae. The trunk segments are wide. Ovigerous legs are found only in males. The female is usually white or cream in colour whilst the male is smaller and often pale brown. **Habitat & ecology** · A lower-shore and shallow sublittoral species, found under flat rocks or attached to its prey, which may include sea anemones, polychaetes such as *Sabellaria* species, hydroids, lucernarians (Stauromedusae), or even sea cucumbers.

Abundance & distribution
Locally common. Found all around the British Isles and Ireland. Distributed from Arctic Norway to southern Spain.

Distinctive features

1. Four pairs of long, slender walking legs.
2. Body slender.
3. Proboscis flanked by two pincer-like feeding appendages.
4. Pinkish-orange.

Distinctive features

1. Body stout, four pairs of thick walking legs appearing distinctly 'segmented'.
2. Proboscis sharply tapering, conical.
3. No palps or chelicerae.

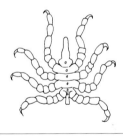

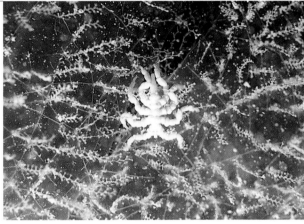

Molluscs

Phylum Mollusca

With about 75 000 living species, this phylum exhibits enormous diversity in both body form and ecology. In the marine environment examples can be found from abyssal depths up to the highest levels of tidal reach. Representatives of the phylum also occur commonly on land and in freshwater. The basic body plan is an **unsegmented**, bilaterally symmetrical, and coelomate one, though many members of the class **Gastropoda** exhibit secondary **asymmetry** as adults. The body consists of a **head**, often closely associated with a muscular **foot**, and a soft **visceral mass** in which the main body organs are situated. The head is often well-developed and houses a protrusible feeding organ (**odontophore**) which includes a **chitinous** toothed ribbon (**radula**) used for scraping algae off rocks, boring into the shell of prey, or other feeding purposes. The foot may be modified for locomotion, burrowing, or feeding. The visceral mass is covered by a **mantle** (**pallium**), a major characteristic of the phylum, and the broad fold of the mantle around the edge of the visceral mass forms a **mantle skirt**. It is the edge of the mantle that secretes another very characteristic structure of molluscs, the calcareous **shell**. The molluscan shell is composed of three layers, an outer organic layer (the **periostracum**), a middle layer composed of columnar **calcite**, and an inner laminated layer that is often **nacreous** (mother-of-pearl effect). The shell, besides serving to protect the softer body parts, is often modified for other functions, such as buoyancy in floating or swimming species. In several groups the shell is internal or completely missing. The gills (**ctenidia**), **osphradia** (sensory organs), and a mucus-secreting **hypobranchial gland** are located in the mantle (**pallial**) cavity into which the reproductive organs, kidneys, and anus discharge. The **coelom** is reduced, **blood** and **coelomic fluid** circulating around the body through an interconnected series of open **haemocoelic** spaces which serve as an efficient hydrostatic skeleton. Most marine molluscs possess separate sexes, although in some families simultaneous or sequential **hermaphroditism** is known. Generally there is a pelagic larval stage in the life-cycle, but fertilisation and development vary enormously throughout the phylum.

Amongst the molluscan classes three, the **Caudofoveata** and **Aplacophora** (elongate, worm-like molluscs with no shell - sometimes placed in a single class) and the **Monoplacophora** (limpet-like molluscs), have no known coastal representatives in northern Europe, but examples from all the other groups are found in north-west European waters. The other classes are the **Polyplacophora** (chitons), **Gastropoda** (snails and slugs), **Bivalvia** (bivalves), **Scaphopoda** (tusk shells) and **Cephalopoda** (octopuses and squids).

Further reading

Graham, A. (1971). British prosobranch and other operculate gastropod molluscs. *Synopses of the British Fauna, New Series*, **2**, 1–112.

Hayward, P. J. (1990). Mollusca II: Bivalvia and Cephalopoda. In *The marine fauna of the British Isles and North-West Europe* (eds P. J. Hayward & J. S. Ryland), Vol. 2, pp. 628–730. Clarendon Press, Oxford.

Hayward, P. J., Wigham, G. D., & Yonow, N. (1990). Mollusca I: Polyplacophora, Scaphoda, and Gastropoda. In *The marine fauna of the British Isles and North-West Europe* (eds P. J. Hayward & J. S. Ryland), Vol. 2, pp. 628–730. Clarendon Press, Oxford.

Thompson, T. E. & Brown, G. H. (1976). British opisthobranch molluscs. Mollusca: Gastropoda. *Synopses of the British Fauna, New Series*, **8**, 1–203.

Thompson, T. E. & Brown, G. H. (1984). *Biology of opisthobranch molluscs, Vol. II*. Ray Society, London.

Class Polyplacophora (chitons, coat-of-mail shells)

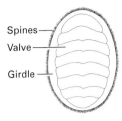

Spines

Valve

Girdle

The general external features of a polyplacophoran.

Polyplacophorans have strongly adhesive, limpet-like habits on hard surfaces. Their oval bodies are covered by dorsal shells composed of eight arched and interlocking plates or **valves**, peripherally embedded in a toughened development of the mantle skirt called a **girdle**. Each of the valves has an anterior **articulamentum** and often notched lateral **insertion plates** which anchor it into the girdle tissues. The girdle is of variable width, depending upon the species, and may be fringed with spines or bear a variety of calcified granules, spines, or small plates on its upper surface. The **foot** is broad and ventral. The small head has neither eyes nor tentacles. The paired lateral, and variable number of, **gills** are situated in a peripheral **pallial groove** located below the edge of the girdle. The sexes are separate.

Found only in marine habitats and mostly in intertidal to shallow sublittoral situations, all chitons are herbivorous grazers feeding on encrusting and filamentous algae. It is possible they may also feed on encrusting, sessile invertebrates such as bryozoans.

FAMILY **Leptochitonidae**

Leptochiton asellus (Gmelin)

Description · A chiton with an elongate oval shape, about 1.5 times as long as broad. The length is up to 19 mm, though usually smaller. The valves are granular and keeled with small posterior knobs. The girdle is narrow and covered with small elongate, ridged rectangular scales. The girdle edge is fringed with tiny spines. The valves are off-white to yellowish, sometimes with dark lines. **Habitat & ecology** · This species is seen on the lower shore but is particularly common subtidally. It is generally found on stones and old shells.

Abundance & distribution
Common on all British coasts. Distributed from Greenland, Iceland, and Spitzbergen in the north to the Atlantic coast of Spain.

FAMILY **Ischnochitonidae**

Lepidochitona cinereus (Linnaeus)

Description · A chiton with a round to oval outline, up to 24 mm in length and about 1.5 times as long as broad. The valves have a low keel and a distinct posterior knob. They are rough to the touch, like fine sand paper. The front valve has 8–9 notches along its front edge and the other valves have one or two notches on each side. The girdle is fairly narrow and finely granulated. The colour of the valves is highly variable with patches and streaks of yellow, reddish-brown, and green. The girdle may also be several colours. **Habitat & ecology** · Occurs intertidally from mid-shore levels to subtidally. Probably the commonest chiton on northern European shores. It is generally found attached to the underside of stones.

Abundance & distribution
Common on all coasts of Britain and Ireland. Distributed from western Norway south to the Mediterranean.

Tonicella rubra (Linnaeus)

Description · A chiton with an elongate oval outline, up to 20 mm in length and about 1.5 times as long as broad. The shell valves are smooth and glossy but have rows of granulation. Along the rear edge of the valves there is a very poorly developed knob. The girdle is fairly broad and finely granulated, with a fringe of minute spines around the edge. The colour of the valves is buff to reddish-brown or deep brown, marbled with white or yellow. The girdle is usually chequered red and white. **Habitat & ecology** · Generally occurs on the lower shore and subtidally. **Similar species** · *T. rubra* resembles *T. marmorea* but this species grows to 40 mm long and the front valve of the shell has eight notches along its leading edge.

Abundance & distribution
Common. Occurs on all British coasts but may be rare in the south-east. Distributed from Britain north to Norway and Iceland.

Distinctive features

1. Valves keeled with small posterior knob.
2. Girdle narrow, with numerous ridged rectangular scales.

Distinctive features

1. Valves keeled with small posterior knob.
2. Front valve with 8–9 notches.

Distinctive features

1. Valves smooth and glossy but have rows of granules.
2. Fairly wide granulated girdle with a fringe of fine spines.

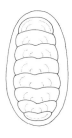

FAMILY **Acanthochitonidae**

Acanthochitona crinitus (Pennant)

Description · A flattened, elongate, and oval-shaped chiton, up to 3 cm long, with the dorsal shell composed of eight interlocked, transverse plates which possess a distinct median longitudinal keel. The girdle or mantle skirt is spiny and also possesses 18 conspicuous tufts of long bristles. The eight shell plates are covered with large, irregularly distributed tubercles of various sizes. The fleshy girdle is typically greyish-brown to dark brown, the tufts of bristles being obvious by their pale grey colour, whereas the shell plates are variously brown, yellowish-brown, or even pinkish. **Habitat & ecology** · Lives clamped to rocks and boulders on the lower shore and in shallow sublittoral situations. **Similar species** · May be mistaken for *A. fascicularis*, although this species tends to be larger (up to 6 cm long) and its shells have a more regular and finer granulation.

Abundance & distribution
Fairly common on most British rocky shores, this species is also found on Atlantic, North Sea, and Channel coasts of northern Europe, in the Mediterranean, and southwards to West Africa.

Class Gastropoda

By far the largest of the molluscan classes, more than 60 000 species have been described worldwide from marine, freshwater, and terrestrial habitats. The body of adults in most groups of gastropods is **asymmetrical**, a consequence of a larval phenomenon called

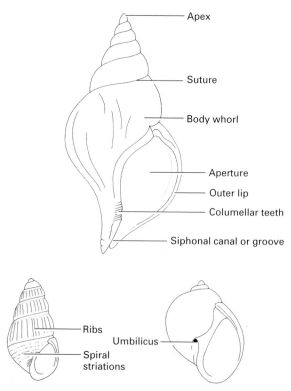

Some of the main external features of gastropod molluscs.

Distinctive features

1. Body oval, elongate, rather flattened.
2. Eight interlocked shell plates with distinct longitudinal keel.
3. Mantle surrounding shell plates with tufts of long bristles.

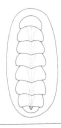

torsion in which the **visceral mass** is rotated through 180°, resulting in the alimentary canal and nervous system becoming looped into a figure-of-eight and the mantle cavity becoming located anteriorly above the head. This phenomenon is very characteristic of gastropod molluscs, though in some groups varying degrees of secondary **detorsion** have occurred. The shell is in a single piece, primitively conical in shape but typically coiled or spiralled; in several groups the shell is reduced or totally lost. The ventral foot is well-developed and used for crawling, burrowing, or swimming depending upon the species concerned. The head is also well-developed and bears **eyes** and **sensory tentacles**. There is usually a pelagic larval stage in the life-cycle, but in several forms the larvae develop inside the egg case and hatch directly as miniature adults. There are three subclasses, the Prosobranchia (sea snails), Opisthobranchia (sea slugs), and **Pulmonata** (air-breathing snails and slugs, mostly terrestrial).

Subclass Prosobranchia Primitively the prosobranch shell is conical, as in limpets, but through evolution has tended to become coiled or spiralled. There may be few or many coils (**whorls**), and shell shape is extremely variable. The last and largest whorl, ending with the shell **aperture**, is called the **body whorl**. The aperture may be simple, oval to rounded, or possess well-developed lips or rims. The lower (ventral)

edge of the aperture may be developed into a distinct groove (**siphonal canal** or groove). Boundaries between whorls are called **sutures**. Typically the shell surface is patterned by a variety of **growth lines** (parallel to the **outer lip** of the aperture), which may be thickened to form **ribs** crossing each whorl, as well as **spiral striations** or **spiralled ridges** parallel to the sutures. On shells with strongly developed ribs and ridges the surface has a chequered (**decussate**) appearance. The shell whorls form around a solid or hollow vertical central column (**columella**); when this is hollow it often opens by a pore (**umbilicus**) at the base of the body whorl. The lip of the aperture adjacent to the body whorl in many forms has distinct ridges (**columellar teeth**) crossing it. In most prosobranchs with a coiled shell, coiling is clockwise (**dextral**), the aperture being to the right of the columella, but **sinistral** (anticlockwise) coiling occurs in some, the aperture then being to the left of the columella. The head, bearing **sensory tentacles** and lateral **eye-stalks**, and foot can be fully withdrawn into the shell, in many forms the aperture then being sealed by a hard, horny **operculum** attached to the posterior dorsal surface of the foot. In the family **Tricoliidae** the operculum is calcified. There are three orders of prosobranchs:

Order Archaeogastropoda Primitive prosobranchs, with the gill paired, single, or replaced by **pallial gills**. The shell may be

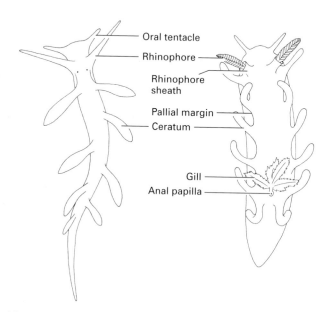

Oral tentacle
Rhinophore
Rhinophore sheath
Pallial margin
Ceratum
Gill
Anal papilla

The external features of two sea slugs (opisthobranchs).

conical or coiled, and an operculum may be present or absent. Radular teeth long and brush-like, employed to sweep food material from rocky surfaces. Gonads and kidneys paired. The order includes ear shells, keyhole limpets, tortoiseshell limpets, limpets, and top shells.

Order Mesogastropoda The largest and most diverse prosobranch order. Members have only a single kidney, gonad, and gill. Feeding types variable, including both herbivores and carnivores. Generally the more specialised the feeding behaviour, the fewer the radular teeth. The group includes chink shells, winkles, mud snails, tower shells, bubble shells, slipper limpets, cowries, and necklace shells.

Order Neogastropoda All are carnivorous, some highly specialised, fast-moving active predators. The radula has few teeth which are modified in each species according to its preferred prey organism. The shell aperture usually has a well-developed siphonal canal. This order includes muricids and whelks.

Subclass Opisthobranchia The Opisthobranchia is a large group, which includes the planktonic sea butterflies, as well as benthic sea hares and sea slugs, and some commensal or parasitic forms (order **Pyramidellimorpha**). A very few opisthobranchs have a conspicuous external shell, some have the shell reduced and internal, but most have no shell. Opisthobranchs as a group are characterised by their nerve loop being untwisted (**detorted**), but the presence of a single gonad and kidney suggests that detorsion is a secondary phenomenon and that the group may have evolved from fully torted prosobranch ancestors. All opisthobranchs are hermaphroditic, their eggs often being laid in conspicuous ribbons or capsules encased in jelly. Most species are carnivorous, though a few are specialised herbivores. Many of the true sea slugs, with no shell, have evolved elaborate defence mechanisms against potential predators, including chemical (toxic) secretions, vivid colour patterns, and, in species which feed on cnidarians, the use of cnidarian nematocysts aggregated into **cnidosacs** at the tips of their **cerata**. Many forms possess obvious external gills.

The systematics of the subclass Opisthobranchia is still under review and some taxonomists do not regard the group as monophyletic. In addition to the Pyramidellimorpha referred to above, there are two entirely **pelagic orders Gymnosomata** and **Thecosomata,** known as the sea butterflies. The **Acochlideacea** or **Acochlidioidea** are small, entirely interstitial opisthobranchs with no shell. The **Aplysiomorpha** or **Anaspidea** are known as the sea hares and these have enlarged **parapodial lobes,** an internal or no shell, and an elongate head bearing rolled **oral tentacles** and **rhinophores.** The **Bullomorpha** usually have an external shell, though it may be internal or absent; the foot may have expanded parapodial lobes, an operculum may be present, and the head forms a flattened **cephalic shield.** This group is also known as the **Cephalaspidea,** and the **Runcinoidea** have been split off from it by some scientists. The **Pleurobranchomorpha** or **Notaspidea** have a flattened body, an internal, external, or no shell, a single, obvious gill projecting on the right side of the body, a head bearing an **oral veil,** and rolled oral tentacles and rhinophores. The **Sacoglossa** have a small or no shell, rolled rhinophores, and small or no oral tentacles.

Finally, the **Nudibranchia,** or true sea slugs, are opisthobranchs with no shell and a very variable body form that may be oval and flattened, or elongate. Many of the nudibranch sea slugs are arguably the most beautifully coloured and patterned of marine invertebrates. Flattened species typically have **papillae** or **tubercles** on their mantle (referred to as the **dorsum** or **notum**). The **gills** of nudibranchs are often arranged in an arc or circle around the **anal papilla,** and many have finger-like extensions of the body wall (**cerata**) on their **pallial margin** (the edge between the dorsum and body sides); the cerata contain lobes of the digestive gland (**hepatopancreas**) and their tips may be armed with nematocysts. The head usually has oral tentacles and rhinophores, the latter being extremely variable in shape and form; they may be swollen or slender, smooth, tuberculate, lamellate, wrinkled, or branched, and may or may not be surrounded by a **sheath** into which they can be withdrawn.

SUBCLASS **Prosobranchia** | ORDER **Archeogastropoda**

FAMILY **Haliotidae**

Haliotis tuberculata Linnaeus
Abalone, green ormer, ormer

Description · This species has a flattened, oval, ear-shaped shell. At one
end the shell forms a flattened tight spiral. Along the other edge runs a
ridge, in which appear holes with raised edges. The shell can reach 10 cm in
length. The outer surface of the shell is rough and variously coloured with
shades of dull greyish-brown and green. Other organisms often colonise
the shell. The inside of the empty shell is bright, iridescent, silvery mother-
of-pearl. The animal is black with numerous tentacles around the margin
of the shell. **Habitat & ecology** · From low shore to shallow subtidal. It
feeds on seaweeds, especially delicate species of red algae. Its eggs and
larvae are pelagic for 3 days after fertilisation before becoming benthic and
completing their development. A smaller species, *H. lamellosa*, occurs in the
Mediterranean.

Abundance & distribution
Uncommon because of over-
collecting. Only occurs in the
Channel Islands and
southwards to the
Mediterranean.

SUPERFAMILY **Patellacea**

FAMILY **Acmaeidae**

Tectura virginea (Müller) **Pink-rayed limpet**

Description · Limpet with a small, delicate, conical shell, with apex often
positioned towards head end. Anterior profile of shell may appear concave,
whilst elsewhere shell is convex. Shell about 10–12 mm long and 4 mm high;
has fine sculpturing of radiating lines and rings and is pale pink, yellow, or
white rayed with pink or brown. Inside of shell is white, though may
appear pinkish or pale green, and may have a red, V-shaped mark near
apex. Mouth has rounded and smooth, lobate lips. Edge of mantle has no
tentacles and is a pale colour, sometimes with white spots. **Habitat &
ecology** · Occurs on lower shore and shallow subtidal, generally on
smooth rocks and stones. Feeds on algae, especially encrusting red species.
Eggs are laid on stones or rocks in a thin mucous sheet, hatching as
planktonic trochophore larvae. **Similar species** · *T. tessulata*, but this
grows larger. Mouth has fringed or crenellate lips and there are tentacles
around margins of mantle.

Abundance & distribution
Frequent. Occurs all around the
coasts of Britain and Ireland.
Distributed from Iceland and
Norway to the Cape Verde and
Azores Islands, including the
Mediterranean.

FAMILY **Patellidae**

Helcion pellucidum (Linnaeus)
Blue-rayed limpet

Description · A beautifully and strikingly marked limpet. The smooth,
cap-shaped shell is up to 15 mm long, thin, and a translucent amber colour
marked with lines of vivid peacock blue spots or streaks which radiate from
the shell apex. The blue markings tend to fade in older individuals, which
may appear a dull greenish- to chalky-white colour. Previously known as
Patina pellucida. **Habitat & ecology** · Found on exposed lower rocky
shores and to sublittoral depths of about 30 m, almost invariably on the
fronds and stipes of large kelp species; exceptionally it may occur on *Fucus
serratus*. Larger adults excavate holes in kelp holdfasts, which can weaken
the holdfast to the extent that it may become torn off during stormy
conditions.

Abundance & distribution
Locally common and
sometimes abundant. Found on
Atlantic coasts from Iceland
and Norway south to Portugal,
but does not occur on Baltic
shores, nor on Belgian or
Dutch coasts.

Distinctive features

1. Flattened, oval, ear-shaped shell.
2. One end of shell forms low tight spiral.
3. Row of holes along one side of shell.

Distinctive features

1. Small limpet.
2. Shell conical with apex towards front.
3. Mouth with rounded smooth lips.
4. No marginal tentacles along mantle edge.

Distinctive features

1. Found almost entirely on large kelp fronds and stipes.
2. Brownish shell marked by streaks or spots of vivid peacock blue radiating from shell apex.

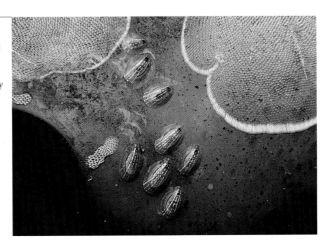

Patella species
Limpets

Description · All patellid limpets have a strong conical shell with radiating ridges. The shell surface may have epiphytes (small seaweeds) or epizooites (barnacles) growing on it. If the underside of the animal is examined a muscular foot is visible around which are small marginal tentacles. The head has an oval-shaped mouth and a pair of tentacles. Differentiating between the species of *Patella* is difficult and usually involves prising the animals off the rock which can kill them. We therefore recommend that unless it is really necessary to identify them to specific level they are just identified to genus.

(a)

(a) *Patella vulgata* Linnaeus

The common limpet. It has a shell up to 5–6 cm long with a tall conical shape in upper-shore individuals, a flatter conical shape in lower-shore and young animals. The outer surface is marked with coarse radiating ridges and distinct growth lines, the undersurface is smooth and greenish-grey. The sole of the foot may be orange but is usually olive green, yellow, or grey, surrounded by translucent grey mantle tentacles.

(b) *Patella depressa* Pennant

The black-footed limpet. This also has a rather flattened conical shell up to 3–4 cm long and finely ridged. Both exterior and interior shell margins may have dark or chocolate-coloured rays or streaks. The underside of the shell rim is deeply and regularly ridged, the darker streaks radiating between the yellowish ridges. The attachment scar on the inner surface of the shell is creamy orange in colour, the foot of the living animal dark olive to greyish-black, with dull white to brilliant white, opaque, marginal mantle tentacles.

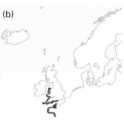
(b)

(c) *Patella ulyssiponensis* Gmelin

The China limpet. This is generally smaller and flatter than the common limpet and has cream-coloured marginal tentacles around the foot. The apex of the shell also tends to be anterior of the midline.

Habitat & ecology · All three *Patella* species are intertidal on rocky shores and are ecologically important animals. They use a very hard-toothed radula to scrape rock surfaces, grazing red and green seaweeds and often limiting algal growth on exposed and moderately exposed shores, particularly *Ulva* and the sporelings of *Fucus* species. The common limpet is found at all exposures and tends to be most numerous at mid-tide levels, though it may be found higher and lower on the shore. The black-footed limpet is preferentially found on exposed or moderately exposed shores and is also commonest around mid-tide levels. The China limpet occurs on moderately sheltered to exposed shores, generally at lower tide levels, but it may be found in rock pools at mid-shore levels. The common limpet changes sex from male to female when about 4 years old, breeding between October and December. It is a free spawner and has pelagic larvae that last a few days.

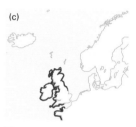
(c)

Abundance & distribution
Patella vulgata (a)

The most common species. Abundant on most rocky shores around Britain and Ireland with a distributional range extending from northern Norway to North Sea, English Channel, and Atlantic coasts of north-west Europe and into the Mediterranean.

Patella depressa (b)

Sometimes locally common, and has a range extending from north Wales (Anglesey) to Atlantic coasts of north-west Europe, and as far east as the Isle of Wight in the English Channel. It is mostly not found on Irish coasts.

Patella ulyssiponensis (c)

Occurs on the south and west coasts of Britain and all around Ireland; distributed south to the Mediterranean.

Distinctive features

1. Conical shell, usually with radiating ridges.
2. Small tentacles around the margin of the foot.
3. Found on the shore. usually firmly attached to rock.

(a)

(b)

(c)

FAMILY **Trochidae**

Calliostoma zizyphinum (Linnaeus)
Painted topshell

Description · Very conical shell with up to 12–13 flattened whorls. Apex of shell quite pointed. Base of shell rather flat and aperture a squarish oval shape. Shell up to 30 mm high. Colour variable, generally pale lilac to flesh-coloured or pale yellow. Whorls of shell marked with reddish-brown or purple irregular spots often flecked with white or pale yellow. Some populations have high numbers of purely violet or white individuals (variety Lyons). Mouth slightly papillate and resembles a T-shape when closed. **Habitat & ecology** · Generally found on the lower shore and shallow subtidal on rocky habitats. *C. zizyphinum* feeds on algae though it may also include sessile invertebrates in its diet. Eggs are laid in strings on the shore and hatch as crawl-away juveniles. **Similar species** · Resembles *C. papillosum*. This species has a more rounded shell base than *C. zizyphinum* and the mouth is densely covered in papillae. It is rarer than *C. zizyphinum* and generally occurs subtidally on soft sediments.

Abundance & distribution
Common all around British Isles and Ireland. Distributed from Norway to the Azores and Canary Islands, including the Mediterranean.

Gibbula cineraria (Linnaeus)
Grey topshell

Description · The somewhat flat shell up to about 1.25 cm tall and similar width, with 5–7 rather compressed whorls ending in a bluntly pointed apex. Whorls smoothly rounded in profile, with inconspicuous sutures. In the centre of shell base a small umbilical pore opens into hollow columella. Greyish-white background shell colour, marked with darker greyish-red or reddish-brown narrow bands. Bands may be faded or damaged, damaged shells often having mother-of-pearl lustre. **Habitat & ecology** · Found on the mid- and lower regions of sheltered rocky shores and sublittorally to depths of 20–100 m, under boulders or stones, and among seaweeds. It may sometimes be found in larger, permanent rock pools on the upper shore. Breeding takes place during the spring and summer months. **Similar species** · Resembles *G. umbilicalis*, but *G. cineraria* is taller and has a less angular last whorl. Also similar to *G. pennanti* but again this species is flatter that *G. cineraria* and with a more angular last whorl.

Abundance & distribution
Sometimes locally quite common, found on Atlantic, English Channel, and North Sea coasts of north-western Europe.

Gibbula magus (Linnaeus)
Turban topshell

Description · The shell, with a stepped, conical profile, is up to 25–30 mm wide but generally not as tall. The 7–8 whorls are joined by distinct sutures, the upper rims of the whorls being regularly and obviously bumpy. The basal umbilical pore is large and distinct. The background colour of the shell is yellowish-white, marked with irregular red, brown, or purple patches. The coloured patches are often faded, particularly when the shell has been taken over by a hermit crab. **Habitat & ecology** · On rocky shores or in mixed sand and mud sediments; found on the lower shore and sublittorally to depths of about 10–20 m. **Similar species** · Closely resembles *G. tumida*, a more northern species found all around Britain. *G. tumida* is much smaller than *G. magus*, only growing to 9 mm in height and with a less papillate snout.

Abundance & distribution
Uncommon. Found all around Ireland; on western British coasts from the Shetland Islands southwards to Swanage in the English Channel; on Atlantic coasts of France, Spain, and Portugal; and in the Mediterranean. It has not been found in the North Sea, nor on

Distinctive features

1. Conical shell with pointed apex.
2. Whorls flattened.
3. Tip of snout slightly fringed.

Distinctive features

1. Shell rather squat, bluntly pointed.
2. Base of shell with small umbilical pore.

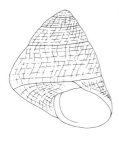

the coast of south Wales.

Distinctive features

1. Shell whorls distinctly stepped in profile.
2. Umbilical pore large, distinct.
3. Upper rims of whorls distinctly and regularly bumpy.

Gibbula umbilicalis (da Costa)
Flat topshell

Description · A bluntly conical shell, up to about 15 mm tall; smoothly rounded shape in profile. There are up to seven whorls, with the base of the shell having a distinct umbilical pore. Background colour pale dull greenish- or creamy-yellow, marked with distinct broad and widely spaced bands of red or purplish-red. **Habitat & ecology** · Sheltered rocky shores from the upper region down to shallow sublittoral situations. Can withstand prolonged emersion and reduced salinities; quite commonly found in upper-shore rock pools. Breeds during summer. **Similar species** · Somewhat resembles *G. cineraria*, but is flatter and more rounded in profile and marked with a pattern of broader and more separated bands. Most similar to *G. pennanti* but in this species the upper whorls tend to be more swollen with prominent sutures and a clearly turreted profile. This species is present only in the Channel Islands and further south on the Atlantic coasts of France, Spain, and Portugal.

Abundance & distribution
Common, often locally abundant. Distribution extends from the Orkney Islands south to Atlantic and Irish Sea coasts of Ireland and north-west Europe, and the western parts of the English Channel. It does not occur in the North Sea or the Mediterranean.

Osilinus lineata (da Costa)
Toothed winkle, toothed topshell, thick topshell

Description · Shell thick, heavy, and distinctly conical, about 25–30 mm tall and wide, with about 5–6 ill-defined whorls. In the centre of the shell base is a small umbilical pore, which may be obscured by growth. The outer lip of the shell aperture appears to overhang the opening; the inner lip has a distinct 'tooth' pointing inwards; the inner surface of the aperture has a mother-of-pearl appearance. The shell is pale greyish-green or light brown with a pattern of purple, green, or reddish-brown zigzags. Often the apex of the shell is worn and appears pearly-yellow or silver in colour. Previously called *Monodonta lineata*. **Habitat & ecology** · An intertidal species found on the middle and upper shore on rocks and boulders, often in rock pools. *O. lineata* feeds on microscopic algal films and small algal plants. The larvae of this species are planktonic and settle low on the shore. The juveniles may be hard to find as they shelter in deep crevices.

Abundance & distribution
Locally fairly common, the distribution extends from north Wales (Anglesey) southwards on Atlantic coasts of north-west Europe and into the western approaches of the English Channel. It also occurs on Atlantic shores of West Africa as far south as Madeira.

ORDER **Mesogastropoda**

FAMILY **Lacunidae**

Lacuna vincta (Montagu) **Banded chink shell**

Description · The broadly conical shell, with about five smooth whorls, is up to 1 cm tall with a pointed apex. The shell aperture is oval. The base of the shell has a small but deep umbilicus. The semi-transparent shells are greenish-yellow, usually with a pattern of reddish-brown bands which follow the spiralling of the whorls. **Habitat & ecology** · A lower-shore and shallow sublittoral species, found on fucoids, red seaweeds such as *Ceramium* and *Polysiphonia*, and on seagrasses. It is sometimes particularly abundant on *Fucus serratus*. The eggs are laid in ring-shaped masses of jelly on algal food between January and early summer. **Similar species** · Easily confused with some rissoid snails, but these are generally smaller.

Abundance & distribution
Locally common but unobtrusive because of its size, with a distribution extending from the west Baltic Sea southwards to Atlantic, North Sea, and English Channel coasts south to Brittany.

Distinctive features

1. Shell bluntly conical, smoothly rounded in profile.
2. Greenish- or creamy-yellow background, marked with broad, widely spaced, red or purplish bands.

Distinctive features

1. Shell thick, heavy and distinctly conical.
2. Inner lip of shell aperture with a distinct 'tooth' pointing inwards.

Distinctive features

1. Shell broadly conical with pointed apex.
2. Semi-transparent greenish-yellow, marked with reddish-brown bands following spiralling of whorls.

Family Littorinidae

Littorinids or periwinkles are important grazers on the shores of northern Europe. *Littorina littorea*, *L. saxatilis*, *L. obtusata*, and *L. mariae* feed on seaweeds and microscopic plants living in a film on rock surfaces. *L. neritoides* eats microscopic algae and lichens because it lives high on the shore. The life histories of these snails vary. *L. littorea* and *L. neritoides* have planktonic larvae, *L. saxatilis* and *L. rudis* bear live young, and *L. obtusata* and *L. mariae* lay eggs on the shore from which crawl-away juveniles hatch.

Littorina littorea (Linnaeus)
Edible periwinkle, common periwinkle

Description · Sharply conical shell, up to 25–30 mm tall, has whorls sculptured with very fine spiralling grooves. Shell colour variable but typically dark blackish- or greyish-brown; some may be reddish. Margins of shell aperture white, outer lip of opening meeting main whorl tangentially. Gill-breathing. **Habitat & ecology** · Commonly eaten in northern European countries. Found from upper shore to shallow sublittoral situations on rocks and boulders, especially when on moderately sheltered shores covered with seaweeds, but also on softer sediments. Gelatinous egg capsules shed directly into sea, and during breeding season it may migrate up and down shore. **Similar species** · Smaller specimens resemble *L. saxatilis*, but in this form outer lip of shell aperture joins main body whorl at right angles rather than tangentially and is protruded at this point. Same feature can be used to distinguish *L. littorea* from *L. nigrolineata*, which tends to be whitish, yellow, or orange-red, and like *L. saxatilis* usually has more heavily sculptured shell than the edible winkle. In *L. rudis* aperture forms a spout where outer lip of aperture meets columella or body.

Abundance & distribution
Abundant on rocky shores of all British and Irish coasts. Distribution extends from White Sea southwards to northern Spain. Does not occur in Mediterranean, and either absent or rare in Channel Islands and Isles of Scilly.

Littorina neritoides (Linnaeus)
Small periwinkle

Description · An air-breathing periwinkle (the gills have been replaced by a pulmonary or lung chamber), the sharply pointed shell is up to about 5 mm tall, with a smooth surface and fragile appearance. The margins of the oval shell aperture are brownish, the colour of the shell bluish-black to brownish-blue. **Habitat & ecology** · Found on the extreme upper shore, and higher under more exposed conditions, living in rock crevices and beneath overhangs, in empty barnacle tests (shells), and in clumps of the lichen *Lichina*. It breeds during late winter, the eggs and larvae being pelagic. The small periwinkle feeds on lichens and microscopic algae. **Similar species** · May be mistaken for smaller specimens of *Littorina saxatilis*, but this form does not extend as high up the shore and has a shell texture which is rough to the touch.

Abundance & distribution
Often common and abundant, though crevice habit often makes it difficult to find. Distributed from Black Sea and Mediterranean to Atlantic coasts of north-west Europe as far north as Norway. Absent from southern North Sea and English Channel. Southern range extends to Azores and Canary Islands.

Distinctive features

1. Shell sharply conical, whorls sculptured with very fine spiralling grooves.
2. Typically blackish- to greyish-brown, occasionally more reddish.

Distinctive features

1. Shell small, sharply pointed, with about five whorls.
2. Typically bluish-black to brownish-blue.
3. Brownish shell-aperture lips.

Littorina nigrolineata Gray
Black-lined periwinkle

Description · Robust shell formed of 5–6 whorls giving almost globular appearance. Shell sculpted with strap-like striations, up to 30 mm tall. Aperture oval, inner lip reflected over columella. Outer lip of aperture meets shell almost at right angles. Shell whitish, yellow to orange, or deep orangey-red with dark brown lines between the striations. **Habitat & ecology** · This species occurs high on rocky shores above the mid-tide level. It lives among fucoids, including *Ascophyllum nodosum* and may even reach into the barnacle – *Fucus spiralis* zone. Eggs laid in pink, jelly-like masses under stones and rocks, hatch as crawl-away juveniles. **Similar species** · Resembles *L. littorea*, but this species lacks the more distinct sculpturing of *L. nigrolineata* and the black lines between the striations. *L. nigrolineata* can be distinguished from *L. saxatilis* by its larger size and that in *L. saxatilis* the outer lip of the aperture is protruded where it meets the columella. *L. saxatilis* also has fewer whorls than *L. nigrolineata*.

Abundance & distribution
Common. Found on all British coasts, possibly with the exception of the south-east. Also occurs on the Atlantic coasts of France.

Littorina obtusata (Linnaeus) **Flat periwinkle**

Description · Shell flat-topped with only suggestion of spire, oval profile, with shallow sutures between whorls. Lips of round shell aperture thick, aperture being smaller than main shell whorl. Colour variable, depending on habitat, with individuals from sheltered shores tending to be a light yellow, orange, green, brown or red, whereas under exposed conditions colours usually darker and often banded or chequered. **Habitat & ecology** · Typically a gill-breathing, mid-shore species, found living on and among brown algae *Ascophyllum nodosum* and *Fucus vesiculosus*, on which it both feeds and lays its oval or kidney-shaped, gelatinous egg-masses. Eggs hatch directly into minute, crawling juveniles. **Similar species** · Closely resembles *L. mariae*, which has rather globular shell with flattened spire and body whorl making up most of shell (b). Aperture oval, and outer lip joins body whorl very high up. Aperture also usually larger than body whorl, differing from *L. obtusata*. However, intermediate shapes are common and reliable identification often needs dissection of sexually mature adults. *L. obtusata*, however, tends not to occur on *F. serratus*, on which *L. mariae* lives, preferring *F. vesiculosus* and *A. nodosum*. *L. mariae* very common, on coasts

of Britain and Ireland; distributed from northern Norway to western Mediterranean.

Abundance & distribution
Locally common. Distribution ranges from northern Norway to south coast of Spain, but not found in the Mediterranean.

Littorina saxatilis (Olivi) **Rough periwinkle**

Description · Shell plump, about 18–20 mm tall, with a low spire of 3–4 whorls which are scored with deep, spiralling grooves and give the shell its characteristic rough texture (a). Ridges between grooves may have distinct crests along their midline. Shell aperture large and rounded, its outer lip meeting main whorl almost at right angles. Outer lip of aperture protruded where it meets columella but does not form spout. Colour variable, usually reddish- to blackish-brown. **Habitat & ecology** · An air-breathing, typically upper-shore periwinkle, found in crevices and cracks of rocks, on stones and boulders, or among brown algae *Pelvetia canaliculata* and *Fucus spiralis*. Sometimes found in upper mid-shore zone or, because of tolerance to reduced salinities (as low as 8‰), on estuarine mudflats. Young born alive. **Similar species** · Closely resembles small, pale specimens of *L. littorea*, from which it can usually be distinguished by angle formed between outer aperture lip and main shell whorl, and also by protrusion of outer lip of aperture when joining columella. *L. rudis* also very similar and in fact may be same species. Main distinguishing feature between these species is outer lip of aperture which, in *L. rudis*, is protruded where it joins

(a)

(b)

Distinctive features

1. Robust globular shell.
2. 5–6 whorls.
3. Outer lip of the aperture meets the shell almost at right angles.

Distinctive features ^(a)

1. Shell flat-topped, almost no spire, oval profile.
2. Main shell whorl larger than rounded shell aperture.
3. Usually yellow, orange, brown, green, or red; often chequered or banded under exposed conditions.

(b)

Distinctive features ^(a)

1. Shell plump, its whorls deeply scored with spiralling grooves and rough to touch.
2. Outer lip of shell aperture joins main shell whorl almost at right angles.
3. Colour variable, usually reddish- to blackish-brown.

columella to form a prominent spout. *L. rudis* is typically reddish-brown and its distribution is similar to *L. saxatilis* except that it does not occur in Mediterranean (b). *L. tenebrosa* is delicate version of more solid *L. saxatilis*; in fact it may represent an estuarine variety of that species. Has elongate, thin, and almost transparent shell, about 15 mm tall. Whorls smooth, marked with fine spiralling lines. Shell aperture small, rounded, and with thin, delicate lips. An uncommon species, found in brackish conditions. Occurs around most coasts of Britain but distribution is uncertain (c).

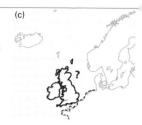

(c)

Abundance & distribution
Often common on all coasts of Britain and Ireland, but unobtrusive. Distribution extends from northern Norway to the Atlantic coasts of Spain, including the western Baltic and the western Mediterranean.

FAMILY **Hydrobiidae**

Hydrobia ulvae (Pennant) **Laver spire shell**

Description · About 5–6 mm tall, shell is slender with a pear-shaped aperture and 6–7 flat-sided whorls which terminate in a blunt apex. Colour varies from dark brown to yellowish-brown. Head tentacles have black rim near their tips; left tentacle thicker than right. Diamond-shaped patch of pigment between eyes. **Habitat & ecology** · Muddy sand and in estuarine muds; able to tolerate fully marine conditions and salinities as low as 1.5‰. Floats under a mucus raft at water surface with incoming tides. The small white sea slug, *Retusa obtusa*, feeds on *H. ulvae*. **Similar species** · Several other mud snails, particularly species of *Alvania* and *Rissoa*, broadly resemble *H. ulvae* and care should be taken with its identification. *H. ventrosa* especially similar but has distinctly swollen whorls and straight outer lip to aperture of shell. This species tends to live in lagoons and ditches. *H. neglecta* is smaller than other *Hydrobia* species, has swollen whorls (not as much as *H. ventrosa*), and pigment patches near tips of tentacles.

Abundance & distribution
Common, sometimes locally abundant (up to thousands of individuals per square metre). Found in northern Norway, southwards on all British coasts, and throughout the Mediterranean, as far south as Senegal in West Africa.

FAMILY **Rissoidae**

Rissoa parva (da Costa)

Description · Sharply pointed, small shell, about 5 mm tall, with about 5–8 smooth whorls. Two main varieties exist, one with vertically marked shallow ribs, the other without ribs.. The shell is semi-transparent and the colour is variable, usually greyish-white to brownish-white or dark brown, often darker towards the shell apex, but there is often a dark brown, comma-shaped mark close to the shell aperture. The aperture of the shell is generally D-shaped. **Habitat & ecology** · An extreme lower-shore to shallow sublittoral (to about 15 m) species, found under stones and boulders or more abundantly with coralline red algae. Sometimes found in rock pools. Rissoids feed on microscopic algae (diatoms), detritus, and fragments of algae. *R. parva* has a pelagic larva. **Similar species** · There are numerous other similar species and varieties of *Rissoa*, *Alvania*, *Cingula*, and *Barleeia*, with which this form may be easily confused. These small gastropods often require specialist knowledge for identification and so may be collectively termed rissoids.

Abundance & distribution
May be common but unobtrusive because of its small size. Its distribution extends from the northern Norway to North Sea, western English Channel, and Atlantic coasts of north-west Europe, and into the Mediterranean.

(b)

(c)

Distinctive features

1. Head tentacles unequal in thickness, the left thicker than the right.
2. Diamond-shaped patch of pigment between the eyes.

Distinctive features

1. Shell small, sharply pointed, whorls marked by shallow vertical ribs.
2. Colour variable, but always a dark brown, comma-shaped mark close to shell aperture.

FAMILY **Barleeidae**

Barleeia unifasciata (Montagu)

Description · Shell a rounded cone shape. Up to five swollen but compressed whorls; shell reaches a length of up to 2–3 mm. Aperture of shell oval with thin lip and slight groove where it joins shell. Shell smooth, varies in colour from dark red, claret, to yellowish-brown or pale brown. Sometimes shell will be banded reddish-brown and white or even be completely white. Body of snail white to yellowish-white but rear half of foot purple and bears a dark red operculum. Formerly known as *B. rubra*. **Habitat & ecology** · Occurs low on shore on seaweeds, especially low-lying red algae, and in rock pools. **Similar species** · Often occurs with *Rissoa parva*, which is often larger than *B. unifasciata* and has 7–8 whorls on its shell. Also similar to the snail *Assiminea grayana*, but this species is also larger, with 6–7 whorls and fine lines on shell, and also only occurs in North Sea. *B. unifasciata* lays egg capsules on seaweed and these hatch as crawl-away juveniles.

Abundance & distribution
Frequent in south-west England and southern Ireland. Also occurs on coast of western Scotland. Distributed south to the Mediterranean.

FAMILY **Turritellidae**

Turritella communis Risso
Auger shell, tower shell

Description · The tall, sharply pointed narrow shell is up to 5–6 cm tall. There are about 20 whorls, each separated from the other by a distinct suture and being marked by 3–6 prominent spiral grooves or ridges. The rounded shell aperture is comparatively small, the opercular plate concave and fringed marginally. Colour variable, usually reddish-brown, brownish-yellow, or white. **Habitat & ecology** · Found partially buried in sublittoral sand and mud to depths of about 200 m. Very lethargic and sits on the seabed filtering seawater for particles of food. May be gregarious, occurring in very large numbers. Egg capsules laid in clusters and hatch into planktonic larvae. Empty shells often found washed up on sandy beaches. **Similar species** · *T. turbona* is very similar, but somewhat smaller and distinguishable by its straight-sided and less obvious whorls, each bearing three main spiral ridges; its distribution is also different in being restricted to the Mediterranean.

Abundance & distribution
May be locally abundant. The distribution extends from northern Norway to the Mediterranean. Rare or absent from the Channel and southern North Sea.

FAMILY **Aporrhaiidae**

Aporrhais pespelecani (Linnaeus)
Common pelican's foot shell

Description · The slender, spired shell is up to about 4 cm tall and arranged with up to ten whorls, which possess thick knobs and finer spiral ridges. The narrow, elongate aperture to the shell has thick outer margins or lips, fanned out into five bluntly rounded points, which become thicker as the animal grows. The uppermost lip extends to halfway up the shell spire, the lower point has a siphonal groove in it. The lips and thick knobs of the shell are white, the smoother parts of the shell typically a pale reddish-brown colour. **Habitat & ecology** · Found only in sublittoral locations on soft sediments. Typically a rather sedentary animal, feeding on fragments of detritus in mud and muddy sand. **Similar species** · *A. serresianus*, occurs in the area. It has a smaller and more delicate shell than *A. pespelecani*. The outer lip of the shell of this species also projects beyond the shell apex.

Abundance & distribution
Not uncommon on many British coasts, though not often found in Channel or North Sea waters, this species has a range extending from the Mediterranean to Atlantic coasts of Norway.

Distinctive features

1. Very small conical-shaped snail.
2. Aperture oval.
3. Rear of foot often purple with a dark red operculum.

Distinctive features

1. Shell tall, narrow, sharply pointed.
2. About 20 whorls, separated by distinct sutures.
3. Whorls marked by 3–6 distinct spiral ridges or grooves.

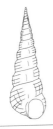

Distinctive features

1. Shell slender, with distinct pointed spire.
2. Shell aperture narrow, flanked by thick margins fanned out into five bluntly rounded points.

FAMILY **Capulidae**

Capulus ungaricus (Linnaeus)
Hungarian cap shell

Description · Shell resembles a cap in which the apex is coiled over backwards. Shell up to 4 cm long, 15 mm high, marked with spiral ridges and fine lines. Edges of ridges and lower edge of shell may appear frilled and are formed by periostracum. Animal has a long, dorsally grooved false proboscis formed by lower lip of mouth. Overall colour of shell white with frilled periostracum of pale brown or brown. Inside shell is a horseshoe-shaped muscle scar from attachment of foot. **Habitat & ecology** · This limpet-like snail occurs on the lower shore or subtidally on rocks, stones or shells. It has the ability to place itself on the margin of the shells of bivalves such as *Modiolus* or *Chlamys*, or the gastropod *Turritella communis* and to feed on mucus and food particles from their mantle cavity. It is capable of collecting food when not associated with these animals. *C. ungaricus* is a protandrous (changes sex from male to female with age) hermaphrodite.

Abundance & distribution
Common all coasts of Britain. Distributed from northern Norway to West Africa. Absent from southern North Sea.

FAMILY **Calyptraeidae**

Crepidula fornicata (Linnaeus)
Slipper limpet, American slipper limpet

Description · The thick, solid, and oval shell is up to 25 mm tall and 5 cm long, with a slightly coiled spire of about two small whorls. The underside of the shell is usually white, the upper surface greenish-brown, yellow, or white, sometimes with reddish markings. The shell aperture is large with a well-developed and obvious internal ledge. **Habitat & ecology** · Found living in groups, often forming chains of individuals living on top of each other, on rocks and shells (e.g. oysters or mussels) in shallow sublittoral situations. In such chains the bottom limpet is female and the oldest; individuals settling on the top begin life as males and change sex as they grow and age. Often a pest in oyster beds where it may overgrow and smother them; as a filter-feeder, it also competes with oysters for food.

Abundance & distribution
An introduced species from America, the slipper limpet is often locally common and abundant. Its European distribution extends from Scandinavia southwards to North Sea, English Channel, Irish Sea, and Atlantic coasts. It is also recorded from the Adriatic and Sicily.

FAMILY **Triviidae**

Trivia monacha (da Costa)
Spotted cowrie, European cowrie

Description · Flattened, egg shape shell, up to about 12 mm long, shiny, and heavily calcified, marked with about 20 close-set transverse ridges. Slightly curved shell opening, a long slit-like aperture, extends along underside. Head, tentacles, foot, and mantle of living animal variably yellow, red, orange, green, or brown, but pale pinkish- to reddish-brown shell is characteristically marked with three dark brown or blackish spots. Previously known as *Cypraea europaea*. **Habitat & ecology** · Lower shore and sublittorally on rocky coasts; also occurs in more sheltered situations, such as lower reaches of estuaries. Usually associated with its prey, ascidians such as *Botryllus schlosseri*, *Botrylloides leachi*, and *Diplosoma listerianum*. It finds live zooid and blocks inhalant siphon from closing with its proboscis, then bites lumps of zooid off and eats them. Also bites hole in test of ascidian colony and lays eggs in this in flask-shaped capsule. Larvae hatch and are pelagic, usually occurring in coastal waters in summer.

Abundance & distribution
Frequent but widespread, locally common. Found on west coasts of Britain and Ireland and in western English Channel. Distributed south to Mediterranean.

Distinctive features

1. Cap-shaped shell.
2. Apex of shell coiled backwards.
3. Long unretractable proboscis.

Distinctive features

1. Shell oval, with wide aperture containing distinct and well-developed inner ledge.
2. Apex of spire with two small whorls.
3. Underside of shell white, upper surface white, yellow, or greenish-brown, sometimes with reddish markings.

Distinctive features

1. Shell marked with numerous close-set transverse ridges, with long, narrow aperture on underside.
2. Pale reddish-brown, with three dark diagnostic spots.

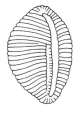

FAMILY **Naticidae**

Polinices catenus (da Costa) **Moon snail**

Description · Shell somewhat resembles *P. polianus* but with taller spire, well-defined sutures, and stepped profile. Outer lip of shell aperture meets body whorl almost at right angles; inner lip barely occludes deep umbilicus. Up to 3 cm tall, pale brown, lighter basally and on inner lip, each whorl marked by row of reddish-brown patches situated close below suture lines. **Habitat & ecology** · Sandy sediments from ELWS to sublittoral depths of about 125 m. Feeds on bivalves by drilling them with its proboscis and radula. Produces collar-like egg capsule made of mucus and sand grains from which crawl-away juveniles hatch (not pelagic larvae). **Similar species** · *P. polianus*, moon snail or Alder's necklace snail, but its shell is pale brown, with five spiral rows of darker brown marks on main whorl but only one row on each spire whorl. Unlike *P. catenus*, *P. polianus* larvae remain in egg case for about 3 weeks before being released for pelagic phase. *P. fuscus* smaller, lacking shell patterning. *P. guillemini* has dark brown columella.

Abundance & distribution
Common off all British coasts, the distribution extends from the Mediterranean northwards to Danish coasts of the Skagerrak.

FAMILY **Epitoniidae**

Epitonium clathrus (Linnaeus)
Common wentletrap

Description · The narrow shell is sharply pointed, up to 4 cm tall and has about ten whorls. Adjacent whorls are sharply separated by sutures, both whorls and sutures being crossed by very conspicuous diagonal ribs. The shell aperture is round, the horny operculum thin and black. The shell may be white, brown, or reddish in colour. Previously known as *Clathrus clathrus* and *Scalar communis*. **Habitat & ecology** · Usually found sublittorally to depths of about 80 m on muddy sand, it may sometimes move up onto rocks at extreme low-water spring tide levels on the shore during its spawning period. The snail is carnivorous, feeding on sea anemones, and has a long proboscis. **Similar species** · About 20 species of *Epitonium* occur in European waters, but none are common. *E. clathrus* may be mistaken for *E. lamellosum*, which is smaller with a less-pointed shell.

Abundance & distribution
Not particularly common, the species has a distribution extending from the Black Sea and Mediterranean northwards to Atlantic, English Channel, North Sea, and western Baltic coasts.

ORDER **Neogastropoda**

FAMILY **Muricidae**

Boreotrophon truncatus (Ström)

Description · Shell tall, sharply pointed, and slightly turreted, up to 1.5 cm long. There are seven whorls marked with longitudinal ridges and deep grooves that extend just below the upper edge of the shell aperture but not to the base of the main whorl. The aperture is oval-shaped, with a short, bent, siphonal canal. The colour of the shell is yellowish-white or flesh coloured with a darker throat. **Habitat & ecology** · Found on the lower shore and sublittorally to 200 m depth on stony or gravelly bottoms.

Abundance & distribution
Locally common. Found on British west coasts and in the northern North Sea. Distributed from the Bay of Biscay to the Arctic. Circumboreal.

Distinctive features

1. Shell globular, but with distinct spire, well-defined sutures, and stepped profile.
2. Outer lip of shell aperture meets body whorl almost at right angles.
3. Pale brown shell with row of reddish-brown patches close below each suture.

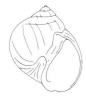

Distinctive features

1. Narrow, sharply pointed shell.
2. Shell whorls with distinct sutures, crossed by conspicuous diagonal ribs.
3. Shell opening round, opercular plate black.

Distinctive features

1. Shell with deep longitudinal grooves and ridges.
2. Colour yellowish-white or flesh coloured.
3. Siphonal groove short, bending away from the plane of the aperture.

Nucella lapillus (Linnaeus) **Dog whelk**

Description · Thick, heavy shell, about 3–4 cm tall, formed from about
five whorls marked with distinct spiral ridges and grooves; in older animals
these may be worn almost smooth. Shell aperture oval but with sharp ends,
its lips thick and obvious; outer lip marked with several transverse ridges or
'teeth'. Siphonal canal at base of aperture is deep and partly closed over by
thickened columella. Opercular plate is tough and a dark reddish-brown.
Shell colour variable, usually greyish-white or creamy-white, but often a
darker grey or patterned with broad spiral brownish bands. Previously
known by several names, including *Thais lapillus* and *N. purpurea*. **Habitat
& ecology** · Essentially a rocky-shore intertidal species, in crevices and
rock pools, or among barnacles and mussels, on which it feeds, mid- to
lower-shore. The small, pale yellow, and vase-shaped egg capsules, about 7
mm tall, are laid in clumps during early spring on the underside of rocks
and boulders; the eggs hatch directly into small, creeping juveniles.

Abundance & distribution
Very common, often abundant
on most rocky shores around
British Isles, except under most
sheltered conditions. Distributed from Greenland and
Iceland to Atlantic coasts of
north-west Europe as far south
as Gibraltar, and to north-east
coast of North America. In

Ocenebra erinacea (Linnaeus)
Sting winkle, oyster drill

Description · Shell up to 6 cm tall, with about five strongly but spirally
ribbed, unevenly sculptured, rough-looking whorls, of which the last is by
far the largest. Dull yellowish-white with dark brown markings. Siphonal
canal at base of aperture open in younger specimens, but closed over and
tubular in older examples. Outer lip of aperture thick and transversely
'toothed', outer edge may have several irregular blunt spines. **Habitat &
ecology** · Muddy gravel, sand, and rocks from lower shore to sublittoral
depths of about 100 m. Migrates inshore during breeding. Serious pest of
commercial oyster farms, drilling oyster shells with its radula and sucking
out flesh in a similar way to *Polinices polianus*. Lays eggs in capsule and they
hatch as crawl-away juveniles. **Similar species** · Several other species of
muricid gastropods with which this form may be confused. *Urosalpinx
cinerea*, the American sting winkle, is an introduction. It has broader and
fatter shell than *O. erinacea*, siphonal canal does not close over, and
sculpturing is more rounded.

Abundance & distribution
Sometimes locally common, the
distribution extends from the
Mediterranean northwards to
Atlantic, English Channel, and
North Sea coasts of north-west
Europe.

Urosalpinx cinerea (Say)
American sting winkle

Description · The shell is up to 4 cm long. There are up to 7–8 rounded
whorls, marked with 9–12 rounded ribs crossed by numerous strong spiral
striae. These ribs do not extend to the base of the main whorl. The aperture
is oval, with a pronounced but short ventral siphonal groove bent towards
the left. The outer lip of the aperture is thick and crenellate. The shell is off
white, buff, or yellowish, often with brown spiral bands. **Habitat &
ecology** · An introduced species from the east coast of the USA. Found on
oysters from the low shore to shallow subtidal. A serious pest on oyster
beds and preys on the oysters themselves. **Similar species** · Resembles
Ocenebra erinacea; distinguished by the closed siphonal aperture in this
species and the heavy irregular sculpturing on the shell. *O. aciculata* also
similar but smaller and in adults the siphonal canal also becomes closed
and has a spiral keel formed by the striae.

Abundance & distribution
Locally abundant. Found only
on oysters in Essex and Kent.

areas locally extinct through poisoning by tributyl-tin (TBT) antifouling paints.

Distinctive features

1. Shell heavy, thick, strong, whorls marked with spiral grooves and ridges.
2. Deep siphonal canal at shell aperture base.
3. Typically greyish-white, creamy-white, dark brown.

Distinctive features

1. Shell spirally ribbed, unevenly sculptured, rough textured.
2. Yellowish-white with dark brown markings.
3. Siphonal canal at base of shell aperture open in young, closed over and tubular in older examples.

Distinctive features

1. Shell sculpturing of ribs and strong spiral striae, not reaching base of main whorl.
2. Shell plump with oval aperture.
3. Short, obvious, siphonal groove bent to left.

FAMILY **Buccinidae**

Buccinum undatum Linnaeus
Buckie, common whelk, edible whelk

Description · Large. Shell generally heavy with strong undulating ribs crossed by numerous spiral ridges. Ribs disappear towards aperture end of shell. 7–8 whorls with body whorl by far the largest and making up most of length, which can reach 11 cm. Shell aperture normally on right, oval, with strongly flared edges. Outer edge of aperture curved inwards near siphonal canal which is short. Shell dirty white, grey or buff body, white to yellowish-white with small black flecks. Operculum thick, ridged with concentric rings; normally various shades of brown. **Habitat & ecology** · Generally subtidal on soft muddy or sandy substrate but also on gravel or rock. A predator or scavenger feeding on worms or bivalve molluscs. Lays clumps of horny eggs. Long valued as food. **Similar species** · These include *Neptunea antiqua* and *Colus* species. *B. undatum* distinguishable by heavily sculptured shell, flared aperture edges, and short siphonal canal. Shells of live and dead *B. undatum* used by other animals for attachment or shelter.

Abundance & distribution
Common around Britain and Ireland but rare off Scillies and Channel Islands. Elsewhere distributed from northern Norway to the Bay of Biscay.

Colus gracilis (da Costa)

Description · Slender and up to 7 cm tall, the 8–10 almost flat-sided whorls of the shell are sculptured with fine spiral grooves and ridges and delicate curving growth lines. The shell spire is sharply pointed, the aperture narrow and ovoid with a broad, curved siphonal opening. The outer lip of the aperture is thin, the inner lip spread closely over the columella. The shell is a pale greyish-white colour. **Habitat & ecology** · Only rarely found intertidally, mostly occurring sublittorally on sand and muddy sand. **Similar species** · Resembles other large whelks. *C. jeffreysianus* is smaller and broader. The siphonal canal is also broader. *C. islandicus* is a larger species, with a long, straight siphonal canal. *Neptunea antiqua* is larger, broader, and the whorls are not flat-sided like *C. gracilis*.

Abundance & distribution
Increasingly more common towards the northern range of its distribution, which extends from the Atlantic coasts of Spain and Portugal northwards to western Norway. Found off all British coasts but less frequently in the south.

Neptunea antiqua (Linnaeus)
Red whelk, buckie

Description · Shell large, up to 15 cm, occasionally 20 cm, tall. Smooth-surfaced whorls marked with fine spiral ridges and grooves. Shell aperture narrowly oval, ventrally tapering to fairly long, curved siphonal canal. Inner surface of aperture reddish-brown, shell itself greyish-white to greyish-brown. **Habitat & ecology** · Never occurring intertidally, found sublit-torally on rock, muddy sand, or gravel to about 100 m or more. Inedible, unlike its relative, *Buccinum undatum*. Spongy and slightly elastic egg-masses, similar to those of *B. undatum*, sometimes found washed up on shore and popularly known as sea wash balls. It is also a carnivore and scavenger. **Similar species** · Very similar to *N. contraria*, but this species has a reddish-brown shell and is sinistrally (left-handed) whorled so that shell aperture is on left side of shell. It also occurs in deep water (100 m +). Also resembles *Colus* species but can grow larger than any of these. *C. jeffreysianus* and *C. gracilis* both have wide, inward-curving siphonal canals, and very flat-sided whorls. *C. islandicus* has long siphonal canal.

Abundance & distribution
May be locally common around northern Britain, less so in the south and off western Ireland. Its geographic range extends from the Bay of Biscay northwards to the Arctic.

Distinctive features

1. Large snail with a heavy-ribbed and ridged shell.
2. Aperture oval with flared margins.
3. Siphonal canal short.

Distinctive features

1. Shell slender, sharply pointed.
2. 8–10 shell whorls almost flat-sided.
3. Siphonal opening wide and curved.

Distinctive features

1. Shell large, smooth-surfaced whorls marked with fine spiral grooves and ridges.
2. Shell greyish-white or greyish-brown.

FAMILY **Nassariidae**

Hinia reticulata (Linnaeus) **Netted dog-whelk**

Description · The brown shell is up to 3 cm tall, fat and conical, with about seven poorly defined whorls. The criss-crossing of surface lines and ribs forms a pattern of small squares. The siphonal canal is oblique and short but deep, the surface of the lips surrounding the oval shell aperture are white; the inner lip is folded back over the lower whorl; the outer lip possesses fine teeth. Previously known as *Nassarius reticulatus*. **Habitat & ecology** · On the lower shore and in shallow sublittoral situations. Found under stones or in crevices, often in muddy, muddy sand, or gravelly conditions crawling along with a siphon held up in the water. Frequently gregarious. *H. reticulata* is a predator of other small invertebrates such as polychaetes and bivalves, and a scavenger. Breeding occurs during the spring and summer, the eggs being laid in neat rows of flat, vase-shaped egg capsules on algae, seagrasses, or stones.

Abundance & distribution
Widespread, sometimes locally common, on all coasts of Britain and Ireland. Distributed from northern Norway and western Baltic Sea to North Sea, English Channel, Atlantic, and Mediterranean coasts of Europe, also to Black Sea, Canary Islands and Madeira.

FAMILY **Turridae**

Raphitoma purpurea (Montagu)

Description · The shell is up to 2 cm long but only 8 mm wide. The shell spire is slender and pointed. The outer rim of the oval shell aperture is thick and transversely ridged whilst the base of the aperture is grooved. The characteristic pattern of sculpturing on the shell surface consists of vertical ribs and transverse ridges, giving the shell an obviously reticulated appearance. The shell is typically reddish-brown in colour whilst the aperture rim and internal surfaces of the shell are white. The animal has a white foot with white chalky speckles. **Habitat & ecology** · Sometimes occurs on the lower shore under stones, in rock crevices, or amongst seagrasses. More usually found subtidally, to depths of 100 m on stones, gravel, or sand. **Similar species** · Resembles *R. linearis* but in this species the ridges and ribs are not as narrow making the shell reticulation less obvious. *R. leufroyi* is smaller than *R. purpurea* and not as heavily sculptured.

Abundance & distribution
Uncommon. Found all around Britain and Ireland. It is distributed from northern Norway to the Mediterranean, becoming more common further south.

SUBCLASS **Opisthobranchia** | ORDER **Cephalaspidea or Bullomorpha**

FAMILY **Acteonidae**

Acteon tornatilis (Linnaeus)

Description · The distinctive shell of this primitive sea slug is up to about 3 cm long, somewhat barrel-shaped, and with up to eight whorls. The teardrop-shaped aperture, through which the animal can fully withdraw into its shell, extends at least half the shell length with its widest part ventrally. It can be closed by an amber-coloured operculum. Shell is glossy pink or pinkish-brown, with a few pale bands of white, grey, or greyish-yellow. The head, which has no tentacles, is flattened and lobed to form a cephalic shield; this and the broad mantle flaps which are folded along the sides of the shell as the animal moves, enable it to be distinguished from prosobranch gastropods with which it might at first be confused. The mantle is white. **Habitat & ecology** · Found in sheltered sandy bays, crawling on lower-shore and shallow sublittoral sandy or muddy sediments as it seeks its tube-dwelling and infaunal polychaete prey, especially *Lanice conchilega* and *Owenia fusiformis*.

Abundance & distribution
Sometimes locally common, this species has a range which extends from Iceland to the Mediterranean and occurs on Atlantic, North Sea and Channel coasts of northern Europe.

Distinctive features

1. Brown shell with reticulate (block-like) sculptured pattern produced by criss-crossing of spiral grooves and ribs.
2. Outer lip of shell aperture with fine teeth.

Distinctive features

1. Shell spire slender, pointed.
2. Shell aperture oval, thick, with transversely ridged outer rim.
3. Shell surface has distinct ribs and ridges.

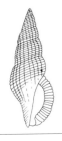

Distinctive features

1. Head lacks tentacles; flattened, lobed to form cephalic shield.
2. Mantle flaps fold along sides of shell as animal moves.
3. Shell barrel-shaped; pinkish, greyish-yellow bands.

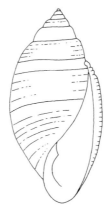

FAMILY **Philinidae**

Philine aperta (Linnaeus)

Description · Body shaped like a flattened egg or rounded diamond shape. It is typically 2–2.5 cm long, exceptionally up to 7 cm, and about half as wide. The soft body encloses a thin, white, reduced shell that is a rounded ear shape. The body consists of a large cephalic shield in front and the mantle, which is wider behind. There are wide parapodial lobes around the sides of the body, which is a translucent greyish-white to yellow. **Habitat & ecology** · Found in sand and muddy sand, extreme lower shore to shallow sublittoral. This animal burrows in search of its prey: polychaetes, bivalve molluscs, and the green sea urchin, *Echinocyamus pusillus*. It lays club-shaped egg masses of up to 50 000 ova that hatch into pelagic larvae after 3–4 days. **Similar species** · There are several other species of *Philine*, all of which are smaller than *P. aperta*. *Scaphander lignarius* is also similar but the shell is heavier and visible in the live animal.

Abundance & distribution
Locally common. Occurs all around the British Isles and Ireland. Distributed from Norway to the Mediterranean.

ORDER **Anaspidea or Aplysiomorpha**

FAMILY **Aplysiidae**

Aplysia punctata Cuvier

Description · Bulky, fleshy body, up to 14–20 cm long, but more usually less than 10 cm. Pair of rolled up oral tentacles on front of head, behind these a pair of shorter rhinophores. Two wing-like parapodial lobes extend down either side of back, joined by narrow band posteriorly. Delicate shell, only about 15 mm wide, almost totally enclosed. Colour extremely variable, depending partly upon algal diet. Younger individuals generally lighter than older specimens, but red, brown, green, purple, or black, with or without mottling or blotching with paler hues, not uncommon. **Habitat & ecology** · Typically among algae in shallow sublittoral situations. Juveniles feed particularly on small red or green algae, general body colour reflecting colour of their diet. Sometimes encountered swimming, and during reproductive period large numbers may be stranded together on shore. When disturbed or threatened, often discharges purple slime for protection.

Abundance & distribution
Frequent, with a distribution extending from the Baltic Sea to Atlantic, Channel, and North Sea coasts of northern Europe, the Mediterranean and southwards to the Canary Islands.

ORDER **Nudibranchia** | SUBORDER **Dendronotacea**

FAMILY **Tritoniidae**

Tritonia hombergi (Cuvier)

Description · An elongate, fleshy, distinctive sea slug, roughly oval in outline, and, at up to 20 cm long, the largest British nudibranch. Young individuals white or colourless, adults brown to purplish-brown to grey, or even yellowish, colour darkening with increase in size. From above, head is hidden by bilobed and very frilly oral veil; behind head tufted and branched rhinophores have short, trumpet-shaped sheaths. Feathery pallial gills arranged along either side of body get bigger and more numerous as animal grows. The back of the animal is covered in soft tubercles or knobs. **Habitat & ecology** · A shallow, sublittoral and rocky shore species, frequently found with its prey, the soft coral *Alcyonium digitatum*. Secretes a defensive mucus when handled that may irritate skin. Lays pinkish spiral bands of eggs that hatch into lecithotrophic planktonic larvae. **Similar species** · Other species of *Tritonia* occur in the north-east Atlantic. These have a similar body structure to *T. hombergi* but are all much smaller, slenderer, and generally smoother in texture.

Abundance & distribution
A fairly common species, with a distribution extending from the Faeroe Islands and Arctic Norway south to all British shores and the Mediterranean coast of Spain.

Distinctive features

1. Body a flattened egg shape, enclosing shell.
2. Shell reduced, thin, white.
3. Body a translucent greyish-white to yellow.

Distinctive features

1. Body bulky, fleshy, parapodial lobes extending either side of back.
2. Head with rolled up oral tentacles at front.

Distinctive features

1. Body an elongate oval shape.
2. Feathery pallial gills along each side of body.
3. Rhinophores tufted, with short, trumpet-shaped sheaths.
4. Colour varying with age, young animals white or colourless, becoming darker brown as they grow.

Tritonia lineata Alder & Hancock

Description · A slender sea slug, growing up to about 3.4 cm long. The head bears four oral processes or blunt tentacles and the rhinophores are branched and have sheaths. There are 4–6 pairs of arborescent gills running along the side of the body and the posterior tapers to a narrow point. The body is translucent white, sometimes tinged with red from the internal organs. A brilliant white opaque line runs from the base of the rhinophores down each side of the dorsal surface, linking the gills and finally meeting in a long point near the end of the body. The tips of the rhinophores may be tinged brown. **Habitat & ecology** · Found subtidally often on rocks with a covering of silt. Its diet is uncertain but it has been found on hydroids, gorgonians, and octocorals such as *Sarcodictyon roseum*.

Abundance & distribution
Frequent. Found all around Britain but rare around Ireland. Distributed from Norway to Brittany.

FAMILY **Dendronotidae**

Dendronotus frondosus (Alder & Hancock)

Description · A narrow-bodied sea slug, up to 5–10 cm long. The head bears branched tentacles, of which there may be up to five pairs depending on the size of the animal. Up to nine pairs of profusely branched and feathery cerata are arranged along the dorsal surface. The rhinophores have long stalks which form flared branched sheaths at the base of the lamellate spindle-shaped clubs. The colour is translucent pink, grey, or white, with white, orangey-red, and brown spots and streaks scattered along the back. **Habitat & ecology** · Found on sand or among rocks in shallow sublittoral situations to depths of about 100 m. Juveniles feed on hydroids such as *Obelia* or *Sertularia*, adults on larger hydroids like *Tubularia larynx* or *T. indivisa*. White or pink eggs are laid in a ribbon during summer and hatch after a month into pelagic larvae.

Abundance & distribution
Uncommon. Found all around the British Isles and Ireland. Distribution extends from the Arctic to the Bay of Biscay.

FAMILY **Dotoidae**

Doto coronata (Gmelin)

Description · Body up to 1.5 cm long; broad head extended as short lobe on each side. 5–8 pairs of knobbed cerata along dorsal surface, each knob marked with a deep red spot. Rhinophores long, smooth, and tapered, with deep, trumpet-shaped basal sheaths. Body white, yellowish, or pink, with dark red or purple blotches. Digestive gland, visible inside cerata, is red or brown. **Habitat & ecology** · Lower shore to shallow sublittoral, usually found on hydroids such as *Hydrallmania falcata*, *Abietinaria abietina*, *Dynamena pumila*, and *Obelia geniculata*. Spawning mass consists of convoluted band containing up to 35 000 or more eggs. These hatch into planktonic larvae. *D. coronata* is almost certainly a species complex. Several species have been separated from it. **Similar species** · At least eight on coasts of north-west Europe: *D. dunnei*, *D. eireana*, *D. hydrallmaniae*, *D. koenneckeri*, *D. lemchei*, *D. maculata*, *D. millbayana*, and *D. sarsiae*. Identification requires careful examination of shape and colour, and a record of hydroid on which it is found. More species may be discovered.

Abundance & distribution
Common on all coasts of Britain and Ireland. Distributed from the Mediterranean north to Spitzbergen, the Faeroes, and Iceland.

Distinctive features

1. 4–6 pairs of arborescent gills along side of body.
2. Four oral tentacles and pair of branched rhinophores with sheaths.
3. Translucent white; bright white line from base of rhinophores along dorso-lateral margin, linking gills.

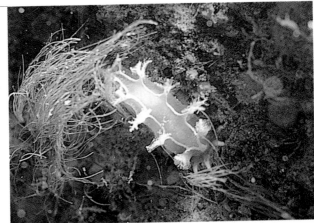

Distinctive features

1. Up to five pairs of head tentacles and nine pairs of cerata.
2. Tentacles and cerata profusely branched.
3. Rhinophore clubs carried on long stalks which form flared sheaths.
4. Colour yellowish-pink or pinkish-white, upper surface with darker, scattered spots.

Distinctive features

1. Head broad, extended as short lobe on each side.
2. Cerata knobbed, each knob with deep red spot.
3. Rhinophores long, smooth, tapered, with trumpet-shaped basal sheaths.

SUBORDER **Doridacea** | SUPERFAMILY **Anadoridoidea**

FAMILY **Goniodorididae**

Goniodoris nodosa (Montagu)

Description · A soft-bodied, but robust looking sea slug. Outline of body an elongate oval, up to about 3 cm long. Mantle edge quite well developed but does not form a long skirt. Low keel may be visible along back, and on rear of animal is a rosette of up to 13 simply branched gills. Small tubercles may also be visible dorsally. Rhinophores lamellate, oral tentacles flattened and point laterally. Translucent white, sometimes with yellowish or pinkish coloration dorsally. Sometimes areas of very transparent skin around rhinophores and gills. Rhinophores may be tinged yellow. **Habitat & ecology** · Generally in shallow subtidal waters of a few metres down to 100 m or more. Feeds on bryozoans such as *Alcyonidium*, *Callopora dumerilii*, and *Flustrellidra hispida* when young and mainly ascidians such as *Diplosoma listerianum*, *Botryllus schlosseri*, and *Dendrodoa grossularia* when adult. Eggs are laid in a horseshoe-shaped mass and hatch into planktonic larvae. **Similar species** · *G. castanea* is similar but reddish-brown and covered in white flecks. This species is rare.

Abundance & distribution
Common. Distributed around all coasts of Britain and Ireland, and from the Faeroes and southern Norway to northern Spain.

Trapania pallida Kress

Description · This sea slug has a slender body and grows to a length of about 2 cm. It has long, bluntly pointed tentacles, rhinophores that are lamellate but which lack sheaths, and a set of branched gills about two-thirds down the body. A pair of thick lateral processes project from the body at the base of the rhinophores and from the gills. The animal is a translucent white with bright white opaque patches on the tips of the tentacles, the rhinophores, the lateral processes, the gills, and the tail. **Habitat & ecology** · A sublittoral species found on sponges and bryozoans. May feed on entoprocts such as species of the genus *Loxocalyx*. **Similar species** · Resembles *Ancula gibbosa* but this species may have up to seven processes projecting from the base of the gills. These processes, the rhinophores, and the tail may be tipped with orange.

Abundance & distribution
Uncommon. Found on west and south-west coasts of Britain and the west coast of Ireland. Distributed south to the Atlantic coasts of Spain.

FAMILY **Onchidorididae**

Acanthodoris pilosa (Abildgaard in Müller)

Description · Up to about 6–7 cm long and half as wide, usually rather smaller. The surface of the soft, textured, elongate, oval-shaped mantle is covered with soft conical tubercles. The head end is rounded, the blunt, rounded oral tentacles usually not being visible from above. There is a pair of large feathery-tipped rhinophores near the front, which may be curved backwards when the animal is active, whilst towards the tail a circlet of up to nine large, trilobed feathery gills surrounds the anus. The colour is variable, but typically white, pale grey, brown to dark purplish-brown or charcoal grey. **Habitat & ecology** · Found on the lower shore and sublittorally to depths of about 170 m, usually feeding on the bryozoans *Alcyonidium* or *Flustrellidra*. Lays ribbon-like egg masses throughout the year that hatch into planktonic larvae. **Similar species** · Can be confused with other dorids but its 'fluffy' appearance is quite characteristic.

Abundance & distribution
Common, although usually not abundant. Found on all British coasts, its distribution extends from Iceland and the Faeroes in the north to Atlantic coasts of Morocco and north-west Europe in the south.

Distinctive features

1. Elongate oval shape.
2. Rosette of up to 13 branched gills.
3. Back smooth but with a scattering of tubercles and a low keel.
4. Lamellate rhinophores and flattened, laterally pointing oral tentacles.

Distinctive features

1. Body uniformly translucent white.
2. Rhinophores and gills flanked on either side by thick lateral processes.
3. Rhinophores not in sheaths but have lamellae towards ends.

Distinctive features

1. Anus at rear surrounded by up to nine trilobed gills.
2. Rhinophores feathery, curved backwards when the animal is active.
3. Body covered in conical tubercles.

Onchidoris luteocincta (M. Sars)

Description · An oval-shaped sea-slug that grows to a length of about 11 mm. The mantle is covered in tubercles or knobs. It has a pair of lamellate rhinophores and, in the rear half of the body, a rosette of up to seven branched gills. The most striking feature of this animal is its coloration: usually white with a wide bright or dark red area in the middle of the back. Around the edges of the mantle, a little bit in, is a yellow band that runs around the body. White individuals do occur, as do various permutations between this and the usual coloration. **Habitat & ecology** · Sublittoral species that feeds on bryozoans such as *Smittoidea reticulata*, *Cellepora pumicosa*, and *Crisia* species. It lays its eggs in a flattened, coiled, white mass. These hatch into planktonic larvae. **Similar species** · There are several similar species of *Onchidoris* and *Adalaria*, but they lack the distinctive coloration of *O. luteocincta*.

Abundance & distribution
Common. Found around most coasts of Britain but rare in the south-east. Occurs all around Ireland and is distributed from Norway to the Mediterranean.

FAMILY **Polyceridae**

Limacia clavigera (Müller)

Description · A robust sea slug growing up to 2 cm long. The foot generally extends beyond the mantle all around the sides and rear of the body. The body is white. The mantle edge forms a series of stout, finger-like processes held erect or bent over the body. These are tipped with yellow or orangey-yellow. The front of the head is also extended in a number of papillate tentacles that are held out horizontally. There are numerous, scattered low bumps on the back, also coloured yellow or orangey-yellow. The rhinophores are lamellate and tipped with yellow. **Habitat & ecology** · Rarely occurs low on the shore, usually subtidal. Generally associated with a variety of bryozoans and sometimes sea pens. Prefers clear, shallow water but may occur to 80 m. **Similar species** · Resembles some *Polycera* species but the body shape and distribution of tentacles and processes are different.

Abundance & distribution
Very common. Occurs all around the British Isles and Ireland. Distributed from Arctic Norway to the Mediterranean, and possibly down the coast of Africa to the Cape of Good Hope.

Polycera quadrilineata (Müller)

Description · Body up to 4 cm long, slender, head bearing 4–6 distinct, finger-like lobes or tentacles. The stout, lamellate rhinophores lack sheaths. Up to 11 branching gills occur, arranged in a tight group posteriorly, flanked by two thick processes. Colour variable: typically body is whitish with streaks of yellow or orange often fused to form up to five longitudinal rows. There are occasionally black streaks; head tentacles and rhinophores may be yellow or orange-tipped or completely yellow or orange; gills are usually tipped in yellow. **Habitat & ecology** · Intertidal and shallow sublittoral (to about 60 m) on rocky coasts. Feeds mainly on encrusting bryozoans, laying white egg masses on bryozoan colonies. These hatch into planktonic larvae. **Similar species** · Resembles *P. faroensis*, but this species has eight or more long head tentacles and a much sparser, blotchy yellow pigmentation. The rare *Trapania maculata* only has two oral tentacles and finger-like processes at the bases of the rhinophores as well as at the gills.

Abundance & distribution
Common, locally abundant, especially during spring and autumn months, this species extends from Greenland, Iceland, and Norway to all British and Irish coasts, and south to the western Mediterranean.

Distinctive features

1. Oval-shaped sea slug.
2. Red patch in middle of the back, yellow band running around mantle edge.
3. Back covered in tubercles.
4. Lamellate rhinophores.

Distinctive features

1. Mantle edge forms a widely spaced series of finger-like processes tipped with yellow.
2. Front of head has several papillate tentacles.
3. Body covered in low, yellow-coloured bumps.

Distinctive features

1. Head bearing 4–6 finger-like tentacles.
2. Gills arranged in a tight group posteriorly, flanked by two thick processes.
3. Rhinophores without sheaths.

FAMILY **Chromodorididae**

Hypselodoris messinensis (van Ihering)

Description · Narrow bodied sea slug with fairly smooth skin (can appear wrinkled). Foot tapers posteriorly and projects beyond the mantle. There is a rosette of up to six branched gills on the rear part of the body. The rhinophores are large and distinctly lamellate. Coloration is striking. Overall it is a bright blue or violet. The mantle margins are yellow or orange. There is a band along the middle of the back, also of yellow or orange. This species grows to about 4.5 cm in length. **Habitat & ecology** · Generally subtidal. Feeds on sponges. **Similar species** · There are several similarly coloured species in the north Atlantic, distributed from the Atlantic coast of France southwards, including *H. webbi*, *H. tricolor*, and *H. villafranca*.

Abundance & distribution
Frequent. Distributed from the Bay of Biscay to West Africa, including the Mediterranean.

SUPERFAMILY **Eudoridoidea**

FAMILY **Archidorididae**

Archidoris pseudoargus (Rapp) **Sea lemon**

Description · The solid body is up to 7–12 cm long, with a distinctly warty dorsal surface. The head has no oral tentacles, but there is a pair of rhinophores which have the appearance of layered discs. Towards the posterior end there is a ring of 8–10 trilobed branching and feathery gills. The general colour is distinctly yellowish, marked dorsally with a highly variable pattern of brown, purple, red, pink, or green blotches. **Habitat & ecology** · Normally found sublittorally, often at considerable depths, on or among rocks, this species moves up to the lower half of eulittoral rocky shores during the breeding season. The broad and ribbon-like egg masses, whitish in colour, are laid in loose coils on rocks and boulders and may be several centimetres in length. Breeding may occur from spring to autumn, depending upon the location. Carnivorous, feeding particularly on encrusting sponges such as *Halichondria*.

Abundance & distribution
Frequent in the intertidal region especially during the breeding season, it occurs off most British shores. Distributed from Iceland and the Faeroes to Atlantic, North Sea, and Channel coasts of northern Europe; it is also found in the Mediterranean.

SUBORDER **Arminacea**

FAMILY **Janolidae**

Janolus cristatus (Delle Chiaje)

Description · Large, reaching 70 mm in length. Elongate oval outline, flattened. Body generally translucent and pale brown or cream. Rhinophores lamellate and darker than rest of body. Between rhinophores is swollen area called sensory caruncle. Most striking feature are the cerata. These are long, swollen, and form band around edge of the animal, even around in front of rhinophores. Narrow, triangular tail projects behind this band of cerata. Each ceratum peppered with bright white pigment around top; apex coloured iridescent blue. Back and rhinophores may also be streaked with white. Oral tentacles are below cerata and finger-like. Front of foot is extended to blunt lateral points. **Habitat & ecology** · Shallow sublittoral, found on rocks and stones under clean, shallow and sheltered waters. Feeds on erect bryozoans such as *Bugula* and *Cellaria*. Eggs laid in linear series of white ovoid capsules, hatching into planktonic larvae. **Similar species** · Only *J. hyalinus* and *Proctonotus mucroniferus*, both of which are rare. Both are speckled brown and cerata have spiky appearance.

Abundance & distribution
Common. Occurs around all of British Isles, except south-east areas where it may be rare. Found all around Ireland. Distributed from southern Norway to Morocco, including the Mediterranean.

Distinctive features

1. Narrow body, tapering at rear where the foot projects beyond mantle.
2. Lamellate rhinophores
3. Rosette of six gills
4. Bright blue or violet colouration with orange or yellow bands.

Distinctive features

1. Head without oral tentacles.
2. Ring of nine feathery gills on back near tail.
3. Body solid in consistency.
4. Colour yellow, marked with highly variable pattern of brown, green, or pink blotches.

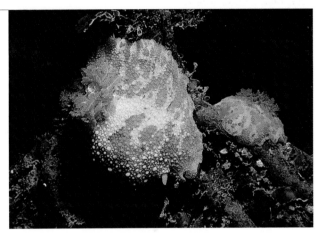

Distinctive features

1. Large sea slug in which swollen cerata run around the entire body.
2. Sensory caruncle between rhinophores.
3. Rhinophores lamellate.

SUBORDER **Aeolidicea**

FAMILY **Flabellinidae**

Coryphella gracilis (Alder and Hancock)

Description · A small sea slug, up to 15 mm long, transparent white but somewhat opaque when carrying developing eggs which appear like opaque white bunches of grapes. The oral tentacles are smooth, the rhinophores slightly wrinkled, both tapering and of a similar length with distal white streaks. There are up to six clusters of cerata, each ceratum bright red to bright green in colour but with a thin band of encircling white just below the tip. **Habitat & ecology** · A shallow sublittoral species, often found feeding on hydroids of the genus *Eudendrium*, and possibly also on *Clytia* and *Halecium* species in deeper water. This species has planktonic larvae. **Similar species** · There are several other species of *Coryphella* with which this form may be confused but all are a larger size than *C. gracilis* at maturity.

Abundance & distribution
Locally common, found on all British coasts. Distributed from the Faeroes and Iceland to the Atlantic coasts of France. Also on eastern American coast.

Coryphella lineata (Lovén)

Description · Slender, up to about 5 cm long, with an obvious head bearing long, distinct, tapering oral tentacles and rhinophores. Along either side of mantle are 5–8 groups of up to about five cerata extending most of body length. Colour pattern usually distinctive. General body translucent white with opaque patches and slender, longitudinal, white line which anteriorly divides to extend up each oral tentacle; a similar line on either side of body which joins midline near front of body. Cerata are white-tipped, but otherwise bright red or reddish-orange. **Habitat & ecology** · Sublittoral, found among hydroids on which it feeds, particularly *Tubularia indivisa*, to depths of about 40 m but exceptionally to over 300 m. Egg mass white or pink spiral, from which planktonic larvae hatch. **Similar species** · Other species of *Coryphella* often very similar in shape and size, but white lines of this species are usually diagnostic. *C. browni* may occur in large numbers with *C. lineata*. Is very similar to *C. lineata* but lacks distinctive white stripes.

Abundance & distribution
Widespread but not usually very numerous. Distribution extends from northern Norway to all British coasts and south to the western Mediterranean.

Coryphella pedata (Montagu)

Description · A narrow-bodied sea slug, up to 5 cm long. The oral tentacles are a similar length or slightly shorter than the wrinkled rhinophores. The cerata are found in up to seven clusters along each side of the body. A characteristic feature of this animal is the overall translucent deep-pink, purple, or violet colour of the entire body. The cerata, tentacles, and rhinophores all have bright white tips. **Habitat & ecology** · Generally subtidal on hydroids such as *Eudendrium ramosum*, *Obelia geniculata*, and *Sertularella gayi*, on which it feeds. The spawn is a coiled string laid amongst the branches of hydroids. The eggs hatch into pelagic larvae. **Similar species** · Only *Flabellina affinis*, found in the Mediterranean. This species has lamellate rhinophores.

Abundance & distribution
Common. Found all around the coasts of Britain and Ireland. Distributed from Norway to the Mediterranean.

Distinctive features

1. Oral tentacles and rhinophores similarly long and tapering, tentacles smooth, rhinophores slightly wrinkled.
2. Cerata bright red or bright green, with band of white near their tips.
3. Up to six clusters of cerata.

Distinctive features

1. Head distinct, with long, tapering oral tentacles.
2. Rhinophores tapering, as long as oral tentacles.
3. Cerata in groups of about five along sides of body, red with white tips.
4. Body translucent whitish, with mid-dorsal longitudinal white line which branches anteriorly to extend along oral tentacles; similar lines occur laterally, meeting mid-dorsal line near front of body.

Distinctive features

1. Narrow-bodied sea slug.
2. Up to seven clusters of cerata along each side of body.
3. Deep pink, purple, or violet colour.

FAMILY **Facelinidae**

Facelina coronata (Forbes & Goodsir)

Description · Slender body, up to 4 cm long. Head has two pairs of tentacles, upper pair much longer than lower, formed by the front of the foot. Rhinophores distinctly lamellate, about half as long as tentacles. Body translucent white, red oesophagus showing through behind rhinophores. Opaque white reproductive organs may show through skin of posterior part of body. Head region usually has iridescent blue sheen, especially around base of oral tentacles, and on cerata. Along back the six groups of cerata have light to dark brown digestive gland visible in them. These have white streaks along frontal aspect; oral tentacles and rhinophores also streaked with white. **Habitat & ecology** · Among rocks and boulders, lower shore to shallow sublittoral. Mostly found feeding on *Tubularia indivisa*, though also on *Obelia* species and *Laomedea flexuosa*. Spawn laid in spiral of up to six whorls. Eggs hatch into planktonic larvae. **Similar species** · Include *Facelina bostoniensis*. This grows up to 5.5 cm long, is much broader in aspect than *F. coronata*, only rarely has blue iridescent pigment, and usually has a patch of white between the rhinophores.

Abundance & distribution
Frequent. Occurs around all coasts of Britain and Ireland. Distributed from Norway to the western Mediterranean.

FAMILY **Aeolidiidae**

Aeolidia papillosa (Linnaeus)
Common grey sea-slug

Description · Large, up to 8–12 cm long. Dorsal surface of body largely covered in long, soft, white-tipped cerata arranged in about 25 closely packed rows on each side, leaving mid-dorsal region uncovered. Head bears two pairs of tentacles, rear pair (propodial tentacles) broad, somewhat triangular, pointing slightly backwards. Rhinophores, positioned dorsally at back of head, smooth and nearly as long as oral (anterior) pair of tentacles. Typically grey, greyish-brown, or purplish-brown, usually with white V-, diamond-, or crescent-shaped patch on head, running out to ends of oral tentacles and back along mid-dorsal line behind head. **Habitat & ecology** · Intertidally at almost all levels below high water and in shallow sublittoral situations, crawling on rocks and boulders, or among seaweeds. Found as deep as 800 m. Feeds on sea anemones, particularly *Actinia* and *Metridium senile*, but also *Actinothoe sphyrodeta* and *Anemonia viridis*. An annual species, living 12–16 months. Eggs laid in spiral of up to 30 000 or more (half a million?) ova, hatching into planktonic larvae.

Abundance & distribution
Common on most British rocky shores, with a widespread distribution extending from Arctic waters, through Atlantic, North Sea, and Channel coasts of northern Europe, southwards to the Bay of Biscay. May also occur in the Pacific.

Class Bivalvia (Pelecypoda)

Bivalve molluscs are characterised by their bilaterally symmetrical, compressed bodies enclosed by a pair of lateral shells (**valves**) which are linked dorsally by a **ligament** and **hinge**. The head is either rudimentary or absent, and possesses neither tentacles nor a radula. The **foot**, typically wedge-shaped, is ventral and not used as a crawling surface as in most gastropods. The gut and visceral mass are enclosed laterally by two extensions of the body wall (the **mantle**), the space between them being the **mantle cavity**. The two edges of the mantle may be partially or completely fused, and in many species are posteriorly

developed into a pair of tubular **siphons**; the ventral siphon is the **inhalant** one, the dorsal the **exhalant**. Siphons may be long or short, contractile and extensile, rigid, quite separate, partially fused, or completely joined, depending upon the species concerned.

Bivalves are mostly sedentary, permanently attached to rocks, burrowed into sand or mud, hidden in rocky cracks or crevices, or simply lying on the substrate surface. Some species are capable of boring into shale or limestone rocks, or wood. All bivalves are **microphagous** filter- or deposit-feeders. Their sexes are usually separate, and the life-cycle typically involves a free-living, planktonic larval stage.

The shell form is often important for

Distinctive features

1. Head with two pairs of tentacles, the upper pair longest.
2. Cerata in about six groups, dark red with white tips.
3. Rhinophores distinctly lamellate.
4. Iridescent blue sheen to head and cerata.

Distinctive features

1. Body dorsally with about 25 rows of long, closely-packed cerata on each side, but mid-dorsal region uncovered.
2. Rhinophores smooth, almost as long as oral tentacles.
3. Propodial tentacles triangular, broad, angled slightly backwards.
4. Typically greyish or brownish-grey, tips of cerata, rhinophores, and tentacles white.

species identification. The mantle is responsible for shell formation, which it achieves by two mechanisms; it synthesises and secretes an organic matrix (**conchiolin**), and then deposits calcium carbonate (**calcite**) onto this matrix. An uncalcified dorsal part of the conchiolin provides an **elastic ligament**, which may be external, internal, or run from one position to the other. Shell growth starts by calcium carbonate being deposited along the free margin of each valve, so that the oldest part of the valves is dorsal where it forms a convex and often very obvious **umbo** or **beak**. **Umbones** on the two valves may be separated by a space (the dorsal **cardinal area**), or the umbones may be close together and the cardinal area is then divided into an anterior **lunule** and posterior **escutcheon**. In many bivalves there is no cardinal area. The ligament joining the two valves is always posterior to the umbones. The two valves may be identical in shape and size (**equivalve**) or dissimilar (**inequivalve**). If the umbo is on the midline, valves are said to be **equilateral**, but if the umbo is anterior or posterior of the midline, valves are **inequilateral**; more often than not the umbo is anterior. Opening of the valves is achieved by the elasticity of the ligament, closure by contractions of the **adductor muscles**, which are usually arranged in pairs (**anterior** and **posterior** adductor muscles). The outer surface of the valves is covered by a horny **periostracum**, which may be thick or thin, coarse or smooth, or bear **periostracal spines**. The surface is also often marked by concentric growth rings or ridges as well as the concentric sculpturing of ridges and grooves typical of many species. **Ribs** radiating from the umbones, often with rows of sharp spines, may also be present.

The inner surfaces of the valves also provide important features of use in identifying the species. The adductor muscles leave scars (**adductor muscle scars**) whose shape, relative size, and position are important. The anterior adductor scar tends to be smaller than the posterior. Extending between the adductor

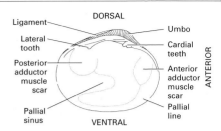

The main internal features of a bivalve mollusc shell.

scars is the **pallial line scar**, which marks the line of attachment of the mantle to the inner shell surface. In many species this line may be

---

SUBCLASS **Protobranchia** | ORDER **Nuculoida**

FAMILY **Nuculidae**

Nucula nitidosa Winckworth

Description · Shells an oval triangular shape, 10–13 mm long, with umbones well posterior to the midline. Outer shell surface marked with faint concentric lines and radiating striations, and coloured white or grey with blue-tinged growth lines. Periostracum is glossy, often with bands of grey or greenish-yellow. Hinge-line has 20–30 anterior lateral and 10–14 posterior lateral teeth. Shell margins finely crenellate. **Habitat & ecology** · Sublittoral, down to about 100 m on fine sand and silt. **Similar species** · These include several other species of *Nucula*. *N. nucleus*, the common nut shell, is a similar size but usually has fewer hinge teeth anteriorly and the periostracum is dull. *N. hanleyi* also tends to have fewer hinge teeth anteriorly, a non-glossy periostracum, and radiating bands of colour from the umbones to shell margin. These may be reddish-brown, purplish-brown, or grey. *N. sulcata* is typically larger and anterior part of hinge-line is often corrugated. *Nuculoma tenuis* has fewer anterior hinge teeth.

Abundance & distribution Common and locally often abundant. Occurs around all British and Irish coasts. Distribution extends from Norway southwards to the Mediterranean and West Africa.

SUBCLASS **Lamellibranchia** | SUPERORDER **Filibranchia**
ORDER **Arcoida**

FAMILY **Glycymeridae**

Glycymeris glycymeris (Linnaeus) **Dog cockle**

Description · Shells equivalve (umbones on the midline), almost circular in outline, up to 65–80 mm in diameter and quite heavy. The inner margins of the valves are distinctly crenellate, appearing almost like the teeth of a cog-wheel. The hinge ligament is external; the hinge on each valve has two rows of up to about 12 teeth. The umbones on the two shells have a slight gap between them. The outer surface of the valves is finely marked with concentric ridges and pale brown to yellowish-brown, often with a pattern of darker brown or purplish-brown concentric zigzagged markings. The inner valve surfaces are white or brownish-white. **Habitat & ecology** · An offshore species, found burrowed just beneath the surface of coarse sandy or gravelly-shell sediments, shallow sublittoral to depths of about 80–100 m. It is commonly eaten in parts of France bordering the Atlantic. **Similar species** · There are about four similar European species, including *G. violascens*, with which the dog cockle may be confused.

Abundance & distribution Widespread and often locally abundant. Occurs all around Britain and Ireland. Distributed from Norway to West Africa, including the Mediterranean.

indented at one end (always posterior), marking the **pallial sinus**, which shows the position of the retracted siphons when the valves are fully closed. A distinction between bivalve families and genera is often possible by the number and type of **hinge teeth**; those located below the umbo are **cardinal teeth**, flanked on either side by anterior and posterior **lateral teeth**. In a number of species the inner portion of the hinge ligament is enclosed by a concave **chondrophore**.

Many species of bivalve molluscs are both common and abundant, in shallow-water marine and estuarine habitats and in deep-sea sediments and even deep-sea hydrothermal vents. In north-west European waters there are representatives of at least six orders and more than 40 families; among the latter, such types as the cockles (**Cardiidae**), dog cockles (**Glycymeridae**), mussels (**Mytilidae**), oysters (**Ostreidae**), scallops (**Pectinidae**), razor shells (**Solenidae**), tellins (**Tellinidae**), and venus shells (**Veneridae**) are particularly well known and several of them are edible and of commercial value.

Distinctive features

1. Shells an oval triangular shape.
2. Umbones far posterior of midline.
3. Outer shell surface grey or white, with bluish growth lines; periostracum glossy.

Distinctive features

1. Shells almost circular in outline.
2. Inner margins of shells resemble cog-wheel teeth.
3. Outer shell surface yellowish-brown marked with concentric, irregular zigzags of darker brown or purplish-brown.

FAMILY **Anomiidae**

Anomia ephippium Linnaeus **Common saddle oyster**

Description · Brittle, almost circular, upper (left) valve is up to 6 cm in diameter, its surface marked with wavy, concentric ridges which typically appear like rough, raised, dull brownish scales, often with a bluish tinge. Valves are unequal, upper convex with three close-set and distinct scars on its inner surface. This overlaps lower (right) flat valve, which has one internal scar and a conspicuous opening through which chalky byssus attachment threads pass from upper valve to substrate. **Habitat & ecology** · Lower shore and in sublittoral situations on rocky coasts, attached to rocks, algal holdfasts and fronds, and other shells. Shape of the oyster is often affected by what it is attached to; when attached to other shells, for example, it often assumes their shape. **Similar species** · Resembles *Monia patelliformis*, but this is more circular in outline and only has two scars on the inside of its left valve. *M. squama* is also more circular;

it does have two scars on the left valve but they are joined.

Abundance & distribution Common. Occurs off all British and Irish coasts, with a distribution extending from Iceland and Norway to West Africa, including the Mediterranean.

ORDER **Mytiloida** | FAMILY **Mytilidae**

Modiolus modiolus (Linnaeus) **Horse mussel**

Description · Shells thick, sub-triangular to rhomboidal in shape, shell margins reaching in front of bluntly rounded umbones. Up to 10–14 cm long, exceptionally to 23 cm, small individuals are bluish, larger examples orangey- to dark brown. Valves similar, without hinge teeth but with distinct ligaments. Young may be brown to olive brown and horny periostracum may bear spines (not in adults). **Habitat & ecology** · Sessile, attached to rocks and other secure surfaces by byssus threads, lower shore and sublittoral to about 150 m, often associated with kelps. Can form reefs when huge numbers of individuals build up a bank raised above level of surrounding seafloor. Such reefs harbour a large diversity of other organisms. Often encrusted with other organisms and commonly infested with the parasitic copepod, *Modiolicola insignis*, and commensal pea crabs *Pinnotheres pinnotheres* and *P. pisum*. Fished commercially as a food in northern Europe. **Similar species** · Similar to *Mytilus* species but these have a thin shell and show differences in the shape and position of the umbones.

Abundance & distribution Common, locally very abundant. Found throughout the north-east Atlantic and from Norway south to the Bay of Biscay.

Mytilus edulis Linnaeus **Common mussel**

Description · Sub-triangular, oval, or ear-shaped shell, 2–20 cm long. Umbones prominent and edge of shell does not pass around them. Shell with thin concentric lines, growth lines distinct. Top of shell can be straight, forming an angle to the posterior margin. Shell pale brown but usually blue or purple to black in adults; the inside is white darkening to blue or purplish around the posterior margins. Mantle edge of live animals yellow-brown. Normally attached to substratum by strong golden threads (byssus). **Habitat & ecology** · Forms large, dense beds or, like *Modiolus modiolus*, raised reefs from the upper shore to shallow sublittoral, especially in sheltered conditions. Important filter-feeder on rocky shores, out-competing barnacles and fucoid algae for space. Beds can be patchy on exposed shores because of cycles of removal of adults and recruitment of larvae. Wild and cultured populations harvested for food. **Similar species** · *Mytilus galloprovincialis*, (b) but the umbones are turned downwards and the shell more rounded. *Modiolus barbatus* and *Modiolus phaseolina* are smaller species that have spiny shells.

(a)

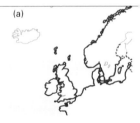

Abundance & distribution Abundant. Occurs around all coasts of Britain and Ireland. Distributed from Arctic Norway to the Mediterranean, including the Baltic sea.

Distinctive features

1. Valves unequal, upper (left) convex, lower (right) flat, with conspicuous hole for attachment threads.
2. Upper shell almost circular, with concentric wavy ridges forming rough, raised scales.

Distinctive features

1. Shells sub-triangular to rhomboidal.
2. Shell margins reach in front of bluntly rounded umbones.

Distinctive features

1. Sub-triangular, oval- or ear-shaped shell.
2. Umbones prominent.
3. Blue, purple, or black, with fine concentric lines.

(a)

(b)

ORDER **Pteroidea**

FAMILY **Ostreidae**

Crassostrea gigas (Thunberg) **Portuguese oyster**

Description · A large species, up to 30 cm long, with thick, broadly, or narrowly oval to ear-shaped shells. The shell surface is coarsely sculptured with concentric ridges and 6–7 thick, bold ribs which commonly give the shell edges a deeply undulating appearance. The surface of the shell may appear frilled with thin raised layers of shell that can be rough or even sharp to the touch. The left, lower, valve is deeply cupped, the upper, right, valve almost flat. On the inner shell surface, which is shiny and nacreous, the single adductor muscle scar is typically deep purple. The outer shell surface is whitish, greyish or pale brown with yellow, brown, purple, or black streaks and patches. **Habitat & ecology** · Living on coarser substrata, lower shore to sublittoral depths of about 80 m. Valued as a food in several European countries. **Similar species** · *C. virginica*, the American oyster, is similar but the shell lacks the bold ribs and wavy edge of *C. gigas*.

Abundance & distribution
Common, locally abundant, especially when cultivated. The natural distribution extends from the Mediterranean to the Bay of Biscay. It has been introduced to various areas such as south-west and south-east English coasts.

Ostrea edulis Linnaeus
Common oyster, native oyster, flat oyster

Description · Up to about 10 cm in diameter. Oval, pear-shaped, or almost circular shells are rough, marked with scaly, concentric, fine radiating ridges. Lower, left valve deeply cupped, smaller right one almost flat. Outer surface of shells varies from dirty white to yellowish, reddish-brown, or bluish-grey. Often pale shells are marked with concentric bands of darker colours. Internally, large, single adductor scar more or less comma-shaped, and white to dull yellowish-white. **Habitat & ecology** · On coarse sediments at ELWS levels on shore and sublittorally to depths of about 50–80 m, often attached to rocks or boulders. Shells often fouled by other organisms; oyster beds can be rich in diversity of other animals. Broods larvae before releasing them into plankton. Highly prized as delicacy, usually from cultured stocks. Inedible when breeding, May-August. **Similar species** · *Crassostrea gigas* usually longer than *O. edulis* and adductor muscle scar tends to be purple or brown. *C. virginica* is more like *C. gigas*, tends to lack ribs and is usually purple or reddish brown. No other similar species, but three varieties are recognised, *O. edulis* var. *adria*, var. *lamellosa*, and var. *tarentina*.

Abundance & distribution
Once locally both common and very abundant, populations since greatly overfished, and now very reduced or extinct. Cultured populations have been devastated by disease such as caused by parasite, *Bonamia ostreae*. Range extends from Atlantic coasts of Norway south

FAMILY **Pectinidae**

Aequipecten opercularis (Linnaeus)
Queen scallop, queenie, frill

Description · Shell rounded, or oval-shaped and biconvex (both valves convex), although left (upper) valve more curved than right (lower) valve. Shell is up to 9 cm long, marked with about 20 distinct radiating ridges and corrugated concentric grooves; margins of shells are crenellated. Hinge-line is marked by a pair of distinct ears; anterior ear sticks out more freely than posterior, with anterior ear of right valve being longer than that of left valve. Colour is variable, but commonly shades of yellow, orange, red, purple, brown, or nearly white, sometimes irregularly patterned or mottled with lighter and darker colours. Previously known as *Chlamys opercularis*. **Habitat & ecology** · Found on coarse gravel and sandy sediments on lower shore and sublittorally to depths of about 200 m. Young scallops attach to substrate by byssus threads, but adults are free and can swim vigorously by 'flapping' the shell. Once extremely abundant, often locally aggregated, commercial exploitation, by dredging, has led to a drastic decline in numbers. **Similar species** · Small specimens may be confused with *Chlamys* species.

Abundance & distribution
Common, locally abundant. Occurs off all British and Irish coasts, with a distribution extending from Norway to the Mediterranean and southwards as far as the Canary Islands.

Distinctive features

1. Shell sculpturing consisting of coarse, concentric ridges and 6–7 bold, thick, radiating ribs.
2. Lower left valve deeply cupped and larger than the almost flat right valve.
3. Adductor muscle scar typically a deep purple.

to Morocco, Mediterranean and Black Sea.

Distinctive features

1. Shells oval, almost circular or pear-shaped.
2. Lower shell larger, deeply cupped, upper shell almost flat.
3. Shell sculptured with irregular, rough, concentric ridges and fine radiating lines.

Distinctive features

1. Shell biconvex, upper (left) valve more curved than lower.
2. Shell hinge with distinct ears, anterior ear more pronounced than posterior.
3. Shell exterior marked with about 20 distinct radiating ridges and corrugated concentric grooves.

Chlamys distorta (da Costa)
Humpback scallop, hunchback scallop

Description · Elongate oval shell, 4–5 cm long, slightly deeper. Umbo of each shell flanked by anterior and posterior ears, anterior longer than posterior and especially so on right (lower) valve. Outer surface of shells sculptured with about 70 rough, spiny, radiating ribs, irregularly worn in larger, older individuals. Shell shape may also be variously distorted or twisted depending on where scallop was attached. Concentric growth lines distinct. Shell colour varies from dirty white to yellow, red, or brown, often mottled with irregular light markings. **Habitat & ecology** · Variously reported as either free-living or attached by byssus threads when young, adults are permanently cemented to hard rocky substrata by their right valve. Often found in kelp holdfasts. Occurs on lower shore and sublittorally, to depths of about 100 m. Breeds throughout much of spring, summer, and autumn, adults maturing as males but changing to females after breeding. **Similar species** · *C. varia* is similar but shell is thin, and narrower than *C. distorta*.

Abundance & distribution
Common on all British and Irish coasts, the distribution extends from Iceland and northern Norway to the Mediterranean and West Africa.

Chlamys varia (Linnaeus)
Variegated scallop

Description · Scallop with a thin, narrow, elongate oval shell, up to 8 cm in length. The dorsal margin of the shell is extended into anterior and posterior ears. The anterior ear is much larger than the posterior. The anterior ear of the right valve is larger than that of the left; it also has a notch, with tiny teeth along its lower edge. The shell is sculptured with 25–35 ribs with concentric growth lines. These may form spines where they intersect the ribs. Colour very variable, often mottled with a mix of dirty white, yellow, orange, pink, red, purple, and brown. **Habitat & ecology** · Lower intertidal to shallow subtidal as deep as 100 m. Most common in rocky or gravelly areas. May be attached by byssus or free swimming. Often found in kelp holdfasts. Similar to *C. distorta* but the shell of this species is thicker, broader, and often distorted.

Abundance & distribution
Common. Occurs off all British and Irish coasts. Distributed south to the Mediterranean and West Africa.

Palliolum tigerinum (Müller)
Tiger scallop

Description · Up to 25 mm in diameter; lower margin of the broadly oval and convex shells forms a semicircle. The outer surface is, unusually for scallops, mostly smooth and marked with fine concentric and radiating lines. In older shells there may be fine marginal ribs. The umbones, situated on the midline, are flanked by tiny posterior and large anterior ears, the latter marked with distinct radiating ribs. The right anterior ear has a byssal notch. Colour very variable: yellow, brown, purple, or sometimes white. It may be blotched or streaked with paler colour which may be in concentric bands, rays or zigzag lines. **Habitat & ecology** · Found on the lower shore and sublittorally to depths of about 100 m, on coarse sand and gravel. **Similar species** · *P. striatum* is smaller than *P. tigerinum* and has small spines on the ribs of the shell. *P. furtivum* has no ribs on the shell. Both are much rarer than *P. tigerinum*.

Abundance & distribution
Locally common. Occurs all around Britain and Ireland. Distributed from Norway to Morocco.

Distinctive features

1. Shells elongate oval, with distinct ears at umbones.
2. Anterior ears larger than posterior, especially on right shell.
3. Shell surface with about 70 coarse, spiny ribs radiating from umbones.

Distinctive features

1. Narrowly elongate oval shape.
2. Thin shell.
3. Anterior ear much longer than posterior.
4. Anterior ear of right valve has notch, and tiny teeth on lower edge.
5. 25–35 ribs with small spines.

Distinctive features

1. Lower half of shell margins forming a semicircle.
2. Umbones flanked by small posterior and large anterior ears.
3. Anterior ears with distinct radiating ribs, right ear with byssal notch.

Pecten maximus (Linnaeus) **Great scallop**

Description · Up to 15 cm in diameter, lower (right) valve deeply cupped, upper (left) almost flat. Both shells externally sculptured with up to 17 thick rounded ribs. Growth rings clearly visible on left and right valves. Umbones, located on midline, flanked on either side by large, similar-sized flat ears. Upper shell rich reddish- or golden-brown, often with paler mottling. Lower shell dirty white to pale brown, sometimes with darker markings. **Habitat & ecology** · Entirely sublittoral, living flat side uppermost in shallow depressions on fine sand and gravel at depths to at least 100 m. If approached carefully mantle of shell may be seen with numerous tiny silvery 'eyes'. Hermaphroditic, breeding commencing when 3 years old. Many natural populations have been reduced by fishing, but still prized as table delicacy, with both adductor muscles and gonad being eaten. Shells often used for ornaments. Sessile invertebrates such as barnacles or tube worms often found growing on shell surface. **Similar species** · *P. jacobeaus* is a similar Mediterranean species, but ribs are square in cross-section.

Abundance & distribution
Locally abundant. Found all around the coasts of Britain and Ireland. Distributed from Norway to the Atlantic coast of Spain. In many areas this species has been heavily overfished by dredging.

SUPERORDER **Eulamellibranchia** | ORDER **Veneroida**

FAMILY **Lucinidae**

Lucinoma borealis (Linnaeus)

Description · Up to 4 cm in diameter, shell thick and almost circular in outline. Small umbones slightly anterior to midline, outer surface sculptured with many fine, concentric ridges; growth lines distinct; the right valve has single anterior and bifid posterior cardinal teeth; the left valve bifid anterior, single posterior. Single anterior and posterior lateral teeth on each valve may be worn and indistinct. Outer shell surface dirty white to yellowish-white. **Habitat & ecology** · Found in sand and gravel on the lower shore and sublittorally to depths of about 100 m. This species has quite specific habitat preferences and is often found in sheltered areas where black, sulfurous-smelling sand is close to the surface. Its tissue contains symbiotic sulfur bacteria which help it to live and grow. **Similar species** · Very easily confused with *Lucinella divaricata*, but none of the cardinal teeth of this species is bifid.

Abundance & distribution
Found from the Mediterranean north to Norway and on all British coasts. May be locally common.

FAMILY **Lasaeidae**

Lasaea rubra (Montagu)

Description · Shells small, only 3 mm long, fat, and with their reddish-brown outer surface marked by fine, concentric ridges. Both valves have single anterior and posterior lateral teeth, the left valve also having a single cardinal tooth. Inner shell surface white. **Habitat & ecology** · Only found intertidally on rocky shore, in barnacle tests, among clumps of the lichen *Lichina*, on algal holdfasts, or deep in crevices, attached by byssal threads. This species can occur high on the shore. It is unusual in that the larvae are brooded in the suprabranchial chamber so there is no planktonic larval stage. **Similar species** · May be confused with *Turtonia minuta*, but this species has three well-developed cardinal teeth on each valve.

Abundance & distribution
Common, locally abundant. Occurs on all British and Irish coasts. Distributed from Norway south to the Mediterranean and Canary Islands.

Distinctive features

1. Upper shell flat, lower shell deeply cupped; both marked with up to about 17 distinct radiating ribs.
2. Umbones on midline, flanked on either side by similarly sized large and flat ears.

Distinctive features

1. Shells almost circular; umbones just anterior to midline.
2. Bifid cardinal teeth anterior on left valve, posterior on right.
3. Shell marked with fine concentric ridges.

Distinctive features

1. Shells small, plump, externally marked by fine concentric ridges.
2. Each valve with only single anterior and posterior lateral teeth, left valve also with single small cardinal tooth.
3. Outer shell surface reddish-brown.

FAMILY **Arcticidae**

Arctica islandica (Linnaeus) **Icelandic cyprine**

Description · The thick, solid, oval shells are up to 125 mm long but not as wide. Both valves are similar, with smooth edges. There are three cardinal teeth on the hinge, with one lateral tooth behind. The prominent forward-pointing umbones are anterior to the midline, with a conspicuous posterior external ligament. The dark, chestnut brown to black and shiny outer shell surface (periostracum) is covered with very fine concentric lines; the inner surface is smooth and white. The periostracum may begin to peel in dead specimens. Previously known as *Cyprina islandica*. **Habitat & ecology** · Burrows in sand, muddy sand, and mud, rarely on the extreme lower shore, much more commonly sublittorally from a few miles offshore to the shelf edge. May be infected with the leech-like nemertean, *Malacobdella grossa*.

Abundance & distribution
Locally common. Occurs around all coasts of Britain and Ireland. Distributed from Arctic Norway southwards to the Bay of Biscay.

FAMILY **Cardiidae**

Acanthocardia aculeata (Linnaeus)
Spiny cockle, red nose

Description · Shells plump, up to 10 cm long, asymmetrical with anterior side rounded and posterior flat-sided, with a marked angle between the hinge-line and edge of the rest of shell. Shell marked with 20–22 radiating deep furrows and ridges, giving rim a toothed appearance (seen as grooves inside). Ridges covered with long, sharp spines. Hinge with two peg-like cardinal teeth (below umbo) on each shell, anterior cardinal tooth of left shell being larger than posterior. Right shell with two anterior and two posterior lateral teeth, left shell only one tooth in each position. Anterior and posterior adductor-muscle scars similar-sized. Shell white on inner surface, yellowish or light brown to reddish-brown or vermilion on external. **Habitat & ecology** · Sublittoral from about 10 m or more depth, in sand, muddy sand, and gravel. **Similar species** · *A. echinata* and *A. tuberculata*, but cardinal teeth on left shell are same size and posterior edge of shell is more rounded.

Abundance & distribution
Around the British Isles restricted to the south and west coasts only. Distributed south to the Mediterranean and north-west Africa.

Acanthocardia echinata (Linnaeus)
Prickly cockle

Description · Plump shells up to about 7.5 cm long with a rounded anterior margin and not so rounded posterior margin. Shell marked by 18–23 sharply defined radiating ridges bearing sharp, pointed spines that are markedly longer near the anterior margin of the shell. Spine bases broad, often fusing with adjacent bases. Grooves formed by ridges are visible inside the shell and run to the middle. Arrangement of hinge teeth is similar to *A. aculeata* except for the anterior and posterior cardinal teeth on the left shell being of a similar size. The prickly cockle is yellowish to dark brown with concentric banding, white inside. **Habitat & ecology** · Sublittoral muddy sand and gravel at depths of 10 m or more. **Similar species** · *A. aculeata* or *A. tuberculata*, but the anterior cardinal tooth of the left shell is larger than the posterior in *A. aculeata*, and the inside of the shells is only grooved to the pallial line in *A. tuberculata*.

Abundance & distribution
Common. Occurs off all coasts of Britain and Ireland. Distribution extends from the Atlantic coast of Norway south to the Canary Islands, including the Mediterranean.

Distinctive features

1. Shells similar, thick, solid, oval.
2. Prominent, forward-pointing umbones anterior to midline.
3. Shell surface glossy, chestnut brown to black.

Distinctive features

1. Shells plump, anterior edge rounded, posterior flat-sided.
2. Marked with radiating grooves and ridges, ridges bearing sharp spines.
3. Anterior cardinal tooth of left shell larger than posterior tooth.

Distinctive features

1. Shells plump, marked with radiating grooves and ridges.
2. Ridges bear sharp, pointed spines.
3. Anterior and posterior cardinal teeth of left shell similar size.

Cerastoderma edule (Linnaeus) **Common cockle**

Description · Broad, thick, oval shells, up to about 5 cm long. Externally each shell marked by about 24 radiating ridges crossed by distinct concentric growth lines. Ridges may bear short, flat knobs. Umbones at hinge slightly anterior to midline of shell. Right valve has two anterior and two posterior lateral teeth; left valve only single anterior and posterior teeth. Each valve has two small cardinal teeth. Inner surface of each shell white, sometimes with brownish markings, grooves matching external ridges being evident for only short distance in from shell margin. Outer surface of shell typically yellowish-brown to dirty brown or light to dark grey, sometimes with pale yellow or white areas. Previously known as *Cardium edule*. **Habitat & ecology** · Lives burrowed in almost all types of sands, including those mixed with significant amounts of mud or gravel, mid-shore level downwards. Commercially harvested for food on many European shores. Can tolerate salinity reductions as low as 10‰, often common in estuaries. **Similar species** · Lagoon cockle, *C. glaucum*, but its shells more triangular in shape and internal grooves extend their full length, beyond pallial line. *Parvicardium* species are also similar, but usually much smaller.

Abundance & distribution
Very common. Occurs all around Britain and Ireland. Distributed from Norway to West Africa, including the Baltic and Mediterranean Seas.

Parvicardium exiguum (Gmelin) **Little cockle**

Description · Shells small, equivalve, obliquely oval but strongly angled and up to 1.3 cm long. Brownish outer surface has 20–22 broad, radiating ribs, formed into small spines in adults, ventrally and anteriorly. Growth lines are visible. Ribs form distinct marginal crenellations around shell but there are no inner grooves matching ribs. Umbones distinctly anterior of midline. Hinge of each valve has two peg-like cardinal teeth; right valve also bears two anterior and one posterior lateral teeth; on left valve there are only single anterior and posterior laterals. **Habitat & ecology** · Lower shore and shallow sublittoral, to depths of about 60 m, found burrowed in muddy sand and gravel. Occasionally occurs in estuaries and brackish conditions. **Similar species** · At least six other species of *Parvicardium* in European waters. Several have the grooves on inside of shell extending deeply into shell. There are also differences in sculpturing on outside of shell.

Abundance & distribution
Common. Found on all British and Irish coasts. Distributed from Norway to the Mediterranean.

FAMILY **Veneridae**

Callista chione (Linnaeus) **Brown venus**

Description · This bivalve has a large oval shell up to 9 cm long. The umbones are prominent and offset towards the anterior. In life the shells are a smooth, polished, glossy golden or reddish-brown, sometimes with darker streaks radiating from the umbones. Young specimens may have rows of vividly coloured spots instead of dark streaks, or three broad white bands. The shell has a fine sculpturing of growth lines and fine concentric lines. Inside the shell is dull white with three cardinal teeth; the left valve has a single, prominent, anterior lateral tooth. **Habitat & ecology** · A sublittoral species found in sand down to 100 m. It becomes more common moving south. **Similar species** · Small specimens somewhat resemble *Chamelea gallina* but the shell in this species is triangular and the area in front of the umbones (lunule) is deeply depressed and heart-shaped.

Abundance & distribution
Uncommon. Found from north Wales southwards to the Channel Islands. Distributed south to the Mediterranean, Canary and Azores Islands.

Distinctive features

1. Growth rings on outside of shells distinct.
2. Umbones slightly anterior to middle.
3. Shells marked with radiating broad ridges which may bear short, flat knobs.

Distinctive features

1. Shells equivalve, obliquely oval with anterior umbones.
2. Outer shell surface with 20–22 broad radiating ribs.
3. Ribs form distinct marginal crenellations around shells.

Distinctive features

1. Large oval shell, valves equal in size and shape; distinct anterior umbone.
2. Smooth glossy shell, golden or reddish-brown with darker streaks radiating from umbone.
3. Fine sculpturing of growth lines.

Chamelea gallina (Linnaeus) **Striped venus**

Description · Broadly triangular shell, up to 4 cm long, with very obvious umbones to one side (anterior) of midline. Posterior margin of shell is roundly curved while anterior is concave. Shell is externally marked with distinct growth lines and very fine concentric sculpturing. Each valve has three cardinal teeth. Pallial sinus is not deep, and U-shaped. Colour is very variable but tends to be dirty white to yellowish with darker streaks of brown or pink. There are usually four broad, dark brown or reddish-brown bands radiating from umbones. **Habitat & ecology** · A lower shore and shallow sublittoral species, found burrowing in coarse sand, fine sand, muddy sand, and shell gravel. **Similar species** · *Dosinia exoleta* is larger and has a deep V-shaped pallial sinus. *Callista chione* can also grow much larger and left valve has a lateral tooth (right a corresponding pit). *Clausinella fasciata* is smaller than striped venus, with flattened sub-triangular shell shape. Other clams with striped shells tend to have a more elongate shape.

Abundance & distribution
Common. Occurs on all British and Irish coasts. Distributed from western Norway south to the Mediterranean and Canary Islands.

Circomphalus casina (Linnaeus)

Description · The almost oval, thick, equivalve shells, up to 5 cm long, are boldly marked with up to 40 concentric ridges of variable width. These are broad, and may be flattened or have the posterior edges sharp and raised. The prominent umbones are bent towards the anterior. Each valve has three cardinal teeth, the left valve also having a small anterior lateral tooth (appears as a small knob). The pallial sinus is short and triangular. Colour yellowish-white or pinkish-white, occasionally rayed reddish-brown.
Habitat & ecology · An entirely sublittoral species, extending out to the edge of the continental shelf, found burrowing in coarse sandy and gravelly substrata. **Similar species** · May perhaps be confused with the warty venus, *Venus verrucosa*, but this species is more globelike than *C. casina*. Also, the concentric ridges of *V. verrucosa* are posteriorly crossed by radiating grooves which yield rounded, warty knobs not found on *Circomphalus*.

Abundance & distribution
Common. Occurs off all British and Irish coasts. Distribution extends from Norway to West Africa including the Mediterranean.

Clausinella fasciata (da Costa) **Banded venus**

Description · A small, solid, compressed sub-triangular shell with prominent umbones, growing to about 2.5 cm long. The sculpturing is of numerous concentric ridges in younger shells with large and small positioned alternately. As the shell grows these are replaced by up to 15 broad, round, concentric ridges. The colour is red, pink, purple, yellow, or brown, typically streaked, rayed, or blotched on a paler background. The margin of the shell may be finely crenellated. There are three cardinal teeth in each valve. The inner surfaces of the shell are dull white. **Habitat & ecology** · Subtidal, to a depth of 100 m or more, living in coarse gravels with sand or shell fragments. **Similar species** · Resembles the striped venus, *Chamelea gallina* but this species has a concave shell anteriorly and finer concentric ridges on the shell.

Abundance & distribution
Common. Found around all coasts of Britain and Ireland. Distributed from southern Norway to the Mediterranean and Canary Islands.

Distinctive features

1. Growth rings on outside of shells distinct.
2. Umbones slightly anterior to middle.
3. Shells with radiating broad ridges, which may bear short, flat knobs.

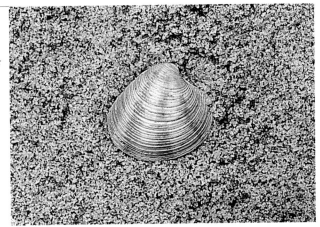

Distinctive features

1. Thick shells, boldly marked with up to 40 broad, flat, concentric ridges of variable width.
2. Umbones distinct, anterior.

Distinctive features

1. Small, solid, sub-triangular shell with prominent umbones.
2. Concentric ridges, broad in older specimens.
3. Slightly crenellated margins.
4. Colour variable, usually in streaks, rays, or blotches on paler background.

Dosinia exoleta (Linnaeus) **Rayed artemis**

Description · Almost circular shells, up to 6 cm in diameter, have small but distinctly projecting anterior umbones just anterior to midline. Shell is concave anterior to umbones and then becomes strongly rounded. Outer shell surface marked with numerous, closely spaced fine concentric ridges and distinct growth lines. Each valve has three cardinal teeth, left valve also having a single, anterior, knob-like lateral tooth. Colour is variable, but commonly with a white, pale yellow or pale brown base colour marked with rays, or blotches of darker pigment. Inner shell surface is glossy. Anterior and posterior adductor muscle scars are similarly sized. **Habitat & ecology** · Found on lower shore and sublittorally to depths of about 100 m, burrowing in muddy, coarse, sandy and gravelly sediments. **Similar species** · Several, particularly the striped venus, *Chamelea gallina*. This species tends to be more angular in outline and has no lateral teeth. The smooth artemis, *D. lupinus*, is also similar, but smaller than *D. exoleta*, and has smoother shell with more concentric ridges.

Abundance & distribution
Common. Found on all British and Irish coasts. Distributed from Norway to West Africa including the Mediterranean.

Mercenaria mercenaria (Linnaeus) **Qahog**

Description · Shells large, sub-triangular, thick, and up to 12 cm long, with prominent rounded umbones located far to the anterior. Outer shell surface with numerous, fine concentric ridges and obvious growth lines. The lunule (hinge area in front of the umbones) is finely striated, deep, and heart-shaped. There are three cardinal teeth on each valve and the hinge plate posterior to these is corrugated. The shell is pale brown to grey, sometimes with brown zigzag markings. The inner shell surface is shiny, with a purplish-blue tinge around the adductor scars. **Habitat & ecology** · A lower-shore and shallow sublittoral clam, found buried in muddy sediments.

Abundance & distribution
Indigenous to the north-east USA but introduced to European waters and now found on the North Sea and English Channel coasts between Netherlands and south England. Introduced populations further north in the River Mersey and River Dee were less successful.

Paphia rhomboides (Pennant) **Banded carpet shell**

Description · Shells elongate oval to oblong shape, up to 6.2 cm long, anterior and posterior margins rounded, sculptured with fine concentric ridges but no radiating lines. Umbones anterior of midline. Three cardinal teeth, middle one on left valve and middle and posterior on right are bifid. Inner shell shiny with pink tinge below hinge, outer surface dirty white, pink, pale brown to brown, typically with streaks, blotches, or rays of dark brown, pale purple, or pinkish-brown. Darker colours often form four radiating darker zigzag bands. **Habitat & ecology** · Lower shore and sublittoral to edge of continental shelf, in coarse sand and gravel. **Similar species** · *P. aurea*, golden carpet shell, is similar but shell is more rounded and umbones are close to midline. *Tapes decussatus* is larger, has a more squared posterior margin, and shell sculpture forms tiny squares or rectangles. In *Venerupis saxatilis* posterior hinge line is straight and pallial sinus extends beyond midline of the shell (not in *P. rhomboides*, *T. decussatus*).

Abundance & distribution
Common. Occurs on all British and Irish shores. Distributed from Norway to north-west Africa, including the Mediterranean.

Distinctive features

1. Shells almost circular, with small but projecting anterior umbones.
2. Shell surface marked with many fine concentric ridges and distinct growth lines.
3. Three cardinal teeth on both valves.
4. Small lateral tooth on left valve.

Distinctive features

1. Shells large, thick, with prominent rounded umbones far anterior.
2. Hinge area in front of umbones deep, heart-shaped, finely striated.
3. Outer shell surface with many fine concentric ridges and obvious growth lines.

Distinctive features

1. Elongate oval shells, with umbones anterior to midline, sculptured with fine concentric ridges only.
3. Shells often with four radiating zigzag bands of darker colour.

Tapes decussatus (Linnaeus)
Chequered carpet shell

Description · Shell is large, broadly oval, and grows up to 7.5 cm long. Umbones are anterior to midline and posterior margin of the shell is quite truncated. Shell has fine sculpturing of concentric striae and radiating lines, giving it a distinctly chequered effect posteriorly. Growth lines are obvious on shell. Colour is yellowish, or light brown with darker markings. Both valves have three cardinal teeth, the middle one of left valve and middle and posterior of right are bifurcated. Inside of shell is glossy white, with yellowish or orange tint. The pallial sinus is U-shaped and does not extend beyond the midline of shell. **Habitat & ecology** · Found on the lower shore and subtidally, living in sand, muddy sand, muddy gravel, or clay. **Similar species** · Resembles the pullet carpet shell, *Venerupis senegalensis*, but this species usually smaller and slightly rounder than *T. decussatus*. Pallial sinus in the pullet carpet shell tends to extend beyond midline.

Abundance & distribution
Frequent. Found mainly on south and west coasts of Britain and Ireland. Distributed south to the Mediterranean.

Venerupis senegalensis (Gmelin)
Pullet carpet shell

Description · Up to 5 cm long, oval-elongate shell marked with fine concentric ridges crossed by radiating lines better developed posteriorly. Umbones anterior to midline. Shells equivalve, edges smooth, with external ligament. Anterior shell margin curved; posterior hinge-line of shell straight, forming distinct angle where it meets posterior shell margin. Each valve has three cardinal teeth, centre one of left and centre and posterior of right being bifurcated. Inner shell surface glossy white, sometimes tinged purplish; outer surface yellowish-white to greyish- or brownish-cream with concentric bands, rays, or other patterns of darker pigment. **Habitat & ecology** · Extreme lower shore to depths of about 180 m, living in shallow burrows in sand or gravel; often attached by byssus threads to stones or shells. **Similar species** · Closely resembles *Paphia rhomboides*, but outer shell surface of this lacks lines radiating from umbones, and posterior margin is rounded. *V. saxatilis* has more truncated posterior margin than *V. senegalensis* and may be an ecotype of this species. *Tapes decussatus* is larger, with bolder radiating lines, giving shell a more chequered appearance.

Abundance & distribution
Locally common. Found off all British and Irish coasts, and from northern Norway to north-west Africa, including the Mediterranean.

Venus verrucosa Linnaeus
Warty venus

Description · The heavy, rounded and equivalve shells are up to 6.5 cm long, their umbones anterior to the midline. The umbone beaks border a lunule, a heart-shaped depression in front of the hinge. Hinge with three cardinal teeth on both valves and external ligament. Shell strongly sculptured with more than 20 pronounced concentric ridges, which posteriorly are broken up by radiating grooves to form distinct tubercles or wart-like knobs. The siphons are fused except at their tips. The outer shell surface is yellowish- or greyish-white with brown markings, the inner surface is white. **Habitat & ecology** · Found on the extreme lower shore to sublittoral depths of about 100 m, in sand or gravel.

Abundance & distribution
Frequent. Occurs on south and west coasts of Britain and Ireland. Distributed south to South Africa, including the Mediterranean.

Distinctive features

1. Large, broadly oval shell.
2. Umbones anterior to midline.
3. Concentric striae and radiating lines on shell, giving chequered effect.

Distinctive features

1. Shells equivalve, oval, umbones anterior to midline.
2. Shell has fine concentric ridges crossed by fine radiating lines.
3. Posterior hinge-line straight, forming angle with posterior shell margin.

Distinctive features

1. Shells equivalve, heavy, rounded, umbones anterior to midline.
2. Shell surface strongly marked by concentric ridges which posteriorly break up to form tubercles.
3. Beaks of umbone border lunule in front of hinge.

Turtoniidae

Turtonia minuta (Fabricius)

Description · The tubby, oval shells, rarely more than 3 mm long, have prominent umbones anterior to the midline. The umbones are also bent over towards the anterior of the shell. There are three cardinal teeth on each valve and the anterior-most on the right valve and posterior-most on the left are small and inconspicuous. Shells are a dull brownish to pink colour, marked with fine concentric ridges and distinct growth lines. Inner shell surface whitish to pale yellow. **Habitat & ecology** · An intertidal species, found in crevices, barnacle tests, and seaweed clumps on rocky coastlines. **Similar species** · May be confused with *Lasaea rubra*, but this species, unlike *T. minuta*, has a left valve with only one small cardinal tooth, and no cardinal tooth on the right valve.

Abundance & distribution
Common and often abundant. Occurs on all British and Irish coasts. Circumpolar distribution, in European waters as far south as Mediterranean.

Mactridae

Mactra stultorum (Linnaeus) **Rayed trough shell**

Description · Shell thin, delicate, swollen, and oval to sub-triangular in shape. Umbones are just anterior of midline. Length up to 5 cm long. Shell is externally marked by fine concentric ridges and obvious growth rings. Left valve has three cardinal and single anterior and posterior lateral teeth; right valve two cardinal, two anterior lateral and two posterior lateral teeth. Anterior cardinal tooth of right valve is parallel to hinge-line. Shell is white to yellowish-white with light reddish-brown rays and, sometimes, a purple tinge around umbones. Shiny inner shell surface has a pale purplish tinge. **Habitat & ecology** · Shallow-burrowing in medium to coarse clean sands, lower shore, and shallow sublittoral. A suspension-feeder, it breeds during spring. Empty shells, that have been drilled by necklace shells, are often found washed up on sandy beaches. **Similar species** · *M. glauca* is larger than *M. stultorum*, but shell is rounder and not as swollen. It is rare and only occurs in Channel Islands and Cornwall in British Isles, and southwards.

Abundance & distribution
Common, locally abundant. Found around the British Isles and Ireland. Distributed from Norway to West Africa, including the Mediterranean.

Spisula elliptica (Brown) **Elliptical trough shell**

Description · Shells thin, 3–4.5 cm long, equivalve, more or less elliptical in outline with an almost smooth, glossy surface marked with very fine concentric grooves and clear growth stages. Umbones almost on midline. Hinge of left valve with three large, fused cardinal teeth which extend almost to the inner edge of the hinge plate; lateral teeth distinctly serrated on their interlocking surfaces. External shell colour pale yellowish-brown. **Habitat & ecology** · Found burrowed in muddy sands and gravels on the lower shore and sublittorally to depths of about 100 m. **Similar species** · May be confused with the thick trough shell, *S. solida*, but *S. elliptica* has more delicate shells and is narrower relative to its length. Also resembles the rayed trough shell, *Mactra stultorum*, which has smooth rather than finely ridged lateral teeth.

Abundance & distribution
Sometimes locally abundant. Occurs off all British and Irish coasts. Distributed from Arctic Norway and Iceland to southern Atlantic coast of Spain. Rare in the western Mediterranean.

Distinctive features

1. Shells small, plump, oval, with obvious umbones anterior to midline.
2. Each valve with three cardinal teeth; though diagnostic, small size makes them hard to see.

Distinctive features

1. Shells thin, delicate, swollen, sub-triangular.
2. Externally pale yellowish-brown, characteristically marked by darker bands radiating from umbones.
3. Anterior cardinal tooth of right valve parallel to hinge-line.

Distinctive features

1. Shells thin, elliptical, umbones almost on midline.
2. Left valve with large, fused cardinal teeth.
3. Lateral hinge teeth distinctly serrated on interlocking surfaces.

Spisula solida (Linnaeus) **Thick trough shell**

Description · Shells sub-triangular, thick, solid, with umbones on midline and coarse, concentric sculpturing with distinct growth lines. Up to 5 cm long. The three cardinal teeth of the left valve are short, extending only half-way to the inner hinge plate rim; the anterior two are fused. Right valve has two short cardinal teeth. The left valve has single, elongate, anterior and posterior lateral teeth, the right valve has paired anterior and posterior lateral teeth. Lateral teeth are serrated or ridged. Outer shell surface brownish or yellowish-white. **Habitat & ecology** · Found burrowed shallowly in sand on the lower shore to sublittoral depths of about 100 m. **Similar species** · May be confused with *Mactra stultorum*, but the cardinal teeth of this species are smooth rather than, as in *S. solida*, ridged. *S. subtruncata* has strong, thick sub-triangular to triangular shells, which are tapered posteriorly and asymmetrical. It grows to about 3 cm long and may be abundant in silty sands.

Abundance & distribution
Common, often locally very abundant. Occurs on all British and Irish coasts. Distributed from sub-Arctic Iceland and Norway as far south as Atlantic Portugal and Morocco, but it is not found in the Mediterranean.

FAMILY **Lutrariidae**

Lutraria lutraria (Linnaeus) **Common otter shell**

Description · Equivalve shells up to 13 cm long, about half as wide; elongate oval outline, umbones anterior to midline. Both ends of shell are open. Left valve with two projecting cardinal teeth forming conspicuous V-shape that fits into similar shaped socket on right valve formed by two cardinal teeth. Also additional very small cardinal tooth on left valve and thin anterior and posterior lateral teeth. Right valve with one posterior lateral tooth. Hinge with both external and internal ligaments. Outer shell surface yellowish-white or brownish-white beneath glossy olive green or greenish-brown periostracum. Shell sculptured with fine concentric lines. **Habitat & ecology** · Found burrowed deep in soft mud or muddy sands on extreme lower shore and to depths of about 100 m. Lives in a deep burrow and maintains contact with surface by partially retractile long, fused siphons. **Similar species** · Some species of *Mya*, but these have finer concentric markings on shell and different teeth pattern. *L. angustior* smaller, but otherwise very similar. *L. magna* a more offshore species, with more concave shell posterior to umbones.

Abundance & distribution
Locally common. Occurs off all British and Irish coasts. Distributed from Norway to West Africa, including the Mediterranean.

FAMILY **Donacidae**

Donax vittatus (da Costa) **Banded wedge shell**

Description · Slender, wedge- or ear-shaped shells, up to 38 mm long, are inequilateral, umbones posterior of midline. Two shells equal (equivalve); anterior side broadly rounded, posterior side more steeply rounded. Ventral margins crenellate. Each valve has two cardinal teeth. Right valve has one anterior, two posterior, lateral teeth. Left valve has single, small anterior and posterior lateral teeth. Outer shell surfaces with numerous, fine concentric ridges and grooves, and very fine lines radiating from umbones. Whitish, yellow, brown, or purple, with pale radiating bands, sometimes pale growth bands. Inner surfaces smooth, tinted pale yellow, orange, or purple. **Habitat & ecology** · Occurs intertidally, from mid-shore down to depths of about 20 m, burrowing in sandy sediments. Particularly common on moderately exposed sandy shores and sandy bays. Drilled empty shells on shore indicate predation by necklace shells. **Similar species** · *D. variagatus* has finer ventral crenellations (almost smooth), and only occurs on Channel Islands, and from southwest coasts of Britain southwards. *Angulus squalidus* also similar, but has different number of lateral teeth on right valve and posterior ventral part of shell and more concave.

Abundance & distribution
Locally abundant. Occurs on all British and Irish coasts. Distributed from Norway to north-west Africa and the Mediterranean.

Distinctive features

1. Shells sub-triangular, thick, solid, umbones on midline.
2. Cardinal teeth on left valve fused, short, extending half-way to edge of hinge plate.

Distinctive features

1. Shells large, elongate oval outline.
2. Both ends of shells open.
3. Outer shell surface brownish, with fine concentric lines.
4. Periostracum olive green or greenish-brown.

Distinctive features

1. Shells wedge- or ear-shaped, ventral margins broadly crenellate.
2. Umbones distinctly posterior of midline.
3. Shell anterior broadly rounded, posterior steeper.

FAMILY **Tellinidae**

Angulus tenuis (da Costa) **Thin tellin**

Description · Irregularly oval shell may reach almost 3 cm. Anterior edge of shell broadly rounded, posterior edge in contrast more sharply angled and truncated. Shells thin, delicate, smooth margined; hinge little evident, although brown hinge ligament, strong enough to hold shells together after animal has died, very obvious behind umbones. Each valve has two cardinal teeth, one being bifid, with single anterior and posterior lateral teeth most obvious on right valve. Shell has glossy, often concentrically banded, appearance, varying from yellowish, orange, pinkish to white; outer and inner shell surfaces similarly coloured. Previously known as *Tellina tenuis*. **Habitat & ecology** · Shallow-burrowed in fine or medium sand from mid-shore level down to shallow sublittoral situations. Young plaice, *Pleuronectes platessa*, feed on its extended siphons, but these rapidly regenerate. **Similar species** · Closely resembles southern species, *A. squalidus*, but this can grow larger, with posterior part of shell convex on side opposite to umbo, giving it hooked appearance. Baltic tellin, *Macoma balthica*, also similar, but has plumper shells, no lateral teeth, and both cruciform muscle scars and hinge ligament are indistinct.

Abundance & distribution
Common, locally abundant. On all coasts of Britain and Ireland. Distributed from Norway to the Mediterranean and southwards to north-west Africa.

Arcopagia crassa (Pennant) **Blunt tellin**

Description · Oval shell, slightly longer than deep, up to about 6 cm long and quite thick. The umbo is slightly to the posterior of the midline. The posterior margin of the shell, on the umbo side, has a shallow dent, concave on the left valve and convex on the right. Shell is sculptured with numerous fine concentric ridges with larger growth lines obvious. Both valves have two cardinal teeth, one of which is bifid on each side. Both valves have single posterior and anterior lateral teeth (small in left valve). The colour of the shell is dirty white or pale brown, often with several irregular rays of red. **Habitat & ecology** · Occurs on the lower shore or sublittorally to offshore. It favours sand or gravel bottoms but also occurs in muddy sands. **Similar species** · *A. balaustina*, but this species is smaller with less obvious growth lines.

Abundance & distribution
Uncommon. Occurs mainly on west coasts of Britain and Ireland. Distributed from Norway to West Africa. Does not occur in the Mediterranean.

Fabulina fabula (Gmelin)

Description · Elongate oval shells thin, brittle, and up to 2 cm long. Posterior end of shell is tapered and curved to the right, whilst anterior end is more steeply curved. Shells are equivalve but inequilateral, hinge-line and umbones being closer to posterior end. There are two cardinal teeth in each valve, as well as anterior and posterior lateral teeth. Outer shell surface is marked with strong growth rings and fine concentric ridges. Right valve only is marked with irregular, wavy striations extending from anterior dorsal to posterior ventral borders. Colour is pearly-white, sometimes tinged with yellow or orange, sometimes in concentric bands. Shell has a reflective lustre. **Habitat & ecology** · Found burrowed in fine and medium sandy sediments on lower shore and in shallow sublittoral situations. **Similar species** · There are about 18 species of European tellins, including *F. fabula*, some of which resemble this form. *Angulus tenuis* is very similar but larger and lacking the wavy striations on the right valve. *Moerella* species also quite similar.

Abundance & distribution
Very common. Occurs around all coasts of Britain and Ireland. Distributed from Norway to north-west Africa and the Mediterranean.

Distinctive features

1. Shell thin, delicate, smooth-margined.
2. Anterior edge of shell broadly rounded, posterior more sharply angled.
3. Hinge ligament distinct, brown, usually keeping shells together after death.

Distinctive features

1. Thick oval shell, longer than deep.
2. Umbo offset to one side.
3. Shallow dent on posterior of umbo side of shell.
4. Two cardinal and one lateral teeth on each valve.

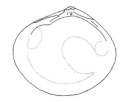

Distinctive features

1. Shells elongate oval, equivalve, posterior end tapered sharply, curved to right.
2. Fine concentric lines and obvious growth rings on outer shell surface..
3. Wavy striations on right shell, from dorsal anterior to ventral posterior margins.

Macoma balthica (Linnaeus) **Baltic tellin**

Description · Shells quite oval, slightly tapered posteriorly. The umbones are just posterior to the midline. The shell is up to 25 mm long, and externally sculptured with fine concentric lines with clear growth lines. Hinge with two small cardinal teeth on each valve, but no lateral teeth. Posterior adductor scar thicker than anterior. The Baltic tellin is very variable in colour, from uniformly snow white through yellow, crimson, and pinkish-brown. It is often marked with lighter and darker concentric bands. There is usually a brown marginal fringe of periostracum. Inner shell surface shiny, white, purple, or pink. **Habitat & ecology** · Burrows in mud and muddy sands intertidally. Often found on tidal flats or in the lower reaches of estuaries. **Similar species** · May be confused with the thin tellin, *Angulus tenuis*, but the Baltic tellin has more prominent umbones and a thicker shell.

Abundance & distribution
Widespread, common, and often very abundant. The range extends from Arctic Norway to all coasts of north-west Europe, including the Baltic, and south to the Atlantic coast of Portugal.

FAMILY **Scrobiculariidae**

Abra alba (Wood)

Description · Thin, brittle, oval shell up to 25 mm long. The colour is white and glossy with a sculpture of fine concentric lines. The umbo is to one side (posterior) of the midline. There is an elliptically shaped depression below the umbo (chondrophore). On the right valve there are two cardinal teeth on the left (anterior) of the chondrophore, one tooth on the left valve. On either side of the shell there is a single lateral tooth, less prominent on the left valve. The adductor muscle scars and pallial line are clear. The pallial sinus is deep and irregular. **Habitat & ecology** · Occurs in extreme lower shore but usually subtidal. Lives in mud and muddy sands and is often gregarious, occurring in very large numbers. **Similar species** · Several similar species occur in the north-east Atlantic. *Abra nitida* and *A. prismatica* tend to be smaller than *A. alba* and have a more elongate shell. *A. tenuis* is triangular, with the umbo roughly on the midline. *Scrobicularia plana* grows larger than *A. alba*.

Abundance & distribution
Common, locally abundant. Occurs all around British Isles and Ireland. Distributed from Norway to the Mediterranean.

Scrobicularia plana (da Costa) **Peppery furrow shell**

Description · Shells thin, broadly oval and flattened, equivalve, up to 6.5 cm long, externally marked with moderately fine concentric sculpturing. Umbones almost on midline, hinge with two cardinal teeth on left valve, one on right. Siphons very long and highly contractile. Brown periostracum on margins of shells, shells glossy white internally, pale greyish-yellow externally, though they may be stained yellow to black from the clay or mud in which the animal is burrowing. **Habitat & ecology** · An intertidal species burrowing 15–20 cm into muddy substrates. Tolerant of reduced salinities and often found in estuaries or salt marshes. Some populations have been found with the nemertean *Tetrastemma fozensis* living in their mantle cavity. The species has long siphons which it extends onto the surface around its burrow, leaving star-shaped tracks when the tide recedes. **Similar species** · There are several other tellins that superficially resemble this species but the oval shape, thin shell, and near middle position of the umbones are quite characteristic.

Abundance & distribution
Common, often locally abundant. Distributed all around the British Isles and Ireland. Distributed from Norway to West Africa, including the southern Baltic and Mediterranean.

Distinctive features

1. Shells plump, almost oval, slightly tapered posteriorly.
2. Umbones just posterior to midline. Hinge with two small cardinal but no lateral teeth.

Distinctive features

1. Oval, thin, brittle shell.
2. Umbo posterior to midline.
3. Elliptical depression beneath umbo.
4. Two teeth below umbo on right valve, one on left.

Distinctive features

1. Shells thin, broadly oval, umbones almost on midline.
2. Left valve has two cardinal teeth, right valve one.
3. Siphons very long, contractile.

FAMILY **Psammobiidae**

Gari costulata (Turton)

Description · Shells an elongate oval shape, up to 2.5 cm long with hinge-line and umbone just posterior to midline. Shells are thin; right valve possesses two bifid cardinal teeth of which anterior is largest. Characteristically there are about 12–20 strong, sharp ribs radiating from umbone to posterior margins of shell. This region of shell is different to the rest, which is relatively smooth and sculptured with fine concentric lines and growth stages. Colour is white, pink, or yellowish, with the rayed area sometimes purplish. Inner shell surface shows outer colour pattern. **Habitat & ecology** · Found subtidally in muddy sands. **Similar species** · Other sunset shells. *G. fervensis* has a steeply sloping posterior end and a prominent ridge from the umbo to the posteroventral border of the shell. *G. depressa* grows to a larger size, is also truncated posteriorly, and lacks the ribs of *G. costulata*. *G. tellinella* is rounded at both ends and lacks strong ribs on the shell.

Abundance & distribution
Uncommon. Found on all British and Irish coasts. Distributed southwards to the Mediterranean.

Gari depressa (Pennant)
Large sunset shell

Description · Elongate oval, compressed shell, growing to 7 cm long. Umbones are anterior to midline. Anterior hinge-line is slightly sloping and anterior edge of shell is rounded. Posterior hinge-line is straight and forms a sharp angle where it joins posterior end of shell, which is truncated. Valves gape posteriorly. Two cardinal teeth on each valve, both bifid on right valve; anterior tooth is bifid on left valve. Shell is sculptured with fine concentric lines that become ridges near margins. Growth lines are distinct. Generally yellowish-white, rayed with purple, brown, or lilac. Inside of shell is glossy and white or yellowish, often tinted purple or bluish. **Habitat & ecology** · Burrowing in sandy bottoms from low intertidal to sublittoral. **Similar species** · Resembles *G. fervensis*, the Faeroe sunset shell, but the latter is smaller and has a distinct ridge running from umbo to posterioventral corner of shell. It is found all around Britain and Ireland but otherwise has a similar distribution to *G. depressa*.

Abundance & distribution
Locally common. Found around south and west coasts of Britain and Ireland. Distributed from western Norway to West Africa, including the Mediterranean.

FAMILY **Solenidae**

Ensis and *Solen* species **Razor shells**

Description · Razor shells have an extremely elongate, narrow shell, with straight or curved margins depending on the species. The shell umbones and ligament are close to the anterior end of the shell and the shell gapes at the anterior and posterior ends. The coloured, glossy periostracum of the shell is often peeling. When alive, razor shells inhabit deep, vertical burrows in sand and usually only a pair of short, fused siphons is visible at the surface. There are four species of *Ensis* and *Solen* off the coasts of northern Europe.

(a) *Ensis arcuatus* (Jeffreys)

This grows to a maximum of 15 cm. The dorsal edge of the shell is straight whilst the ventral margin is distinctly curved and both ends are obliquely truncated. The colour is cream or pale brown with reddish or brown streaks. The periostracum is usually pale golden brown, yellow-brown, or grey.

(a), (b), (c)

(d)

Distinctive features

1. Umbone just posterior to midline.
2. 12–20 strong, sharp ridges radiating from umbone to posterior margin of shell.
3. Elongate oval.

Distinctive features

1. Elongate oval, compressed shell shape.
2. Anterior edge rounded, posterior truncated.
3. Valves gape posteriorly.

(a)

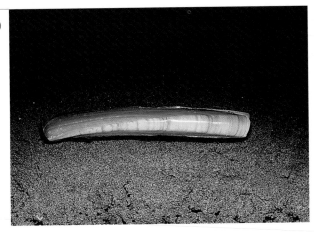

(b) *Ensis ensis* (Linnaeus)

The common razor shell, it grows up to 12.5–13 cm long. The shell has evenly and equally curved concave dorsal and convex ventral margins and tapers towards the square posterior end. The anterior end is rounded. The periostracum is greenish-yellow to golden brown in colour. The outer surface of the shell is whitish with red or brown markings.

(c) *Ensis siliqua* (Linnaeus)

The pod razor shell grows up to 20 cm long. The dorsal and ventral shell margins are parallel and straight whilst the anterior and posterior ends are similar, being quite square. The periostracum is a glossy green or yellowish-green. The outer shell surface is whitish, marked with reddish-brown patterns and fine vertical and horizontal lines.

(d) *Solen marginatus* Montagu

The grooved razor shell grows up to 12–12.5 cm. The shell is narrow, parallel-sided with anterior and posterior edges almost straight. There is a conspicuous and very characteristic groove or furrow just behind the margin of the anterior end of the shell. The shells are marked externally with fine lines and with a glossy periostracum that is pale olive to yellowish-brown in colour.

Habitat & ecology · The razor shells are found on the lower-shore to shallow sublittoral habitats, in vertical burrows in fine sandy and muddy sediments. When uncovered by the receding tide the animals may be seen on approach by a sudden squirt of sandy seawater. Razor shells are harvested for their flesh but it is difficult to remove them from their burrows because the enormous foot can be inflated by hydrostatic pressure and grips the sides of its burrow very firmly. These animals have been overfished in some areas.

(b)

Abundance & distribution
All the razor shells are common and sometimes locally abundant. All *Ensis* species are found all around Britain and Ireland. *E. arcuatus* (a) is distributed from Norway to the Atlantic coast of Spain. *E. ensis* (b) and *E. siliqua* (c) are distributed from Norway to Africa including the Mediterranean. *Solen marginatus* (d) occurs in southern Britain, to the Clyde on the west coast and Essex on the east coast. It is distributed from western Norway to West Africa including the Mediterranean and the southern Baltic.

Phaxas pellucidus (Pennant)

Description · Shells slender and resembling a pea pod. The dorsal edge is straight, the ventral edge convex, anterior and posterior borders smoothly rounded. Up to 4 cm long, the diagnostic character for the species is the arrangement of the hinge teeth. The left valve has two cardinal teeth, the posterior bifid, and a single short posterior lateral tooth, all grouped together. The right valve has a single cardinal and one lateral tooth. The outer surface of the shells, sculptured with fine, oval, concentric ridges, is pale yellow to pale brown, sometimes marked with pink. **Habitat & ecology** · An entirely sublittoral species to depths of about 100 m, found in fine mixed sandy sediments.

Abundance & distribution
Common, locally abundant. Found on all British and Irish coasts. Distributed from Norway to north-west Africa, including the Mediterranean.

Distinctive features (c)

1. Shells very elongate and narrow with straight or curved margins.
2. Ligament and umbones of shell close to anterior end.
3. Shell gaping at anterior and posterior ends.
4. Burrowing in sand, sometimes with a pair of short fused siphons visible at the surface.

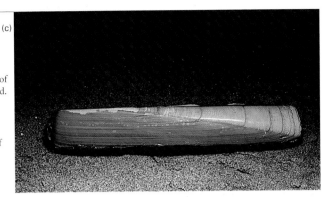

(d)

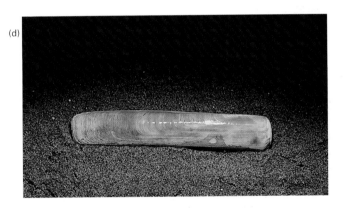

Distinctive features

1. Shells slender, pod-like, upper margin straight, lower margin convex.
2. Hinge teeth arranged as close-set single cardinal and lateral on left valve, two short cardinal and single lateral in one group on right valve.

ORDER **Myoida**

FAMILY **Myidae**

Mya arenaria Linnaeus **Sand gaper**

Description · Shells up to 15 cm long, equivalve but inequilateral, with umbones posterior to midline. Shells thick and strong, anteriorly broadly rounded but posteriorly tapered. Outer surface marked with rough concentric ridges and radiating striae. Chondrophore of left valve spoon-shaped and projecting at right angles to hinge-line. The siphons are fused, long, and leathery, and reach to the surface. Brownish-white to dark brown in external colour, the inner shell surface is pale brown. **Habitat & ecology** · Found on the lower shore and sublittorally to depths of about 70 m, in firm mud, muddy sands, and gravels, often on estuarine flats. This species became extinct off the coasts of north-west Europe during the last ice age but was reintroduced during the 17th century. **Similar species** · Somewhat resembles the blunt gaper, *M. truncata*, but this species is smaller with an abruptly truncated posterior end.

Abundance & distribution
Common, frequently abundant. Occurs around all coasts of Britain and Ireland. Distributed from the North Sea south to northern France, including the Baltic Sea.

Mya truncata Linnaeus **Blunt gaper**

Description · Solid shells up to 7–7.5 cm long. Anterior edge of shell is rounded, the posterior is truncated. The left valve not as convex as the right. Viewed from the posterior end the closed shells have a wide and obvious gape. The umbones are just posterior to the midline. The left valve has a distinctive spatulate chondrophore at right angles to the hinge. Shells with both internal and external hinge ligaments. Leathery fused siphons connect the shell to the surface of the substrate. These are not fully retractile. The colour is a dirty creamish-white to brown with an olive brown periostracum. **Habitat & ecology** · Burrows in muddy and sandy sediments from the middle shore to sublittoral depths of about 70 m. The species appears to be less tolerant of reduced salinities than *M. arenaria*. **Similar species** · Somewhat similar to the sand gaper, *M. arenaria*, but with shells more a rounded rectangular shape. The straight posterior margin usually distinguishes the two species.

Abundance & distribution
Locally common. Occurs off all British and Irish coasts. Distributed from the North Sea to the Bay of Biscay.

FAMILY **Corbulidae**

Corbula gibba (Olivi)
Basket shell, common basket shell

Description · Up to 15 mm long, the shells are thick and broadly oval or triangular. The umbones are on the midline. The right valve is deeply convex, its lower edge overlapping that of the less convex and narrower left valve. The hinge ligament is situated in a groove in the left valve. The right valve has a single, large cardinal tooth and single anterior and posterior lateral teeth. The left valve has no teeth. Both valves have a triangular chondrophore. The outer shell surfaces are sculptured with concentric coarse grooves and ridges; the left shell is also marked with a small number of radiating lines and a long ventral periostracal fringe. The periostracum is brownish, the shell surface whitish with yellowish or red marks. **Habitat & ecology** · A lower-shore and sublittoral species, found buried in muddy sands and gravels. May be found buried in clay, often near seaweeds.

Abundance & distribution
Locally common. Occurs all around Britain and Ireland. Distributed from Norway to West Africa, including the Mediterranean.

Distinctive features

1. Shells thick, strong; umbones just posterior to midline.
2. Chondrophore of left shell spoon-shaped, projecting at right angles to hinge-line.

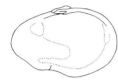

Distinctive features

1. Left shell not as convex as right.
2. Posterior edge of shells sharply truncate, hind margin almost straight.

Distinctive features

1. Broadly oval or triangular shell.
2. Right valve overlaps left valve, enclosing it.
3. Right valve with single large cardinal tooth, anterior and posterior lateral teeth; left valve with no teeth.
4. With concentric grooves and ridges.

FAMILY **Hiatellidae**

Hiatella arctica (Linnaeus) **Wrinkled rock borer**

Description · Up to 4 cm long, the thick equivalve shells are an irregular or rounded, rectangular shape with their umbones located near the anterior margin. The outer shell surface is rough and marked with thick, irregular concentric ridges. Two characteristic coarsely toothed ridges extend posteriorly and posteroventrally from the umbones. The left valve possesses two cardinal teeth, the right valve only one; the hinge ligament is external. In larger shells both the umbones, the external ridge teeth, and the cardinal teeth are often worn. The inner shell surface is pale greyish-brown to white, the outer yellowish-white to a dark reddish-brown. **Habitat & ecology** · A lower-shore and sublittoral species, either found attached by its byssus threads in rock cavities, crevices, and on algal holdfasts, or in holes bored into chalk, limestone, or New Red Sandstone. Its habitat is often associated with appreciable amounts of muddy silt. Often responsible for the holes found in limestone pebbles and small rocks.

Abundance & distribution
Locally common. Occurs on all coasts of Britain and Ireland. Distribution extends from Arctic Norway south to the Mediterranean and West Africa.

FAMILY **Pholadidae**

Barnea candida (Linnaeus) **White piddock**

Description · Thin, brittle shell that is elongate with rounded ends, up to 6.5 cm long. The umbones are about a third of the way from the anterior end of the shell. The valves gape posteriorly and the dorsal part of the anterior shell is folded over. An accessory plate, the protoplax, is positioned in front of the umbones. The shell is sculptured with concentric ridges and radiating lines. Where the lines cross the ridges, especially anteriorly, they form pointed spines. The shell is white, with a yellowish or brownish periostracum. **Habitat & ecology** · A boring bivalve that burrows into wood, peat, and soft rock from the lower shore to the sublittoral. **Similar species** · *Petricola pholadiformis*. This species does not have the protoplax, the shell does not gape, and it lacks the spines on the shell. It is also restricted to south-east and south coasts of Britain.

Abundance & distribution
Frequent, locally common. Occurs off all British and Irish coasts. Distributed from Norway to West Africa, including the Mediterranean.

Pholadidea loscombiana Turton

Description · Shells an elongate oval shape, up to 4 cm long, thin and brittle, with sharply truncate posterior margin. Umbones anterior to midline. In young individuals the widely gaping anterior end, forming the pedal gap, is obliquely truncate, but during growth the gap is closed by the formation of an additional part of each valve, the callum. The siphons are enclosed at their base by two additional plates, forming the cup-shaped siphonoplax. Outer shell surface has a distinct groove or furrow extending from umbones to ventral margin, otherwise marked by corrugated, concentric ridges which anteriorly bear tubercles. The outer shell surface is brownish, the inner white. **Habitat & ecology** · A lower-shore and shallow sublittoral species, found in compacted mud, clay, peat, and softer rocks.

Abundance & distribution
Uncommon, but may be locally common. Found on south-west coasts of Britain and Ireland, also off parts of western Scotland and off the coast of Co. Antrim. Distributed from Britain to the Mediterranean and West Africa.

Distinctive features

1. Shells irregular, rounded, rectangular shape.
2. Shell surface has thick, irregular, concentric ridges.
3. Coarsely toothed ridges extend posteriorly and posteroventrally from umbones.

Distinctive features

1. Elongate, thin, brittle shell with rounded ends.
2. Umbones a third along body.
3. Dorsal part of anterior of shell folded over.
4. Spines on shell where radiating lines cross concentric ridges.

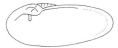

Distinctive features

1. Elongate oval shells; posterior edge straight, sharply truncate.
2. Siphons enclosed by pair of calcareous accessory plates.
3. Outer shell surface with distinct groove from umbones to ventral margins.

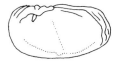

Pholas dactylus Linnaeus **Common piddock**

Description · Grows up to 15 cm long. Shell equivalve, elongate, plump and rounded. Ventral shell margin anteriorly deeply concave and often crenellate. The posterior end of the shell is rounded, the far anterior and swollen umbones are folded back (reflected) over the shells with up to 10–12 vertical septa between each fold and umbo. Shells anteriorly with a wide pedal gape, posteriorly not gaping. Dorsally there are three accessory shell plates. Outer shell surface sculptured with concentric and radiating ribs that may form small spines anteriorly where they cross. This assists in drilling into the substrate. On the inside of each shell there is a single free tooth (apophysis). The long, fused siphons are enclosed by a horny sheath. Internal shell surface white, outer surface greyish- or yellowish-white. The living animal is phosphorescent. **Habitat & ecology** · Lower shore and shallow sublittoral, found bored into softer rocks, shale, peat, harder sands or, less commonly, wood.

Abundance & distribution
Locally common. Found in south-west and southern Britain, and all around Ireland. Distributed south to north-west Africa, including the Mediterranean.

Zirfaea crispata (Linnaeus) **Oval piddock**

Description · Thin, obliquely-oval to wedge-shaped shell, up to 9 cm long. Anterior end, through which the foot is protruded, is widely gaping and obliquely truncated. Posterior end, through which two long and very contractile siphons protrude, also gapes widely. Outer shell surface sculptured with numerous concentric wavy ridges and radiating ribs, forming small, sharp spines anteriorly where they intersect, separated from the smoother posterior region by a distinct groove that extends from the umbones to the ventral border. Yellowish- to greyish-white, the inner surface white. The highly contractile siphons are fused. **Habitat & ecology** · Bores into peat, clay, compacted mud, or soft rocky substrates, such as shale, less commonly into wood, on the lower shore and in shallow sublittoral situations. Some populations harbour large numbers of the entocommensal nemertean species, *Malacobdella grossa*, in the mantle cavity, but there is rarely more than a single adult nemertean per host.

Abundance & distribution
Common, locally abundant. Occurs all around Britain and Ireland. Distributed from Norway to the Bay of Biscay.

FAMILY **Teredinidae**

Xylophaga dorsalis Turton

Description · Globular, thin, and brittle trilobed shell that gapes anteriorly. The anterior lobe is triangular with horizontal ridges. The middle lobe is formed of the anterior disc, which is elongate with angled ridges, and a median disc that is formed by a concave band with horizontal lines. The anterior lobe and middle lobe give the anterior of the shell a distinctly right-angled indent. The posterior lobe is continuous with the median disc and is large, making up half the shell. The outer shell surface is greyish to brownish. **Habitat & ecology** · A wood-boring species, found in drifting wood. Not uncommonly found in driftwood washed ashore. **Similar species** · *X. praestens*, but this species is very rare. It gapes both anteriorly and posteriorly.

Abundance & distribution
Widespread in the north-east Atlantic, from Iceland and Norway to all British and Irish shores, south into the Mediterranean.

Distinctive features

1. Umbones far anterior, reflected over shells.
2. Four dorsal accessory plates.
3. Outer shell surface with concentric, radiating ribs, anteriorly coarser and used in boring.

Distinctive features

1. Shells obliquely oval- or wedge-shaped.
2. Shell with concentric wavy ridges and radiating ribs anteriorly forming small spines.
3. Groove running from umbones to ventral shell margin.

Distinctive features

1. Shells highly modified, trilobed, anterior edge with a right angled indent.
2. Posterior end of shells has wide gape.
3. Inner surface of shells with wide ridge running from umbones to ventral border.

Teredo navalis Linnaeus **Great shipworm**

Description · Much reduced, trilobed, shell, up to 2 cm long, enclosing only part of the long, worm-like body at innermost end of tube. Anterior lobe of shell triangular and a similar size to elliptical posterior lobe (auricle). Middle lobe has a narrow, concave, median disc. Valves have a long and curved inner tooth (hypophysis). Mantle secretes a hard, chalky substance coating inner tube surface as animal burrows; tubes up to 60 cm long and 8 mm diameter. Open end of tube can be closed by a pair of hard plates up to 5 mm long (pallets), when siphons are withdrawn. Shells white, soft body tissues brownish. **Habitat & ecology** · The most common and destructive shipworm, boring permanent tubes into wooden structures such as pier pilings or boat hulls, using shell as a drill. **Similar species** · *Nototeredo norvegica*, but auricle is much smaller than anterior lobe of shell. Also resembles *Xylophaga dorsalis*, but posterior lobe of shell is relatively large, comprising nearly half shell.

Abundance & distribution
Locally common, sometimes abundant in driftwood. A cosmopolitan species found around all coasts of Britain, Ireland, and Europe.

SUBCLASS **Anomalodesmata** | ORDER **Laternulacea**

FAMILY **Thraciidae**

Thracia convexa (Wood)

Description · The shell has a sub-rectangular shape but without a truncate posterior margin and is notably swollen. (a) The umbones are roughly on the midline and the shell is sculptured with fine concentric ridges and lines. Inside the shell is a shallow pallial sinus. The length is up to 6 cm. The shell is a pale yellowish-brown. **Habitat & ecology** · Occurs subtidally, but is rarely found because it burrows deeply into the sediment. **Similar species** · There are several similar species of *Thracia*. *T. phaseolina* (b) and *T. villosiuscula* have truncated posterior edges to the shells and a very deep pallial sinus extending to just below the chondrophore. *T. pubescens* has a shallow pallial sinus like *T. convexa* but the posterior margin is sharply truncate. *T. distorta* lives in crevices and its shells may have an irregular outline.

Abundance & distribution
Uncommon. Found all around the British Isles and Ireland. Distributed south to the Mediterranean.

Class Scaphopoda (tusk shells)

Scaphopods possess elongate bodies housed in a tapering cylindrical shell which is open at both ends. The mantle cavity extends the full length of the shell, forming **inhalant** and **exhalant** openings through which the respiratory water currents are circulated. Tusk shells have no **gills**. The head and closely associated foot are protruded from the wider, anterior end of the shell. The head bears numerous sensory tentacles and, around the mouth, short ciliated tentacles (**captacula**) which are employed in food selection. All scaphopods are **microphagous detritus feeders**. The short, cylindrical foot is employed for burrowing into the soft sediments in which the animals live head-down.

Distinctive features

1. Shells trilobed, much reduced.
2. Anterior and posterior lobes of shells similar size, triangular in shape.
3. Open end of tube can be closed off by pair of calcareous plates.

Distinctive features

1. Rectangular, swollen shell not truncated posteriorly.
2. Umbones roughly on midline.
3. Shell sculptured with concentric ridges and lines.
4. Shallow pallial sinus.

Dentalium vulgare (da Costa) **Tusk shell**

Description · Shell resembles a slightly curved horn, tapering gently towards the posterior end which has marked longitudinal striations. The shell ends in a short, pipe-like circular aperture. The shell is thick and is a dull white with a few concentric lines. The length of the shell can reach 6 cm and is 6 mm wide at the anterior end. **Habitat & ecology** · Occurs offshore where it lives on sand. **Similar species** · There are several similar species in the north-east Atlantic. *D. entalis* is similar but the shell is smaller, more curved, and lacks the longitudinal striations at the posterior end. The posterior aperture is also oval and has a notch in it. This species can be common and occurs around most of Britain but is rare in the south. It is distributed in the north-east Atlantic as far south as Portugal. Other species are much smaller (less than 1 cm).

Abundance & distribution
Uncommon. Occurs in the Channel, southern North Sea, south-west Britain, and off the west coast of Ireland. Distributed south to the Mediterranean.

Class Cephalopoda (octopus, squid)

Cephalopods are the most highly modified and advanced of the molluscan groups and include the bulkiest living invertebrates. Their body is either sac-like or cylindrical, the anterior head actually being ventral, the posterior end dorsal. Most living cephalopods (with the notable exceptions of the tropical genus *Nautilus* and the tropical and warm temperate octopod genus *Argonauta*) have no external shell. Instead they have an internal **pen** or **cuttlebone**, a light calcareous structure which provides rigidity and firmness to the body but also serves as an extremely finely balanced **buoyancy organ**. In some cephalopods, especially the octopods, the internal shell is vestigial or completely absent. The well-developed head bears a pair of large, complex **eyes** and a mouth with a pair of tough **jaws** resembling the beak of a parrot. Most cephalopods have modified **salivary glands** associated with their mouth which secrete a **venom** used to incapacitate the prey. The cephalopod **radula** functions like a tongue. The head and visceral region of the body are not delimited from each other. The thick, muscular **mantle** completely encloses the body; the mantle epidermis contains **chromatophores**, pigmented structures which, by expansion or contraction, can make the animals change colour or appear darker or lighter. The ventral **mantle cavity** contains the

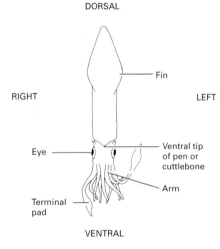

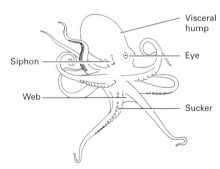

The main external features of decapod (*top*) and octopod (*bottom*) cephalopod molluscs.

Distinctive features

1. Shell resembles a slightly curved horn.
2. Shell tapers towards one (posterior) end.
3. Shell has longitudinal striations at the posterior end and a circular posterior aperture.

excretory and reproductive openings as well as the ctenidia and anus. Water, actively pumped into the mantle cavity, is forcibly expelled by muscle contractions through a short, often very flexible, **funnel**; this water propulsion device is usually used for rapid escape movement, although cuttlefishes and squids have **lateral** or **terminal fins** on their bodies which they use for normal locomotion. The sucker-bearing **tentacles** (arms) join directly with the head, the **suckers** sometimes being armed with **chitinous** hooks or spines. Octopuses possess eight arms, squids and cuttlefishes an extra pair of longer arms provided with suckers on their **terminal pads**; these longer and retractile arms are used to seize prey. Cephalopods also possess an **ink sac**, from which a dense, dark ink cloud is discharged to mask their escape when they are threatened. The sexes are separate in all members of the class, males in most species easily being recognised by one of their arms being specialised (**hectocotylous**) for transferring packets of sperm to the female.

All cephalopods are predatory, octopuses and cuttlefishes feeding mainly on crustaceans, particularly crabs, whereas the faster-moving pelagic squids have a wider variety of swimming prey. The class contains two extant suborders, the Nautiloidea (nautiluses), which contains about six species restricted to the Indo-Pacific, and the Coleoidea, which comprises four orders, the **Sepioida** (cuttlefishes), the **Teuthoida** (squids), **Octopoda**

(Octopuses) and the **Vampyromorpha** (vampire squids):

Sepioida Body short, dorsoventrally flattened with lateral fins. The shell is internal, calcareous, straight or coiled, and often chambered, or it may be absent altogether. There are eight arms and two long retractile tentacles.

Teuthoida Body elongate and cylindrical with lateral or terminal fins and with an internal shell reduced to a cartilaginous pen. Mouth surrounded by eight sucker-bearing arms and two longer, non-retractile tentacles.

Octopoda Body sac-like, with thin external, vestigial internal shell or shell absent. There are no fins but the eight arms linked at the bases by a web of skin. The arms are provided with suckers.

Vampyromorpha Deep-sea cephalopods with a plump body and four pairs of equal arms linked by an extensive web of skin. There is a single pair of rounded fins and a pair of retractile filaments. The shell is vestigial; there is no hectocotylus and the ink sac is degenerate.

SUBCLASS **Coleoidea** | ORDER **Sepioida**

FAMILY **Sepiidae**

Sepia officinalis Linnaeus **Common cuttlefish**

Description · Body broadly oval, almost rectangular, rather flattened, up to 30–40 cm long. Fin runs around entire ventral mantle margin. Dorsal mantle edge forms obvious lobe between eyes. A conspicuous ventral funnel used for jet propulsion. Tentacles have four longitudinal rows of suckers. Two long retractable tentacles have up to six suckers, distinctly larger than others. These usually held tucked-up next to mouth and used to catch prey. Laminate, internal shell (cuttlebone) almost parallel-sided, posteriorly rounded rather than pointed. Typically mottled greyish-brown or striped blackish-brown dorsally, paler to whitish ventrally. Colour used for communication and can change quickly, along with body texture. Courting males may exhibit striking patterns of stripes alternating purplish-brown and white. **Habitat & ecology** · From shallow sublittoral to depths of about 250 m, on sand or mud sediments, or free swimming; also in eel-grass beds. During summer it moves inshore; spawns gregariously. Eggs attached to clumps of seaweed or rope, look like bunches of black grapes. **Similar species** · Two occur south-west of Britain, *S. elegans* and *S. orbignyana*.

Both have acute lobe projecting from anterior dorsal edge of mantle between eyes.

Abundance & distribution
Sometimes locally abundant, especially during breeding season. Occurs on all coasts of Britain and Ireland. Distributed from southern Norway to

FAMILY **Sepiolidae**

Sepiola atlantica d'Orbigny **Little cuttlefish**

Description · Body rather short, fat, sac-like, up to 5 cm long, with flap-like, irregularly rounded, lateral fins which do not extend full body length. Dorsal mantle margin fused to head between eyes; ventral edge straight, thickened, with short, broad siphon. Tentacles bear 2–8 rows of suckers. Often pale ventrally, pale dorsally spotted with dark brown pigment spots (chromatophores). **Habitat & ecology** · Essentially shallow sublittoral; also occurs in intertidal rock pools. Usually found swimming close to seabed above sand, particularly in sheltered bays. **Similar species** · Include *S. aurantiaca*, but this is distinguishable by ventral edge of mantle margin, which has distinct cleft. *Sepietta* species also similar but dorsal pair of tentacles joined by a membrane for part of their length. Also resembles *Rossia macrosoma*, but dorsal mantle margin not fused with head and has continuous, well-marked lip. Tentacles of this species only have two longitudinal rows of suckers. Body a mottled brown. Has similar distribution to *S. atlantica* but is also found in Mediterranean.

Abundance & distribution
Locally common. Found around all coasts of Britain and Ireland. Distributed from Iceland and Norway to Morocco, not including the Mediterranean.

ORDER **Teuthoida**

FAMILY **Loliginidae**

Loligo forbesii Steenstrup **Common squid**

Description · Grows up to 60 cm long. Mantle cylindrical, tapering to point at posterior tip. Fins diamond-shaped, running from posterior tip of body to about two-thirds of body length. Middle of anterior dorsal part of mantle extended into bluntly pointed lobe that projects to level of eyes. Arms about twice length of body. One pair of tentacles longer than rest, and end in club-like pad. This has rows of suckers, the middle ones of which are less than twice diameter of marginal suckers. Base colour greyish-white, densely spotted with reddish-brown. Skin often lost in dead animals so they appear white. **Habitat & ecology** · Pelagic. May come inshore to reproduce and then die. Eggs laid in bunches and resemble long, white, pod-like tubes. Commercially valuable and fished off all coasts of Europe. **Similar species** · *L. vulgaris*. Middle suckers of club are 3–4 times wider than marginal suckers. It occurs from the south and west coasts of Britain and Ireland, southwards.

Abundance & distribution
Common, often abundant. Occurs throughout the north-east Atlantic to off the coasts of Portugal, including the Mediterranean and the Azores.

Mediterranean and South
Africa.

Distinctive features

1. Dorsal lobe of mantle
   forms a distinct lobe
   between the eyes.
2. Tentacles with four longitudinal rows of suckers.
3. Lateral fins extend from
   rear of head to posterior
   tip of body.

Distinctive features

1. Rounded lateral fins do
   not extend full body
   length.
2. Ventral mantle margin
   forms short, broad
   siphon.
3. Dorsal mantle margin
   fused with head.
4. Tentacles with 2–8 rows of
   suckers.

Distinctive features

1. Large squid with
   diamond-shaped fins.
2. Ten tentacles, one pair
   longer than rest, with
   median suckers less than
   twice diameter of
   marginal suckers.

ORDER **Octopoda**

FAMILY **Octopodidae**

Eledone cirrhosa (Lamarck) **Curled octopus**

Description · Up to 50 cm long, the eight tentacles are slender and tapering, sometimes with their tips curled up when the animal is at rest. The tentacles bear a single row of suckers and have a maximum spread of about 70 cm. The body is soft and sac-like, either warty or smooth-surfaced. The colour is mainly a reddish-brown to pinkish-red above, often mottled with white, and whitish below. **Habitat & ecology** · Usually sublittoral, occasionally found on the extreme lower shore, among rocks and boulders. Often seen by divers at night. It feeds voraciously on crustaceans such as small crabs.

Abundance & distribution
Locally common. Found on all British and Irish coasts. Distributed along the coast of north-west Europe, not including the Mediterranean.

Octopus vulgaris Lamarck
Common octopus

Description · Up to 1 m in total length but often no more than 60 cm, with a maximum tentacle spread about three times this but usually less. Soft, sac-like body may be warty on dorsal surface or smooth as animal can change texture of its skin. Tentacles are stout, thick, and strong, with two longitudinal rows of suckers. Colour is variable according to mood and where animal is, but typically greyish-yellow to brownish-green, usually strongly mottled. **Habitat & ecology** · Occurs off rocky coasts in the shallow sublittoral to depths of about 100 m. It is often found in a protective lair camouflaged with arranged stones and boulders. This hiding place is often given away by the remains of crabs and other Crustacea lying around the burrow. Very intelligent animals that may curiously investigate divers who approach carefully. **Similar species** · *Eledone moschata*, but this has only a single longitudinal row of suckers on its tentacles and is dark brown, with darker brown flecks.

Abundance & distribution
Locally common. Rare in Britain, where it occurs on south and south-west coasts. Distributed from the southern North Sea to the Mediterranean and southwards to South Africa.

Distinctive features

1. Tentacles bear a single row of suckers.
2. When at rest, ends of long tapering tentacles typically curled up.
3. Colour reddish-brown above, white below.

Distinctive features

1. Tentacles thick and strong, with two longitudinal rows of suckers.
2. Body sac-like, dorsally warty.

Horseshoe worms, lamp shells, and bryozoans

Phylum Phoronida (horseshoe worms)

Sedentary, coelomate and worm-like animals, the **Phoronida** have elongate cylindrical bodies which bulge posteriorly to form an **ampulla**, used for anchoring themselves in their tubes. Surrounding the mouth, which is covered by a small lip or flap (**epistome**), a horseshoe-shaped or crescentic crown of numerous long and ciliated tentacles arranged on two ridges forms the **lophophore**, used for filter-feeding. The lophophore can be spread out for feeding or folded up when the animal withdraws into its tube, but it cannot be **introverted** (turned inside-out). The **coelomic** cavity of the lophophore (**mesocoel**) is separated from that of the body (**metacoel**) by an oblique septum, the metacoel usually being subdivided longitudinally into four compartments by **oral** and **anal mesenteries**. Two nephridia are associated with the lateral mesenteries, one opening on each side of the anus. Eggs may be shed through the nephridia and externally fertilised, developing to form a characteristic planktonic larva (**actinitrocha**), or they may be brooded in the dorsal part of the lophophore. Some phoronids reproduce asexually by propagation.

Phoronids are often inconspicuous, although sometimes forming abundant and dense colonies. They secrete a membranous tube within which they live, either embedded vertically in muddy sand or bored into shells or limestone rocks. Part of the tube may be free above the burrow opening; when it is, it is usually camouflaged by shell fragments and sand grains. A small phylum, with only about 20 species known worldwide, perhaps five species of phoronids occur around the British Isles and in northern Europe, all being members of the genus *Phoronis*.

Together with the Brachiopoda and Bryozoa, the Phoronida are members of the lophophorate phyla and all have a lophophore and a number of other shared features. These phyla are likely to have arisen from a common ancestor in the very distant past.

Further reading

Emig, C. C. (1979). British and other phoronids. *Synopses of the British Fauna, New Series*, 13, 1–57.
Ryland, J. S. (1990). The lophophorate phyla: Phoronida, Bryozoa, and Brachiopoda. In *The marine fauna of the British Isles and North-West Europe* (eds P. J. Hayward & J. S. Ryland), Vol. 2, pp. 794–838. Clarendon Press, Oxford.

Phoronis species

Description · Popularly known as horseshoe worms, these sedentary, worm-like animals either live in vertical membranous tubes which they secrete, or bore into shells or limestone substrata. Phoronids typically have a long, plump body posteriorly swollen to act as an anchor. Mouth, at top of tube, surrounded by lophophore formed of numerous, long ciliated tentacles. Usually a conspicuous white. **Habitat & ecology** · Two European species, *P. hippocrepia* and *P. ovalis*, bore into limestone rocks, mollusc shells, or thicker crusts of calcareous red algae, such as, *Lithothamnion* species. *P. hippocrepia* has a markedly horseshoe-shaped lophophore when viewed from above whereas in *P. ovalis* tentacles form a roughly circular-shaped crown which only curves inwards slightly at one point. Remaining species of phoronids live in vertical tubes in muddy sand, amongst seagrasses, or in reefs of polychaete *Sabellaria*. Depending upon species, they may occur intertidally at extreme lower-shore level to depths of 50 m or more; *P. muelleri* known to occur as deep as 140 m. **Similar species** · There are at least five European species of *Phoronis*, three of which are known to occur in British waters. Their identification requires specialist knowledge and careful examination of their anatomy.

Abundance & distribution
Although inconspicuous, phoronids may be locally both common and very abundant. The European representatives, depending upon the form, are distributed between the west coast of Sweden and the Mediterranean.

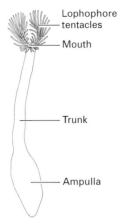

Some of the main externally visible parts of a phoronid.

Distinctive features

1. Worm-like; long, plump body.
2. Mouth surrounded by circular or horseshoe-shaped structure, the lophophore, composed of numerous long, ciliated tentacles.
3. Lives either in vertical, membranous burrows or bores into calcareous substrata, including limestone rocks and mollusc shells.

Phylum Brachiopoda
(lamp shells)

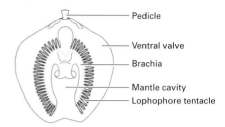

Brachiopods superficially resemble bivalve molluscs in being sessile and possessing a **shell** composed of two **valves**. The valves, however, are only thinly calcified, often with scattered uncalcified areas which give them a speckled (**punctate**) appearance. The valves are always **inequivalve**, the larger valve being ventral, the smaller dorsal. Brachiopods attach themselves to rocks and boulders by a fleshy stalk (**pedicle**) which extends from between the valves. The body is enclosed by two **mantle lobes**, which secrete the valves, the **mantle cavity** they contain being mostly filled by the **lophophore**.

The main features of a brachiopod with the smaller, dorsal valve removed.

This is an essentially horseshoe-shaped feeding structure with long, ciliated tentacles (**filaments**) carried on arms (**brachia**) which may be long and coiled. Water currents set up

CLASS Articulata | ORDER Terebratulida

FAMILY Cancellothyrididae

Terebratulina retusa (Linnaeus)

Description · Valves plump, oval, and almost pear-shaped, up to 33 mm long by 25 mm wide. Deeper, convex, and larger lower valve has large foramen or pore close to narrower end. Upper valve uniformly convex, tapering posteriorly. Anterior margin of shell may be rounded, straight, or even slightly concave in outline. The surfaces of both valves have distinctive growth lines and are finely ribbed with radiating lines that extend from the hinge-line to the anterior edges of the valves. The shell is generally whitish but not uncommonly tinged with yellow or rust red. Internally the lophophore is horseshoe-shaped. **Habitat & ecology ·** Found on stones and often associated with beds of the bivalve mollusc *Modiolus*, but also with hydroids and deep-water coral reefs. Also on vertical rock faces, from shallow sublittoral situations at least 15 m deep to offshore depths of 200 m.

Abundance & distribution
May be locally common and abundant, especially at greater depths, with a distribution extending from Norway and west coasts of the British Isles and Ireland to the Mediterranean.

Phylum Bryozoa
(Ectoprocta, Polyzoa)

Bryozoans are all sessile and colonial, comprising communities of separate individuals (**zooids**) held together by the zooid walls. The zooids show polymorphism, either functioning as ciliary feeding zooids (**autozooids**) or having specialised functions (**heterozooids**). The anterior portion of the body forms an **introvert**, called the **tentacle sheath**, into which the **lophophore** and its ciliated **tentacles** can be rapidly withdrawn if the animal is disturbed. The lophophore is circular or bell-shaped, with the **mouth** at its base opening into a U-shaped gut; the **anus** thus opens close

to the mouth but outside the lophophore. Each zooid in the colony secretes its own outer wall, often called a **zooecium**, in contrast to the soft body parts that constitute the **polypide**. Depending upon the species, the zooecium may be lightly or strongly calcified, cuticular, or gelatinous with pliant walls. Some zooids have beak-like structures called **avicularia**. These are functionally analogous to the pedicellariae of echinoids and serve a protective function crushing settling larvae of fouling organisms of the limbs of predators such as seaspiders. Each zooid possesses its own nerve net and gonads, colonies but not necessarily individual zooids being **hermaphroditic**. Embryos are usually brooded, either by the tentacle cilia transport the suspended detritus on which brachiopods feed. Sexes are separate, with external fertilisation of the eggs and a **planktonic** larval stage in the life-cycle.

Brachiopods are normally found attached to rocks dredged up from deeper water, such as on the continental slopes, but some can be found in more shallow situations closer inshore. Except in tropical habitats, they are rarely common. There are about 300 living species known worldwide, a very small number compared to the thousands known only as fossils. The group, a geologically ancient one, dominated seas during the **Palaeozoic** and **Mesozoic** eras but declined after the **Jurassic**. There are about ten species around the British Isles, the phylum being divided into two classes, of which the Articulata is the largest:

Inarticulata Valves not hinged but held together by muscles, gut U-shaped and with an anus.

Articulata Valves hinged but not held together by a ligament, gut looped but with no anus.

Further reading

Brunton, C. H. C. & Curry, G. B. (1979). British brachiopods. *Synopses of the British Fauna, New Series*, 17, 1–57.

Ryland, J. S. (1990). The lophophorate phyla: Phoronida, Bryozoa, and Brachiopoda. In *The marine fauna of the British Isles and North-West Europe* (eds P. J. Hayward & J. S. Ryland), Vol. 2, pp. 794–838. Clarendon Press, Oxford.

Distinctive features

1. Shells plump, oval, almost pear-shaped.
2. Lower shell larger than upper.
3. Surface of shells finely ribbed.

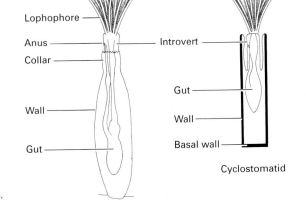

The main features of ctenostomatid (Gymnolaemata) and cyclostomatid (Stenolaemata) bryozoans.

Ctenostomatid

Cyclostomatid

within the maternal zooid or in special **brood chambers**, sexual reproduction giving rise to a larva which **metamorphoses** into an **ancestrula**. Asexual budding by an ancestrula ultimately leads to the formation of the colony, which thus genetically forms a single individual (though different colonies may fuse).

Bryozoan colonies exhibit a very wide range of shapes and sizes. Many form irregularly outlined encrusting sheets or nodules, or are soft, fleshy, and lobed, whilst others produce erect growths that may be like stiff twigs or look like diffuse or bushy tufts. The colonies are found attached to almost any suitable surface, such as rocks and boulders, algal fronds, or mollusc shells. Intertidal colonies are commonly found on larger algae, such as fucoids or laminarians, and are often abundant on rocky shores. Although some of them are inconspicuous, several hundred species occur in European seas. Some bryozoans have a distinctly shaped colony, but for their certain identification examination of the zooids is necessary, a hand lens usually being adequate. The simplest or basic zooid form is probably cylindrical and erect, but more often individuals are squat and attached to their neighbours, forming extensive encrusting mats or layers. Two classes of marine Bryozoa are found in British waters.

CLASS **Stenolaemata** | ORDER **Cyclostomata**

FAMILY **Crisiidae**

Crisia eburnea (Linnaeus)

Description · Forms dense, tufted colonies up to 2 cm high, with distinctly curved branches. The colony is usually attached by a single stem with a few rootlets. The internodes are short and consist of 5–7 incurved zooids. The joints between the nodes are often yellowish or yellowish-brown, but may be colourless. The zooids arise alternately on the main axes except in the distal parts of the colony, where all the zooids arise from the same side. Gonozooids are narrow, pear-shaped, and carried on a short tube. **Habitat & ecology** · Found on the extreme lower shore and in shallow sublittoral situations to at least 50 m depth. Grows on a variety of substrate types, including red algae, hydroids (*Halecium*, *Abietinaria*, *Hydrallmania* and *Sertularella* species) and bryozoans (*Cellaria* and *Flustra* species).

Abundance & distribution
Common. Found around all coasts of Britain and Ireland. Distributed from Arctic Norway to the Mediterranean.

CLASS **Gymnolaemata** | ORDER **Cheilostomatida** | SUBORDER **Malacostegina**

SUPERFAMILY **Membraniporioidea**
FAMILY **Electridae**

Electra pilosa (Linnaeus) **Hairy sea-mat**

Description · Forms mat-like, silvery-grey, encrusting colony, with very irregular and angular outline, sometimes somewhat star-shaped. Colonies may form broad sheets or, on smaller algae, are cylindrical around frond. Zooids are squat, about 0.5 mm long and have an extensive, oval frontal membrane. Each zooid has two small blunt spines at one end and a single, long, and obvious spine at the other, with up to 11 other short spines distributed around edge. About one-third of frontal surface of colony is lightly calcified, and covered with large numbers of scattered pores. **Habitat & ecology** · Lower-shore to shallow sublittoral, encrusting stones and boulders or seaweeds, particularly *Fucus serratus*, kelps, *Chondrus crispus*, and *Gigartina stellata*. In southern North Sea it forms ball-shaped colonies, often with a central piece of substrate; during summer enormous numbers of these 'pilosa balls' may be stranded on shore. The sea slug, *Adalaria proxima*, feeds on this as well as other bryozoan species.

Abundance & distribution
Abundant. Found around all British and Irish coasts. Occurs in all temperate seas.

Stenolaemata Zooids long, slender, and cylindrical, with strongly calcified wall. A single order, **Cyclostomatida**.

Gymnolaemata Zooids cylindrical or squat, walls calcified, cuticular, or gelatinous. The two orders in this class are the **Cheilostomatida** and **Ctenostomatida**.

Further reading

Hayward, P. J. (1985). Ctenostome bryozoans. *Synopses of the British Fauna, New Series*, **33**, 1–169.

Hayward, P. J. & Ryland, J. S. (1979). British ascophoran bryozoans. *Synopses of the British Fauna, New Series*, **14**, 1–312.

Ryland, J. S. (1990). The lophophorate phyla: Phoronida, Bryozoa, and Brachiopoda. In *The marine fauna of the British Isles and North-West Europe* (eds P. J. Hayward J. S. Ryland), Vol. 2, pp. 794–838. Clarendon Press, Oxford.

Ryland, J. S. & Hayward, P. J. (1977). British anascan bryozoans. *Synopses of the British Fauna, New Series*, **10**, 1–188.

Distinctive features

1. Dense, tufted colonies with incurved branches.
2. Internodes short with 5–7 incurved zooids.
3. Joints at nodes yellowish, yellowish-brown, or colourless.

Distinctive features

1. Forms irregular, encrusting growths.
2. Each zooid with a single very long spine or bristle at one edge.
3. Silvery-grey.

FAMILY **Membraniporidae**

Membranipora membranacea (Linnaeus) **Sea-mat**

Description · Forms a variably sized, encrusting colony, often with a lacy appearance. Colonies may reach a considerable size. The zooids are rectangular, with short spines or tubercles at their corners. The lateral walls contain vertical uncalcified bands which provide the colony with flexibility. The more or less rectangular membranous area covers the whole of the frontal surface. Typically a pale greyish-white colour. **Habitat & ecology** · A lower-shore to shallow sublittoral species, very characteristically found encrusting the fronds and other parts of kelps, less often on other brown seaweeds such as *Fucus serratus*. A rapidly growing bryozoan whose colony can spread several millimetres per day, especially when fed on by sea slugs. This species is eaten by the sea slug, *Polycera quadrilineata*. **Similar species** · Very similar to *Electra pilosa*.

Abundance & distribution
Common and often locally abundant. Found all around Britain and Ireland. The distribution extends throughout the north-east Atlantic region as far south as the Mediterranean coasts of Europe.

SUBORDER **Neocheilostomatina** | SUPERFAMILY **Flustroidea**

FAMILY **Flustridae**

Chartella papyracea (Ellis & Solander)

Description · Forms small, delicate, bilaminar colonies which appear as whitish tufts of narrow fronds up to 10 cm tall. The fronds are profusely branched. Zooids are rectangular, up to 0.5 mm long, and possess a slender spine at each corner. Ovicells, in which the embryos are brooded, are hemispherical and underlie the surface of the colony. The embryos are orange. **Habitat & ecology** · Found on the lower shore or, more usually, subtidally at depths of 10–50 m. It is usually attached to hard surfaces such as boulders and stones. May be common on moderately exposed shores. **Similar species** · *C. barleei*, but this species lacks spines on the zooids.

Abundance & distribution
Locally common. Found in southern Britain, the Irish Sea, and southern and western Ireland. It is distributed south to the coast of Spain.

Flustra foliacea (Linnaeus) **Hornwrack**

Description · Colonies form stiff but flexible erect, greyish to yellowish-grey or greyish-brown bushy clumps up to 10–20 cm tall, with broad, flattened, and lobed fronds bearing zooids on both sides (bilaminar). The fronds may form palmate or, less commonly, undivided or split into very narrow branches. The distal end of each zooid is bordered by 4–5 short, thick spines. Avicularia with brown, rounded beaks are located at the bifurcations of the zooid rows. Egg-shaped ovicells open distally to the zooid operculum and contain pale orange embryos. When alive the bryozoan has a distinctly lemony scent. **Habitat & ecology** · An entirely sublittoral species to depths of 100 m, typically attached to stones, boulders, and shells, and may form dense beds when growing in current-swept locations. Faded and dried specimens are very commonly found washed up on the shore among strandline debris.

Abundance & distribution
Abundant. Found all around Britain and Ireland. Distributed from the Barents Sea and Arctic Norway to all north-west European coasts as far south as the Bay of Biscay.

Distinctive features

1. Encrusting, irregularly shaped colonies, often rather lace-like.
2. Zooids rectangular, with short spines at corners.
3. Pale greyish-white.

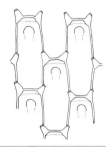

Distinctive features

1. Colonies form bushy, whitish tufts of highly branched, narrow fronds.
2. Zooids rectangular with slender spine at each corner.

Distinctive features

1. Colonies form stiff, erect, broad-lobed fronds.
2. Zooids distributed on both sides of fronds.
3. Greyish to yellowish-grey.
4. Living specimens have lemony smell.

SUPERFAMILY **Cellaroidea**

FAMILY **Cellariidae**

Cellaria fistulosa (Linnaeus)

Description · Forming large, ivory-white, clump-like growths of densely branching tufts up to 10 cm tall. Sometimes colonies are more branching and diffuse. The branches are formed of narrow, cylindrical internodes 5–8 mm long and 0.5–1 mm in diameter, linked by short, chitinous nodes. Each internode contains 5–6 whorls of hexagonal zooids, opening on all surfaces of the branches, whilst between zooids the small, rectangular avicularia possess short, almost elliptical mandibles pointing towards the tip of the branch. The internodes are cylindrical and slender. **Habitat & ecology** · Living in shallow coastal and offshore depths to at least 80 m. This species tends to settle on other sessile organisms such as hydroids or other bryozoans and often grows down until secondarily attached to the surrounding substrate. **Similar species** · May be mistaken for other *Cellaria* species but can be distinguished by the shape of the internodes.

Abundance & distribution
Locally common. This bryozoan is found all around Britain and Ireland. It is distributed south to Spain and the Mediterranean.

SUPERFAMILY **Buguloidea**

FAMILY **Bugulidae**

Bugula flabellata (Thompson in Gray)

Description · Dense, tufted colonies, formed from broad, flat, rather wedge-shaped branches containing up to eight rows of zooids. Zooids at margins of branches have three spines at outer corner, two at inner, zooids away from margins have two spines on each corner. Avicularia (polymorphic zooids often important for identification), marginal ones very much larger than central, have long, hooked beaks. Colonies up to 2–3 cm high, buff colour alive, drying to grey if washed up on shore dead. **Habitat & ecology** · Lower shore and shallow sublittoral, on rocky surfaces. May cause fouling. **Similar species** · Resembles *B. plumosa* in tufted appearance, but this has spirally arranged branches arising from a mass of tangled rootlets and grows to height of 8 cm, with outer distal angle of each zooid developed into finger-like spine and avicularia small and lateral, with slightly down-curved tip. Resembles other bugulid species, but usually distinguishable by numbers of zooid spines and rows, and avicularia size and shape.

Abundance & distribution
Common, found on all British rocky coasts with a range extending from the Shetland Islands southwards to the Mediterranean. Has been transported to other parts of the world as a fouling organism on ship hulls.

SUBORDER **Ascophorina** | INFRAORDER **Umbonulomorpha**

SUPERFAMILY **Lepralielloidea**

FAMILY **Umbonulidae**

Umbonula littoralis Hastings

Description · A heavily calcified species forming thick, orange-coloured encrustations. The zooids are large, with about 20 conspicuous marginal pores. There are no ovicells, but the reddish embryos are easily visible inside the zooids during the autumn and winter months. The frontal surface of zooids is completely calcified with a nodular surface bordered by the marginal pores, and often a single rounded avicularium. **Habitat & ecology** · A lower-shore to shallow sublittoral species, found growing on hard surfaces, kelp holdfasts, or the buttons of the brown alga *Himanthalia elongata*. **Similar species** · May be confused with *U. ovicellata*, but this species is rare, possesses ovicells, and has fewer marginal pores, which are bordered by thick, calcified, ridges.

Abundance & distribution
Common. Found on most British coasts, with a range extending from Atlantic coasts of Norway south to the coasts of Brittany.

Distinctive features

1. Forms densely branching, erect tufts.
2. Branches with cylindrical internodes possessing 5–6 whorls of hexagonal zooids.

Distinctive features

1. Branches of colony erect, broad, flat, rather wedge-shaped.
2. Avicularia with long, hooked beaks.
3. Marginal zooids with three outer corner spines, two inner; innermost zooids with two spines on each corner.

Distinctive features

1. Colony forms thick, heavily calcified, orange encrustations.
2. Zooid frontal surface with nodular border; often single, rounded avicularium.
3. Reddish embryos visible inside zooids during autumn and winter.

INFRAORDER **Lepraliomorpha** | SUPERFAMILY **Smittinoidea**

FAMILY **Celleporidae**

Omalosecosa ramulosa (Linnaeus)

Description · An encrusting or cylindrical base gives rise to a branched growth that resembles the antlers of a deer or a small branching coral. The tapering branches are cylindrical and divide dichotomously in different directions to give a roughly spherical colony up to 5 cm in diameter. The zooids are disposed all around the branches. The colour is a dirty white. **Habitat & ecology** · A subtidal bryozoan that either arises from rock or shelly gravel or grows around another bryozoan or hydroid or on the holdfast of kelp. It occurs down to a depth of approximately 80 m.

Abundance & distribution
Common. Found all around Britain and Ireland. Distributed from western Norway to Mauritania, including the Mediterranean.

SUPERFAMILY **Schizoporelloidea**

FAMILY **Hippoporinidae**

Pentapora fascialis (Pallas) **Ross-coral**

Description · Forms erect, flat, bilaminar plates that are rigid and folded into an approximately domed-shaped structure, rather like a coral head or a flower. The plates are highly irregular in shape and fuse often. An alternate growth form is of elongate, irregularly divided branches. The zooids are visible to the naked eye and are an elongate hexagonal shape. The overall colour of the colony is orangey-red to buff, sometimes with light and dark concentric bands. Colonies may grow to 30 cm in diameter and to 10 cm or more in height. **Habitat & ecology** · A subtidal species found attached to shells, stones, boulders, and rock. Colonies may be conspicuous in size and numbers in some localities.

Abundance & distribution
Locally both common and abundant. Found on south-west British coasts and south and west coasts of Ireland. Distributed south to the Mediterranean.

ORDER **Ctenostomatida** | SUBORDER **Carnosa**

FAMILY **Alcyonidiidae**

Alcyonidium diaphanum Lamouroux **Sea chervil**

Description · Uncalcified, highly variable in shape and appearance, its different forms probably representing three or more currently indistinguishable species, i.e. sea chervil is probably a species complex. Colonies may be lobed or branched, rounded or elongate, cylindrical or flattened, smooth or knobbly, but are typically translucent amber or honey colour, firmly gelatinous in texture, with surface that is not tuberculate. Each zooid has 15–17 tentacles. Colonies grow from narrow stalk; frequently 15 cm long but may reach length of 50 cm. Identified by some authors as *A. gelatinosum*, a related species. **Habitat & ecology** · Extreme lower shore and in shallow sublittoral situations, attached to shells, stones, rocks, or boulders, but also on shelly or gravelly bottoms. Frequently becomes detached and may be stranded on shore, sometimes in large quantities. Skin dermatitis, 'Dogger Bank Itch', is apparently caused by an allergic reaction to this species but seems to be confined to North Sea.

Abundance & distribution
Common, locally abundant. This species is found off all coasts of Britain and Ireland, and along most north-west European coasts.

Distinctive features

1. Branched growth form that resembles the antlers of a deer.
2. Roughly spherical colony up to 5 cm in diameter.

Distinctive features

1. Rigid, flat, bilaminar plates, folded into dome or crown shape, like coral head.
2. Plates often fused.
3. Zooids elongate, hexagonal shape.

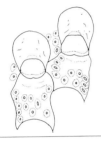

Distinctive features

1. Shape extremely variable.
2. Honey or translucent amber in colour.
3. Firmly gelatinous in texture.

Alcyonidium hirsutum (Fleming)

Description · Surface of colony has a furry or velvety texture. Zooids are box-shaped, each one bordered by spherical or conical polymorphic kenozooids (feeding zooids [=autozooids grouped at distal ends of stolonic segments]). Colony typically forms small patches or broad spreading sheets, but may develop erect and fleshy lobes in some situations. **Habitat & ecology** · An intertidal bryozoan typically found on the alga *Fucus serratus* but less commonly on *Gigartina* or *Chondrus* species. It tends to form fleshy lobes on small specimens of *Chondrus*. **Similar species** · *A. parasiticum* tends to grow on animals such as the hydroids *Tubularia indivisa* or *Hydrallmania falcata* or on erect bryozoans such as *Cellaria* species. It forms thick, smooth, cylinder-like colonies around these animals. The colour is typically grey or greyish-brown and the surface is coated with accretions of fine sand or silt. Single encrusting colonies are up to 2–3 cm long and 5 mm thick. *A. parasiticum* is distributed from Norway and Iceland to the Channel.

Abundance & distribution
Common. Found on all British and Irish coasts. Distributed from the Barents Sea to Brittany.

FAMILY **Flustrellidridae**
Flustrellidra hispida (Fabricius)

Description · An uncalcified bryozoan species, forming thick-lobed patches on large algal fronds or cylindrical colonies on smaller ones. The colonies have a distinctly furry appearance. The bell-shaped lophophore of each zooid, composed of ciliated tentacles, is easily visible to the naked eye. The rough-feeling surface texture results from the spiny kenozooids. There are no avicularia. **Habitat & ecology** · Found only in the intertidal region, growing as an epiphyte on algae, particularly *Fucus serratus* or, less commonly, forming cylindrical growths on *Chondrus* and *Gigartina* species. The onchidorid sea-slug, *Adalaria proxima*, feeds on this epiphytic bryozoan as well as other species, but it does not occur south of Britain.

Abundance & distribution
Common. Found on all British and Irish coasts. Distributed from the White Sea and Arctic Norway to the Brittany coasts of France. Also found in the western Atlantic as far south as Woods Hole.

Distinctive features

1. Surface of colony has a velvety texture.
2. Zooids box-shaped, bordered by spherical or conical kenozooids.

Distinctive features

1. Forms thick, furry, uncalcified colonies.
2. Epiphytic, especially on *Fucus serratus.*
3. Lophophore, composed of ciliated tentacles, visible to naked eye when extended.

Echinoderms

Phylum Echinodermata

Essentially, the **Echinodermata** comprise animals with five different basic body forms, but all are united by a number of common features. All show **pentasymmetry** (radial symmetry based on five **rays**), exemplified by the classes **Asteroidea** (starfish) and **Ophiuroidea** (brittlestars), which typically possess five arms radiating from a central disc. All echinoderms have a skeleton composed of calcareous plates (**ossicles**). The ossicles may be linked by flexible body-wall tissues, as in starfish, be closely jointed and form a rigid **test**, as in the class **Echinoidea** (sea urchins), or be few in number and widely spaced, rarely completely missing, so that the body is soft and pliable as in the **Holothurioidea** (sea cucumbers). The outer body surface may be covered in calcareous spines, between which are often found large numbers of thin-walled protuberances (**papulae**) which function as gills, or **pedicellariae**, minute, mobile-jawed structures used for keeping the body surface free of debris or for keeping intruders at bay. Each of the five rays comprises a narrow band of small plates, called an **ambulacrum**, which have pores through which long, flexible, and contractile **tube feet** project. Tube feet typically end in sucker-like tips. In starfish and brittlestars the ambulacra are located on the lower (**adoral** or **adambulacral**) surface of the body and the tube feet are used primarily for locomotion. However, in the sea urchins the ambulacra commence at five small **ocular plates** surrounding an **anal opening** on the upper, **aboral**, surface and basically extend around the body to the mouth; to some extent employed for movement, the tube feet more often anchor the sea urchin to its surroundings. In this case bands of larger plates, called **interambulacra**, also extend between the ambulacra. The tube feet of echinoderms are operated by an internal **water vascular system**. This consists of a **ring canal** surrounding the mouth, from which a **longitudinal** vessel radiates out below each ambulacrum to connect with each of the tube feet. A **stone canal** links the ring canal to a sieve plate (**madreporite**) situated in the body wall,

usually on the aboral surface. In sea urchins, however, the largest of the five **genital plates**, situated around the anus, between the ocular plates, is perforated and doubles as a madreporite. When water is drawn in through the madreporite the tube feet are extended, fine control being achieved via a system of valves and chambers.

Echinoderms usually possess separate sexes, external fertilisation and seasonal reproduction. In the Echinoidea eggs are released and hatch into a planktonic larva, but many Asteroidea and Ophiuroidea brood their eggs, which then hatch as advanced juveniles.

Feeding specialisations in the phylum are extremely varied. Larger, regular sea urchins, for example, are typically browsers or grazers of algae and sessile invertebrates, whereas most starfish are predators on polychaete annelids, bivalve molluscs, or other starfish; sea cucumbers are microphagous filter- or deposit-feeders and brittlestars, depending upon the species, may show almost any one of the above feeding adaptations.

Echinoderms form an exclusively marine group of invertebrates, none being recorded from fresh- or brackish-water habitats. Worldwide, there are about 7000 living species. Their often large size, slow-moving habits, and bright coloration make them conspicuous members of the benthos. The five classes within the phylum are the **Asteroidea** (starfish, sea stars), **Crinoidea** (feather stars, sea lilies), **Echinoidea** (sea urchins), **Holothurioidea** (sea cucumbers), and **Ophiuroidea** (brittlestars).

Further reading

Moyse, J. & Tyler, P. A. (1990). Echinodermata. In *The marine fauna of the British Isles and North-West Europe* (eds P. J. Hayward & J. S. Ryland), Vol. 2, pp. 839–71. Clarendon Press, Oxford.

Class Crinoidea (feather stars, sea lilies)

Primitive echinoderms, with a cup-shaped body (**calyx**) bearing ten flexible and feathery arms (two from each **ambulacrum**), which possess numerous slender, lateral branches (**pinnules**) formed of small, articulated plates. The mouth is on the upper surface of the calyx, the ambulacra extend along the inner surface of each arm. Crinoids may be either permanently attached to the substrate by a

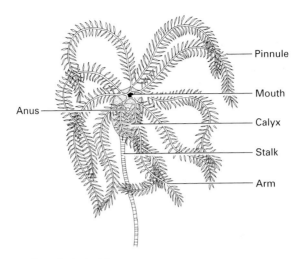

The external features of a stalked crinoid.

jointed stalk (**stalked crinoids**) or temporarily
attached by several unbranched and prehensile
hooked **cirri** which often have a claw-like end
(**stalkless crinoids**). Although stalked crinoids
are not found in British coastal waters, representatives of one stalkless family, the
Antedonidae, with perhaps five local species,
may be encountered in lower shore rock pools
or shallower sublittoral situations. Both
specific and generic diversity increase in
deeper off-shore waters.

ORDER **Comatulida**

FAMILY **Antedonidae**

Antedon bifida (Pennant) **Feather star**

Description · Small cup-shaped body; ten pinnate arms with side branches, giving an overall feathery appearance. Arms prehensile and it can swim (poorly) by undulating arms. Arms may reach 10 cm in length, but generally less. Also has up to 30 (usually 25) shorter prehensile, simple, arms projecting from around lower part of body. Mouth and anus located on upper part of body. Varies from rose to deep purple, yellow, or orange; dark pinkish-red commonest. Arms often banded alternately dark and very pale; body may be mottled overall. **Habitat & ecology** · Subtidal from 5–200 m depth, exceptionally to 450 m depth. Occurs on variety of substrates including rock, algae, and sessile organisms in moderately exposed to sheltered habitats, occasionally in large numbers. Carries eggs until hatched into larvae. Juvenile stage stalked; may occur in large numbers on other organisms in vicinity of adults. Parasitic polychaetes of genus *Myzostoma* may be found on the animal's body.

Abundance & distribution
Common, locally abundant. Found around all coasts of Britain except for the east Coast, south of Northumbria to the Channel. Distribution is from the Shetland Islands south to Portugal.

Class Asteroidea (sea stars, starfish)

Most Asteroidea exemplify the basic penta-symmetry of the echinoderms, typically possessing flat bodies with five, sometimes more, heavy and broad **arms** which grade outwards from an indistinct central disc. The arms are called **rays** and their axes **radii**, whilst areas of the central disc between the arms comprise the **interradial** regions. The **ambulacra** are located in grooves on the lower (**adoral**) surface of the arms and possess either two or four rows of tube feet. The ambulacral groove is often fringed by spines and the upper (**aboral**) margin of each arm may be edged with large **marginal plates**. The aboral surface is usually covered with spines and tubercles, including a special type with a flat top bearing a bunch of spiny processes resembling miniature paint brushes (**paxillae**). Small, sac-like gills (**papulae**) occur between the aboral spines, as do the **pedicellariae** which, in the asteroids, are always two-jawed but come in two basic types, either **crossed** (with a scissors action) or **straight** (with a tweezers action). Starfish can usually regenerate lost or damaged arms and several species are often found with an irregular arm number. The mouth is in the centre of the lower surface (variously known as the **oral**, **ambulacral**, or **actinal** surface), the upper surface being called **aboral** or **abactinal**.

Five orders of north-west European asteroids occur in coastal waters. The **Paxillosida** have numerous paxillae on the upper surfaces and tube feet without suckers. The **Valvatida** have suckers on the tube feet and always an anus present. The **Velatida** have a large disc and five to many arms, and tube feet in two rows with suckers. The **Spinulosa** are characterised by generally lacking pedicellariae, and the **Forcipulata** are armed with crossed pedicellariae. Asteroids are not uncommon in intertidal rock pools or sublittorally.

Distinctive features

1. Small, cup-shaped.
2. Up to ten relatively long, feathery arms.
3. Up to 30 small, prehensile arms projecting from lower part of body.

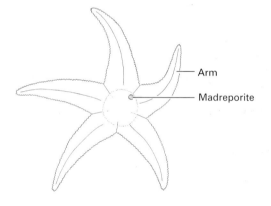

Arm

Madreporite

Papula or gill

Coelom

Radial water vascular canal

Ossicle

Pedicellaria

Gut caecum

Ampulla

Spine

Tube foot

The typical appearance of an asteroid echinoderm (*top*) viewed from the aboral surface, with a diagrammatic transverse section through one of the arms (*bottom*), showing some of the terms referred to in the text.

ORDER **Paxillosida**

FAMILY **Luidiidae**

Luidia ciliaris (Philippi)

Description · Extremely large, growing to up to 60 cm across, usually with seven (rarely eight) arms, which may be of different lengths or shapes because of regeneration. Arms taper only in outer part and fringed with long, stiff white spines (4–5 per lower marginal ossicle) that are not all aligned in one direction. Dorsal surface may be brick red, orange, or orangey-brown, ventral surface paler. **Habitat & ecology** · Mainly subtidal to 400 m depth, but may occur at ELWS. Generally found on sand, sand-scoured rock, or gravel, often without mud. Voracious feeder, preying on other echinoderms such as *Ophiothrix, Spatangus purpureus, Echinocardium* species, *Asterias rubens, Thyone fusus, Cucumaria* species. Occasionally feeds on bivalves such as *Pecten* species. In southern Britain it breeds in summer; in the Mediterranean, November-January. **Similar species** · Include *Luidia sarsi*, but this only has five arms. *Astropecten irregularis* is also similar but this has five short, stiff arms with large, rectangular marginal plates. *Solaster endeca* has seven or more arms but no fringe of spines around margin.

Abundance & distribution
Common around all coasts of Britain apart from southern North Sea. Distributed from Faeroe Islands to Mediterranean, Canary Islands, Azores, and possibly Cape Verde Islands.

FAMILY **Astropectinidae**

Astropecten irregularis (Pennant)

Description · A stiff, star-shaped species with five rather short arms, usually up to 10 cm across but may reach 20 cm. Arms are an elongate triangular shape, with a double row of distinctive plates around the margin (superomarginal and inferomarginal plates). Arms are fringed with a horizontal row of long spines, 4–5 for each marginal plate, the third being the longest. Superomarginal plates often bear a short, conical spine. The rest of the dorsal surface is granular. Colour reddish-violet, pale violet, yellow, or sand-coloured. May have a purple mark in the centre of the disc and purple tips to the arms. **Habitat & ecology** · Subtidal, on sand and sandy mud, and usually partially buried, from 10–1000 m depth. Occasionally encountered at ELWS. Feeds voraciously on molluscs, echinoderms, crustaceans, annelids, and even fish. It swallows its food whole. Dioecious, with pelagic larval stage. **Similar species** · *Luidia ciliaris* and *L. sarsi*, but these lack the obvious large, marginal plates of *A. irregularis*.

Abundance & distribution
Common around all coasts of Britain. Distribution is from Norway to Morocco and the Cape Verde Islands. A subspecies occurs in South Africa.

ORDER **Valvatida**

FAMILY **Asterinidae**

Anseropoda placenta (Pennant)
Goose foot starfish

Description · A distinctively flattened starfish that reaches about 20 cm across. It has five short webbed arms that give the animal a pentagonal to sub-pentagonal shape. Dorsal surface is red and this is generally most intense in the centre, margins, and a median line along each arm. The 'webs' between each arm can be paler red to almost white. Occasionally individuals are orange or pink. The ventral surface is usually yellowish with a band of red around the margins. The ventral surface may vary to pink or grey. The surface of this starfish has a granular texture. **Habitat & ecology** · Occurs subtidally at depths of 10–500 m. Unconfirmed records from the Mediterranean suggest this may extend to 600 m. Usually found on sand with gravel or shell and some mud. Small specimens may hide under shells. Feeds on crustaceans (amphipods, cumaceans, mysids, crabs, hermit crabs), molluscs, and echinoderms. No similar species in shallow water.

Abundance & distribution
Frequent. Found all around the British Isles but not in southern North Sea. Distribution extends from the Faeroes south to Sierra Leone, including the Mediterranean.

Distinctive features

1. Large size.
2. Seven arms.
3. Fringe of stiff white spines along margins.

Distinctive features

1. Rigid, star-shaped species.
2. Large marginal plates around arms.
3. Arms fringed by long spines.

Distinctive features

1. Very flattened starfish.
2. Five webbed arms giving a pentagonal or sub-pentagonal shape.

Asterina gibbosa (Pennant) **Cushion starfish**

Description · A small, compressed, 'cushion'-like species, up to 5 cm across, with five arms and a sub-pentagonal shape. The ventral surface is flat. The dorsal surface, swollen towards the centre and more flattened towards the tips of the arms, is spiny with a rough texture. Colour usually greenish-brown (khaki), olive green, pale brownish-orange, or greenish-yellow. The margins of the arms may appear orange. The ventral surface is usually paler. **Habitat & ecology** · Intertidally this species is usually found during the day in rock pools, crevices, and under stones. Subtidally it occurs down to 125 m depth. It feeds on dead plants and animals. It is a protandrous hermaphrodite and when the female is shedding eggs it may be accompanied by 2–3 functional males. Eggs are attached in small groups under stones and hatch directly into small starfish. **Similar species** · *A. phylactica*, from which it may be distinguished by its larger size and uniform coloration. The two species can be confused when small.

Abundance & distribution
Common on west and south coasts of Britain but not in the North Sea. Distribution is from the west coast of Scotland to the Canary Islands and Azores, including the Mediterranean.

Asterina phylactica Emson and Crump
Small cushion starfish

Description · Tiny, compressed, 'cushion'-like species, up to 15 mm across, with five arms and a sub-pentagonal shape. The ventral surface is flat. The dorsal surface is swollen towards the centre and becomes more flattened towards the tips of the arms. Dorsal surface is greyish-green with a conspicuous, dark, star-shaped marking over the central area. Ventral surface pale. **Habitat & ecology** · Locally common intertidally on moderately exposed shores at HWNT level, especially on algae or in coralline turf on the tops and sides of rocks but also in rock pools. Occurs subtidally to at least 18 m. Simultaneous hermaphrodite which broods its eggs. These hatch directly into small starfish. **Similar species** · Resembles *A. gibbosa* but grows to a much smaller size and has a distinctive star-shaped marking on the dorsal surface.

Abundance & distribution
Uncertain because this species was only recently distinguished from *A. gibbosa*. Occurs in west Wales, Irish Sea, southern Ireland, south-west England, south-west France, and the northern Adriatic.

FAMILY **Poraniidae**

Porania pulvillus (Müller)
Red cushion starfish

Description · A stout species with five arms, which grows up to a diameter of 12 cm. The arms are short and the disc large. The starfish is smooth to the touch and its dorsal surface is only interrupted by clusters of white, yellowish, or transparent soft papulae. This species is usually a very striking and vivid bright red though it may be purple, orange, or yellow. Dorsal surface is often marked with white or yellowish spots, and white or yellowish streaks often run from the margin towards the centre of the animal. Ventral surface is pale. **Habitat & ecology** · Sublittoral, at depths of 10–1000 m, but reported to be more common in the shallower part of this range. Often occurs on exposed rocks but may also be found among kelp holdfasts or on coarse or muddy substrates. Reported to feed on detritus and on the soft coral, *Alcyonium digitatum*. It is a sexually reproducing species with pelagic larvae.

Abundance & distribution
Occurs frequently on north, west, and south coasts of Britain, but absent from the North Sea south of the Moray Firth. Distributed from Norway to northern Spain.

Distinctive features

1. Small, with compressed 'cushion' shape.
2. Sub-pentagonal in shape.
3. Coloration fairly uniform.

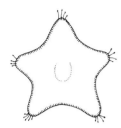

Distinctive features

1. Tiny species with compressed 'cushion' shape.
2. Conspicuous star-shaped marking on dorsal surface.

Distinctive features

1. Stout, cushion-shaped starfish.
2. Dorsal surface mainly smooth to touch.
3. Usually a vivid red colour.

ORDER **Velatida**

FAMILY **Solasteridae**

Crossaster papposus (Linnaeus) **Sun star**

Description · Large, reaching up to 35 cm in diameter. Usually has 10–13 arms but occasionally 8–14. Dorsal surface is covered in narrow bars of ossicles forming an irregular reticulation. These enclose membranous spaces in which papulae are distributed. Dorsal surface can be various shades of yellow, red to purple, or even dirty brown. Usually red or pale orange, patterned with concentric rings of light and dark colour. Madreporite often forms a conspicuous white spot. Ventral surface yellow or whitish. **Habitat & ecology** · Occasionally occurs on lower shore, but usually subtidal to depths of 900 m or more. Found in areas subject to moderate current flow, often on rocks or boulders, or on brittlestar beds. Feeds on other echinoderms, especially the starfish *Asterias rubens*, holothurians, and molluscs. Reported to be a pest on oyster beds. **Similar species** · *Solaster endeca*, but this tends to have fewer arms, and these are slenderer and more tapered than *C. papposus*. The surface texture of *S. endeca* tends to be rough rather than spiny.

Abundance & distribution
Common around all coasts of Britain. Distribution is circum-boreal, but in the north Atlantic it occurs from Iceland and Scandinavia down to northern Brittany.

Solaster endeca (Linnaeus)
Purple sun star

Description · Fairly large species that grows to up to 40 cm diameter and usually has 9–10 arms but may have up to 13. The arms are short and thick and the disc is large. The dorsal surface is covered in very short, small spines that make it rough to the touch. Colour is variable and ranges through dirty cream and orangey-red to bright pinkish-purple. The ventral surface is pale and the tips of the arms are often turned upwards to reveal the underside. **Habitat & ecology** · Occurs on lower shore but usually subtidal down to about 500 m depth. Often found on muddy gravel or on silty rocks. A voracious predator on other echinoderms and has been observed eating animals nearly as large as itself. Breeds March-April, and young starfish hatch directly from eggs without a pelagic stage.

Abundance & distribution
Found frequently on the north and west coasts of Britain and in the Irish Sea. Does not occur in the southern North Sea or Channel. Distribution is circumboreal. Occurs northwards from Britain into the Arctic.

ORDER **Spinulosida**

FAMILY **Echinasteridae**

Henricia oculata (Pennant) **Bloody Henry**

Description · Stiff, moderately sized, five-armed starfish, with very small disc; usually grows to 12 cm in diameter (possibly larger). Arms cylindrical in cross-section, broad at base, tapering evenly to rounded tips. Surface of starfish has rough sandpaper-like feel, and dorsal surface covered in scattered groups of opaque spines with numerous irregular points, and covered in skin (needs hand lens). Dorsal surface various shades of red, orange, brown, purple, and yellow; ventral surface often paler. **Habitat & ecology** · Generally subtidal to 180 m depth, but may be found at ELWS. On hard bottoms, in rock pools, and amongst kelp species. Common on shell gravel. A typical species of sites exposed to strong water movement. Dioecious: fertilises eggs externally and has planktonic larvae. It uses mucus to trap food particles in water (suspension feeder). **Similar species** · Very difficult to separate from *H. sanguinolenta* with which it may co-occur. This has glassy spines, not covered with skin, on dorsal surface, which come to 5–6 (sometimes 3–5) flared points. Accurate identification may need hand lens.

Abundance & distribution
Common on all coasts of Scotland, Shetland Islands, Ireland, north-east and west coasts of England, and the western half of the Channel and northern France.

Distinctive features

1. 10–13 (sometimes 8–14) arms.
2. Dorsal surface covered in bars of ossicles forming reticulated pattern.
3. Often a pattern of pale and darker concentric rings.

Distinctive features

1. 9–13 arms.
2. Arms short and thick.
3. Surface feels rough to touch.

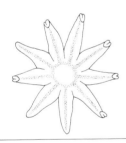

Distinctive features

1. Stiff; five arms.
2. Small disc.
3. Sandpaper surface texture.
4. Arms cylindrical in cross-section.
5. Irregular opaque, skin-covered in spines on dorsal surface.

ORDER **Forcipulata**

FAMILY **Asteriidae**

Asterias rubens Linnaeus **Common starfish**

Description · Usually 25–30 cm wide, although can be up to 50 cm across.
Tapering arms of active specimens may be curled up at tips. Both arms and
plump central disc are covered on their upper surfaces by irregularly
shaped spines that are encircled by pedicellariae. There is also a prominent
madreporite on aboral surface of central disc. Colour varies from pale
brown to a purple or violet hue, although bright orange or orangey-yellow
is more typical. Deep water examples tend to be very pale. **Habitat &
ecology** · Found on a wide range of hard substrata including mussel or
oyster beds, and less frequently on softer sediments. On rocky shores it is
most easily found by searching rock pools from mid-shore downwards, or
by turning over boulders. Occurs from mid-shore to sublittoral depths of
400 m or more. Two crustacean species, the amphipod, *Pariambus typicus*,
and the semi-parasitic copepod, *Scottomyzon gibbosum*, may be found
attached to the spines on upper surface of the body.

Abundance & distribution
Common. Found on most
British and Irish coasts. Its
range extends from Iceland, the
White Sea, and the western
Baltic Sea southwards to West
Africa (Senegal).

Leptasterias muelleri (Sars)

Description · Moderately sized starfish that grows up to 20 cm diameter
but is typically smaller (6 cm). Arms of moderate length, somewhat swollen
at base and tapering very little towards the tips. The dorsal surface is
densely packed with spines and generally the spaces between these are only
occupied by a single papula. Spines may appear to be in longitudinal rows
in small specimens. Dorsal surface is pink, pale red to various shades of
purple or violet, becoming whitish towards tips of arms. A green form
occurs in shallow water or intertidal habitats. **Habitat & ecology** · Found
intertidally under rocks and in rock pools. Intertidal and shallow forms
may be green because of the presence of a unicellular green alga in the
body. Occurs subtidally to 800 m. This species broods its young, which are
released as tiny starfish. **Similar species** · Resembles *Asterias rubens* but
distinguished from it by the densely packed spines on the dorsal surface
and presence of single papulae in spaces between spines.

Abundance & distribution
Occurs around Scotland and
south-west Ireland, and in the
Irish Sea. Distribution is from
the Arctic to the Irish Sea.

Marthasterias glacialis (Linnaeus)
Spiny starfish

Description · May reach 80 cm diameter, usually with five arms, occasionally eight. Disc small; arms are long, tapering distally to blunt tips. Arms
have five conspicuous, longitudinal rows of heavy spines, one mid-dorsal
and two, one upper marginal and one lower marginal, on each side. Each
larger spine surrounded by wreath of granular material, a cluster of crossed
pedicellariae. More smaller spines distributed between three main rows.
Animal greenish-grey, pale blue, brownish, yellow, or even red. Spines
usually white and pedicellarial cushion may be whitish, grey, or brown.
Ventral surface pale. **Habitat & ecology** · May occur low on shore, but
generally sublittoral down to 180 m depth (rarely exceeds 50 m). Usually
lives on rocky areas, but found on range of habitats, including muddy
substrates or gravel. Voracious predator and scavenger, feeding on fishes,
crustaceans, echinoderms such as *Asterias rubens*, and molluscs. Has pelagic
larval stage and around UK breeds in summer. In Mediterranean reported
to have two breeding seasons, one in summer, one in winter.

Abundance & distribution
Common on all British coasts
except eastern part of the
Channel and western North Sea.
Distributed from Finnmark to
the Cape Verde Islands,
Canaries, and the Azores,
including the Mediterranean. It
occurs in the Gulf of Guinea on
offshore islands.

Distinctive features

1. Usually five arms.
2. Bright orange above, paler below.

Distinctive features

1 Moderately sized starfish with five arms.
2. Dorsal surface covered in densely packed spines; single papulae in spaces between.

Distinctive features

1. Conspicuous, longitudinal rows of heavy spines along arms.
2. Large spines surrounded by a 'cushion' of pedicellariae.

Stichastrella rosea (Müller)

Description · A moderately sized starfish growing up to 30 cm in diameter. It has a small disc and five gently tapering, stiff, slender, blunt-ending arms. The dorsal surface is covered in plates that are conspicuously arranged in irregular longitudinal and transverse rows. The dorsal surface is coloured pink, orangey-red or yellowish. The ventral surface is pale.
Habitat & ecology · Sublittoral species, found from 4–366 m depth on sand, sandy mud, shelly sand, or stones. It breeds August–September and has a pelagic larva.

Abundance & distribution
An uncommon species, found around all coasts of Britain except for the Channel and southern North Sea. Distribution is from the Lofoten Islands to the Bay of Biscay.

Class Ophiuroidea (brittlestars)

The **Ophiuroidea** are characterised by five long, slender, and flexible arms radiating from a distinct, flattened, and typically almost circular central disc. The disc regions between the arms correspond to **interradii**. The mouth, at the centre of the disc underside, is bordered by five interradial **jaws** whose tips bear **teeth** in a single or double row (**teeth papillae**). The **aboral** disc surface is characterised by a series of calcareous plates or scales, the pattern of which is often helpful in their identification. The central, or **primary plate** is surrounded by concentric circles of **secondary plates**, and pairs of **radial shield** plates lying adjacent to the base of each arm on the aboral surface. These aboral plates, except for the radial shields, are often covered with scales, teeth, small spines, or granulations. The flexibility of the arms is due to their 'segmented' structure, each segment being constructed of four plates,

one **dorsal**, one **ventral**, and two **lateral**. Segments usually carry fans of rigid or articulated **spines** on each side. On the underside of each arm there are two series of tube feet which extend through pores or holes in each segment; these holes can be closed off by flaps (**tentacle scales**). The **madreporite** in ophiuroids is on the oral surface, forming one of the **oral shields** that partially enclose the mouth.

The ophiuroids comprise the largest class of living echinoderms, with about 1800 species worldwide but only about 20 around British coasts, where they are usually found on the lower shore or subtidally on soft or rocky substrates, and also burrowed in softer sediments. During their breeding season enormous numbers may be found, albeit for only a few days, congregated around boulders and rocks partially embedded in muddy sand. The class is divided into two orders, **Ophiurae** and **Euryalae**.

Distinctive features
1. Gently tapering, stiff, slender arms.
2. Dorsal surface covered in plates in longitudinal and transverse rows.

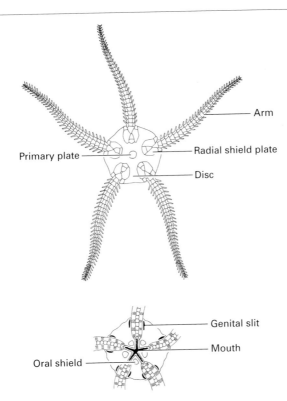

An ophiuroid in aboral view (*top*), showing some of the main external features, with an oral view of the disc (*bottom*).

<u>ORDER</u> **Ophiurae**

<u>FAMILY</u> **Ophiolepidae**

Ophiura albida Forbes

Description · Small brittlestar, with disc diameter up to 15 mm. Disc is covered with coarse scales. Radial shields small, and usually nearly joined in their outer part. Length of arms is about four times disc diameter. Dorsal and ventral plates of arms have convex outer edge. There are combs of 8–12 short papillae at base of each arm, and three spines on each side of each arm segment. Usually reddish-brown, with pair of white marks at base of each arm. **Habitat & ecology** · Subtidal, generally on muddy sands or gravel or on silt covered rocks, usually in shallow water but sometimes down to 200 or even to 850 m depth. Breeds in summer and has a pelagic larva. This ophiuroid feeds on small food particles in the sediments. It also hosts the intermediate stages of several parasites of fish including flatworms and nematodes. **Similar species** · *O. robusta* may occur on the north-east coasts of Scotland. This species has very poorly developed combs of papillae on the arms.

Abundance & distribution
Common around all coasts of Britain. Distributed from northern Norway to the Mediterranean. Also occurs in the Azores and the Baltic, as far east as Bornholm. Does not occur in Greenland.

Ophiura ophiura (Linnaeus)

Description · Large brittlestar, up to 35 mm disc diameter. Upper disc surface has conspicuous scales. Radial shields large, about half disc radius and may just touch above base of arms. Arm length about 3.5 times disc diameter. Dorsal plates of arms rectangular in shape, and towards disc 4–5 times broader than long. Ventral plates of arms twice as broad as long, with convex outer edge. They are not contiguous but separated by pair of sharply defined, pore-shaped grooves. Pair of combs of up to 30 papillae occurs at base of each arm. Three spines may be found on each side of each arm segment. Often reddish or reddish-brown, greyish-brown, or sandy orange, may have spotted appearance. Ventral surface generally pale. **Habitat & ecology** · Lower shore to about 200 m depth, on sand or muddy sand. Active species that may live 5–6 years. Breeds in summer around Britain and has pelagic larva. Can feed in variety of ways, either as scavenger or predator or by collecting food particles from water column.

Abundance & distribution
Common all around Britain. Distributed from the Lofoten Islands off Norway to the Mediterranean and as far south as Madeira. Occurs on Danish coasts but not in the Baltic.

<u>FAMILY</u> **Ophiocomidae**

Ophiocomina nigra (Abildgaard)

Description · Large brittlestar with a disc of up to 25 mm in diameter. The disc lacks scales and plates and appears finely granular. The dorsal arm plates are broad and rounded, the ventral arm plates are rounded on the outside edge but obtuse on the inner. There are 5–7 fairly long spines on each side of each arm segment. The length of the arms is up to five times the disc diameter. The colour in life may be black, brown, grey or even pink, and may be spotted. **Habitat & ecology** · Subtidal, 0–400 m, though rare below 100 m. Often found on stony or rocky bottoms, in areas sheltered or slightly exposed to current. May occur at high densities with other species such as *Ophiothrix fragilis* and is also tolerant of reduced salinities. Noted for being a good climber. It may extend its arms into the water as a suspension feeder or eat algae or dead animals. It has a pelagic larva.

Abundance & distribution
Common, locally abundant, all around the west and south coasts of Britain. On the east this species only occurs as far south as the coast of Durham. Elsewhere it is distributed from Norway to the Mediterranean and the Azores.

Distinctive features

1. Disc covered with coarse scales.
2. A pair of white marks at the base of each arm.
3. Radial shields small.
4. A pair of combs of 8–12 papillae at the base of each arm.

Distinctive features

1. Large disc.
2. Conspicuous scales on disc dorsal surface.
3. Ventral plates of arms separated by pore-shaped grooves.
4. Pair of combs at base of each arms with 30 papillae.

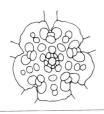

Distinctive features

1. Large brittlestar.
2. Smooth disc without scales or shields.

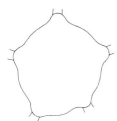

Ophiopsila aranea Forbes

Description · Medium to large brittlestar with a disc diameter of up to 15 mm. The disc lacks scales and appears very finely granular. The radial shields are separated and fairly narrow and straight. Arm length is proportionally long, up to seven times the disc diameter. The dorsal plates of the arms are elongate oval-shaped, more rounded further out. The ventral plates of the arms have a slightly concave outer edge. There are 6–8 small spines on each side of each arm segment.**Habitat & ecology** · Subtidal, 25–185 m depth. Occurs on hard substrates, especially in crevices from which it extends its long arms. At the Mewstone Ledges in Plymouth Sound, SW Britain it occurs in crevices in shale. The arms are very fragile. **Similar species** · Closely resembles *O. annulosa*, though this species has 11–12 spines on each side of each arm segment.

Abundance & distribution
Rare but locally abundant. Only occurs off south-west coast, especially at Mewstone Ledges and Stoke Point grounds near Plymouth. Distribution includes west coast of Ireland, and from Channel to coast of North Africa and Mediterranean. Also found in Azores.

FAMILY **Ophiotrichidae**

Ophiothrix fragilis (Abildgaard)

Description · Large, disc up to 20 mm diameter. Disc (illustrated) usually covered with short spinelets and longer, slender spines. Radial shields conspicuous, large (up to two-thirds disc radius), naked, separated, roughly triangular. Arm length up to five times disc diameter. Dorsal plates of arms approximately diamond-shaped, with more or less distinct longitudinal keel. Ventral plates rectangular, with depression proximally and slightly concave outer edges. Arms distinctly spiny, each segment generally with seven glassy spines, on each side, which increase in length from innermost to outermost spines. Colour varies from uniform dark violet, to various shades of red, yellow, orange, brownish-grey, or almost white. Arms often banded light and dark. **Habitat & ecology** · From lower shore generally to 150 m, though as deep as 350 m. On shore and in shallow water may be under boulders or amongst other sessile animals. Subtidally, on range of substrates, but including rocks, coarse gravels, sandy or shelly sediments, and even mud. Offshore, may form large beds with densities over 10 000 individuals/m². Separate sexes. Around Britain breeds in summer, producing pelagic larva. Feeds by holding several arms into water column and capturing food particles, or feeds on small invertebrates such as polychaete worms, crustaceans, and mussels. **Similar species** · *O. luetkeni* occurs off west coast of Ireland in water over 150 m deep.

Abundance & distribution
Very common around all coasts of Britain. Distribution extends from Lofoten Islands and Iceland down the coast of Africa to the Cape of Good Hope. Also occurs in the Mediterranean and Azores.

Distinctive features

1. Disc lacks scales.
2. Radial shields narrow, separate.
3. Arms long in proportion to disc diameter.
4. Lives in crevices with arms extended into water.

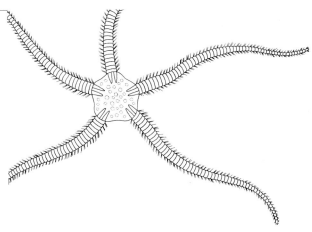

Distinctive features

1. Arms with conspicuous glassy spines.
2. Large, conspicuous, separate radial shields.
3. Disc covered in small spines.

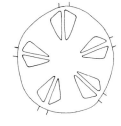

FAMILY **Ophiactidae**

Ophiopholis aculeata (Linnaeus)

Description · Large brittlestar, with a disc up to 20 mm diameter. Dorsal surface covered in plates separated by small, granular scales and spinelets. Plates may form the shape of a ten-pointed star. Radial shields not visible. The body may bulge between the arms. Dorsal plates of arms large, transverse oval shape, surrounded by small, granular plates. Ventral plates of arms almost rectangular, may be separated by a small depression. 6–7 thick, compressed spines each side of each arm segment. Arm length up to four times disc diameter. Colour highly variable but usually various shades of red or purple. Disc may be bluish, arms often banded with paler and darker colours. **Habitat & ecology** · Subtidal to 1880 m depth, though rare below 300 m. On hard substrates often in crevices or holes in rocks with just the arms projecting out. Breeds June-July and has a pelagic larva. **Similar species** · *O. balli* is very similar though smaller when mature. Juvenile specimens are very difficult to distinguish from *O. aculeata*.

Abundance & distribution
Common around most coasts of Britain but rarer off the south coast. Distribution is circumpolar but in the Atlantic this species reaches its southern limit on the south coast of Britain.

FAMILY **Amphiuridae**

Amphipholis squamata (Delle Chiaje)

Description · Extremely small. Disc is circular and up to only 4–5 mm in diameter. Disc is covered in small scales on dorsal and ventral sides and radial shields are up to a third of diameter of disc and joined throughout their length. Length of the arms is up to four times diameter of disc. Dorsal plates of arms are rounded triangular-shaped; ventral plates are triangular with excavate outer edges. There are four, farther out three, short conical spines on each side of each segment of arms. Colour greyish-white or bluish-grey. **Habitat & ecology** · Found intertidally on lower shore but further up shore in rock pools. Lives under stones and rocks, but especially common among coralline algae. Subtidally, reported as occurring down to 250 m. Like *Amphiura filiformis*, it is bioluminescent. It is also hermaphroditic, and viviparous. A parasitic copepod, *Cancerilla tubulata* lives on ventral side of arms of *A. squamata* and another species lives in the bursa.

Abundance & distribution
Very common around all coasts of Britain. This species has a cosmopolitan distribution in temperate and warm seas.

Amphiura brachiata (Montagu)

Description · Medium sized, disc reaching 13 mm diameter. Disc covered in scales on dorsal and ventral surfaces. Radial shields on dorsal surface small, smooth, separated. Scales of ventral surface and margins of dorsal surface have small tubercle, giving them slightly spiny appearance. Arms very thin and flexible, up to 15 times disc diameter. Plates on dorsal surface of arms short, nearly rhombic; those on ventral surface also short and nearly rectangular. In proximal parts of arm these may bear a median keel and pair of lateral keels. Each arm segment bears up to 12–13 short, conical, arm spines on each side. Bluish-grey to brownish-grey. **Habitat & ecology** · Lower shore and subtidally to 40 m. Lives in sand buried to about 10 cm, with its long flexible arms protruding from surface. May be found with urchin, *Echinocardium cordatum*. Two species may be found living commensally with it: bivalve, *Mysella bidentata*, and polynoid polychaete, *Harmothoe lunulata*.

Abundance & distribution
Common, locally abundant. Occurs on south and west coasts of Britain. Distributed around coast of Ireland, and from west coast of Sweden to French coast. Also reported from west coast of Denmark and Dogger Bank.

Distinctive features

1. Dorsal surface of disc covered in large plates.
2. Radial shields not visible.
3. Often in crevices or holes in rock.

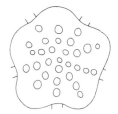

Distinctive features

1. Very small, pale.
2. Scale-covered disc.
3. Radial shields joined throughout length.
4. 3–4 conical spines on each side of each arm segment.

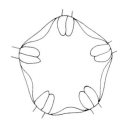

Distinctive features

1. Scale-covered disc.
2. Scales on ventral surface and margin of disc have tubercles.
3. Up to 13 short conical spines on each arm segment.
4. Usually buried in sand with arms projecting from seabed.

Similar species · *A. chiajei*, but lacks tubercles on ventral and marginal scales and only has up to six spines on each side of each arm segment. *A. filiformis* has similar habit to *A. chiajei* in lying buried with its long delicate arms protruding. It only has scales on dorsal surface, ventral surface being delicate and easily damaged. Like preceding species, *A. filiformis* is reddish- or greyish-brown; is also bioluminescent.

Class Echinoidea (sea urchins)

In the **Echinoidea** the skeletal **ossicles** are closely jointed to provide a usually rigid **test** which may be **spherical, ovoid**, or flattened, and **discoid** in shape. The test in some groups exhibits the perfect **pentasymmetry** which is characteristic of the echinoderms as a whole; this occurs in the **regular urchins**. Other groups, however, have a secondary superficial **bilateral symmetry** and comprise the **irregular urchins**. Five rows of **ambulacral plates** are penetrated by holes through which the **tube feet** emerge, one from each hole. The five **interambulacral plates** are usually covered with often very mobile **spines** which articulate on a rounded knob or **spine boss**. Between the spines up to five distinct types of short-stalked, three-jawed **pedicellariae** are usually present, together with small, flexible, stalked, globose **sphaeridia** which may function as **statocysts**. In regular urchins the aboral **anus** is surrounded by five large **genital plates**, one of these forming the **madreporite**, and five smaller **ocular plates**. On the oral (lower) surface the mouth is bordered by a tough but flexible **buccal membrane**, with the complex and highly characteristic five-rayed jaw or toothed apparatus (**Aristotle's lantern**) situated at its centre. Five pairs of **buccal**

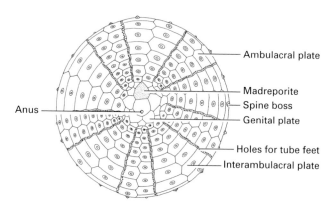

Anus —
— Ambulacral plate
— Madreporite
— Spine boss
— Genital plate
— Holes for tube feet
— Interambulacral plate

The test of a sea urchin with spines removed, showing the main external features viewed aborally.

SUBCLASS **Euechinoidea** | SUPERORDER **Echinacea** | ORDER **Diadematoidea** |
SUBORDER **Camarodonta**

FAMILY **Echinidae**

Echinus esculentus Linnaeus

Description · Large, radially symmetrical, with globe-shaped test that is sometimes depressed or sub-conical. Test usually red, but may be pink, pale purple, or even pale green. May reach 176 mm in diameter. Spines fairly short (a centimetre or so), all of same size, and usually reddish with a violet point. When the urchin is dead, spines usually all fall off and the test is covered with white lumps or tubercles. **Habitat & ecology** · Generally on rocks, boulders, and other hard substrata from low intertidal down to 40 m. Rarer deeper, but recorded to 1200 m. Omnivorous, feeding on algae, and encrusting animals such as bryozoans and barnacles. Parasitised by nematodes, flatworms; polychaete, *Flabelligera affinis*, lives amongst its spines. Breeds early summer and has pelagic larva. Gonads eaten in some European countries. Has been over-collected for marine curio trade on British coasts.

Abundance & distribution
Very common. Occurs all around Britain and Ireland but absent from the eastern part of the Channel. Also found from northern Norway and Iceland to Portugal. Does not occur in Mediterranean.

tube feet emerge from the buccal membrane, which also has five pairs of branched **gills** situated at its margin. Irregular urchins do not have this jaw apparatus, and their mouth and anus have moved to different sites on the test.

Sea urchins typically feed by browsing on seaweeds, including some of the larger brown algae. As with other groups, echinoid taxonomy is currently under review because of recent investigations. Traditionally echinoids are subdivided into five orders, of which the **Cidaroidea** and **Diadematoidea** are radially symmetrical regular urchins, while the **Cassiduloidea**, **Clypeasteroidea**, and **Spatangoidea** comprise the secondarily bilaterally symmetrical irregular urchins. Neither the Cidaroidea nor Cassiduloidea have known representatives occurring in shallow European waters. In more recent classification schemes the cidaroid echinoids have been placed within the subclass **Perischoechinoidea**, and the other species in the subclass **Euechinoidea**. The majority of European echinoids have been grouped within the superorder **Echinacea**, which includes most common regular urchins, and the superorder **Gnathostomata**, containing irregular urchins, including the order **Clypeasteroidea**.

Distinctive features

1. Large urchin.
2. Globe-like shape.
3. Spines fairly short and of equal length.

Paracentrotus lividus (Lamarck)

Description · A small- to medium-sized urchin with a radial test that is rounded but compressed. The primary spines are fairly long and robust and appear to form longitudinal rows. The test can be up to 7 cm in diameter. The colour of the urchin is highly variable but can be dark violet, brownish, or olive green. The test is green. **Habitat & ecology** · This species is found on the low shore boring into rocks, in Ireland usually in rock pools, down to shallow sublittoral depths. The holes just fit the urchin and there are usually many individuals in a single locality. They provide a painful surprise for unsuspecting bathers. In many localities in Ireland and throughout the Mediterranean this species has been collected for food. The gonads are considered a delicacy in some European countries.

Abundance & distribution
Locally abundant. Generally does not occur in Britain but may be in a few scattered localities off west coast of Scotland. Occurs on west coast of Ireland, south to Morocco. Especially common in Mediterranean, Canary Islands, and Azores.

Psammechinus miliaris (Gmelin)

Description · A fairly small urchin that grows to a maximum of 50 mm diameter. The test is radially symmetrical and rather depressed. The spines are closely spaced, short, and robust. The test and spines are usually greenish but the spines have a violet point. **Habitat & ecology** · Generally found intertidally under rocks and stones, and amongst seagrass and algae. It may occur down to a depth of 100 m. Reproduces in early summer and has a pelagic larva. **Similar species** · Resembles small *Echinus esculentus* and it may form natural hybrids with this species. *E. esculentus* has a more globe-shaped test than *P. miliaris* and is generally much larger. *P. microtuberculatus* occurs in the Mediterranean.

Abundance & distribution
Common. Found all around coasts of Britain and Ireland. Elsewhere, it occurs from Trondheim Fjord to Baltic and North Seas. Also found in Iceland, on the coast of Morocco, and the Azores. Does not occur

---

SUPERORDER **Gnathostomata** | ORDER **Clypeasteroida**

FAMILY **Spatangidae**

Echinocardium cordatum (Pennant)

Description · Fawn-coloured, heart-shaped, with thin test and dense covering of yellow spines. Can reach up to 90 mm but usually smaller. There is conspicuous indentation in one end of urchin that marks anterior ambulacral plate. **Habitat & ecology** · Buried in sand, at depths of about 10–20 cm. Occurs intertidally down to about 230 m. Often occurs in high numbers. Its presence may be detected by a depression at the surface. It lives in burrow and feeds by extending long tube feet of anterior ambulacral plate to surface through a hole, which extends to bottom of the surface depression. Breeds in summer and has pelagic larva. A small amphipod, *Urothoë marina*, and bivalve, *Tellimya ferruginosa*, may be found with it. **Similar species** · Two in British Isles, *E. flavescens* and *E. pennatifidum*. Neither have conspicuous indentation at front of urchin. *E. flavescens* has large spines scattered in interambulacral areas on dorsal surface, *E. pennatifidum* only has long spines in anterior ambulacral area and nowhere else on dorsal surface.

Abundance & distribution
Common around all coasts of Britain. In the Atlantic, found south from Tromsö in Norway to South Africa. It occurs all around the world except in polar seas, hence is not found in Greenland or Iceland.

Distinctive features

1. Radial test that is rounded but compressed.
2. Primary spines long and robust, in longitudinal rows.
3. Usually inhabits shallow holes bored into rock.

in Greenland or the Mediterranean.

Distinctive features

1. Radially symmetrical test.
2. Test is depressed.
3. Size up to 50 mm diameter.

Distinctive features

1. Heart-shaped test.
2. Dense covering of yellow spines when alive.
3. Indentation in one end of the test.
4. Lives buried in sand.

Spatangus purpureus Müller

Description · A large, bilaterally symmetrical, somewhat flattened, heart-shaped urchin. May grow up to 12 cm in length. The test is covered in fine spines with larger, long curved spines projecting from the dorsal surface. This urchin is a conspicuous violet or purple colour and the larger spines may appear whitish. **Habitat & ecology** · Found from lower tidal zone to 900 m depth. Generally occurs buried in coarse sand or gravel, feeding on detritus and other species such as *Echinocyamus pusillus*. Breeds in summer and has a pelagic larva. A small bivalve mollusc, *Montacuta substriata*, may occur on the spines of this urchin.

Abundance & distribution
Common around all coasts of Britain though may be locally abundant. Elsewhere it occurs from the North Cape and Norway down to the north coast of Africa, including the Azores and Mediterranean. It does not occur in Greenland.

Class Holothurioidea (sea-cucumbers)

Holothurians are elongate echinoderms, rounded or slightly oval in section, with their lower (ventral) surface marked by three longitudinal rows of tube feet (**trivium**) and their upper (dorsal) surface by two rows (**bivium**), although tube feet may occur anywhere over the body surface or be completely absent. The skin of sea cucumbers may be thick and tough, or thin and delicate. Although it contains large numbers of calcareous **ossicles** or **deposits**, it is usually flexible. Beneath the skin a layer of **circular muscles** has five **radial muscles** which extend the full body length.

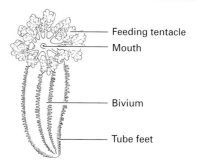

The general external appearance of a sea cucumber.

The mouth is anterior, sometimes slightly dorsal or ventral, and surrounded by variable

ORDER **Aspidochirota**

FAMILY **Holothuriidae**

Holothuria forskali Delle Chiaje **Cotton-spinner**

Description · Large, growing up to 30 cm in length. Dorsal surface is rounded, the skin thick, soft, and covered in conical papillae. Ventral surface is flattened, with 3–4 longitudinal series of tube feet. The middle series may be divided in two by a naked median space. Dorsal surface often black, though some individuals are paler, tending to brown. Tips of papillae white to pale blue. Ventral surface often a dirty yellow or pale brownish colour. Has up to 20 small, shovel-shaped tentacles around the mouth. These are usually yellow but may be black. **Habitat & ecology** · Found on rocky substrates from extreme low water to about 70 m depth. Favours rocks covered in a layer of silt. Breeds in summer. When irritated it may eject sticky white threads that dart through the water like arrows to entangle potential predators. In the Mediterranean a parasitic fish may be found living inside this sea cucumber. The fish enters and exits the sea cucumber via the anus.

Abundance & distribution
Common along south-west coast of Britain and west coast of Ireland. Found around Atlantic coasts of Europe, in the Mediterranean, and in the Azores and Madeira.

Distinctive features

1. Heart-shaped, flattened urchin.
2. Violet or purple in colour.
3. Dorsal surface covered in short spines with some longer curved spines present.

numbers of **feeding tentacles** which may be bushy, feathery, **digitate** (finger-like), or shield-shaped; tentacle shape, constant at the order level, is thus of taxonomic significance. The mouth, tentacles, and anterior portion of the body comprise an **introvert**, which can be retracted by special **retractor muscles**. The mouth leads into an **oesophagus** that is surrounded by a **calcareous ring**, usually consisting of five **radial** and five **interradial** pieces. Behind the calcareous ring is the **water vascular ring**, from which radial **water vessels** lead off to connect with **tentacle canals**. In some groups **tentacle ampullae** arise from the tentacle canals; if present, they lie free in the body cavity. The **gut** is long and looped,

ending in a **cloaca** in which the **respiratory trees** are located.

Feeding strategies are diverse in members of this group, holothurians being filter-, suspension-, or deposit-feeders. The animals are sedentary in habit, typically occurring on softer sediments, beneath boulders, in crevices, or amongst algal holdfasts. Representatives of three orders are found in British waters:

Aspidochirota Holothurians with well-developed respiratory trees and shield-shaped oral tentacles.

Dendrochirota Holothurians with bushy oral tentacles.

Apoda Holothurians with no tube feet.

Distinctive features

1. Dorsal surface of body covered in conical papillae.
2. Ventral surface flattened, with 3–4 longitudinal series of tube feet.
3. Small, shovel-shaped tentacles around mouth.
4. May eject sticky fluid if handled.

ORDER **Dendrochirota**

FAMILY **Cucumariidae**

Aslia lefevrei (Barrois)

Description · Body almost cylindrical, with tube feet in distinct double rows though some occur between rows. Skin tough, leathery, and may be wrinkled, usually a brown to dirty brownish-white colour, turning black on exposure to air. Body up to 15 cm long. Usually only tentacles and anterior part of the body are visible. Up to ten tentacles, mottled dark brown, grey, or black, with pale edges. Each tentacle, up to 10 cm long, consists of a main branch with many irregular branches. **Habitat & ecology** · Occurs in crevices from intertidal to a maximum of about 30 m depth. **Similar species** · Very similar to *Pawsonia saxicola* but this species has distinctive white body coloration.

Abundance & distribution Not common. Occurs in scattered localities on the west coasts of Britain and Ireland. Locally may be common (e.g. Plymouth). Elsewhere, only found on the Atlantic coasts of France.

Neopentadactyla mixta (Östergren)

Description · Body elongate, cylindrical, and tapering at both ends. Tentacles form two rings of ten, outer ring larger than inner ring. Tentacles finely arborescent, up to 10 cm long. Body up to 25 cm long, and either white with varying amounts of brown flecks on the tentacles, or yellowish-violet with dark tentacles. Tube feet in six longitudinal, double series along the body. **Habitat & ecology** · Lives in a burrow with its tentacles held in the passing current, usually in coarse gravel or maerl but also muddy or sandy bottoms. Found at depths of *c.*20–200 m. **Similar species** · *Thyone fusus*, but this only has a single ring of ten arborescent tentacles. It occurs in less exposed habitats than *Neopentadactyla* and is found in mud or shelly or sandy mud. The body is white, grey, or red and extremely delicate; tentacles are brown. Distributed all around Britain apart from the southern North Sea. Also from Trondheim in Norway to the Mediterranean and Madeira.

Abundance & distribution Uncommon but may be locally abundant. Found off south, west, and north-east coasts of Britain. Elsewhere it is known from the Faeroes, Norway, and the Atlantic coast of France.

ORDER **Apoda**

FAMILY **Synaptidae**

Labidoplax digitata (Montagu)

Description · A slender, soft-skinned species, up to 20–30 cm long. Each of the 12 tentacles possesses four short digits. There are no locomotory tube feet. Body is a dark pink, red, reddish-brown, or purple overall, though this may appear mottled with paler colour. The skin is barely translucent. The internal skeleton consists of small, three-dimensional, anchor-shaped structures, called deposits, which have short handles. **Habitat & ecology** · Found burrowed in fine, muddy sand between the lower shore and sublittoral depths of about 70 m. A sedentary species feeding on organic surface deposits. Breeds in summer and produces a pelagic larva. **Similar species** · May be confused with *Leptosynapta inhaerens*, but in this species the tentacles possess 10–14 short, finger-like digits and the body surface is both distinctly sticky to the touch and partially transparent.

Abundance & distribution Not common, this sea cucumber is found on the west coasts of Britain from Brixham to the Shetland Islands. Found in Ireland, and on the Atlantic coasts of Europe southwards to the Mediterranean.

Distinctive features
1. Ten mottled, dark, branched tentacles.
2. Tube feet in distinct double rows.
3. Body brown to dirty brownish-white.

Distinctive features
1. Elongate, cylindrical body tapered at both ends.
2. Concentric rings of ten arborescent tentacles.

Distinctive features
1. Oral end with 12 tentacles, each with four short digits.
2. Skin very slightly translucent, dark pink, red, reddish-brown, or purple.

Leptosynapta inhaerens (Müller)

Description · Slender, soft, worm-like species that lacks tube feet. Body is pale pink and translucent with longitudinal stripes that represent longitudinal bands of muscle. There are 10–13 tentacles, usually 12. Tentacles have 5–7 pairs of digits, with the outermost ones being longer than the inner, and a single unpaired terminal digit that is the longest. Length is up to 30 cm, but usually 10–18 cm. **Habitat & ecology** · Lives buried in mud, sand, or gravel from the intertidal to about 50 m depth. May be found amongst detached algae or in seagrass beds. It is a hermaphrodite, and though it has small eggs undergoes direct development. Numerous different parasites or commensal species, from several phyla, may be found on or in this holothurian. **Similar species** · Resembles *Labidoplax digitata* though this species tends to be darker and more opaque than *L. inhaerens* and has fewer digits on the tentacles. Also similar to *Leptosynapta bergensis*, which has 8–11 pairs of digits on the tentacles.

Abundance & distribution
Common along the west coast of Britain from Plymouth to the Shetland Islands. Also recorded from north-east Britain (Firth of Forth, St Andrews). Elsewhere distributed from northern Norway to Brittany.

Distinctive features

1. Soft, slender body.
2. Tube feet absent
3. Usually 12 tentacles at end of body, each with 5–7 pairs of digits and one unpaired terminal digit.

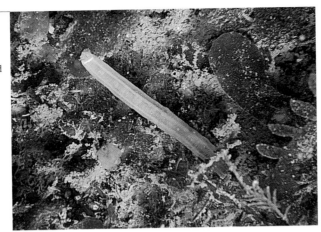

Ascidians and fishes

Phylum Chordata

Subphylum Tunicata (Urochordata) (sea squirts, tunicates)

Class Ascidiacea (ascidians)

Though not looking like chordates as adults, nearly all **tunicates** have **tadpole**-like larvae with **chordate** tails. The adult body of **ascidians** is enclosed by a **test** (**tunic**) produced by the underlying **mantle**. Depending upon the species, the test may be thick or thin, opaque or transparent, clean or with sand grains or various invertebrates attached to it. There are two openings to the body, an inhalant **oral siphon** and exhalant **atrial siphon**, both of which can be contracted and closed by a **sphincter** of muscles. Much of the body cavity is occupied by a basket- or mesh-like **branchial sac** (**pharynx**) which serves both as a **respiratory structure** and a **filter-feeding** device, to trap particulate material suspended in the water. The branchial sac wall is perforated by large numbers of ciliated **stigmata**; the cilia create the water currents that enter the ascidian body through the oral siphon with its ring of **oral tentacles**, pass through the stigmata, and then exit via

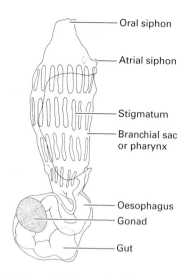

Some of the main features of a solitary ascidian.

the atrial siphon. At the base of the branchial sac a short **oesophagus** leads into the looped **gut**, the anus opening just below the atrial siphon. All ascidians are **hermaphroditic**, the gonads generally being located within or close to the loop of the gut. Larger, solitary ascidians generally shed their eggs into the sea, but smaller species (including most colonial forms) typically incubate their embryos, either in the atria or the basal part of the test.

Ascidians are sessile chordates, most living in intertidal to shallow coastal waters permanently attached to almost any suitable

---

ORDER **Enterogona** | SUBORDER **Aplousobranchia**

FAMILY **Cionidae**

Ciona intestinalis (Linnaeus)

Description · Solitary ascidian. Body is elongated and cylindrical but can contract to some extent. Test is soft, smooth, and transparent with a gelatinous texture. It is attached to substratum by bottom of left side or by base. Branchial siphon is terminal, long, and tubular, with eight lobes. Atrial siphon is just below the branchial and generally shorter in length with lobes. Yellowish or yellowish-green, and there may be bright yellow around margins of siphons with orange spots between lobes. It can grow up to 12 cm long. **Habitat & ecology** · Found on low shore and subtidally to over 500 m depth. *C. intestinalis* grows on rocks, stones, and algae. It is particularly found on man-made structures such as harbour structures, buoys, and ship bottoms. It may be through attachment to ships that this species is so widespread. Once the animal has exceeded 2 cm in height it reproduces throughout year. The tadpole larva can remain swimming for up to a day and a half.

Abundance & distribution
Common, locally abundant. Found all around Britain and Ireland. Distributed from Arctic Norway to the Mediterranean. Also occurs in the western Atlantic, Pacific, and Indian Oceans.

type of substrate, such as under large boulders, in permanent rock pools, under rock overhangs, on algal fronds or among their holdfasts, on mollusc shells, or on pier pilings. Some larger species are solitary, others form densely packed aggregations or communities, but many are colonial with the constituent individuals (**zooids**) living in a communal tunic. In colonial ascidians the zooids, which are produced by **budding**, often live in an ordered series, each with its own oral siphon but sharing a communal atrial siphon with other members of the colony. Zooids may grow from stolons or a basal mat, project from a common tunic, or be fully embedded in it. The identification of ascidians often depends upon a microscopic examination of the zooids, though some species have characteristic external features that are reliable enough for them to be identified. In north-west European waters representatives of two orders are widespread; in the **Enterogona**, with ten families, the gonads are essentially situated in the gut loop, whereas in the **Pleurogona**, with three families, gonads are associated with the mantle wall.

Further reading

Knight-Jones, E. W. & Ryland, J. S. (1990). Hemi-chordata and Urochordata. In *The marine fauna of the British Isles and North-West Europe* (eds P. J. Hayward & J. S. Ryland), Vol. 2, pp. 872–904. Clarendon Press, Oxford.
Millar, R. H. (1970). British ascidians. *Synopses of the British Fauna, New Series*, 1, 1–92.

Subphylum Cephalo-chordata (lancelets)

In the lancelets the larval **notochord** persists into the adult form and there is no cartilaginous or body skeleton. The slender body is tapered at both ends, the adult generally resembling a fish with no paired fins, eyes, or nostrils. The **mouth** is located ventrally between a pair of lateral expansions that comprise an **oral hood**, fringed with **cirri**. The pharynx forms a perforated **branchial sac**, surrounded by an **atrial chamber** for about two-thirds of the body length, ending at a small **atriopore**. The edges of the flat ventral surface below the atrial chamber form **metapleural folds** that extend from the mouth back to behind the atriopore. The **dorsal fin** extends the full body length to merge directly with the **caudal fin**, a **ventral** (**median**) **fin** extending forwards from the caudal fin to end at the atriopore.

The cephalochordates contain only a single order, **Amphioxi**, with examples of only one family, the **Branchiostomidae**, being found in British waters.

Further reading

Ryland, J. S. (1990). Cephalochordata and Euchordata. In *The marine fauna of the British Isles and North-West Europe* (eds P. J. Hayward & J. S. Ryland), Vol. 2, pp. 905–51. Clarendon Press, Oxford.

Distinctive features

1. Solitary.
2. Elongated, soft, gelatinous test.
3. Attached by bottom of left side or base.
4. Transparent, often with yellow or orange markings around siphons.

FAMILY **Diazonidae**

Diazona violacea Savigny

Description · A colonial ascidian. It forms globular, or rather flattened colonies up to 20 cm tall and 40 cm diameter, with the base narrower than the top. Individual zooids within the colonies may be 5 cm high, their branchial region, about 2 cm long, usually extending above the colony surface. Terminal inhalant and exhalant openings are close together at the tip of the protruded branchial region. The colonies have a translucent green colour with yellowish or cream-coloured zooids. **Habitat & ecology** · Grows on rocks, boulders, or stones, often in stronger currents, at sublittoral depths of 30–200 m.

Abundance & distribution
Locally common. Found off south-west and west coasts of Britain and all around Ireland. Distributed south to the Mediterranean.

FAMILY **Clavelinidae**

Clavelina lepadiformis (Müller) **Light-bulb ascidian**

Description · Colonial ascidian in which the individual zooids are almost free. The zooids are connected at the base through a stolon-like network of test material. Colonies often form clusters, though only a few individuals may be found in a loose array. The zooids are elongate and almost cylindrical. The branchial siphon is terminal; the atrial siphon is quite close to the branchial. Test is smooth and remarkably transparent. Through it intensely bright-white lines run the length of the zooid and around the margin of the siphons. These mark certain internal structures. In some specimens these lines may be yellow or pink. The abdomen may be yellowish-brown and red eggs or tadpole larvae may be visible through the test. Grows up to about 3 cm long. **Habitat & ecology** · Occasionally in rock pools on the low shore but generally in shallow subtidal habitats down to 50 m. Often found growing on rock, especially ledges, but also on stones and man-made structures such as harbour walls.

Abundance & distribution
Common. Found all around Britain and Ireland. Distributed from Norway to the Mediterranean and Azores Islands.

FAMILY **Polyclinidae**

Aplidium proliferum (Milne Edwards)

Description · Compound ascidian forming fleshy, ovoid or club-shaped colonies. These may form several clumps arising from single stalk-like base. Colonies up to 4–5 cm high. Zooids 8–12 mm long, arranged irregularly around several common pores (cloacae). Colony tests smooth, transparent, yellowish, greyish, or orange. Zooids may be bright red. Has large tadpole larva, with body (minus tail) up to 1 mm long. **Habitat & ecology** · Lower shore and subtidally in depths of less than 50 m. Often occurs under rocks, stones, and shells; also grows on algae or sponges. **Similar species** · Encrusting *A. nordmanni* may be same species. It lacks stalked base of *A. proliferum* and forms broad, lobate, flat-topped colonies. *A. glabrum* and *A. densum* have non-stalked colonies with sand coated sides. *A. pallidum* forms small, flat, yellowish-buff colonies. *A. punctum* forms slender club-shaped, stalked colonies, often in rock crevices. These are attached to sand covered base. *Morchellium argus* also very similar, but stalks sand covered, and colony tops cream-coloured with red spots.

Abundance & distribution
Common. Occurs on the south and west coasts of Britain and all around Ireland. Distributed from western Norway to the Mediterranean.

Distinctive features

1. Colonial ascidian.
2. Colonies globular or flattened with base narrower than top.
3. Colony a translucent green, with yellowish or cream zooids.
4. Branchial region of individuals, with inhalant and exhalant apertures close together, protrude above general colonial surface.

Distinctive features

1. Colonial ascidian in which the zooids are nearly free.
2. Shape elongated and roughly cylindrical.
3. Test transparent, usually with bright white, sometimes yellow or pink, lines running along the length and around the siphons.

Distinctive features

1. Compound ascidian.
2. Colonies ovoid or club-shaped, several arising from common stalked base.
3. Smooth, transparent test, yellow, grey, or orange.

Morchellium argus (Milne Edwards)

Description · Colonial ascidian. Colonies of this species have an elongated, cone-shaped stalk, up to 1 cm in diameter, and a club-shaped to rounded head up to 3 cm across. They can reach 8 cm long but are usually around 4 cm. Where the stalk is attached to the rock it sends out branching fibres. The stalk is usually covered in fine sand. The head is transparent and generally a creamy colour but with numerous fine red spots. The stalk is red with a yellowish tint under the sand grains. **Habitat & ecology** · From low shore to shallow subtidal. Generally attached to sides and undersides of stones, rock, and rock overhangs. Particularly common under wave-swept overhangs at low water mark. **Similar species** · Resembles species of *Aplidium*, but the sand covered stalk and red spots on the head are distinctive.

Abundance & distribution
Common, locally abundant. Found on the west and south-west coasts of Britain, all around Ireland, and in north-west France.

Sidnyum turbinatum Fleming

Description · A colonial ascidian. The colonies are often club-shaped or globular, sometimes quite elongated, up to 40 mm high and 15 mm wide. Several usually arise from a network of creeping fibres. The colonies comprise 6–12 zooids arranged around a common cloacal opening, the margins of which may be raised and undulating. Individual zooids are about 5 mm long. The test is transparent and gelatinous, and an orange or greyish-white colour. **Habitat & ecology** · Found on the low shore and in shallow water, but may occur as deep as 200 m. It is usually attached to stones, rock, and algae, and is often in rock crevices. **Similar species** · *S. elegans*, but the colonies are broader and more cushion-like, with fewer occurring in one place.

Abundance & distribution
Frequent. Found all around the British Isles and Ireland but rare on North Sea coasts. Distributed from Norway to the Mediterranean.

FAMILY **Didemnidae**

Didemnum coriaceum (Von Drasche)

Description · Compound ascidian. The colonies are thin, hard, and encrusting, with a rough leathery surface. The colonies are up to 3–4 cm wide and about 2 mm thick. The zooids are usually grouped in clusters of 5–8 with a common cloacal opening. The surface of the colony has many pores in it. The colour varies from white or greyish to violet. **Habitat & ecology** · On lower shore and sublittorally on rocks, and on and underneath stones. Frequently inhabits kelp holdfasts. **Similar species** · The systematics of this group is confusing, and different species are very difficult to separate. *D. maculosum* can only be distinguished from *D. coriaceum* by characteristics of the tadpole larvae, otherwise they are the same. *D. fulgens* is also similar but tends to be thin and orange in colour.

Abundance & distribution
Locally common. Found on south and west coasts of Britain and all around Ireland. Distributed from western Norway to the Mediterranean.

Distinctive features

1. Colonial ascidian.
2. Elongated, cone-shaped stalk with a rounded head.
3. Stalk covered in fine sand grains.
4. Head creamy with fine red spots.

Distinctive features

1. Colonial, forming club-shaped or globular colonies.
2. 6–12 zooids arranged around central cloacal opening with raised undulating margins.

Distinctive features

1. Compound ascidian.
2. Colonies encrusting, to 2 mm thick.
3. Texture hard and leathery, coloured white, greyish, or violet.

Diplosoma spongiforme (Giard)

Description · Compound ascidian. The colonies form thick (*c.* 6 mm) encrusting, irregular, cushion-like mats somewhat resembling a sponge. The texture is soft and translucent, often a greyish colour, sometimes with whitish or blackish speckles. The individual zooids are tiny, up to about 1.5 mm long, and the siphons open at the surface of the colony as tiny pores. **Habitat & ecology** · Generally subtidal to 40 m depth, found growing on rock, often over other encrusting animals. Rarely grows on algae. **Similar species** · *D. listerianum* forms thin (< 2 mm) sheeting, transparent colonies with brown or grey speckles. It has common cloacal openings that are often raised. This species is generally found growing on algae or seagrasses. *D. singulare* forms small, thin, transparent colonies with yellowish-orange zooids (when alive).

Abundance & distribution
Locally common. Found off south-west and west coasts of Britain and Ireland. Distributed south to the Mediterranean.

Lissoclinum perforatum (Giard)

Description · A colonial species forming thin, encrusting, flattened sheets up to 2 mm thick, typically irregularly lobed but less than 3 cm across. The mouth openings of the individual ascidians appear as regularly distributed black spots over the colony surface, between which are the larger, slit-like atriopores (exhalant apertures) that are shared by several individuals and have a coarser pattern. The colonies are typically white or a pale yellowish-brown colour. **Habitat & ecology** · An ELWS and shallow sublittoral species found colonising rocks but, more commonly, occurring on kelp holdfasts, especially of *Laminaria digitata*.

Abundance & distribution
Locally common on south and west coasts of Britain and all around Ireland. Distributed south to the Mediterranean.

SUBORDER **Phlebobranchia**

FAMILY **Perophoridae**
Perophora listeri Forbes in Forbes & Hanley

Description · A very distinctive ascidian that may be identified by its pale yellow, rather transparent, ovoid zooids, about 4 mm high, which are widely but regularly arranged on slender stalks growing from a creeping stolon. The siphons of the zooids are large and obvious, the branchial sac easily visible with its four rows of slits or stigmata. **Habitat & ecology** · A lower-shore to shallow sublittoral species, found encrusting rocky surfaces, hydroid colonies, and smaller algae.

Abundance & distribution
Locally common. Found in the Irish Sea and Channel coasts of Britain and reported from the east coast of Britain and Ireland. Distributed south to the Mediterranean.

Distinctive features

1. Colonial ascidian.
2. Colony forms a sponge-like mat, up to 6 mm thick.
3. Colour greyish, with white or black speckles.

Distinctive features

1. Colonial, forming thin, flattened, encrusting sheets.
2. Mouth openings of individual ascidians appearing as regularly distributed spots over surface of colony.
3. Larger atriopores, shared by several individuals, slit-like and with a coarser pattern.

Distinctive features

1. Zooids ovoid, pale yellow, rather transparent.
2. Zooids on slender stalks, growing regularly from creeping stolon.
3. Branchial sac of each zooid with four rows of slits.

FAMILY **Corellidae**

Corella parallelogramma (Müller)

Description · Solitary ascidian. The body is oval or squarish, and generally laterally compressed. The attachment point is at the base. The branchial siphon is terminal, though offset to one side. The atrial siphon is offset to the other side and slightly below the level of the branchial siphon. The test is hard but thin. The test is the most striking feature of this species: it is generally transparent and bright crimson; yellow or white pigment flecks can often be seen through it. The branchial basket with its meshwork of vessels may also be obvious. This species grows to about 5 cm in height. **Habitat & ecology** · Found subtidally to depths of more than 150 m. It is usually attached to stones, shells, or to algae such as kelps, often in more offshore, clearer waters.

Abundance & distribution
Frequent. Found around all coasts of Britain and Ireland. Distributed from northern Norway to the Mediterranean.

FAMILY **Ascidiidae**

Ascidia conchilega Müller

Description · A solitary ascidian. The body is elliptical or oblong and rather elongate. It is usually attached by almost all of its left side. The branchial siphon is terminal and the atrial siphon is about two-thirds down the body and quite long. The body is up to 6 cm long. The test is cartilaginous and thin but the free surface is usually rough and may or may not be covered in shell fragments. The colour is greenish, sometimes with vivid pink eggs showing through the test of the attached side. **Habitat & ecology** · From the lower shore down to over 1000 m depth. It is usually attached to stones or shells, and often underneath large stones.

Abundance & distribution
Common. Found off all coasts of Britain and Ireland. Distributed from Norway and the Faeroes to the Mediterranean.

Ascidia mentula Müller

Description · A solitary ascidian that grows up to 18 cm long. The body is elongated and a rounded-rectangular shape. It is attached by the left side. Each siphon is small, more or less appearing as a bump with a pore in it. The branchial siphon is terminal, the atrial siphon half to two-thirds down the body. The test is thick, cartilaginous and translucent, with a rough, slightly wrinkled, or knobbly surface. The colour is greenish to pink. The tadpole larva is up to about 8 mm long. **Habitat & ecology** · Occurs on the lower shore and subtidally to 200 m depth. Usually attached to rock, large shells, or stones. **Similar species** · *A. virginea* is rectangular and has a smooth test. It is rose red in colour and the mantle, seen through the test, is transparent with red veins. *A. obliqua* and *A. prunum* are both more ovoid in shape and only found from the Shetland Islands northwards.

Abundance & distribution
Common. Found all around Britain except on North Sea coasts. Found all around Ireland. Distributed from Norway to the Mediterranean and Black Sea.

Distinctive features

1. Solitary.
2. Body oval or squarish, laterally flattened.
3. Test transparent, with bright red, yellow, or white markings visible through it.

Distinctive features

1. Solitary.
2. Attached by almost all left side.
3. Test cartilaginous, rough, may be covered in shell fragments.
4. Attached to stones or shells.

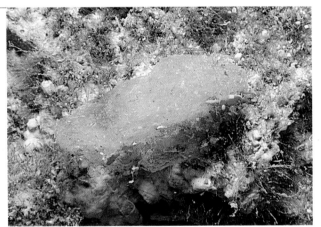

Distinctive features

1. Solitary.
2. Elongated rectangular body attached by left side.
3. Test thick, cartilaginous, rough with slightly wrinkled or knobbly surface.
4. Sometimes large (18 cm).

Ascidiella aspersa (Müller)

Description · A solitary ascidian with an elongated oval body, up to 13 cm long, usually attached by the base. In soft substrates, such as clay, the attachment point may be extended as a stalk several centimetres long. Test cartilaginous and covered in small papillae, often also encrusted with other animals such as colonial ascidians. Branchial siphon terminal, atrial siphon about one-third of the body length down. Usually greyish but may vary from blackish to whitish. **Habitat & ecology** · Intertidal and subtidal to depths of more than 50 m, though most common in shallow water. Attached to stones, clay, algae, and man-made structures such as wharf pilings. May form large clumps of individuals, especially in estuaries. **Similar species** · Resembles *A. scabra*, but this species is generally attached by a large part of its left side rather than the base. The siphons are also usually closer together than in *A. aspersa*.

Abundance & distribution
Common, locally abundant. Found on south and west coasts of Britain and all around Ireland. Distributed from Norway to the Mediterranean and Black Seas.

Phallusia mammillata (Cuvier)

Description · A large, solitary ascidian. The body is a rounded oblong shape and up to 14 cm high. The test is smooth, thick, cartilaginous and covered with large, prominent, rounded bumps. The branchial siphon is terminal and the atrial siphon about halfway down the body. The animal is attached obliquely by the base. The colour is dark brown to milky- or bluish-white, paler specimens being typical of deeper water. **Habitat & ecology** · Found on the lower shore and subtidally to 180 m depth. Often on stones lying in clay or mud.

Abundance & distribution
Frequent. Found off south-west and western Britain and Ireland. Distributed south to the Mediterranean.

ORDER **Pleurogona** | SUBORDER **Stolidobranchia**

FAMILY **Styelidae** | SUBFAMILY **Styelinae**

Dendrodoa grossularia (van Beneden)
Baked-bean ascidian

Description · Solitary ascidian, up to 25 mm long, often occurring in dense aggregations. Shape varies, from depressed hemispherical or dome shape with wide base to more elongated cylindrical or bean shape with narrower base. Attachment point is at base. Branchial siphon may be more or less terminal or offset to one side depending on shape of individual. Atrial siphon is generally offset to one side, at a similar level or below level of branchial siphon. Siphons are distinctly four-sided or lobed. Test is smooth and generally red, reddish-brown, or orange. The tadpole larvae are large with a spherical body and may swim for several hours after escaping from atrium. **Habitat & ecology** · Found on low shore and subtidally to 1000 m. Grows on rock, stones, shells, on other animals such as ascidians, and on algae. May form extensive sheet-like aggregations. **Similar species** · *Distomus variolosus*, but this forms fused clusters of zooids, is generally smaller than *D. grossularia*, and has hard texture. Found especially on kelp holdfasts.

Abundance & distribution
Common, locally abundant. Found all around Britain and Ireland, though more common on west and south-west coasts. Distributed from the Arctic to Brittany.

Distinctive features

1. Solitary ascidian.
2. Cartilaginous test covered in small papillae, often encrusted in other animals.
3. Attached by the base.

Distinctive features

1. Large solitary ascidian.
2. Body covered in large, rounded bumps.

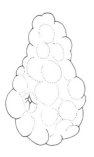

Distinctive features

1. Solitary, often in dense aggregations.
2. Hemispherical or dome-shaped to more elongated.
3. Four-sided siphonal openings.
4. Red, reddish-brown, or orange.

Styela clava Herdman

Description · A solitary species, up to 12 cm tall, with an elongate, club-shaped body borne on a tough, slender, wrinkled stalk; the body surface is leathery and corrugated, with a greenish-brown and hairy appearance. **Habitat & ecology** · An introduced species originating in the Pacific Ocean, found as a fouling species on submarine aquatic surfaces in warm, sheltered docks. Also occurs in sheltered estuaries, such as Salcombe.

Abundance & distribution
May be locally common, with a distribution from Portsmouth to Milford Haven; introduced from the Pacific by shipping.

SUBFAMILY **Polyzoinae**

Distomus variolosus Gaertner

Description · A colonial ascidian. The colony forms an encrusting mass of zooids. Each zooid is hemispherical or globular, sometimes more elongated, and up to 1 cm high. Zooids are attached by their base and/or sides but are mostly free. The branchial and atrial siphons are both on the top of the test and off-centre, with the atrial siphon slightly lower then the branchial. The texture is hard and sometimes rough. The colour of this species is red, dull cherry red, brick red, or brown. **Habitat & ecology** · Found at extreme low water but usually subtidal in shallow water. This species grows on rocks and stones but is very often found growing on the holdfasts of kelps or around the bases of hydroids. **Similar species** · May be confused with *Dendrodoa grossularia* but this species is larger, with a softer texture. Clustered colonies are formed by budding in *Distomus*.

Abundance & distribution
Locally common. Found on south-west coasts of Britain and Ireland. Distributed south to Portugal.

Stolonica socialis Hartmeyer

Description · This species forms clusters connected by creeping stolons that form the base. Individuals may be close together or spaced further apart. They are ovoid or rectangular, up to 2 cm tall. The siphons are small and close together on top of the body. The test is smooth, generally without adhering sand, but the stolons are sand-coated. Small buds may be seen around the bases of individuals in winter. The colour is often bright orangey-yellow, but may be brownish. The tadpole larvae are large with a body length of about 1 mm. They swim for several days after release. **Habitat & ecology** · Generally subtidal, at depths of 5–35 m. It is found attached to rock, stones, and under ledges, especially where there is high water movement. **Similar species** · May be confused with *Distomus variolosus* but this species tends to have a hard, leathery test. *Dendrodoa grossularia* is also similar but does not arise from a network of stolons.

Abundance & distribution
Frequent. Found in south-west Britain and Ireland, and in Brittany.

Distinctive features

1. Body club-shaped, borne on tough, slender stalk.
2. Solitary in habit.
3. Body appears rather hairy, greenish-brown in colour.

Distinctive features

1. Colonial ascidian.
2. Colony an encrusting mass of mostly free globular zooids, up to 1 cm high.
3. Test is hard and red in colour.
4. Often on kelp holdfasts.

Distinctive features

1. Forms clusters of individuals connected by basal stolons.
2. Shape ovoid or rectangular, with small siphons at top.
3. Bright orangey-yellow.

Botryllinae

Botrylloides leachi (Savigny)

Description · Compound ascidian. Colonies are flat, thin to thick, and encrusting, rather cushion-like, usually with one axis much longer than the other. The zooids are arranged in two parallel rows, like a ladder, that run in an irregular winding pattern within the test, though they may be so crowded that any pattern is obscured. The individual zooids are up to 3 mm long, but not as wide. There is a common cloacal cavity between the two rows of zooids. The colour of the colony tends to vary between grey, yellow, orange, or reddish-brown. **Habitat & ecology** · This species is found from the low shore to shallow subtidal, underneath and on top of stones, on other animals, and on algae. It is also found in estuaries. The tadpole larvae are brooded in a sac and burst through its walls into the common cloacal cavity before swimming away. **Similar species** · Resembles *Botryllus schlosseri*, but in this species the zooids are arranged in a star-like pattern around a common cloacal pore.

Abundance & distribution
Common. Found all around Britain and Ireland. Distributed from northern Norway to the Mediterranean and Black Seas.

Botryllus schlosseri (Pallas)

Description · Forms flat, encrusting, cushion-like fleshy colonies up to many centimetres across. The zooids are distinctly arranged in a star-shaped pattern around a common pore. There are usually 3–12 zooids in each group. The zooids are much longer than broad. The test is smooth and transparent and the colour is extremely variable. Colonies may be greenish, deep violet, blue, bright to dull yellow, brown, or red, sometimes with black intermixed. The tadpole larvae have a body about 0.5 mm long. **Habitat & ecology** · Found on the lower shore and shallow intertidal habitats. It is usually attached to rock, on or underneath rocks and stones, or on algae, seagrass, or other animals such as ascidians. It also attaches to man-made structures such as harbour walls or wharf pilings, and the bottom of boats and ships. **Similar species** · *Botrylloides leachi*, but in this species the zooids are arranged in two parallel rows.

Abundance & distribution
Very common. Found all around Britain and Ireland. Distributed from Arctic Norway to the Mediterranean and Black Seas. Also found on the east coast of the USA.

Pyuridae

Pyura squamulosa (Alder)

Description · A solitary ascidian, with an ovate or compressed globular shape, reaching 25 mm in height. It is attached by a broad base. The siphons are at the top of the body and well separated. The test is tough, quite smooth, with small, scattered, scaly platelets not giving a tessellated appearance. The body has a violet tinge and violet stripes on the siphons. **Habitat & ecology** · This species occurs on the low shore and in shallow subtidal situations. It grows on shells and stones. **Similar species** · Several other species of *Pyura* occur in northern Europe. *P. tessulata* is the only other one with platelets. It is hemispherical in shape, or very flattened, with the siphons separated by a large space. This species is covered in closely packed oblong or hexagonal platelets, giving it a tessellated appearance.

Abundance & distribution
Frequent. Found on south, west, and north coasts of Britain, and all around Ireland. Distributed south to the Mediterranean.

Distinctive features

1. Compound ascidian.
2. Cushion-like test, with two parallel rows of zooids winding in an irregular fashion throughout.

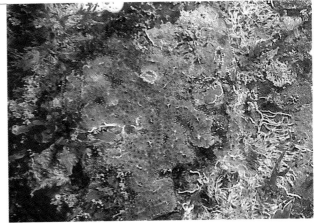

Distinctive features

1. Compound ascidian.
2. Forms a flat, encrusting, cushion-like colony.
3. Zooids arranged in a conspicuous star shape around a common pore.

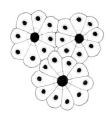

Distinctive features

1. Solitary ovate or globular ascidian.
2. Test is tough, smooth with scattered scaly platelets.
3. Siphons with violet stripes.

FAMILY **Molgulidae**

Molgula manhattensis (De Kay)

Description · Solitary ascidian. Body rounded, and 1–3 cm high. Siphons are positioned on top of body with bases close together. These may be short or as long as half body length. Body soft; test covered with fibrils to which sand and other particles may attach. Grey to greenish-blue. **Habitat & ecology** · Lower shore and subtidally to about 90 m. May be attached to stones, algae, or man-made structures such as harbour walls or underneath ships, or loosely attached in sand. Common in estuaries where may form large clusters. Seems to tolerate reduced salinities and pollution. **Similar species** · *M. occulta* common and similar size, but siphons short and body always completely covered in sand grains, mud or shell fragments. *M. oculata* occurs from south-west Britain southwards. It grows up to 7 cm high, with distinct space between siphons. *M. citrina* small, with hard, greenish test, sometimes with sand grains adhering. *M. complanata* fairly small, with well separated siphons. Also often has adherent sand particles.

Abundance & distribution Common. Found all around Britain and Ireland. Distributed from northern Norway to Portugal. Also found in the west Atlantic.

Subphylum Euchordata (Vertebrata)

Chordates with an internal skeleton composed either of **cartilage** or **bone**.

Pisces (fishes)

Though widely regarded as a single group of vertebrates, the name 'Pisces' does not comprise a natural taxonomic grouping but three distinct groups of fishes, regarded by different authors either as classes or subclasses. One group, the **Cyclostomata**, comprises fishes with no jaws (**agnathous**) such as the Lamprey (*Lampetra fluviatilis* [Linnaeus]) parasitic on other fish, broadly eel-like in shape but with neither paired fins nor scales, with a round **suctorial** mouth and seven pairs of **branchial** openings (**gill slits**); it is not covered further in this book. The other two groups, possessing paired fins and jaws are the **Chondrichthyes** (sharks, skates, and rays, with a cartilaginous skeleton) and the **Osteichthyes** (with a bony skeleton).

Further reading

Dipper, F. (1987). *British sea fishes*. Underwater World Publications, London.
Ryland, J. S. (1990). Cephalochordata and Euchordata. In *The marine fauna of the British Isles and North-West Europe* (eds P. J. Hayward & J. S. Ryland), Vol. 2, pp. 905–51. Clarendon Press, Oxford.

Whitehead, P. J. P., Bauchot, M.-L., Hureau, J.-C., *et al.* (eds)(1989). *Fishes of the north-eastern Atlantic and the Mediterranean*. Vols 1–3. UNESCO, Paris.

Class Chondrichthyes (sharks, skates, rays)

Also known as **elasmobranchs**, the skeleton and fin rays in the **Chondrichthyes** are composed of **cartilage**, and the typically rough skin contains **placoid scales** (**dermal denticles**) which resemble tiny teeth. The paired **pelvic fins** are always located well behind the paired **pectorals**. In fast swimming forms, such as sharks, the first **dorsal fin** is large and obvious, with the **upper lobe** of the **tail fin** being larger than the lower and internally supported by the hind end of the backbone, whereas in the dorsoventrally flattened skates and rays the dorsal and tail fins are reduced or absent. In males the pelvic fins possess finger-like extensions (**claspers**) which are used as **copulatory organs**. The mouth is typically on the underside of the head. On either side of the body there are five to seven **gill openings** placed just in front of the pectoral fins. Members of this class do not possess a **swim-bladder**, but their intestine contains a characteristic **spiral valve**.

Examples from five orders of elasmobranchs occur in north-west waters, all being found subtidally. The orders are the **Lamniformes**, containing the families **Carcharinidae** (sharks) and **Scyliorhinidae** (bottom-dwelling sharks), the **Rajiformes**, with a single family, the

Distinctive features

1. Solitary.
2. Rounded body.
3. The siphons are on top of the body with bases close together.
4. Sand grains may adhere to fibrils on the body surface.

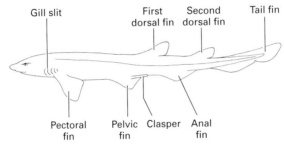

The main external features of a shark, one of the cartilaginous fish.

Rajidae (skates and rays), the **Squaliformes**, with two families, **Squalidae** (spiny sharks) and **Squatinidae** (monkfishes), the **Myliobatoidei** with the family **Dasyatidae** (stingrays), and the **Torpediniformes** with the family **Torpedinidae** (electric rays).

ORDER **Lamniformes**

FAMILY **Scyliorhinidae**

Scyliorhinus caniculus (Linnaeus) **Dogfish**

Description · Small shark with short, blunt snout. Skin has sandpaper texture. Nostrils joined to snout by shallow channels covered by flaps. Has two small, rounded dorsal fins set well back on body. Origin of second dorsal fin level with hind end of base of anal fin. Body sandy, brown, grey, or blue-grey, covered in numerous small, dark spots. Underside paler, not marked with spots. May grow up to 1 m long. **Habitat & ecology** · Lives on seabed, especially in sandy, muddy, or gravelly areas from below intertidal to 110 m depth. May be especially common in areas of rock mixed with patches of sand. Lives on bottom living invertebrates, such as molluscs and crustaceans, and fish. Oviparous, laying egg cases November-July. These often seen attached to kelp holdfasts or washed up on beach. It is most active by night. **Similar species** · Nursehound, *S. stellaris*, but this has larger dark spots or patches, and origin of second dorsal fin is in front of end of base of anal fin.

Abundance & distribution
Very common. Found all around the British Isles and Ireland. Distribution is from southern Norway south to Senegal, including the Mediterranean.

Scyliorhinus stellaris (Linnaeus) **Nursehound**

Description · A small shark with a short, blunt snout. The nostrils are not joined to the mouth by channels although this species does have distinctive nasal flaps. The dorsal fins are small and rounded and set well back on the body. The origin of the second dorsal fin lies in front of the end of the base of the anal fin. The upper surfaces of the body are sandy-coloured or greyish with large dark rounded spots. Some specimens are completely black. The underside is pale and unmarked. The nursehound may grow to a length of over 160 cm. **Habitat & ecology** · Found on the seabed in areas that are generally considered as rough or rocky, from shallow water to 65 m depth. It feeds on bottom-living animals such as molluscs, crustaceans, and bottom-dwelling fish. This species is oviparous.

Abundance & distribution
Occurs frequently around all coasts of Britain and Ireland, although it is rare in the Shetland Islands. Elsewhere this species is distributed from southern Norway to Morocco, including the Mediterranean.

FAMILY **Carcharinidae**

Galeorhinus galeus (Linnaeus) **Tope**

(a)

Description · A slender shark that may grow to 2 m in length. It has a relatively long snout and sharp, triangular-shaped teeth. The first dorsal fin is large and triangular and originates over the rear edge of the pectoral fins. The second dorsal fin is smaller and about the same size as the anal fin. The colour is grey to brown on the top and sides, whitish on the underside. **Habitat & ecology** · Tope (a) occur inshore in the summer. They feed on fish, squid, and bottom-living invertebrates such as molluscs and crustaceans. Tope are ovoviviparous and give birth to 20–40 young, known as pups.

Abundance & distribution
Frequently encountered, and occurs around all coasts of Britain and Ireland. The species is distributed from northern Norway to Madeira but is uncommon in the Mediterranean. It also occurs in the Indian and Pacific Oceans.

Distinctive features
1. Small, with blunt snout.
2. Two small, rounded dorsal fins set well back on body.
3. Origin of second dorsal fin level with hind end of base of anal fin.
4. Body covered in small spots.

Distinctive features
1. Small, with blunt snout.
2. Two small rounded dorsal fins set well back on body.
3. Origin of second dorsal fin in front of hind end of base of anal fin.
4. Body covered in large spots.

Distinctive features (a)
1. Slender, shark-like shape.
2. First dorsal fin larger than second.
3. Second dorsal fin same size as anal fin.

(a)

Similar species · The smooth hound, *Mustelus mustelus* (b), and the spurdog, *Squalus acanthias*. The smooth hound has a blunter snout than the tope and two dorsal fins that are of almost equal size. The spurdog does not have an anal fin.

(b)

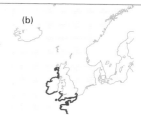

ORDER Squaliformes

FAMILY Squatinidae

Squatina squatina (Linnaeus) **Angel shark, monkfish**

Description · An extremely flattened shark with a blunt nose and a broad and flattened head which somewhat resembles a ray. Mouth is wide and terminal in position. Eyes are on dorsal surface of head with a pair of large spiracles positioned behind them. Pectoral and pelvic fins are large compared to overall size of body. Pectoral fins extend in front of the back of head, though they are separate from head. Hind tips of pelvic fins reach to level of origin of first dorsal fin. Dorsal fins are small and rounded and there is no anal fin. Lower caudal lobe of tail is longer than upper. Colour greenish-brown with darker spots and speckles. May grow to 2.5 m long.
Habitat & ecology · Lives on the seabed, preferring sandy or muddy bottoms. It typically occurs in depths of 5–100 m. Feeds on bottom-living animals such as other fish, molluscs, and crustaceans. Ovoviviparous, giving birth to young 20–30 cm long.

Abundance & distribution
Rare. Distributed around all coasts of Britain and Ireland. Elsewhere distributed from the southern North Sea southward to the coasts of Mauritania and the Canary Islands. Also found in the Mediterranean and Black Seas.

ORDER Rajiformes

FAMILY Rajidae

Raja batis Linnaeus **Skate**

Description · Elongated, pointed snout, broadly kite-shaped with acutely pointed outer corners. Anterior margins of body may be distinctly concave. Upper surface partly prickly in adults but may be smooth in juveniles. Adults may have row of 12–18 large thorns along tail, usually with 1–2 thorns between dorsal fins. Lower edges of tail may also have thorns. Underside smooth in juveniles but may feel prickly in adults. Upper surface ranges from olive grey to brown, with scattering of paler spots or blotches. May also be oval-shaped eye spot on each side of dorsal surface. Underside grey to bluish-grey. May grow to over 2.5 m. Egg cases also very large.
Habitat & ecology · Bottom-living down to 600 m, though usually found above 200 m. Feeds on variety of bottom-living animals, including fish. Is oviparous and egg cases resemble those of dogfish, but are larger.
Similar species · Include the thornback ray, *R. clavata*, but this has large thorns scattered over dorsal surface.

Abundance & distribution
Frequent all around British Isles and Ireland, though rare in southern North Sea and parts of Irish Sea. Elsewhere distributed from northern Norway to coasts of Morocco and Madeira. Also recorded from Faeroes, Iceland, and rarely in western part of Baltic.

(b)

Distinctive features

1. Flattened body.
2. Shark/ray cross.
3. Pectoral fins reach in front of back of head.
4. Lower caudal lobe of tail fin longer than upper.

Distinctive features

1. Ray with elongated snout.
2. 12–18 large thorns along tail.
3. Usually 1–2 thorns between dorsal fins.

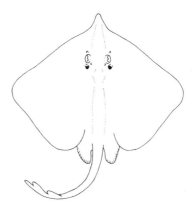

Raja clavata Linnaeus **Thornback ray**

Description · Blunt snout and typical diamond shape with pointed outer corners. Upper surface always prickly, even in juveniles. Row of 30–50 thorns from back of head to first dorsal fin, with 0–2 thorns between first and second dorsal fins. In adults, also scattering of large 'buckler' thorns, backward pointing, with swollen base. Underside of fish also often prickly and may have scattering of large thorns. Upper surface usually various shades of brown to grey, mottled with dark and light spots or blotches, or producing marbled pattern. Small specimens, especially, may have distinctive yellow spots. Underside off-white to grey with dark margins; tail may be marked with light and dark crossbars. Can grow to over 90 cm.
Habitat & ecology · On seabed to depth of about 300 m. May lie covered in sand during day, feeding at night on range of bottom-living animals; perhaps has preference for Crustacea. Oviparous, laying up to 150 egg cases a year. Resembles other rays found in area, but distinguished by large thorns scattered on upper surface.

Abundance & distribution
Common all around coasts of Britain and Ireland. Distributed from Norway and south of Arctic Circle, and Iceland to South Africa and into south-west Indian Ocean. Rarely found in western Baltic, but occurs throughout Mediter-

Raja naevus Müller & Henle **Cuckoo ray**

Description · A ray with a short snout. Upper surface covered in tiny spines. Two rows of thorns run along mid-line of body and extend along tail. There are additional rows of thorns on the tail, which may thus have 4–5 rows in total. Just behind the head there is also a patch of thorns, often triangular in outline, and a complete row of 9–13 thorns along the inner margin of each eye. The coloration of the species is distinctive: base colour of upper surface ochre to brownish-grey, with two large, black, distinctive eyespots marked with yellow lines or patches that form a marbled effect. Underside whitish to greyish. The cuckoo ray grows to a length of 70 cm.
Habitat & ecology · Lives on the seabed at 20–250 m depth and feeds on a variety of bottom-dwelling animals. The ray is oviparous, laying up to 100 egg cases throughout the year. Similar to other species of rays but may be distinguished by its distinctive eyespots and the double row of thorns on the upper surface and patch of thorns behind the head.

Abundance & distribution
Common, occurring around all coasts of Britain and Ireland. Elsewhere distributed from southern Norway and the Kattegat to northern Africa and the western Mediterranean.

Raja undulata Lacepède **Undulate ray**

Description · Up to 1 m long, with a short snout. The front edges of the wings are sinuous in shape. The dorsal surface is covered in tiny spines apart from bare areas on the central and rear parts of the disc. Along the mid-dorsal line, from some distance behind the eyes, there is an irregular row of spines that runs all the way back to the dorsal fins. There are also spines around the eyes and in several rows along the tail. The dorsal fins are small and there are also a few spines between these. The colour pattern is distinctive. The base colour is various shades of brown, usually with long, dark, wavy lines around which are rows of white spots. The underside of the body is white. **Habitat & ecology** · Common, but rarely seen because it prefers water deeper than 40 m. Lives on the bottom in muddy or sandy areas down to about 200 m. It eats various invertebrates and fish.

Abundance & distribution
Common. Found around south-west Britain and southern Ireland. Distributed south to Mauritania, including the western Mediterranean.

ranean and the western part of Black Sea.

Distinctive features

1. Upper surface has scattering of large 'buckler' thorns.
2. Row of 30–50 thorns from nape to first dorsal fin.
3. Upper surface always prickly.

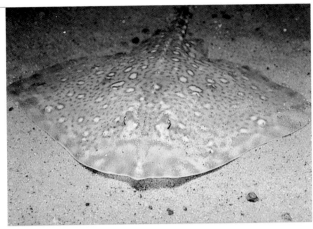

Distinctive features

1. Two rows of spines along mid-line of back.
2. A patch of spines behind head.
3. Two distinctive black eyespots marked with yellow.

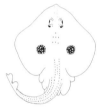

Distinctive features

1. Brown; long, wavy dark lines around which are white spots.
2. Row of spines along midline.
3. Dorsal fins separate with few spines between.

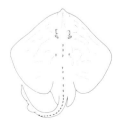

Class Osteichthyes (bony fishes)

In this group of fishes the skeleton and fin rays are composed of **bone**, though the fin rays may be soft. The body surface is usually covered by rounded, overlapping **bony scales**. The paired **pelvic fins** are often somewhat anterior to the paired **pectorals**. The mouth is typically at the front of the head. The filamentous **gills** open on each side of the body by a single aperture, covered by an **operculum**. A gas-filled **swim-bladder**, associated with the foregut, is usually present and used for adjusting **buoyancy**, though it may be missing from inshore species living in rough water. In

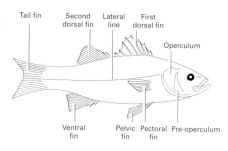

The main external features of a typical bony fish.

ORDER Clupeiformes

FAMILY Clupeidae

Clupea harengus Linnaeus **Herring**

Description · Fairly slender, with rounded belly and forked tail. Body laterally compressed, with single, small dorsal fin originating just in front of, or level with, pelvic fins. These are small and positioned on hind part of belly. Head fairly small; mouth has projecting lower jaw. Gill covers lack bony striations. Dark blue on back, fading to silver elsewhere. May reach about 40 cm. **Habitat & ecology** · Generally offshore, to depth of 250 m. May form enormous shoals, but seriously depleted by overfishing. Fish gather to spawn either inshore or offshore and shed millions of eggs that sink to bottom and stick to gravel, shells, and stones. Female may produce 50 000 eggs. Larvae pelagic. Adults feed on planktonic animals such as copepods, small shrimps, amphipods, ctenophores, and small fish. **Similar species** · Sardine, *Sardina pilchardus*. This has distinctive bony striations on gill cover with dorsal fin beginning well in front of pelvic fin. Also resembles sprat, *Sprattus sprattus*, which has sharp keel of scales along belly.

Abundance & distribution
Abundant around all coasts of Britain and Ireland. Elsewhere distributed from Spitsbergen and the White Sea to the Bay of Biscay.

Sprattus sprattus (Linnaeus) **Sprat**

Description · A small fish, covered in silvery scales. The body is elongated, laterally compressed and tapering at both ends. The head is roughly triangular with a projecting lower jaw. There is a single dorsal fin and a forked tail fin. Along the belly is a distinctive sharp keel of scales. The sprat is a silvery colour, with bluish back and greenish flanks. It may reach 16 cm but is usually somewhat smaller. **Habitat & ecology** · This is a shoaling species, often found in shallow water near the coast. It feeds on microscopic planktonic plants when young but adults eat planktonic animals such as copepods. The sprat is tolerant of reduced salinities. **Similar species** · Resembles the sardine, *Sardina pilchardus*, but this tends to be slenderer and more rounded than the sprat. It also lacks the sharp keel of scales along the belly. The herring, *Clupea harengus*, also lacks this sharp keel of scales and tends to grow larger than the sprat.

Abundance & distribution
Common, locally abundant. Found off the south coasts of Britain and Ireland. Distributed from southern Norway to Morocco, including the Baltic, Mediterranean, and Black Seas.

most bony fishes a longitudinal sensory system (**lateral line**) is usually visible along each side of the body, which responds to changes in water pressure caused by currents and eddies.

The bony fishes exhibit a great diversity in body shape and size and in their ecology. In north-west European waters examples from 13 orders are frequently encountered. These orders are the **Anguilliformes** (eels), **Atheriniformes** (garfish, smelt), **Clupeiformes** (herring, sprat, and other shoaling pelagic species), **Gadiformes** (cod, whiting), **Gasterosteiformes** (sticklebacks), **Gobiesociformes** (clingfish, suckerfish), **Lophiiformes** (anglerfish), **Perciformes** (horse mackerel, mullet, butterfish), **Pleuronectiformes** (turbot, flounder, plaice),

Salmoniformes (salmon, trout, the **anadromous** [moving into rivers to spawn] fishes), **Scorpaeniformes** (gurnards, sea scorpions), **Syngnathiformes** (pipefish), and **Zeiformes** (John Dory).

Distinctive features

1. Single dorsal fin.
2. Silvery scales.
3. Projecting lower jaw.

Distinctive features

1. Small, silvery, streamlined.
2. Single dorsal fin, forked tail fin.
3. Lower jaw projecting.
4. Sharp keel of scales along belly.

ORDER **Anguilliformes**

FAMILY **Congridae**

Conger conger (Linnaeus) **Conger eel**

Description · Typical elongated eel-shape, though body can be extremely massive and heavy in appearance. Front end of body is circular in cross-section becoming laterally compressed towards rear. Dorsal fin begins just behind level of pectoral fins and extends right around body, being continuous with anal fin. Pectoral fins are sharply angled. Large mouth. Dark grey or brown to black, sometimes with paler underside. May reach 3 m in length, and possibly over 100 kg in weight. **Habitat & ecology** · Common, usually found in rocky areas and very commonly on shipwrecks. Often observed poking head out of a crack or hole, or even pipes. Despite its aggressive appearance it is harmless unless provoked and will often tolerate close proximity of divers. A nocturnal predator, coming out at night to prey on fish, crustaceans, and cephalopods such as octopus. It has a complex life history involving a migration to oceanic spawning grounds. The pelagic larva is called a leptocephalus.

Abundance & distribution
Common around all coasts of Britain and Ireland. Distributed from southern Iceland and Norway to Senegal. Also found in the Mediterranean, Madeira, and the Azores.

ORDER **Syngnathiformes**

FAMILY **Syngnathidae**

Syngnathus acus Linnaeus **Greater pipefish**

Description · Extremely elongated, narrow, pipe-like body. Snout in front of eyes extremely elongated and more than half head length long. Tiny, upturned mouth positioned at end of snout. Slight hump on head behind eyes. Has dorsal fin and small, fan-shaped, tail fin. Body ridged, especially in front half. Dark brown or greenish-brown. Sometimes body looks banded, and ridges along body may be marked with thin, pale blue lines. Underside of body may be paler. Grows up to 46 cm long. **Habitat & ecology** · Generally subtidal to maximum depth of 90 m. Found in wide variety of habitats but seems very common amongst seaweeds and seagrass. Feeds on planktonic animals such as copepods and fish larvae. Like other pipefish, female lays eggs in pouch on male, where they are fertilised. Young develop in pouch until few centimetres long. **Similar species** · Nilsson's pipefish, *S. rostellatus*. Snout less than half head length and lacks hump behind eyes. Deep-snouted pipefish, *S. typhle*, has laterally compressed snout with ridge along middle of upper surface. Length of snout more than half the head.

Abundance & distribution
Common around all coasts of Britain and Ireland. Distributed from southern Norway to Senegal, and from Namibia to South Africa.

Nerophis lumbriciformis (Jenyns)
Worm pipefish

Description · Very slender and elongate, worm-like fish. Head is extremely small with a short snout turned distinctly upwards. There is a single, small dorsal fin but the anal and tail fins are absent. Dark brown, varying to black or olive in shade. Body sometimes marked with pale spots or stripes. Underside may be yellowish-brown to golden brown. May grow to a length of 17 cm. **Habitat & ecology** · Amongst seaweeds in rocky areas on the shore and down to 30 m depth. Often very well camouflaged so may be difficult to see. Feeds on very small crustaceans such as copepods. The female lays eggs in a groove on the male's belly and the male looks after the eggs and young until they reach about 1 cm, when they are released and become planktonic. **Similar species** · The straight-nosed pipefish, *N. ophidion*, is very similar but has a straight snout and can grow to about 30 cm length.

Abundance & distribution
Frequent around most coasts of Britain and Ireland. Rare on east coast of Britain. Distributed from southern Norway to Morocco.

Distinctive features

1. Eel-shaped body.
2. Dorsal fin continuous with anal fin, and begins just behind pectoral fin.

Distinctive features

1. Very elongate, narrow.
2. Elongate snout more than half head length.
3. Ridged body.
4. Hump on head behind eyes.
5. Tail fin present.

Distinctive features

1. Very slender, worm-like body.
2. Short snout that is distinctly turned upwards.
3. No anal or tail fin.

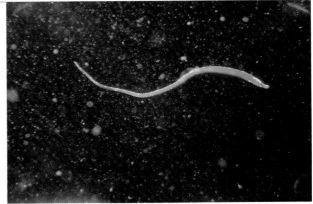

ORDER **Gasterosteiformes**

FAMILY **Gasterosteidae**

Spinachia spinachia (Linnaeus)
Fifteen-spined stickleback

Description · Elongate, slender body. Head small, elongated in front of eyes. Mouth very small, positioned at end of body. Dorsal fin roughly triangular-shaped. In front of it is row of 14–17 small spines. Anal fin almost mirrors dorsal fin but on underside of body. Two small spines in front of anal fin, one nearer level of pectoral fins. Body becomes extremely narrow just before tail fin. Greenish-brown to dark brown on upper surfaces and sides, becoming paler below. Grows up to 22 cm long. **Habitat & ecology** · Intertidally in rock pools, or subtidally down to 10 m or so. Found amongst seaweeds or seagrasses, either solitary or in pairs. Male builds nest in late spring to early summer in seaweed, constructed by sticking together pieces of algae. Eggs laid in nest, guarded by male. Feeds on small invertebrates such as copepods and polychaete worms. **Similar species** · None, although three-spined stickleback, *Gasterosteus aculeatus*, usually associated with freshwater in Britain, may be found in sea. It has deeper body, more arrow-shaped head, and only three spines in front of dorsal fin.

Abundance & distribution
Frequently encountered around all coasts of Britain and Ireland. Distributed from northern Norway to the Atlantic coasts of France.

ORDER **Gadiformes** | FAMILY **Gadidae**

Gadus morhua Linnaeus **Cod**

Description · Bulky. Large head with single barbel under chin. Upper jaw projects forward of lower; mouth large. Three dorsal fins, first triangular, second and third rounded and more elongated. Two anal fins. Tail fin ends with flat edge or is slightly concave. Obvious pale lateral line, curving after first dorsal fin. Sandy yellow or brown, sometimes with greenish tinge. Upper parts often mottled with darker colour such as brown or pinky-brown. Underside usually white. Can grow to nearly 2 m. **Habitat & ecology** · Generally near bottom, from shallow subtidal to at least 600 m. Younger cod usually seen inshore, particularly in winter. Commercially valuable; has been overfished in many areas. Usually found in shoals; breeds on specific spawning grounds. Female may lay 6 million eggs. Eggs and larvae are planktonic, sometimes occurring in very large numbers. Eats wide variety of fish and invertebrates such as shrimps, amphipods, and polychaete worms. Also cannibalistic.

Abundance & distribution
Common around all coasts of Britain and Ireland. Elsewhere found off northern Russia, Spitzsbergen, Iceland, and Greenland, south to Bay of Biscay. Also in north Pacific.

Gaidropsarus mediterraneus (Linnaeus)
Shore rockling

Description · Elongate body, round in cross-section, up to about 25 cm long. Head tapers to a fairly narrow tip with a small mouth. Below chin is a single barbel, above is a pair of long barbels. There are two dorsal fins; first has a single long ray followed by short rays; second is long, running almost to base of tail. Body dark brown or reddish-brown. **Habitat & ecology** · Intertidal rock pools and rocky areas down to about 30 m depth. Feeds on other fish, invertebrates, and algae. Spawns offshore; eggs and larvae planktonic. **Similar species** · Three-bearded rockling, *G. vulgaris*, also has three barbels, grows to over 40 cm, and occurs offshore at depths of 10–120 m. It has a large mouth and is pale pink to pale pinkish-brown, with dark brown blotches on upper body surfaces. Five-bearded rockling, *Ciliata mustela*, has one barbel below mouth and two pairs above. It is rich reddish-brown, sometimes with a paler bronze belly.

Abundance & distribution
Common on south and west coasts of Britain and all around Ireland. Distributed from the Orkney Islands to Spain, including the Mediterranean, Adriatic, and Black Seas.

Distinctive features

1. Very elongate, slender body.
2. 14–17 spines in front of dorsal fin.
3. Body becomes very narrow before tail fin.

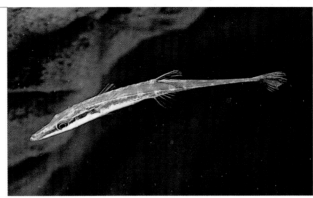

Distinctive features

1. Large head; upper jaw forward of lower.
2. Single barbel under chin.
3. Three dorsal, two anal, fins.
4. Obvious curved, lateral line.

Distinctive features

1. Head with three barbels.
2. Elongate body.
3. First ray of first dorsal fin longer than rest.
4. Long second dorsal fin.

Molva molva (Linnaeus) **Ling**

Description · Elongate fish with a large head and the upper jaw projecting beyond the lower. A barbel is present below the mouth. Two dorsal fins, the second of which is very long. There is also a single, long anal fin. A mottled yellowish-brown or golden brown to greenish on the upper parts of the body becoming paler on the sides and almost white on the belly. Can reach a length of nearly 2 m. **Habitat & ecology** · Occurs at depths of 10–400 m. Inshore animals tend to be immature. They are often observed as solitary fish on rocky areas, particularly underneath overhangs or around shipwrecks. Ling spawn offshore and a single female may release a staggering 20–60 million eggs. Eggs and larvae are planktonic. Ling feed on other fish, and invertebrates such as crustaceans and echinoderms. They are caught by commercial fishing boats. **Similar species** · The hake, *Merluccius merluccius* is superficially similar, but it lacks a barbel.

Abundance & distribution
Frequent around all coasts of Britain and Ireland. Distributed from the Barents Sea and Iceland to Gibraltar. Rare in the Mediterranean.

Pollachius pollachius (Linnaeus) **Pollack**

Description · Laterally compressed, reaching 1.3 m. Large, pointed head and large eyes. Mouth large with protruding lower jaw. No barbels. Three dorsal fins; first triangular, other two less tall but longer. Two anal fins and broad tail with convex outer edge. Lateral line distinct, curved part-way along body. Brown or green on back, paling to light silvery-green or silvery-white on sides. Larger individuals usually darker. **Habitat & ecology** · Above kelp forests, rocky ground, or shipwrecks, from shallows down to 100 m. Carnivorous: may dart in to snap up sand eels or other small fish in sandy gullies surrounded by rock and kelp. Spawns early in year, eggs and larvae planktonic. Popular with anglers, also commercially fished. **Similar species** · Saithe, *P. virens*; this has straight lateral line and lower jaw nearly same length as upper. In whiting, *Merlangius merlangus*, upper jaw projects in front of lower and lateral line curved about halfway along length. Others in cod family have barbels under mouth (cod, haddock, bib, poor-cod). Haddock, *Melanogrammus aeglefinus*, has dark spot on side, and black lateral line.

Abundance & distribution
Very common around all coasts of Britain and Ireland. Distributed from northern Norway and Iceland to the Bay of Biscay.

Trisopterus luscus (Linnaeus) **Bib, pout**

Description · Deep-bodied fish, almost diamond-shaped. Relatively small head with barbel under chin. Upper jaw forward of lower jaw. Three dorsal fins, the first being triangular and tallest. Two anal fins, first longer than second. Colour pattern usually distinctive. Base colour very pale brown or pale pinkish-brown, with darker, copper-coloured, saddle-like markings or broad vertical bars along entire body length. Sometimes these bars also very pale or even not visible. Also often dark spot at base of pectoral fin. Grows up to 45 cm. **Habitat & ecology** · Young often seen in shoals, sheltering inside or around shipwrecks or amongst rocks. Older, larger fish tend to occur in deeper water down to 100 m. Feeds on bottom-living inverte-brates, such as crustaceans, molluscs, and other fish, sometimes squid. Spawns in deeper water in spring. **Similar species** · Include other members of cod family, especially poor-cod, *T. minutus*. This tends to be overall copper colour, without vertical bands. Some pale bib can be particu-larly difficult to differentiate from poor-cod.

Abundance & distribution
Common to locally abundant around all coasts of Britain and Ireland. Distributed from southern Norway to Morocco, including western part of Mediterranean.

Distinctive features

1. Elongate body.
2. Large head with barbel beneath mouth.
3. Two dorsal fins, the second long.

Distinctive features

1. Pointed head with large eyes.
2. Three dorsal fins, first triangular.
3. Two anal fins.
4. Lower jaw protrudes ahead of upper.
5. Lateral line curved.

Distinctive features

1. Deep, diamond-shaped body.
2. Three dorsal fins; first tall, triangular.
3. Upper jaw longer than lower.
4. Barbel under chin.
5. Vertical dark bars on body.
6. Dark spot at base of pectoral fin.

Trisopterus minutus (Linnaeus) **Poor-cod**

Description · Slender fish with a relatively small head and a barbel under the chin. The upper jaw of the mouth is forward of the lower jaw. There are three dorsal fins, the first of which is triangular and the tallest. There are two anal fins, the first longer than the second. The colour pattern is a yellowish-brown to bronze red on top, and a coppery colour on the flanks. The underside is paler. Poor-cod grow to a maximum length of 26 cm.
Habitat & ecology · Like the bib, small poor-cod are often seen in and around wrecks, or in large cracks or crevices in rocky areas. Larger fish occur down to 300 m. Poor-cod breed in spring in deep water. Like bib they feed on invertebrates such as decapod crustaceans and smaller fish.
Similar species · Poor-cod closely resemble bib, *T. luscus*, but lack the dark vertical bars usually visible on this species.

Abundance & distribution
Very common to locally abundant around all coasts of Britain and Ireland. Distributed from mid-Norway to Morocco, including the western Mediterranean.

ORDER **Zeiformes**

FAMILY **Zeidae**

Zeus faber Linnaeus **John Dory**

Description · Very distinctive, with a very deep, round, but laterally flattened body. Head is large, as is the upturned, protrusible mouth. The first rays of the dorsal fin are extremely long, whilst the back half is much shorter. The first rays of the anal fin are also long and spiny. Around the body runs a double row of thick spines beneath the dorsal and above the anal fins. The pelvic fins are large. Mottled yellow to golden brown with a yellow-edged black spot on each side of the body. Mottling is of a paler colour. Grows up to 66 cm. **Habitat & ecology** · Subtidal to 400 m. Solitary John Dory may be seen hovering in sandy areas between seaweed-covered rocks. A predaceous fish, it hunts other species by stealth. Difficult to see when head-on because of the narrowness of the body. It breeds in the summer, probably only off southern areas of the UK. There are no similar species.

Abundance & distribution
Frequent around most coasts of Britain and Ireland, though rare in North Sea. Distributed from southern Norway to South Africa, including the Mediterranean, Black Sea, Madeira, the Canary Islands, and the Azores.

ORDER **Perciformes**

FAMILY **Polyprionidae**

Polyprion americanus (Bloch & Schneider) **Wreckfish**

Description · A large, heavily built fish up to 2 m in length. The head is large with a lower jaw longer than the upper. The forehead is distinctive with a slight dip just above the level of the eyes, which are very large. The front gill cover is serrated on the back edge whilst the main gill cover has a rough bony ridge roughly level with the eye. The dorsal fin is bilobed with large spines in the anterior part. Adults are dark brown or bluish-grey whilst juveniles tend to be marbled with light and dark shades. **Habitat & ecology** · Lives above sandy, muddy, or rocky bottoms at depths of 40–1000 m. The adults tend to be solitary and live near the bottom but younger fish may be gregarious and more pelagic. The fish gets its name from the habit of living under floating wreckage or seaweed. It feeds on invertebrates such as molluscs and crustaceans, and fish.

Abundance & distribution
Locally common. Found on west, north-east and south coasts of Britain and all around Ireland, though rare inshore. Distributed from southern Norway to South Africa, including the Mediterranean, Azores, Canaries and Cape

Distinctive features

1. Three dorsal fins; first tall, triangular.
2. Upper jaw longer than lower.
3. Barbel under chin.
4. Coppery overall; no distinctive markings.

Distinctive features

1. Deep, laterally compressed, round body.
2. Large head with large upturned mouth.
3. Yellow-edged dark spot on side.

Verde Islands. Also found in the western Atlantic.

Distinctive features

1. Outline of forehead with dip above eyes.
2. Rear edge of front gill cover toothed.
3. Main gill cover with longitudinal bony ridge at eye level.
4. Large, heavy-bodied; large eyes.

FAMILY **Moronidae**

Dicentrarchus labrax (Linnaeus) **Bass**

Description · Streamlined; can appear heavy-bodied, especially larger specimens. Body covered in small but obvious silvery scales giving fish an overall silver colour. Upper parts may be bluish or greenish; may be dark patch on edge of gill covers. Two dorsal fins, the first having spiny rays. Head large, with large mouth. Close inspection reveals spines on lower edge of gill covers. Can grow up to 1 m. **Habitat & ecology** · Subtidal, found over various bottom types down to 100 m. Also associated with rocky reefs and shipwrecks. Younger fish may occur in very shallow water, estuaries, or lower reaches of rivers. Adults are large predators that take variety of fish, but young also feed on invertebrates such as shrimps. Breeds inshore, releasing floating eggs that hatch into larvae which remain within sheltered areas such as estuaries. **Similar species** · Mullet, particularly *Chelon labrosus*, but this has small mouth, flat head, and thick lips. Spotted bass, *D. punctatus*, also occasionally found in western Channel. Adults have small black spots scattered over body and spot on gill covers is black and distinct.

Abundance & distribution
Locally common. Found all around coasts of Britain and Ireland but more common off south and west coasts. Elsewhere distributed from southern Norway to Senegal. Also found in Mediterranean, Black Sea, and Canary Islands.

FAMILY **Carangidae**

Trachurus trachurus (Linnaeus)
Scad, horse mackerel

Description · Very streamlined body, compressed laterally. Head is blunt arrow-shape with relatively large eyes. First dorsal fin sail-like, and very close to second dorsal fin which is longer. Anal fin also long and tail fin deeply forked. Body narrows markedly towards tail. A row of narrow, shield-like scales along lateral line. Bluish-green to black on upper surfaces, paling to silvery on sides. May appear metallic greenish or bluish depending on light. May reach 60 cm, though usually much smaller. **Habitat & ecology** · Lives in shoals in coastal waters but found down to 500 m. Sometimes seem to associate with offshore banks or shipwrecks. Feeds on planktonic crustaceans, squid, and other fish. Spawns during summer and has planktonic eggs and larvae. **Similar species** · Include the mackerel, *Scomber scombrus*, but this has distinctive zebra-stripe markings along the back and a series of small finlets after second dorsal fin. Horse mackerel is commercially fished but less valued than the mackerel.

Abundance & distribution
Common around all coasts of Britain and Ireland. Distributed from southern Norway and Iceland to the Cape Verde Islands. Also found throughout the Mediterranean.

FAMILY **Mullidae**

Mullus surmuletus Linnaeus **Red mullet**

Description · Has distinctive pair of long barbels, longer than pectoral fins, under mouth. Head fairly small but with steeply sloping front and eyes positioned towards top of head. Two sail-like dorsal fins, forked tail. Body scaly. Reddish or pinkish overall, with lateral stripes of yellow. First dorsal fin often yellowish with darker markings. Underside white or pale blue. Can grow to 40 cm length. **Habitat & ecology** · Lives on bottom, in depths of only a few metres down to 100 m. Usually inhabits soft bottoms such as sand, though occurs amongst rocks in sandy areas. Often seen swimming along bottom, moving its long barbels rapidly back and forth in sand searching for food, which mainly consists of small invertebrates and occasionally fish. Spawns in early summer. Eggs laid on bottom but larvae planktonic. **Similar species** · *M. barbatus* also occurs around British coasts. Front of head almost vertical and barbels shorter than pectoral fins. Both species are commercially valuable but not fished around Britain as too rare.

Abundance & distribution
Locally frequent, mainly on south coasts of Britain and Ireland. Distributed from southern North Sea to Senegal, including the Mediterranean and Black Seas.

Distinctive features

1. Streamlined shape.
2. Body covered in silver scales.
3. Large head and mouth.
4. Two dorsal fins; first has spiny rays.
5. Spines on lower part of gill cover.

Distinctive features

1. Very streamlined, laterally compressed body.
2. First dorsal fin sail-like, second longer.
3. Row of narrow, shield-like scales along lateral line.
4. Deeply forked tail fin.

Distinctive features

1. Pair of long, tentacle-like barbels under mouth.
2. Steeply sloping front edge of head.
3. Two dorsal fins.

FAMILY **Sparidae**

Sparus aurata Linnaeus **Gilt-head sea bream**

Description · Laterally compressed body with ovoid outline. Snout and forehead steeply sloped. The lips are large, with the upper jaw slightly protruding over the lower and the front of the head lacking scales. The jaws bear strong, sharply pointed front teeth with flatter crushing teeth behind. The gill covers are smooth. The body is greenish above and silvery on the flanks and beneath. There is often a large dark mark at the origin of the lateral line, and a golden-coloured bar across the forehead. May exceptionally grow to 70 cm length but is usually half this. **Habitat & ecology** · Lives in shallow water, especially over sand and in seagrass beds, down to 150 m. It may enter estuaries. Feeds on invertebrates, especially mussels, other fish, and even plants. It is a protandrous hermaphrodite. **Similar species** · The black sea bream, *Spondyliosoma cantharus* but this has a depression in the forehead above the eye, and lacks the distinctive markings of the gilt-head sea bream.

Abundance & distribution
Common. Found in southern Britain and occasionally Ireland. Distributed southwards to the Cape Verde Islands, including the Mediterranean and Canary Islands.

FAMILY **Labridae**

Centrolabrus exoletus (Linnaeus) **Rock cook**

Description · A laterally flattened, small fish, possessing a small mouth with thick lips and a fairly small head. There is a single long dorsal fin, and fairly large pectoral fins with which the animal usually swims. Reddish-brown, fading to yellowish on the extremities and around the belly and underside. In summer the males become vividly coloured with blue to violet stripes especially around the mouth and head. May reach 16 cm in length though adults are usually smaller. **Habitat & ecology** · Frequently seen amongst kelp or in seagrass beds. Sometimes approaches divers closely, especially during the breeding season, and may be territorial.

Abundance & distribution
Locally common. Found around all coasts of Britain and Ireland but rare on the east coasts of England and eastern part of the Channel. Elsewhere is distributed from central Norway to Portugal and the east coast of Greenland.

Crenilabrus melops (Linnaeus) **Corkwing wrasse**

Description · Laterally flattened body; fairly small head and mouth; thick lips. Body deep, covered with large, obvious scales. Single, long dorsal fin, fairly large pectoral fins usually used for swimming. Brown, greenish-brown, green, or reddish. Often crescent-shaped dark mark behind eye which may be brown, black, dark red, or blue. Also often dark spot in middle of tail base. Head may have bluish or greenish stripes. Grows to about 15–20 cm. **Habitat & ecology** · Subtidal in depths of 1–30 m; occasionally in rock pools. Often gregarious; generally occurs amongst seaweed-covered rocks or seagrass beds. Male builds nest, for egg-laying by female, which it guards vigorously. After mating with one or more females, males tend fertilised eggs. Occasionally 'sneaker' males resembling females fertilise eggs guarded by larger male. Larval fish planktonic, settling inshore in late summer or autumn. Feeds on various small invertebrates. **Similar species** · Rock cook, *Centrolabrus exoletus*, and goldsinny wrasse, *Ctenolabrus rupestris*; distinguishable from both by its deeper body and dark spot in middle of base of tail (less obvious in dark specimens).

Abundance & distribution
Common around all coasts of Britain and Ireland. Elsewhere distributed from middle of Norway to Morocco. Also occurs in southern Baltic, western Mediterranean, Adriatic, and around Azores Islands.

Distinctive features

1. Laterally compressed body with a deep ovoid outline.
2. Steeply sloped forehead, mouth with large lips and pointed teeth.
3. Silvery, with a dark patch at the origin of the lateral line and a golden bar across the forehead.

Distinctive features

1. Small size.
2. Small mouth with thick lips.
3. Laterally flattened.
4. Single dorsal fin.

Distinctive features

1. Laterally flattened.
2. Single, long dorsal fin.
3. Small mouth, thick lips.
4. Dark spot in middle of base of tail.

Ctenolabrus rupestris (Linnaeus) **Goldsinny wrasse**

Description · A laterally compressed, slender fish, with a small head and mouth. Has a single dorsal fin, and a pair of large pectoral fins used for swimming. Usually a golden or reddish-brown, though some specimens appear greenish. Belly usually pale. Characteristic black spot at top of base of tail and another one at front of dorsal fin (not visible if dorsal fin is held down). Grows to about 18 cm. **Habitat & ecology** · Subtidal at depths of 1–50 m; also found in rock pools. Favours rocky, seaweed-covered habitats, especially where there are many hiding places. Also found on quite exposed subtidal reefs. The male defends territory during mating season, though eggs are pelagic. Feeds on a variety of small invertebrates, including worms, molluscs, bryozoans, and crustaceans. These fish are very curious and may be difficult to photograph underwater because they are so busy investigating the camera! **Similar species** · Difficult to confuse with other wrasse species because of slender shape, distinctive colour, and black spot on tail.

Abundance & distribution
Locally common. Found all around Britain and Ireland though rare on east coast because of lack of suitable habitat. Elsewhere it occurs from central Norway to Morocco, and in Mediterranean, Adriatic, and Black Seas, and in southern Baltic.

Labrus bergylta Ascanius **Ballan wrasse**

Description · Very bulky. Large head; mouth with very thick lips, containing white pointed teeth. Single long dorsal fin and pair of large pectoral fins used to swim with paddling motion. Dorsal fin rays extremely bony and sharp; can cause injury if fish handled incorrectly. From very dark brown or green, sometime mottled with dark and light patches, through various shades of reddish-brown, to orangey-brown, orange, red, or pinkish-red. Body often covered with pale or white spots. Juveniles small, often deep green. Can grow to 60 cm length; largest wrasse found around British Isles. **Habitat & ecology** · Generally subtidal amongst kelp-covered rocks in all conditions of exposure. Young often found amongst algae in rock pools. Feeds on molluscs such as mussels, and crustaceans like crabs and barnacles. Can crush food with strong teeth in mouth and throat. Very strange life history: starts as female, changing to male after several years. Eggs laid in nests of seaweed built in rock crevices, guarded by male.

Abundance & distribution
Very common around all coasts of Britain and Ireland in suitable habitat. Elsewhere distributed from central Norway to Atlantic coasts of Spain, and Atlantic islands of Azores, Madeira, and Canaries.

Labrus bimaculatus Linnaeus
Cuckoo wrasse

Description · Slender, with long, pointed head and thick-lipped mouth. Single, long dorsal fin and pair of pectoral fins, used for swimming with characteristic paddle-like motion. Markings highly characteristic. Female (a) overall pinkish-red, red, or orangey-red; three black or dark brown saddle-like blotches on rear half of back. After each dark blotch is blotch of white or pale golden yellow. Male (b) one of most spectacularly coloured British fishes. Body base colour often yellow, orange, or red, sometimes tinged with blue or green. Head and flanks often lined with turquoise blue stripes and spots, and fins with deep sky blue colours. Intensity of coloration varies with breeding condition. May reach about 35 cm. **Habitat & ecology** · Subtidal from just below low water to 200 m. Like ballan wrasse, some change from female to male after exceeding a certain size. Lay eggs in nests of seaweed on seabed, defended by males. Eats invertebrates such as crustaceans and molluscs, and small fish. Can be extremely curious of divers. Coloration makes it hard to confuse with other species.

Abundance & distribution
Frequent around all coasts of Britain and Ireland where there is suitable habitat. Elsewhere distributed from mid-Norway to Senegal, including Madeira and the Azores.

Distinctive features

1. Slender, laterally compressed body.
2. Single, long dorsal fin.
3. Black spot at top of tail base.
4. Black spot at front of dorsal fin.

Distinctive features

1. Thick lips.
2. Very bulky appearance.
3. Single long dorsal fin.

Distinctive features

1. Slender, with long pointed head.
2. Single, long dorsal fin.
3. Thick lips.
4. Distinctive colour pattern (see description).

FAMILY **Ammodytidae**

Ammodytes tobianus Linnaeus **Sand eel**

Description · Silvery, slender, long, eel-like fish. Tail forked; dorsal fin long, generally equal in height for entire length. Anal fin shorter, grows along rear third of body. Jaw pointed; lower jaw protrudes ahead of upper. Belly scales arranged in chevrons (only visible on close examination); lateral line simple. Sandy-coloured. Rarely exceeds 20 cm. **Habitat & ecology** · Inshore from intertidal zone down to about 30 m. Prefers sandy areas such as bays and beaches but also occurs in rocky areas interspersed with sandy gullies. Divers often see at a distance as shimmering schools and may even see them dart into sand if endangered by predatory fish. Female lays eggs in sand, producing 4000–20 000. Preys on zooplankton and large microscopic plants. **Similar species** · *A. marinus* similar but generally occurs offshore. Head distinctly dark above, paler below; belly scales loosely arranged. Up to 25 cm. *Gymnammodytes semisquamatus* also offshore species, distinguishable from *A. tobianus* and *A. marinus* by branched lateral line. Golden brown; up to 28 cm. *Hyperoplus immaculatus* and *H. lanceolatus*, both known as greater sand eel. *H. immaculatus* occurs inshore and offshore; preys on lesser sand eels.

Dark greyish-brown; up to 35 cm. *H. lanceolatus* has distinctive dark spot on either side of snout. Generally occurs inshore; up to 40 cm.

Abundance & distribution
Very common. Occurs around all coasts of Britain and Ireland. Elsewhere distributed from

FAMILY **Trachinidae**

Echiichthys vipera (Cuvier) **Lesser weever**

Description · Elongated body. Head has upturned mouth and eyes at top of head. Two dorsal fins: first black, sail-like, with sharp, spine-like rays; second long, running almost to tail. Pectoral fins rounded. Gill covers have sharp, backward-pointing spine. Overall, a yellowish- or sandy brown, with brown spots, especially on upper body. Grows to about 15 cm long. **Habitat & ecology** · Seabed, in sandy areas from very shallow water to about 50 m. A predator of small invertebrates and other fish. Most active at night. Spines of first dorsal fin and on gill covers can inject poison. They bury themselves in sand, so bathers may step on them, receiving very painful sting. Not usually dangerous but medical attention should be obtained. If not available, poison can be counteracted to some extent by immersion of affected area in hot water (not burning temperature). **Similar species** · The greater weever, *Trachinus draco*, which grows larger. Also, its first dorsal fin is not entirely black and body usually has a pattern of diagonal dark stripes.

Abundance & distribution
Locally common. Occurs around all coasts of Britain and Ireland. Elsewhere this species is found from the Skaggerak south to Morocco and the Canary Islands, and throughout the Mediterranean and Adriatic.

FAMILY **Scombridae**

Scomber scombrus Linnaeus **Mackerel**

Description · Very streamlined, elongate, slender, narrowing markedly from middle of body to tail. Head relatively small; mouth quite large with small teeth lining jaws. First dorsal fin small, roughly triangular. Second set well back from first and followed by very small finlets. Very deeply forked tail fin. Anal fin almost mirrors second dorsal fin in position and shape. Body covered in very tiny scales. Upper body deep bluish-green with charac-teristic pattern of diagonal black stripes. Flanks silvery, sometimes with greenish tint and almost silvery-white belly. Colours may change dramati-cally after death. Can grow to over 60 cm but 35–40 cm more usual. **Habitat & ecology** · Swims in shoals in mid-water. Occurs inshore in late summer but migrates to deep water on edge of continental shelf to spawn, April–June. Eggs and larvae planktonic. Fast swimming predator; preys on smaller fish and planktonic animals, especially crustaceans. Is eaten by larger fish and mammals, such as dolphins. Occasionally beach themselves in large numbers in shallow bays. Commercially valuable; under considerable pressure from fishing fleets. **Similar species** · Spanish mackerel, *S. japonicus*, similar shape, but belly marked by wavy lines and/or spots.

Abundance & distribution
Locally abundant around all coasts of Britain and Ireland. Distributed from the White Sea to Morocco, including the Azores, southern Baltic, and most of the Mediterranean and Black Seas.

northern Norway to Spain, including most of Baltic. In Mediterranean, only recorded from Balearic Islands.

Distinctive features
1. Slender, long, silvery, eel-like fish.
2. Belly scales arranged in chevrons.
3. Simple lateral line.

Distinctive features
1. Elongated shape.
2. Upward-pointed mouth.
3. Eyes towards top of head.
4. First dorsal fin black, sail-like, with sharp spines.

Distinctive features
1. Very streamlined.
2. Second dorsal fin well separated from first, and followed by tiny finlets.
3. Characteristic black stripes along back.

FAMILY **Gobiidae**

Gobius niger Linnaeus **Black goby**

Description · Large head; thickset, tapering body. Eyes positioned at top of head; lips of mouth large, with quite fat 'cheeks'. Two dorsal fins with no gap between. First has elongated fin rays, giving sail-like shape. Second is elongated, and both fins have dark patches on front upper corners. Body scaly and an overall brown with dark brown or black patches, especially along sides. Underside usually paler. Can grow to about 17 cm. **Habitat & ecology** · Occasionally intertidal, but generally subtidal to maximum of 75 m. Lives on bottom, favouring sandy or muddy habitats. Also amongst seagrass beds or seaweed, in estuaries, saline lagoons, and sea-lochs as tolerant of low salinities. Eats small invertebrates, especially crustaceans, molluscs and polychaetes, and small fish. Lays eggs in shells or under stones, guarded by male. **Similar species** · Resembles giant goby, *G. cobitis*. Rare in UK; lacks elongated fin rays of black goby, and usually lives on rocky habitats. Also similar to painted goby, *Pomatoschistus pictus*; has rows of black spots on fins, and usually much smaller than black goby.

Abundance & distribution
Common species around all coasts of Britain and Ireland. Distributed from southern Norway to Mauritania, including the southern Baltic, Mediterranean, and Black Seas, and the Canary Islands.

Gobius paganellus Linnaeus **Rock goby**

Description · Large head, thickset, tapering body. Like other gobies, has eyes positioned at top of head, large cheeks, and thick-lipped mouth. Pectoral fins relatively large and paddle-shaped and upper rays are free throughout most of their length. Two dorsal fins, second being longer than first. Colour highly variable: pale to dark mottled brown, purplish-brown, or even black. Usually upper part of first dorsal fin pale; may even become orange in breeding males. Grows to about 12 cm. **Habitat & ecology** · Mostly intertidal in rock pools or beneath rocks. Also in shallow subtidal habitats down to about 15 m, especially in sheltered situations. Feeds on small invertebrates such as crustaceans and polychaetes, small fish, and even seaweed. Eggs may be seen stuck to underside of rocks, on shells, or on sea squirts, in patches of up to several thousand. **Similar species** · Include giant goby, *G. cobitis*, though this generally lacks pale upper margin of first dorsal fin. Black goby also similar, but generally found in sandy or muddy habitats.

Abundance & distribution
Common on west and south coasts of Britain and all around Ireland. Elsewhere distributed from Scotland to Senegal. Also found in the Mediterranean, Azores, Madeira, and the Canary Islands.

Gobiusculus flavescens (Fabricius) **Two-spot goby**

Description · A small, slender species with a small head. Eyes are positioned towards top of head and mouth has fairly thick lips. There are two dorsal fins, second longer and slightly taller than first. Markings are characteristic. Base colour is generally reddish-brown, with pale saddle marks along back. Sides are marked with pale blue and dark brown stripes. There is a large black spot, sometimes partially outlined in yellow, at base of tail, and males have a second dark spot on sides of body, under first dorsal fin. Belly is pale pink or whitish. **Habitat & ecology** · Intertidal in deep rock pools, especially where they have large amounts of seaweed. Generally subtidal down to about 20 m. Often observed by divers in groups hovering around kelps, individuals maintaining position by regular fin 'twitches'. It also occurs above seagrass beds. Feeds on planktonic animals such as copepods, amphipods, and larvae. Eggs are laid in early summer on smooth substrates, especially in hollow holdfasts of *Sacchoriza polyschides*.

Abundance & distribution
A common species around all coasts of Britain and Ireland. Elsewhere distributed from northern Norway and the Faeroe Islands to the Atlantic coasts of Spain. Also found in the western Baltic, but not the south-east North Sea.

Distinctive features
1. Large head, thickset body.
2. Eyes at top of head, fat cheeks.
3. Two dorsal fins.
4. First dorsal fin has elongated fin rays.

Distinctive features
1. Large head, thick-set body.
2. Eyes at top of head; fat cheeks.
3. Two dorsal fins, first with pale upper margin.

Distinctive features
1. Small size.
2. Two dorsal fins.
3. Dark spot at base of tail.
4. Eyes positioned towards top of head.
5. Large lips.

Pomatoschistus minutus (Pallas) **Sand goby**

Description · Small, elongate, with small head, fat cheeks, eyes positioned towards top. Large-lipped mouth. Area from head to first dorsal fin and breast scaled. Two dorsal fins, first longer than second. Pectoral fins relatively large, rounded. Anterior edge of pelvic fins joined, frilled. Single anal fin. Pale sandy brown or grey with darker vertical bars and patches or spots varying in strength. Both sexes have dark spot on rear edge of first dorsal fin, dark triangular spot at base of tail; underside of head and breast dark. Up to 9.5 cm long. **Habitat & ecology** · Mid-tide level down to 20 m or more. Sandy or muddy habitats but less tolerant of low salinities than common goby, and found lower in estuaries. Feeds on small invertebrates such as amphipods and copepods. Lays eggs under stones or shells in spring or summer. Planktonic larvae. **Similar species** · Common goby, *P. microps*, closely resembles sand goby in wild. Lacks scales on head to first dorsal fin and on breast. Anterior edge of pectoral fins simple. *P. norvegicus* also similar, but tends to be translucent and lacks scales on breast.

Abundance & distribution
Abundant around all coasts of Britain and Ireland. Distributed from northern Norway to south coast of Spain. Also southern Baltic Sea and parts of north-west Mediterranean and Black Seas.

Pomatoschistus pictus (Malm) **Painted goby**

Description · Small, elongate. Eyes towards top of head; fat cheeks. Area from head to first dorsal fin and breast lacks scales. Two dorsal fins, second longer than first. There is a single anal fin and pectoral fins are relatively large and rounded. Pelvic fins joined. Pale sandy brown to yellowish-brown overall, with pattern of dark brown lines formed by scale edges. Saddle-like, paler patches along back, and four dark, double-streaked spots along sides. Two dorsal fins have several rows of very dark spots. May also be dark spot at base of tail. Can grow to 9–10 cm. **Habitat & ecology** · Subtidal to depths of 50–55 m, on gravelly or shelly bottoms or coarse sand. Occasionally found in rock pools. Feeds on small invertebrates, especially crustaceans such as amphipods and copepods. Breeds spring to early summer; eggs laid under shells where guarded by male. Hatch into planktonic larvae. **Similar species** · Common goby *P. microps*, and sand goby, *P. minutus*. Both lack large spots on dorsal fin. Lozano's goby, *P. lozanoi*, also very similar but has scales between head and first dorsal fin.

Abundance & distribution
Common around Britain except for east coast. Common around Ireland and distributed from southern Norway to north coast of Spain. Also found in parts of northern Mediter-ranean.

Thorogobius ephippiatus (Lowe) **Leopard-spotted goby**

Description · Elongated but thick-set, tapering body. The eyes are positioned at the top of the head and the lips of the mouth are large with quite fat 'cheeks'. There are two dorsal fins between which there is no gap. The second dorsal fin is longer than the first. The pelvic fins are joined to form a disc. The body is scaly. The overall colour is often pale brown with large orange, brick red, or blackish spots all over the body. However, the overall colour may be a slate grey to bluish-grey with dark brick red or blackish spots. Can grow to a length of 13 cm. **Habitat & ecology** · Generally subtidal in rocky habitats. Often seen on ledges near crevices or holes, or at the bases of submarine rock faces. Occasionally found in lower-shore rock pools. Feeds on small crustaceans, polychaetes, molluscs, and seaweed. The distinctive colour pattern makes it easy to distinguish from other species of goby.

Abundance & distribution
Frequent around all coasts of Ireland and Britain apart from the North Sea, south of St Abbs. Distributed from Britain to northern Mediterranean, including Madeira, and the Canary and Salvage Islands.

Distinctive features

1. Small, elongate fish.
2. Eyes towards top of head.
3. Head to first dorsal fin and breast with scales.
4. Two dorsal fins
5. Anterior margin of pelvic fins joined, frilled.

Distinctive features

1. Small, elongate.
2. Eyes near top of head.
3. Head to first dorsal fin and breast without scales.
4. Two dorsal fins with rows of dark spots.

Distinctive features

1. Elongate, thick-set body.
2. Eyes at top of head, fat cheeks.
3. Two dorsal fins.
4. Covered in distinctive dark spots.

FAMILY **Callionymidae**

Callionymus lyra Linnaeus **Common dragonet**

Description · Rather flattened and elongate. Head almost triangular from above; eyes on upper surface of head. Two dorsal fins: first sail-like, with very long first ray; second reaches along most of back but not as high as first. Fins often folded down when fish on bottom. Skin has no scales. Females and immature males blotchy brown to greenish-brown; mature males vivid golden brown with various blue spots and stripes, especially around head. Males grow to about 30 cm and females 20 cm. **Habitat & ecology** · Bottom-living, in sandy or muddy habitats down to 430 m. Complex mating behaviour, involving inter-male fighting and courtship between males and females. Eggs and larvae planktonic. Feeds on small invertebrates such as molluscs and crustaceans living on or in seabed. May 'follow' divers, or swim just ahead, coming to rest periodically on sediment a few metres ahead. **Similar species** · Two in British Isles. Reticulated dragonet, *C. reticulatus*, has four (males) or two (females) horizontal rows of dark spots on dorsal fins. Generally found deeper. Spotted dragonet, *C. maculatus*, is smaller, orangey-brown with dark patches along dorsal surface, and less common.

Abundance & distribution
Very common around all coasts of Britain and Ireland. Elsewhere distributed from southern Iceland and central Norway to Mauritania, including the northern

FAMILY **Blenniidae**

Lipophrys pholis (Linnaeus) **Shanny**

Description · Relatively large head and thickset, tapering body. Eyes are set towards top of head and mouth is large with thick lips. A single, long dorsal fin with a shallow notch about half way along body. Body is smooth and coloration extremely variable. Ground colour usually green, brown, or greyish, with darker colours and sometimes with pale spots. Dark saddle-like blotches are often positioned along length of body and a diffuse, dark marking may be present on front of dorsal fin. Grows to maximum of 16 cm. **Habitat & ecology** · Common intertidally and subtidally down to about 30 m. May be found in rock pools, under stones, amongst algae, in cracks, and in crevices in man-made structures such as piers. Lives on bottom-living invertebrates such as molluscs and crustaceans, and seaweed. Eggs are laid under stones, or in crevices and guarded by male. May bite if handled – or out of curiosity! All other blennies have tentacles on their heads so no similar species.

Abundance & distribution
Very common around all coasts of Britain and Ireland. Elsewhere distributed from southern Norway to Morocco, including Madeira, but not generally found in the Mediterranean.

Parablennius gattorugine (Linnaeus)
Tompot blenny

Description · Elongate, sturdy-looking body, with fairly large head. Eyes near top of head. Around nostrils is pair of small, branched tentacles. On top of head, between eyes, are large pair of branched, feathery tentacles. Mouth relatively large, with large lips. Single, long, dorsal fin with slight notch halfway along. Pectoral fins large, rounded. Single, long anal fin. Generally reddish-brown with vertical dark brown bands along body. Basic colour mottled, with paler or darker spots or reticulations. Grows to about 30 cm. **Habitat & ecology** · Intertidally in rock pools or subtidally, especially amongst seaweed-covered rocks. Often lives in holes or crevices, and commonly observed on shipwrecks peering out of small holes or pipes. Feeds on small invertebrates such as crustaceans and echinoderms. Female lays eggs in hole or crevice. Male guards eggs until hatched. Larvae are planktonic. **Similar species** · Montagu's blenny, *Coryphoblennius galerita*. This has fringe of very short tentacles running along mid-line, behind head. Also similar to Yarrell's blenny, *Chirolophis ascanii*. First few rays of dorsal fin have tufted, feathery tips.

Abundance & distribution
Common on west and south coasts of Britain and all around Ireland. Very rare or absent from North Sea. Distributed from west coast of Britain and Ireland to Morocco, western Mediterranean and Adriatic Sea.

Mediterranean, Black Sea, Azores, and Madeira.

Distinctive features

1. Flattened body.
2. Triangular head.
3. Two dorsal fins, first one tall and sail-like.

Distinctive features

1. Single dorsal fin with notch.
2. Large head.
3. Eyes at top of head.
4. Mouth with thick lips.

Distinctive features

1. Elongate but sturdy body.
2. Small pair of feathery tentacles around nostrils.
3. Large pair of feathery tentacles on top of head, between eyes.

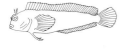

FAMILY **Anarhichadidae**
Anarhichas lupus Linnaeus **Wolf-fish**

Description · The wolf-fish has a rather elongate body, up to 1.25 m long. The head is huge, with large lips. The pointed canine teeth are also large, and often protruding. Snout is blunt. There is a single, long dorsal fin running most of the body length, and a long anal fin. The pectoral fins are large and rounded. The skin is tough and wrinkled and usually bluish-grey, though sometimes yellowish. There may be a series of darker vertical bars along the body. **Habitat & ecology** · This ferocious looking fish lives mainly in rocky areas, though it can be found over sandy or muddy bottoms. It is carnivorous, using its powerful jaws to break up hard-shelled molluscs, crabs, and sea urchins. The wolf-fish usually lives in deep water (to 500 m) but off Scotland and further north it may be found in shallower water (12 m or less).

Abundance & distribution
Frequent. Found all around Britain and Ireland but usually in deep water. Distributed from the White Sea and Spitsbergen to the Channel.

FAMILY **Pholididae**
Pholis gunnellus (Linnaeus) **Butterfish, gunnel**

Description · Very elongate body, laterally compressed. Head very small, with small mouth. A single dorsal fin running from behind head to tail fin. Anal fin runs from about halfway along body to tail fin. Overall, a brown, reddish-brown to pinkish-red colour. Body exceptionally smooth and slippery. A series of dark brown, spots extend along back, often outlined in yellow. Rest of body may be marked with dark vertical stripes or patches. A dark band runs through eye. Can grow to 25 cm. **Habitat & ecology** · Commonly found on rocky shores in rock pools, amongst seaweed, or under rocks. It occurs subtidally down to 100 m in rocky areas, though it may be found in other habitats. Feeds on small invertebrates such as crustaceans, molluscs, and polychaete worms. Eggs are laid in a clump amongst rocks, in shells, or in burrows of other animals. Are guarded by both parents until they hatch into planktonic larvae. There are no similar species.

Abundance & distribution
Very common around all coasts of Britain and Ireland. Elsewhere distributed from the White Sea and Iceland to the Bay of Biscay.

FAMILY **Mugilidae**
Chelon labrosus (Risso) **Grey mullet**

Description · Broad head, flat between eyes, and small mouth with thick lips. Body is roughly cylindrical in cross-section and covered with large, round, silvery scales. Two dorsal fins, both of which are fairly small. First is sail-like, with only four fin rays. Upper surfaces of fish are dark bluish-grey with silver coloured flanks and silvery-white belly. May grow to over 70 cm in length. **Habitat & ecology** · Inshore. Often seen in estuaries, or around boats in marinas or harbours. Juveniles may be found in rock pools. Feeds on bottom, or 'sucks' food from water surface. Eats algae, small invertebrates, and detritus. Regarded with suspicion as food in parts of British Isles and Ireland as it eats 'rubbish'. **Similar species** · Two off coasts of Britain. Golden grey mullet, *Liza aurata*, has thin lips and golden patch on operculum. Thin-lipped mullet, *L. ramada*, also has thin lips and may have weak, longitudinal, dark stripes along body. Both rarer than grey mullet, and *L. ramada* generally only occurs in southern British Isles.

Abundance & distribution
Very common around all coasts of Britain and Ireland. Distributed from southern Norway and southern Iceland to Senegal and the Cape Verde Islands in the south. Also found throughout the Mediterranean and in the northern Red Sea.

Distinctive features

1. Elongate, heavy body with long, continuous dorsal fin.
2. Huge head; blunt snout, large lips, large pointed teeth.
3. Rounded pectoral fins.

Distinctive features

1. Elongate, laterally compressed body.
2. Small head.
3. Single, long dorsal fin.
4. Dark, saddle-like markings along back.

Distinctive features

1. Flat head, thick lips.
2. Cylindrical body in cross-section.
3. Large, silvery scales.
4. Two small dorsal fins, first sail-like.

<small>ORDER</small> **Scorpaeniformes**

<small>FAMILY</small> **Triglidae**

Eutrigla gurnardus (Linnaeus) **Grey gurnard**

Description · Head large compared to body. Head covered in bony plates with ridges and spines. Underside of head flat. Two separate dorsal fins, first with fairly stiff spines, second with soft rays. Pectoral fins large; first three rays form separate, finger-like feelers. Anal fin elongated. Breast of fish scaleless, belly partially scaled. Lateral line scales slightly larger than normal body scales, but each has distinct spine. Grey to greyish-brown, sometimes with reddish tinge. Upper body parts usually covered in pale spots and may be blotched with patches of darker and paler colour. Often distinctive dark patch on rear part of first dorsal fin. Underside pale. May grow to 50 cm, but usually smaller. **Habitat & ecology** · On bottom in sandy or muddy areas; also on gravelly substrates or where mix of rock and sand. Occurs at depths of 10–200 m. Feelers detect prey, such as fish, molluscs, and crustacea below seabed surface. Larval stage pelagic and fish migrate to bottom as juveniles. Like other members of this group, can emit grunting or growling noise.

Abundance & distribution
Common. Found all around coasts of Britain and Ireland. Distributed from Norway to Morocco; also western Baltic, Mediterranean and Black Seas, and Madeira.

Trigla lucerna Linnaeus **Tub, sapphirine gurnard**

Description · Grows to about 75 cm with large, bony, triangular head about one-quarter of body length. Upper profile of snout in front of eyes slightly concave. Upper tip of snout (pre-orbital) forms sharp angle and is spiny. Pectoral fins as long or longer than head and overlap anal fin. First few rays of pectoral fin modified into finger-like feelers. Two dorsal fins, first of which shorter but taller than second, with very spiny rays. Pink or reddish-brown, sometimes mottled and golden to white ventrally. Pectoral fins always brilliantly marked with blue. May be almost completely blue or have blue edges, often spotted with white or green and sometimes with rear edge having wide blackish patch. **Habitat & ecology** · Subtidal on sandy or muddy bottoms down to 300 m. Juveniles occur as shallow as 5 m, sometimes in estuaries, but adults are most common below 20 m. Feeds on bottom-living crustaceans, molluscs, and other fish. **Similar species** · The red gurnard, *Aspitrigla cuculus*.

Abundance & distribution
Common. Found all around Britain and Ireland though more common in south. Distributed from western Norway to West Africa, including the Mediterranean and Black Seas.

<small>FAMILY</small> **Cottidae**

Taurulus bubalis (Euphrasen) **Sea scorpion**

Description · Spiny looking. Large head, with eyes positioned towards top. Mouth large with large lips and head covered in small protuberances. Small flap of skin, which may resemble spine from a distance, at corners of mouth. Several larger spines on gill covers including one particularly long spine. Two spiny dorsal fins; pectoral fins large and rounded. Colour patterning highly variable. Ground colour can be brown or greenish-brown, green, or red, mottled with paler and darker colours often resembling colour of background habitat. Belly can be yellowish. Maximum size 17.5 cm, though usually smaller. **Habitat & ecology** · Intertidally in pools on rocky shores, and down to 100 m, usually on rocky bottoms. Often seen amongst seaweed and may be found under rocks. Feeds on various invertebrates including crustaceans, molluscs, polychaete worms, echinoderms, and other fish. Eggs laid in crevices or on seaweed in spring. Larvae are planktonic. **Similar species** · Bull rout, *Myxocephalus scorpius*, but it grows larger and lacks flap of skin at corner of mouth.

Abundance & distribution
Common around all coasts of Britain and Ireland. Distributed from northern Norway and Iceland to the north-west Mediterranean, including the southern Baltic.

Distinctive features

1. Large bony head with spines.
2. Two separate dorsal fins.
3. First three rays of pectoral fins form finger-like feelers.
4. Lateral line scales slightly larger than body scales and spiny.
5. Dark blotch on first dorsal fin.

Distinctive features

1. Sharp spines on upper snout tip.
2. Front dorsal fin taller than posterior; prominent spiny rays.
3. Pectoral fins brilliantly marked blue; as long or longer than head and overlapping anal fin.

Distinctive features

1. Spiny.
2. Large head with spines; eyes towards top of head.
3. One of spines on gill covers particularly large.
4. Flap of skin at corners of mouth.

FAMILY **Agonidae**

Agonus cataphractus (Linnaeus)
Pogge, armed bullhead

Description · Up to 15 cm long, the large head bears numerous ventral barbels and smaller, spine-like protrusions on the upper tip of the snout. Behind the head the body is distinctly humped dorsally, then tapering sharply to a long, slender tail region. There are two dorsal fins, and the pectoral fins are large. The surface of the body is completely encased in bony plates. The pogge is typically a rather mottled dark brown. **Habitat & ecology** · Found in shallow water to depths of 500 m, typically associated with soft substrata and often burrowed into mud or sand, including under estuarine conditions.

Abundance & distribution
Not common, with a range extending from the western Baltic and Atlantic coasts of Scandinavia southwards to Channel, North Sea, and Atlantic coasts of the British Isles.

FAMILY **Liparidae**

Liparis montagui (Donovan) **Montagu's sea snail**

Description · A small, tadpole-shaped fish. The head is relatively large and broad compared to the elongated and tapering body. On the underside is a sucker formed from the pelvic fins. There is a single long dorsal fin and the anal fin is also elongated. The skin of liparids is scaleless and can appear smooth and 'flabby'. The colour varies, and can be various hues of brown, yellow, red, or green. The fish grows to a length of about 10 cm. **Habitat & ecology** · On rocky shores and down to 30 m depth, clinging to the underside of rocks or onto algae. May be found curled up. These small fish feed on small crustaceans. They breed early in the year, laying their eggs on seaweeds. These hatch into planktonic larvae. **Similar species** · *L. liparis* also occurs around Britain. This is generally found subtidally and can be distinguished from Montagu's sea snail because the dorsal and anal fins are joined to the tail fin.

Abundance & distribution
Common around all coasts of Britain and Ireland but rare in south-east Britain. Elsewhere distributed from northern Norway and Iceland to the Bay of Biscay.

FAMILY **Scophthalmidae**

Psetta maxima (Linnaeus) **Turbot**

Description · A flatfish with the eyes on the left side of the body. The head is relatively large and the mouth is also large. The body is very rounded in outline and the eyed-side is covered in scattered bony tubercles. The dorsal fin of the turbot is simple. The colour of the turbot is grey, grey brown or brown with numerous dark and pale spots of various sizes, but mainly small. The fish can be extremely hard to see because it can be so well camouflaged. The underside is white. Note that cultured turbot can have strange colour patterns because of their artificial diet. Turbot can grow to a length of about 1 m. **Habitat & ecology** · Subtidal on sand and gravel but also muddy bottoms down to 70–80 m depth. Turbot are also often found in estuaries. They have a large mouth and eat a variety of other fish species but may also take invertebrates such as crustaceans and bivalve molluscs. Turbot spawn in late spring to summer and eggs and larvae are planktonic. A single female may lay up to 15 million eggs. **Similar species** · The brill, *Scophthalmus rhombus* (Linnaeus) is very similar to the turbot in appearance but the first rays of the dorsal fin are branched giving a frilled appearance. A subspecies of turbot, *Psetta maxima maeotica*, living in the

Black Sea, has larger bony tubercles than the northern European/Mediterranean *Psetta maxima maxima*.

Abundance & distribution
Frequent around all coasts of Britain and Ireland. Elsewhere distributed from northern Norway to Iceland to Morocco, including the Mediterranean, Black Sea and southern Baltic.

Distinctive features

1. Large head; numerous ventral barbels.
2. Body posteriorly tapering sharply behind distinctly humped back.
3. Two dorsal fins.
4. Body encased in bony plates.

Distinctive features

1. Tadpole-shaped fish.
2. Sucker on underside.
3. Single long dorsal fin, not joined to the tail fin.

Distinctive features

1. Flatfish with eyes on left side of head.
2. Rounded body shape.
3. Large mouth.
4. Bony tubercles scattered over body.

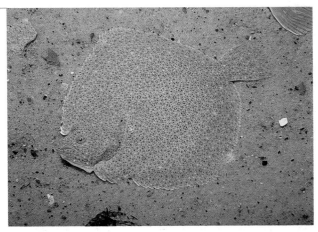

Zeugopterus punctatus (Bloch) **Topknot**

Description · The dorsal fin of this flatfish starts anteriorly between the mouth and upper eye; the pelvic and anal fins are attached to each other. The oval body is sinistral, i.e., the left side is uppermost. The upper body surface is blotched with irregular patches of brown shades, with bands or belts of darker pigmentation extending from either side of the eye sockets, and with a dark region behind the curve of the lateral line. The rear margins of the scales covering the body are toothed. Grows up to 20 cm long. **Habitat & ecology** · Bottom-dwelling among rocks from shallow water to depths of about 40 m,

Abundance & distribution
May be locally common, with a distribution extending from the Atlantic coast of Europe northwards from the Bay of Biscay to the western Baltic Sea.

FAMILY **Pleuronectidae**

Limanda limanda (Linnaeus) **Dab**

Description · A flatfish with eyes on right side. Body oval; upper surface feels rough to touch. Mouth small, reaching to just beyond front of right eye. Pelvic fins separate and distinct from anal fin. Sandy brown on upper surface, sometimes with small rusty orange spots or darker patches. Lower surface white. Occasionally pectoral fin orange. Pale lateral line, distinctly curved above pectoral fin. **Habitat & ecology** · From just below low tide mark to about 100 m depth. Lives on seabed on sand, and feeds on smaller fish and invertebrates such as crustaceans, molluscs, and echinoderms. Spawns in early part of year, producing planktonic eggs and larvae. Caught commercially. **Similar species** · These include plaice, *Pleuronectes platessa*. This is generally wider than dab, has straighter lateral line, and row of bony knobs on back of head. Flounder, *Platichthys flesus*, also similar, but this has rows of bony tubercles at bases of anal and dorsal fins, and lateral line tends to be less curved than in dab.

Abundance & distribution
Abundant around Britain and Ireland. Elsewhere distributed from the White Sea and Iceland to the Bay of Biscay.

Pleuronectes platessa Linnaeus **Plaice**

Description · Eyes on right side of body. Row of bony tubercles behind eyes. Mouth reaches to level of eyes. Outline of body, with fins, oval. Small fin just before anal fin. Lateral line very slightly curved above pectoral fin. Greyish- or greenish-brown with bright orange or reddish-orange spots, sometimes with smaller white spots. Underside white. Grows up to 1 m but usually less than half this. **Habitat & ecology** · Seabed, on sand, gravel, or mud from very shallow water down to 100 m or more. Younger fish may be found in sandy intertidal pools, and on sand lying amongst rocks. Feeds on variety of bottom-living invertebrates, including molluscs and polychaete worms, and small fish. Spawns late winter; planktonic eggs and larvae. Female lays up to 500 000 eggs. Very important commercially. **Similar species** · Include flounder, *Platichthys flesus*, dab, *Limanda limanda*, rough dab, *Hippoglossoides platessoides*, witch, *Glyptocephalus cynoglossus*, and lemon sole, *Microstomus kitt*. Plaice distinguishable by spine in front of anal fin and row of bony tubercles behind eyes.

Abundance & distribution
Very common around all coasts of Britain and Ireland. Distributed from the White Sea to Morocco, including the northeast Mediterranean and Iceland.

Distinctive features

1. Dorsal fin anteriorly commencing between mouth and upper eye.
2. Left-hand side of body uppermost.
3. Pelvic and anal fins attached to each other.

Distinctive features

1. Eyes on right side.
2. Upper surface rough.
3. Mouth small, just reaching front edge of right eye.
4. Lateral line curved above pectoral fin.

Distinctive features

1. Eyes on right side of body.
2. Row of bony tubercles behind eye.
3. Orange spots cover upper surface of body.

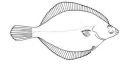

FAMILY **Soleidae**

Solea solea (Linnaeus) **Sole**

Description · Eyes on right side of body. Head rounded, mouth small and semicircular. Pectoral fins fairly small; slightly fewer rays on left (lower) side than eyed side. Often has dark mark on edge of pectoral fin on eyed side of body. Dorsal fin reaches around to almost front end of body. Greyish-brown to reddish-brown, with irregular dark markings. Can grow to 70 cm. **Habitat & ecology** · On seabed from lower shore (young fish) down to about 200 m, on sandy and muddy substrates; also in sandy patches amongst rocks. Feeds on small, bottom-living invertebrates, such as polychaete worms, crustaceans, and small molluscs. Around Britain usually spawns spring to early summer. Eggs released at spawning grounds offshore and, along with larvae, are planktonic. **Similar species** · Solenette, *Buglossidium luteum*, thickback sole, *Microchirus variegatus* and sand sole, *Solea lascaris*. Solenette much smaller than the adult sole, lacks a dark marking on pectoral fin, pectoral fin on lower side of body greatly reduced. Thickback sole grows to about 20 cm in length, has dark transverse bands

across body, extending on the dorsal and anal fins as dark blotches. Sand sole usually smaller than Dover sole and similar shape but front nostril of the lower side is distinctly enlarged. Thickback and sand soles live in deep water.

ORDER **Gobiesociformes**

FAMILY **Gobiesocidae**

Diplecogaster bimaculata (Bonnaterre) **Two-spotted clingfish**

Description · Small. Head wider than rest of body. Head slopes steeply towards front, but not flattened. So named because of sucker beneath front end of body, allowing it to cling to rocks. Rest of body, behind head, laterally compressed. Dorsal, anal, and tail fins separate. Usually overall reddish-brown, red, or pale reddish-brown often with dark patches along back. Ventral surface usually paler, sometimes yellowish. Male has purple spot outlined with yellow behind pectoral fins. **Habitat & ecology** · Intertidally on low shore in rock pools or under rocks. Single fish may guard eggs under rock. These hatch into planktonic larvae. **Similar species** · Cornish clingfish, *Lepadogaster lepadogaster purpurea*, but has dorsal, tail, and anal fins joined. Mouth also flattened like a duck's bill, with pair of feathery structures in front of eyes and blue spots behind head. Connemara clingfish, *Lepadogaster candollei*, resembles Cornish clingfish, but dorsal, tail, and anal fins not joined. Also lacks tentacles in front of eyes and pair of blue spots behind head. Small-headed clingfish, *Apletodon microcephalus*, very

similar to, and difficult to distinguish from, two-spotted clingfish. Males lack purple spot behind pectoral fins.

Abundance & distribution
Locally frequent. Found around the south-west and west coasts of Britain and all around Ireland. Elsewhere occurs from Norway to the Mediterranean.

Lepadogaster lepadogaster purpurea (Bonnaterre) **Cornish clingfish**

Description · Small. Head wider than rest of body. Head flattened, especially towards front end where mouth almost resembles duck's beak. Small feathery tentacle in front of each eye. So named because it has sucker beneath front end of body, allowing it to cling to rocks. Rest of body, behind head, laterally compressed. Dorsal, anal, and tail fins continuous. Overall reddish-brown, red, or pale reddish-brown to dirty yellow. Body often marked with spots or stripes; often a pair of blue spots behind head, outlined with yellow, red, or black. Grows to about 7 cm. **Habitat & ecology** · Intertidally in rock pools or under rocks. Single fish may guard eggs under rock. These hatch into planktonic larvae. **Similar species** · Several in British Isles. Connemara clingfish, *Lepadogaster candollei*, but dorsal, tail, and anal fins separate. Also lacks tentacles in front of eyes and pair of blue spots behind head. Two-spotted clingfish, *Diplecogaster bimaculata*, has shorter head, without bill-like, flattened snout. Also has much shorter dorsal and anal fins than in Connemara clingfish, and male has purple spot behind pectoral fin.

Abundance & distribution
Locally frequent. Found around south-west and west coasts of Britain, and all around Ireland. Elsewhere occurs from Shetland Islands to Senegal, including Canary Islands.

Abundance & distribution
Frequent around all coasts of Britain and Ireland. Distributed from southern Norway to Senegal including most of the Mediterranean and the southwestern Black Sea.

Distinctive features
1. Eyes on right side of body.
2. Head rounded; small semicircular mouth.
3. Pectoral fin on eyed side with dark marking on edge.

Distinctive features
1. Head wider than body.
2. Sucker beneath front of body.
3. Dorsal, tail, and anal fins separate.
4. Male with purple spot behind pectoral fins.

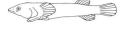

Distinctive features
1. Head wider than body.
2. Front of head flattened, resembling duck's bill.
3. Sucker beneath front of body.
4. Dorsal, tail, and anal fins continuous.

ORDER **Lophiiformes**

FAMILY **Lophiidae**

Lophius piscatorius Linnaeus
Angler, monkfish

Description · Massive flattened head; extremely large, gaping mouth, hundreds of inwardly pointing teeth. Rod with feathery end on head just above mouth. Behind this, 3–4 further spiny rods running along mid-line. Front of head forms semicircle; around bottom edge there is a frill of branching bits of skin. Pair of large pectoral fins behind head. Rest of body much narrower than head and more cylindrical in cross-section. Again, lower edges lined by fringe of branched bits of skin. Dorsal fin on tail section. Colour very variable, highly cryptic. Varies through brown, reddish-brown, green, or grey, almost always blotched with darker colours. Lower surface white. Can grow to 2 m. **Habitat & ecology** · On bottom, from a few metres to 500 m or more in various habitats. Ambush predator, lying camouflaged and waving rod-like lure on head to attract smaller fish, which are snapped up when close enough. Inwardly curved teeth ensure no escape and fish are swallowed whole. Has been known to eat seabirds. Spawns offshore. Eggs and young planktonic. **Similar species** · *L. budegassa* occurs further offshore. Has very small, simple dorsal spines compared to *L. piscatorius*. Both species fished commercially; usually only tail section sold as monkfish.

Abundance & distribution
Common around all coasts of Britain and Ireland. Elsewhere distributed from northern Norway to the Straits of Gibraltar, including the Mediterranean and Baltic Seas.

Distinctive features

1. Massive head.
2. Rod-like lure on top of head, with feathery end.
3. Very large mouth; inwardly curved teeth.

Flotsam and jetsam

Egg mass of *Buccinum undatum* (Linnaeus)

Description · Egg masses of the common whelk are often washed up on the shore. They resemble a mass of yellowish-white purse-like capsules, each about 7–8 mm across. The eggs are laid on the seabed and juvenile whelks hatch directly from them. When dried they have a rough texture.

Mermaid's purse

Description · These are the egg cases of cartilaginous fish, particularly rays and dogfish. They are generally rectangular, flattened, sac-like structures with horns or tendrils growing out of the corners. Usually dark brown or black but slightly transparent. They have a tough texture, becoming brittle if dried. The egg cases contain a single developing fish which, if alive, can be seen moving within the case. The eggs are laid around the bases of kelps or other objects on the seabed.

Sea slug egg string

Description · The egg strings of sea slugs are often seen on the shore and by divers. They have a variety of structures, from simple tangled strings to more elaborate adherent horse-shoe or spiralled egg masses. Sea slugs often pair to lay egg strings and sometimes aggregate in very large numbers during the breeding season. Often planktonic larvae hatch from these egg masses.

Eulalia viridis (Linnaeus) egg mass

Description · The egg masses of the green-leaf worm are common on rocky shores. They resemble small bag-like masses of green slime or mucus.

Cuttlebone

Description · The cuttlebone is the internal shell of a cuttlefish. These animals only live for a few years and when they die the body decomposes, releasing the buoyant cuttlebone. In life the cuttlebone is used by the cuttlefish to regulate its buoyancy, acting like a fish's swim bladder. In certain areas, such as south-west Britain, large numbers of cuttlebones may be washed up on the shore, giving an indication of how many cuttlefish live in the nearby sea.

Acknowledgements

During the course of putting together this book the authors have obtained help from many people. In particular we would like to thank the following for specialist taxonomic advice: Algae – Dr J.M. Jones; Porifera & Hydrozoa – Jenny Mallinson; Anthozoa – R.L. Manuel; Mollusca – Dr Andy Brand; Bryozoa – Dr Peter Hayward; Ascidiacea – Dr John Bishop. We would also like to thank Dr David Gibson and all the staff at the North Queensferry and Ellesmere Port Deep-Sea World Aquariums, and Dr Louise Allcock at the National Museums of Scotland. Comments from anonymous referees were invaluable in the initial stages of development of this book. Paul Chandler, Peter Pool, Peter Hayward and Peter Cotton also provided helpful comment on the design and concept of the book at an early stage. We would also like to thank Dr Jack Lewis for permission to redraw Fig. 3 from his 1964 book *The ecology of rocky shores.*

Photographs of *Enteromorpha linza, Codium bursa, Jania rubens, Adocia cineria, Adamsia carciniopados, Physalia physalis, Pagurus prideuxi, Munida rugosa, Osilinus lineata, Epitonium clathrus, Goniodoris nodosa, Octopus vulgaris, Ophiura albida, Paracentrotus lividus, Ascidia conchilega, Ctenolabrus rupestris, Labrus bimaculatus* (male) and *Mullus surmeletus* were taken by Alex Rogers.

We also gratefully acknowledge the following for allowing us to use their photographs (numbers in parentheses refer to the appropriate page number): David Barnes, *Limnoria lignorum* (213); Andy Brand, *Lepas anatifera* (175), *Atelecyclus rotundatus* (203);

Ken Collins, *Ciocalypta penicillus* (79) *Maxmuelleria lankesteri* (141), *Scalpellum scalpellum* (175), *Dicentrarchus labrax* (395), *Gobius paganellus* (403); Sue Daly, *Loligo forbesii* (313), *Lepadogaster lepadogaster* (417); Tom Dickie, *Neoturris pileata* (117); Jenny Mallinson, *Suberites domuncula* (71), *Callianassa subterranea* (189); Lois Nickell, *Pennatula phosphorea* (107); Christine Ryan, *Aphrodita aculeata* (145); Erling Svensen, *Clava multicornis* (117), *Nereis diversicolor* (151), *Nereis virens* (151), *Pandalus montagui* (187), *Doto coronata* (259), *Facelina coronata* (269), *Ophiopholis aculeata* (349), *Clupea harengus* (385), *Ammodytes tobianus* (401); Steve Widdicombe, *Goneplax rhomboides* (207), *Philine aperta* (257), *Phallusia mammillata* (371); Mark Woombs, *Virgularia mirabilis* (109), *Halecium halecinum* (119), *Nephrops norvegicus* (191), *Nymphon gracile* (221), *Tritonia hombergi* (257), *Amphiura brachiata* (349), *Raja naevus* (383) *Nerophis lumbriciformis* (387), *Zeus faber* (393), *Centrolabrus exoletus* (397), *Lipophrys pholis* (407).

Dr Alex Rogers would like to acknowledge Professor Patrick Holligan for use of facilities at the School of Ocean & Earth Science, University of Southampton, during final preparations of this book. He would also like to thank the Marine Biological Association of the UK and the Natural Environment Research Council for Research Fellowships during this time.

Finally we would all like to thank the staff of OUP for their assorted assistance and patience.

Index

Page numbers in **bold** indicate the main references to the species listed